DECISION METAPHORS: PARADIGMS, THEORIES, AND RESEARCH RESULTS

AHMED RIAHI-BELKAOUI

CONTENTS

PREFACE

A metaphor is basically a way, linguistically or non-linguistically, to refer to one thing in terms of another. A metaphor has two parts:

1. A tenor also referred to as a ground or a target, is basically the subject or dependent variable in need to be explicated by another part.
2. A vehicle also referred to as a figure or source is basically the independent variable or attributes used to explicate the tenor.

This book approaches decisions and decision making as a metaphor where the tenor is the decision and decisions attributes as the vehicle.

1. The first decision metaphor will show that a decision is a function of diagnostic and redundant cues. Focusing on the representation of the policy-capturing process, Chapter 1 examines the Brunswik lens model.
2. The second decision metaphor will show that a decision is the result of making risky choices. As a result Chapter 2 covers the models that are used to predict or describe how individuals make risky choices. It focuses on the expectation models or expected utility models in general and the subjective expected utility model in particular, as the latter is the most researched paradigm in the risky choice literature.
3. The third decision metaphor will show that a decision may be the result of elicitation and revision. As a result Chapter 3 covers the subjects of probability elicitation and revision as studied and evaluated in behavioral decision theory.
4. The fourth decision metaphor will show that a decision is the end result of the application of a heuristic or bias. As a result chapter 4 covers the heuristics and biases individuals seem to employ in order to reduce cognitive processes to simpler, more manageable judgmental operations.
5. The fifth decision metaphor will show that a decision is the end result of a cognitive process. As a result Chapter 5 covers the application of cognitive science in decision making.

6. The sixth decision metaphor will show that a decision is the end result of a functional fixation situation. Accordingly, Chapter 6 covers the literature on functional and data fixation.
7. The seventh decision metaphor will show that a decision is the end result of a slack behavior. Accordingly, Chapter 7 covers the literature on the practice of slack.
8. The eighth decision metaphor will show that a decision is the end result of a cognitive process. Accordingly, Chapter 8 will cover a cognitive relativism model.
9. The ninth decision metaphor will show that a decision is the end result of a cultural process. Accordingly, Chapter 9 will cover a cultural relativism model.
10. The tenth decision metaphor will show that a decision is the end result of a linguistic process. Accordingly, Chapter 10 will cover a linguistic determinism model.
11. The eleventh decision metaphor will show that a decision is the end result of an organizational culture. Accordingly, Chapter 11 will cover an organizational culture determinism model.
12. The twelfth decision metaphor will show that a decision is the end result of following contractual covenants. Accordingly, Chapter 12 will cover on contractual relativism model.

Many people helped in the development of this book. They have my best gratitude. Finally, thanks to Elizabeth Alvarez for her professional help.

CHAPTER 1
THE LENS PARADIGM

A large portion of human judgment research in psychology has focused on building mathematical models that can predict human judgment from explicit information cues. This research has been applied to various fields such as accounting and auditing, management, medical diagnosis, and judicial decision making.

The major task in this type of research is to capture the judgment policy of an individual who has been provided with values or information cues that are supposed to assist him or her in judgment or prediction. The task is also referred to as the building of "policy-capturing' models. These models are intended to represent the relationships between the judgment and the cues rather than to explain the actual mode of information processing used to form judgments. Hoffman uses the term *paramorphic representation* to refer to the model that represents the relationship rather than the exact cognitive process. The model shows the judge's use of one particular combination of the information. Hoffman describes such models as follows:

Mathematical models are designed to provide a scheme whereby one set of events may be satisfactorily predicted from another, and whereby testable derivations may lead to more complete theoretical understanding of the phenomena. Such models, therefore, constitute a level of description and explanation which suffices for scientific purposes. It is not required of any models that they bear any semblance of some "actual" state of affairs, either within the organization or elsewhere, nor would this necessarily lead to a better understanding of nature.[1]

The model, therefore, describes what is observed about certain properties or characteristics of the judge and also assists in the making of predictions. It is, however, inevitably incomplete, for other properties of the judgment remain undescribed; this explains the use of the term *paramorphic representation*. As Einhorn states:

Even if a model is highly accurate in describing the judgmental process, it does not necessarily mean that the process has actually worked in exactly the way the model has specified. Different models may be equally powerful with respect to describing the process. It, therefore, seems that accurately describing the process is at least necessary although not sufficient for describing the underlying cognitive processes.[2]

Therefore, it is the representation of the policy-capturing process that is of concern in this chapter. In addition, the chapter examines the Brunswik model used in this type of research and the various conceptual and methodological ramifications resulting from its use.

BRUNSWIK'S LENS MODEL

First proposed by Brunswik, whose philosophy of probabilistic functionalism led him to study the organism's successes and failures in an uncertain world, the lens model relies on multiple regression as a model for human use of information.[3] Its applications include depth perception,[4] person perception,[5] clinical inference,[6] and conflict resolution,[7] to name some of the early applications in psychology. As will be seen in Chapter 2, its applications in accounting and auditing are various and numerous. The model is designed for use in the investigation of judgment situations where humans infer the current state of an environment event from information cues from the environment which probabilistically relate to the environmental event. It has been adequately described by Beach[8] and Dudycha and Naylor.[9]

Exhibit 1.1 provides a description of the lens model based on Dudycha and Naylor. As shown in the exhibit the world is divided into two parts: (1) the left side, representing the environmental or predictive ability system, which describes the relationship between an information set (X) and the individual judgment or prediction (Y_s).

On the left side, the correlation or validity coefficient, r_{ie}, known as the ecological validity of the cue, represents the relationship between each cue and the environmental event to be predicted. The left side is also summarized by the multiple regression equation:

$$\widehat{Y}_e = b_{1e}X_1 + b_{2e}X_2 + \cdots + b_{ke}X_k$$

Exhibit 1.1
Diagram of Lens Model

Environmental or "Predictive Ability" System

Behavioral or Decision Maker System

Information Set

$R_e = r_{Y_e \hat{Y}_e}$
Environmental Predictability

Environmental Event = Y_e

Predicted Environmental Event = $\hat{Y}_{e(1)}$

r_{1e}
r_{2e}
r_{je}
r_{1e}
r_{ij}

X_k
$\cdot$ $\cdot$ X_j
X_i
$\cdot$ $\cdot$
X_2
X_1

r_{1s}
r_{2s}
r_{js}
r_{is}

$r_a = r_{Y_e Y_s}$

$G = r_{\hat{Y}_e \hat{Y}_s}$

User Prediction = Y_s

Predicted User Prediction = $\hat{Y}_{s(2)}$

$r_s = r_{Y_s \hat{Y}_s}$
Response Linearity

(1) $\hat{Y}_e = b_{1e}X_1 + b_{2e}X_2 + \ldots + b_{ke}X_k$

Matching Index

(2) $\hat{Y}_s = b_{1s}X_1 + b_{2s}X_2 + \ldots + b_{ks}X_k$

where $\widehat{Y}_e$ is the predicted environment event, X_i is the informational cues used, and b_i is the regression coefficient or weight assigned to the cues by the model. The model on the left side is also known as the mechanical model, that is to say, the best multiple regression predictions of $\widehat{Y}_e$ obtained by a statistician using the cues. The environmental multiple correlation or environmental predictability, R_e, measures the relationship between the best prediction of the distal variable $\widehat{Y}_e$ and the distal variable Y_e.

On the right side of the model, the correlation coefficient, r_{is}, known as the utilization coefficient, represents the relationship between each cue and the individual's prediction. The right side is summarized as follows:

$$\widehat{Y}_s = b_{1s}X_1 + b_{2s}X_2 + \cdots + b_{ks}X_s$$

where $\widehat{Y}_s$ is the statistician's optimal regression of subjects' judgments, X_i is the informational cues used, b_i is the regression coefficient or weight assigned to the cues by the individual, and r_{is} is the utilization coefficient. The model on the right side is known as the judgment model or policy-capturing model, that is to say, the statistician's optimal regression prediction of subjects' judgments. The subject's multiple correlation or response linearity, R_s, measures the relationship between best prediction of subject's responses $\widehat{Y}_s$ and the subject's responses Y_s.

Given the values of Y_e, $\widehat{Y}_e$, Y_s and $\widehat{Y}_s$, six judgment indices may be computed to evaluate the quality of an individual's judgments or predictions:

- *A matching coefficient*, $G = r\widehat{Y}_e\widehat{Y}_s$, represents the extent to which the linear weightings of the two systems match one another. It is the relationship between the best prediction of subject's responses, $\widehat{Y}_s$, and the best prediction the distal variable $\widehat{Y}_e$.
- *An achievement index*, $r_a = rY_eY_s$, represents the relationship between subject's responses and the distal variable. It is a measure of accuracy.

- *An optimality index*, $r_0 = r\hat{Y}_e Y_s$, represents the relationship between subject's responses Y_s and the optimal prediction of the distal variable from the cues, $\hat{Y}_e$.
- An index, $r'_a = r Y_e \hat{Y}_s$, represents the relationship between the distal variable and the best prediction of subject's response.
- The other two indices, R_e and R_s, were defined earlier.

The six indices apply to linearly predictable relations and dependencies. To expand the model to express nonlinear cue utilization, Hursch et al. introduced a C coefficient.[10] C is the correlation between the residual which cannot be linearly predicted in the criterion and the residual which cannot be linearly predicted in the judgment. In other words, the index C is the correlation between the variance unaccounted for by multiple correlation in the mechanical model and the variance unaccounted for in the subject's model. C varies between +1.0 and -1.0 and is a general measure of nonlinearity. If C is zero a problem of interpretation arises. As stated by Einhorn:

The results because $C = 0.00$ can occur for a variety of reasons such as the nonlinearity used by the subject in combining cues does not match the nonlinearity involved in the ecological validity between distal stimulus and cues at the lens; *or*, the variance that is left after one takes out the linear effect (as shown by the multiple correlation), is random error variance and not variance due to nonlinearity. There is no way of knowing which interpretation is correct.[11]

A high C indicates the presence of nonlinearity, the need for an examination of the original regression, and the possible inclusion of nonlinear terms in the model.

Because the major use of the lens model is to assess the prediction by users and test the information content of the information cues provided, the relevant index of usefulness is the prediction achievement index (r_a), which means prediction accuracy. A formulation of r_a in terms of all the other indices was provided by Tucker as:[12]

$$r_a = G R_e R_s = C \sqrt{1 - R_e^2} \sqrt{1 - R_s^2}$$

This equation expressing r_a in terms of all the other indices has been labeled as the lens model equation. Its benefits are expressed as follows:
It demonstrates that achievement is a function of statistical properties of the environment (R_e), as well as the statistical properties of the subject's response system (R_s), the extent to which the linear weightings of the two systems match one another (G), and the extent to which nonlinear variance of one system is correlated with nonlinear variance of the other (C).[13]

Assuming nonlinearity is negligible, the lens model equation explains achievement (r_a) in terms of the other components of the model as follows:

$$r_a = GR_eR_s$$

In other words, achievement depends on accuracy of cue weighing, predictability of the environment for predictive ability of the information, and predictability of the individual (consistency).

In the multiple cue probability learning literature, the index R_s is called cognitive control and the interpretation of the lens model equation becomes:

$$r_a = GR_eR_s$$

or Achievement = Task Knowledge X Task Predictability X Cognitive Control.

The relative importance given each cue on the right side of the lens model is, as seen earlier, represented by the $b_{i,s}$ values and the utilization coefficient, $r_{i,s}$. An alternative index, called relative weight, was proposed by Hoffman:[14]

$$RW_{is} = \frac{b_{i,s}r_{i,s}}{R^2_s}$$

Given that the sum of relative weights is 1.0, the relative weight corresponds to the relative contribution of each cue as a proportion of the predictable linear variance.

Other alternatives provided by Darlington include: r, the zero-order correlation coefficient (or its square); b, the standardized regression weight (or its square); br, claimed to sum to R_s^2 even when cue intercorrelations are nonzero; r_p, the part-correlation coefficient (or its square); and the sum of the independent and joint effects of a "contribution to variance" measure.[15]

MULTIPLE REGRESSION MODELS OF THE JUDGE

The lens model, as seen earlier, can be used to study the effect of the decision maker's environment on his or her performance. Given the judge's prediction or judgment, Y_s, on an event given a set of cues X_i, the purpose of multiple regression method as a framework for policy capturing is to derive the weights $\beta_i, \beta_2 \ldots \beta_n$ for the cues, $X_1, X_2 \ldots X_n$ and an additive constant β_0 so that the resultant $\hat{Y}_{.s}$, which is defined by the multiple regression equation

$$\hat{Y}_{.s} = \beta_0 + \beta_1 X_1 + \beta_2 X_2 \ldots + \beta_n X_n$$

predicts a specific distal variable with a minimum sum of squares. The model is known as the linear model of the lens model. If the distal variable to be predicted by the judge is classified into categories, the linear discrimination model, rather than the multiple regression equation, is used to analyze the way the cues are weighted.

Researchers in accounting and psychology have found these linear models to be successful at predicting various types of judgments. However, when asked, judges indicated that their use of cues may be in a nonlinear fashion. One type of nonlinearity is the *curvilinear* one. The capturing of policy under a curvilinear model requires the addition of exponential terms as predictors in the judge's policy equation (e.g., b_{si}, X^2_i, X^3_i, etc.) A second types of nonlinearity is the *configural* one, where the judge's use of an informational cue varies according to the nature of other available information. The amendment to the policy-capturing equation is generally accomplished by the addition of cross-product terms (e.g., $b_{sij} X_i X_j$).

In other words, the use of a linear model may occur even when there are curvilinear or configural relationships in the ecological part of the lens (the left side).

The policy-capturing models examined so far, whether linear, curvilinear, or configural, are known to be compensatory in the sense that a high value on a cue tends to offset a low value on another cue. The linear compensatory models are not the only combination models available, as various non-compensatory models have been proposed.[16] These models include the conjunctive, disjunctive, and lexicographic.

The lexicographic model assumes that attributes are evaluated on the basis of the most important variable before proceeding to the next ordered variable.

The conjunctive model assumes that the individual requires some minimal value for each cue resulting in a minimum evaluation function (for example, in the selection of a research assistant one may require a minimum level of expertise in statistics, computer science, and economics).

The disjunctive model assumes that the individual makes a judgment on the basis of the "best" cue, resulting in a maximum evaluation function.

While the disjunctive model cannot be represented mathematically, the conjunctive, disjunctive, and compensatory models can be defined in terms of one-parameter function by assuming a general evaluative function:

$$V(X) = \left(\sum X_i^r\right)^{1/r}$$

If $r = 1$, the function becomes compensatory; if r tends to $+\infty$, $V(X)$ becomes a maximum function and disjunctive model. If r tends to $-\infty$, $V(X)$ becomes a minimum function and conjunctive model.

Einhorn compared the conjunctive and disjunctive models with the linear model in a decision task to see which provides a better fit of the data.[17] His subjects were fit better by the conjunctive model than by the linear model, particularly in a job preference task. Einhorn criticized the notion of cognitive complexity and mathematical complexity going hand in hand, arguing that the nonlinear, noncompensatory models may be more simple, cognitively, than the linear model despite their greater mathematical complexity. To extend Einhorn's findings, Goldberg investigated which of five models (linear, conjunctive, disjunctive, logarithmic, and exponential) provides the most accurate representations of the differential diagnoses made by each of 20 clinical psychologists, based on the Minnesota Multiphasic Personality Inventory (MPPI) profiles of patients.[18] The computation and formula for each of the models are as follows:

$$\text{linear: } \hat{y} = \sum_{i=1}^{k} b_i X_i$$

$$\text{conjunctive: } \log \hat{y} = \sum_{i=1}^{k} b_i \log N_i$$

$$\text{disjunctive: } \log \hat{y} = \sum_{i=1}^{k} b_i \log(a_i - X_i)$$

$$\text{logarithmic: } \hat{y} = \sum_{i=1}^{k} b_i \log X_i$$

$$\text{exponential: } \hat{y} = \sum_{i=1}^{k} b_i X_i$$

The linear model provided a better representation of the judgments made by all clinicians than the conjunctive, disjunctive, and exponential models. Only the logarithmic model appears to provide some competition to the linear model. Goldberg concluded:

In this sense, then, Einhorn's approximations of the conjunctive and disjunctive strategies, as well as the logarithmic and exponential models used in the present study, all lead to arbitrary findings, as long as the cues and the responses are not measured on ratio scales. And, since few psychological variables are even measured with such precision, Einhorn's models must be viewed as but crude first approximations to the sort of model needed to capture the notion of conjunctive and disjunctive decision strategies.[19]

The added contribution of nonlinear models was, however, found to be minimal in most other studies, adding little or no increase of predictable response variance to that contributed by the linear model. While the findings do not preclude the existence of configural judgment processes they show the linear model to account for all but a small fraction of predictable variance in judgments across a wide spectrum of tasks. The following measures are presented in support of the superiority of the linear models:

(a)Human judges behave, in fact, remarkably like linear data processors, but somehow they believe that they are more complex than they really are; (b) human judges behave, in fact, in a rather configural fashion, but the power of the linear regression model is so great that it serves to obscure the real configural processes in judgment; (c) human judges behave, in fact, in a decidedly linear fashion on most judgmental tasks (their reports not withstanding), but for some kinds of tasks they use more complex judgmental processes.[20]

While Goldberg[21] and Hoffman[22] believe that the reason for the success of the linear model corresponds to reason (b), Dawes and Corrigan proposed that linear models worked because the situations in which they have been investigated are those in which: "(a) the predictor variables have conditionally monotone relationships to criteria (or may easily be rescaled to have such a relationship); (b) there is error in the dependent variable; (c) there is error in the independent variables; and (d) deviations from optimal weighting do not make much practical difference."[23] In spite of this assessment linear models continue to be used to represent human judgment policies.

ANALYSIS-OF-VARIANCE MODEL OF THE JUDGE

As seen earlier the accuracy of prediction resulting from the use of a multiple regression model suggests that judges are primarily linear in their use and combining of cues. It does not, however, preclude the possible existence of meaningful nonlinear cue use. Configurality means that the judge's interpretation of an informational cue varies, depending upon the nature of other available information. Naturally, the linear model can be made sensitive to configurality by the incorporation of nonproduct terms in the policy equation of the judge. However, a better modeling approach in the presence of configurality is the analysis of variance (ANOVA). As Hoffman et al. state:

If judgment stimuli (cues) are regarded as categorical treatment factors rather than as continuous random variables, and if the judgments made to the cues are considered as dependent variables, then the elegant inferential and descriptive capabilities of the ANOVA technique can be applied to the study of judgment. The application is simple and direct: one prepares multi-dimensional judgment stimuli by constructing all possible combinations (patterns) of the cue levels in a completely crossed factorial design. Such a set of patterns is of necessity orthogonal in the cue dimension.[24]

Therefore, the ANOVA model requires two important characteristics of the cues describing the events being judged: the level of the cues must be categorical (e.g., high vs. low) rather than continuous and the cues must be uncorrelated or orthogonal. ANOVA has the potential to describe both the linear or main effect of the cues and their nonlinear or interaction effect.

The importance of individual or patterned use of a cue, relative to the importance of other cues, is provided by an index (w^2).[25] It provides an estimate of the proportion of total variation in an individual's judgments that can be predicted from a knowledge of the particular levels of a given cue or a pattern of cues. Its interpretation has been emphasized as follows:

Its interpretation is analogous to the interpretation of the squared product-moment correlation as a proportion of variance explained and to Hoffman's index or relative weight when the latter is calculated for orthogonal cues. The w^2 makes possible the interpretation of the effects of

ANOVA variables in terms of degree, rather than in terms of level of significance.[26]

For example, suppose a judge was asked to predict bankruptcy on just two factors, profit and liquidity, each of which could be either up (+) or down (-) for a given firm, on a scale varying form 1 (very unlikely) to 7 (very likely). The ANOVA model, if adopted, yields

$$J_{ijk} = M + \alpha_j + \beta_k + \gamma_{jk} + e_{ijk}$$

Where
J_{ijk} = bankruptcy judgment
M = mean judgment on all firms
α_j = main effect of profit
β_k = main effect of liquidity
γ_{jk} = interaction effect of profit and liquidity
e_{ijk} = random error.

Factorial designs are used in ANOVA models of the judge allowing the assessment of the linear and nonlinear effects of each cue.[27] When the large number of cues makes factor designs unmanageable, fractional factorial designs may be more practical.[28] An argument for fractional factorial designs goes as follows:
In this method, the experimenter confounds those higher order interactions presumed to have negligible effects with main effects and lower order interactions. This is accomplished by judiciously omitting certain of the stimulus combinations from the set of all possible patterns. For many judgment situations, the assumption that higher order interaction effects are negligible is probably a reasonable one.[29]

MULTIDIMENSIONAL SCALING MODEL OF THE JUDGE

If the object of the study is to evaluate the impact of cues on a comparison between different distal variables, then multidimensional techniques rather than multiple regression should be used for the modeling of policy judgments. The concept of multidimensional scaling deals with procedures for identifying people's perceptions and preferences of stimuli as relations or points in a multidimensional space, the dimensions of which are perceived to be attributes of the stimuli.[30] Basically, subjects are asked to assign similarity or dissimilarity judgments to all pairs of concepts, objects, or distal variables. The similarity judgments are usually interpreted as "psychological distances" to be scaled by multidimensional scaling techniques. They are assumed to represent a type of "mental map" used by the respondent to view pairs of concepts that are near to each other as similar and pairs of concepts that are far from each other as dissimilar. If the respondent is able to provide numerical measures as similarity judgments, then multidimensional scaling techniques may be used to construct a "physical" multidimensional map whose interpoint distances most closely relate to the input data.[31]

Different computer-based algorithms have been developed to obtain appropriate geometrical representations of psychological data. One model is the TORSCA nonmetric scaling routine.[32] Given $n(n-1)/2$ similarity/dissimilarity measures, the TORSCA program first yields a set of orthogonal coordinates for the final configuration and then estimates the dimensionality of the data using stress as a measure of the goodness of fit. Another model used in accounting research is the INDSCAL model.[33] In contrast to the TORSCA solution, the stimulus configuration obtained from the INDSCAL algorithm is uniquely oriented. The INDSCAL model assumes that all individuals share a common perceptual space, but assigns different weights or saliences to the different dimensions of the group stimulus space. Thus, using a set of N individuals' dissimilarities matrices, a three-way matrix of respondent by stimulus similarities judgment, the INDSCAL model gives an algorithm which permits a group stimulus space; that is, all individuals share a common perceptual space and a set of N subjects' saliences $W_{it,}$ which are the individual's differential weights given to the various dimensions. Those dimensional weights or saliences for each individual are used to measure the effect of different informational cues on the judge's predictions or perceptions.

Multidimensional scaling techniques were used by (1) Gooding[34] to quantify investors' perceptions of common stock in terms of risk and return on dimensions, (2) Belkaoui and Cousineau[35] to compare the differential impact of accounting information and non-accounting information relative to stock perception and to evaluate the effect of stock image, conveyed by stock name alone, when other accounting and non-accounting information is available, (3) Libby[36] to evaluate bankers' and auditors' perceptions of the message communicated by the audit report, (4) Green and Mahareshwari[37] to quantify common stock perception and preference, (5) Belkaoui[38] to investigate the interprofessional linguistic communication of accounting concepts, (6) Pratt[39] to investigate the determinants and relationships of postcognitive structure to perceived information use and predictive accuracy, and (7) Bailey et al.[40] to investigate the effects of audit report wording changes on the perceived message.

The purpose of multidimensional scaling in all these accounting research studies was to discover previously unknown structures, thereby providing new scientific insight.[41] Yet its role in research has been criticized for several reasons: the models, although mathematically elegant, have little or no theoretical basis;[42] there is no basis for assuming a particular functional form for the monotone relationship between similarity and distance;[43] it may not be applicable to all psychological domains and processes; and the models are computer dependent, with different computers yielding different results[44] or with solutions not converging to an optimal solution.[45] Given these limitations and doubts, Watkins[46] warned accounting researchers using multidimensional scaling techniques to be aware of the assumptions, difficulties, and demands required by these techniques. If his advice is followed, then multidimensional scaling models offer good alternatives to regression models when cues are unquantified and ill-defined and when the data base consists of similarity ratings between pair of concepts.

CONJOINT MEASUREMENT MODEL OF THE JUDGE

Conjoint measurement is another approach to the quantification of judgmental data the requires only rank-ordered input to yield interval-scaled output. As a method, it is concerned with the joint effect of two or more independent variables as the ordering of a dependent variable. It overcomes the problems associated with the main assumptions in regression analysis and analysis-of-variance models that the variables that enter the proposed functional relation can be measured independently and objectively and that validity of the composition principle can be tested directly.[47] As such, it solves the management and the composition rule simultaneously by constructing measurement scales for the relevant variables so that the composition principle is satisfied. It allows the determination of the component utilities or part-worth functions and the functional form which combines components into an overall judgment. The composition rules in three variables or functional forms include:

additive rule: $X + Y + Z$
distributive rule: $(X + Y)Z$
dual-distributive rule: $XY + Z$
multiplicative rule: XYZ

Conjoint measurement investigates what properties of the ordering of the dependent variable should be satisfied so that it can be represented numerically according to the proposed combination rule. The five necessary and sufficient properties for ordinal relation are single-factor independence, joint independence, double cancellation, distributive cancellation, and dual-distributive cancellation.[48]

There are two basic complementary approaches to the use of conjoint measurement: axiomatic and numerical. The axiomatic approach searches for the existence of interval scales for component attributes which combine according to a presumed functional form.[49] The numerical approach makes an assumption about one of the functional forms, then searches for the best-fitting component scales using, as a search criterion, the minimization of a "badness of fit" measure, known as stress.[50]

JUDGMENT RESEARCH RELATED ISSUES
Research Objectives

The various models presented for a study of judgment suggest the following research questions:
Upon what information is the judgment based?
What is the judgmental law?
By what process is the law accomplished?
What affects the judgment?
By what process are the effects on judgment accomplished?
Why doesn't a human make optimal judgments?
Can a machine (algorithm) make good judgments?
How do humans do simply what seems complex?[51]

Each of these questions and their subjects have been examined in the human information processing literature in both accounting and psychology as shown in Exhibit 1.2. Although the listing is not exhaustive, it indicates the wealth of issues in need of examination to better understand the judgment process. Of major importance is the issue of judgment agreement and judgment accuracy.

Judgment agreement was studied in terms of *stability*, or agreement over time for the same judge relying on the same cues and data, *consensus*, or agreement across judges relying on the same cues and data, and *convergence*, or agreement across data sources for the same judge at one point in time.

Where accuracy is lacking, three approaches have been proposed: replacement of judges by their models, the use of composite judgments, and the alternative specifications of weighting parameters. These approaches are examined next.

Judge versus Model of Judge

The regression model of the subject captures the policy of the clinical judge and is the judge's model. Using the model to replace the judge in the prediction process is known as bootstrapping. The overwhelming finding is that the model often outperforms the judge as a decision maker. This is generally determined by comparing the individual's accuracy ($r_a = r_{yeys}$) with the accuracy of the individual's regression model $r'_a = r_{yeys}$) In the prediction of distal variables. The general superiority of the bootstrapping model over the decision maker has been explained as follows:

Exhibit 1.2
Classification of Information Processing Variables

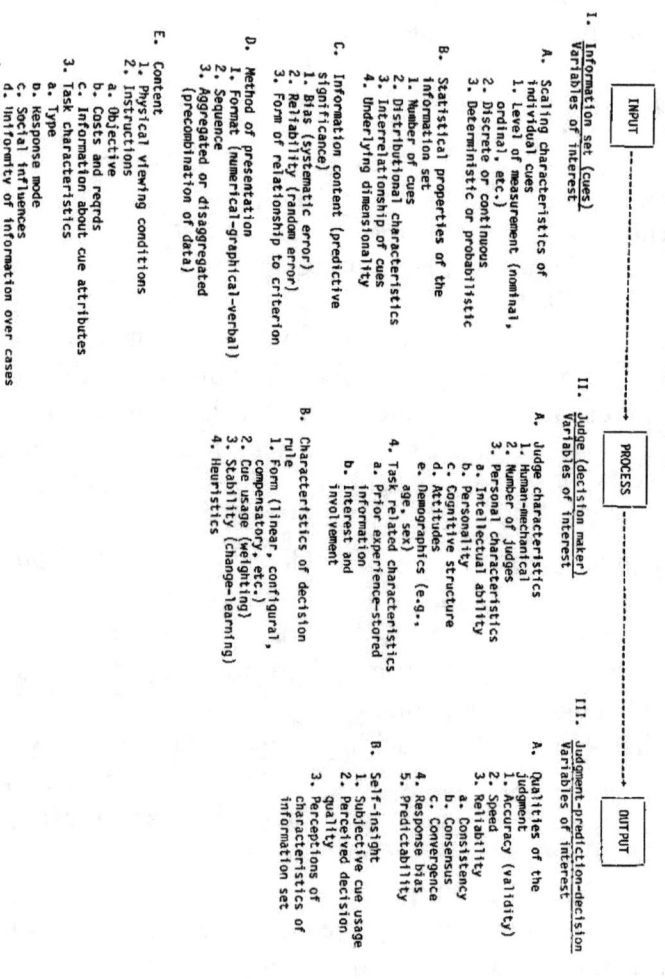

```
┌───────┐        ┌─────────┐        ┌────────┐
│ INPUT │ ─────▶ │ PROCESS │ ─────▶ │ OUTPUT │
└───────┘        └─────────┘        └────────┘
```

I. Information set (cues)
   Variables of interest

A. Scaling characteristics of individual cues
   1. Level of measurement (nominal, ordinal, etc.)
   2. Discrete or continuous
   3. Deterministic or probabilistic

B. Statistical properties of the information set
   1. Number of cues
   2. Distributional characteristics
   3. Interrelationship of cues
   4. Underlying dimensionality

C. Information content (predictive significance)
   1. Bias (systematic error)
   2. Reliability (random error)
   3. Form of relationship to criterion

D. Method of presentation
   1. Format (numerical-graphical-verbal)
   2. Sequence
   3. Aggregated or disaggregated (precombination of data)

E. Content
   1. Physical viewing conditions
   2. Instructions
      a. Objective
      b. Costs and reqrds
      c. Information about cue attributes
   3. Task characteristics
      a. Type
      b. Response mode
      c. Social influences
      d. Uniformity of information over cases
   4. Feedback

II. Judge (decision maker)
    Variables of interest

A. Judge characteristics
   1. Human-mechanical
   2. Number of judges
   3. Personal characteristics
      a. Intellectual ability
      b. Personality
      c. Cognitive structure
      d. Attitudes
      e. Demographics (e.g., age, sex)
   4. Task-related characteristics
      a. Prior experience-stored information
      b. Interest and involvement

B. Characteristics of decision rule
   1. Form (linear, configural, compensatory, etc.)
   2. Cue usage (weighting)
   3. Stability (change-learning)
   4. Heuristics

III. Judgment-prediction-decision
     Variables of interest

A. Qualities of the judgment
   1. Accuracy (validity)
   2. Speed
   3. Reliability
      a. Consistency
      b. Consensus
      c. Convergence
   4. Response bias
   5. Predictability

B. Self-insight
   1. Subjective cue usage
   2. Perceived decision quality
   3. Perceptions of characteristics of information set

Source: Libby, R. and R. L. Lewis, "Human Information Processing Research in Accounting: The State of the Art in 1982," Accounting, Organizations, and Research (December 1982), p. 253. Reprinted with Permission.

A mathematical model by its very natures is an abstraction of the process it models; hence, if the decision maker's behavior involves following valid principles but following them poorly, these valid principles will be abstracted by the model- as long as the derivations from these principles are not systematically related to the variables the decision maker is considering.[52]

Goldberg uses the lens model equation to specify the conditions under which models will outperform judges as follows:[53]

$$GR_e(1 - R_s) > C\sqrt{1 - R_e{}^2}\sqrt{1 - R_s{}^2}$$

Notice that with $R_e = 1.0$, i.e., when the criterion is perfectly predictable from the linear model, and the judge has any positive validity, the model will outperform the judge. Similarly, as R_s approaches 1.0 and the judge becomes more linearly predictable, the predictions of the judge become less distinguishable from the model, leading to the disappearance of the differences between judge and model. Empirical results have verified the conditions and the overwhelming superiority of model over judge, which led one researcher to make the recommendation of "getting the human decision maker out of the decision process at the earliest possible moment."[54]

Camerer also uses the lens model to specify the conditions for the success of bootstrapping models.[55] If $r_z = C(1-R_e{}^2)^{1/2}$, then the necessary condition for bootstrapping model success is:

$$\Delta > 0, \text{if } r_z < GR_e(1 - R_s)/(1 + R_s)^{1/2}$$

or

$$\frac{d\Delta}{dG} > 0, \frac{d\Delta}{dR_e} > 0, \frac{d\Delta}{dR_s} < 0, \frac{d\Delta}{dr_z} < 0$$

The evidence supported the model for r_z, R_s, and R_e, but not for G, leading Camerer to propose that bootstrapping models will outperform judges in tastes with a wide range of lens model variable values.[56]

The superiority of models of judges over judges is only part of the debate. Another part of the debate, known as the clinical versus statistical prediction, has not been resolved, although in an extensive study Meehl concluded that there exists, "depending upon one's standards for admission as relevant, from 16 to 20 studies involving a comparison of clinical and actuarial methods, *in all but one of which the predictions made actuarilly were either approximately equal or superior to those made by a clinician."[57] The solution proposed to the two debates is to combine the individual and the statistical or mechanical model."* The real issue is not to find the proper sphere of activity for clinical predictive methods and for statistical ones, conceived in ideal-type terms as antithetical. Rather, we should try to find the optimal combination of actuarially controlled methods and sensitive clinical judgment for any parts under predictive enterprises."[58] Eight combinations were proposed by Sawyer after distinguishing between modes of data combination (clinical or statistical) and modes of data measurement (clinical or statistical):

1. *Pure clinical*: clinically collected data, clinically combined.
2. *Trait ratings:* clinically collected data, mechanically combined.
3. *Profile interpretation*: mechanically collected data, clinically combined.
4. *Pure statistical*: mechanically collected data, mechanically combined.
5. *Clinical composite*: both methods of data, clinically combined.
6. *Mechanical composite*: both kinds of data, mechanically combined.
7. *Clinical synthesis*: a prediction produced by mechanical combination is treated as a datum to be combined clinically with other data.
8. *Mechanical synthesis*: a prediction produced by clinical combination is treated as a datum to be combined mechanically with other data.[59]

The framework applied to 45 studies showed a clear superiority for mechanical modes of data collection and combination and suggested that the clinician is more likely to contribute through observation than integration.

Composite Judgments

Another decision aid developed within the regression paradigms is the idea of equal-weighted cue models.[60] Basically, it consists of computing the group's mean judgment for each cue-level combination, which is equivalent to weighting all the individuals' judgments equally. The technique definitively avoids the problem of weighting the judgments of different people differently. In addition, it can be proven analytically that the validity (as measured by the correlation between the judgment and criterion) of the group's mean judgment will be greater than or equal to the average of the validities of the individual judgments ($r_{xy} \geq \widetilde{r_{x_1y}}$).[61] The superior accuracy of the aggregate or composite judgments has been well-documented. One limitation of the composite judgment may be its relatively higher cost than the alternative of using modeling on a particular individual. The use of one particular individual is, however, subjective and may not lead to the choice of the most accurate individuals. One way of reducing the cost of using n judges to develop a composite judge is to reduce the number of judges and eventually determine the optimal number of judges necessary. Libby and Blashfield investigated the effect of group size on the incremental accuracy of a mathematical composite.[62] In all three tasks investigated, they found that equal-weighted composites of three judges were substantially more accurate than individual judges.

Alternative Specifications of Weighting Parameters

One issue of importance in the specification of judgment models in accounting is the weighing parameters which represent the extent to which the judge uses each cue in making judgments. Three types of weighting schemes have been used in multiattribute decision making: regression weighting, equal weighting, and subjective weighting.

Regression weighting is the most popular in human information processing research and provides an "optimal" weighting scheme. One significant problem associated with the use of regression weights, however, is the loss of predictive power found when regression weights derived from one sample of data are used for prediction purposes on a different sample of data. The decrease or "shrinkage" in the coefficient of multiple determination (R^2) is known to occur because of the overfitting of the original sample and/or the presence of outliers in the original sample.[63] While the amount of shrinkage that will obtain on a different sample can be found via several formulas,[64] a formula developed by Wherry[65] can be used to estimate the R^2 in the population using certain parameters of the sample as follows:

$$\widehat{R^2}_\alpha = 1 - \{(1 - R^2[N - 1/N - n - 1])\}$$

where

$\widehat{R^2}_\alpha$ = Estimate of the "adjusted" R^2, i.e., the true value of R^2 in the population
R^2 = Sample coefficient of multiple determination
N = Number of observations used to estimate the multiple regression
n = number of independent variables in the equation

The decrease in $\widehat{R^2}_\alpha$ appears to be a decreasing function of N and R^2 and an increasing function of n. Ashton showed empirically that the decrease in $\widehat{R^2}_\alpha$ is quite sizable for low to moderate values of R^2 unless a combination of large N and small n is present.[66]

Equal or unit weightings have been proposed as an alternative to regression weighting. Equal weighting implies that all variables are assigned equal weights while unit weighting implies that all the variables are assigned a weight of ± 1.0. Unit weighting is just a special case of equal weighting and implies the same results.[67] Equal- or unit-weighting models have been found to produce predictions that correlate highly with those from other linear models and predict a criterion as well as the multiple regression model.

Subjective weighting has also been proposed as an alternative to regression weighting. Various methods have been used to obtain the subjective weights. One way is to infer from written or verbal descriptions. Other methods include Likert scales, paired comparisons, relative frequency approaches, and other scaling methods.[68] The method found most easy to administer and most understood by subjects is the "100 point" method whereby individuals are asked before and/or after completing the task to allocate 100 points across the cues consistent with the relative importance placed on each cue. Once determined, the subjective weights are compared to the statistical or objective weights obtained by relating actual subject judgments to the data as the cues are made available to the subjects (i.e., standardized regression coefficient if regression has been used, W^2 if ANOVA has been used, saliences if multidimensional scaling techniques have been used). This comparison of the subjective and objective weights determines the degree of "self-insight" of the judge in the usage of the cues made available. If an individual provides subjective cues that are found to correspond to the objective cues, he or she is considered to possess good self-insight into the weighting and combination of data. In general, two statistical methods are used for the comparison. One method consists of determining the degree of association between the subjective weights and the objective weights. A second method consists of comparing the ability of linear models to explain the variance in subject judgment distributions using subjective and objective weights as coefficients. The evidence from the literature shows that (1) with some exceptions the relationship between subjective and objective weights is a poor one and (2) subjects tend to frequently overestimate the importance of low-correlation cues and underestimate the importance of high-correlation cues.[69]

Given these three types of weighting systems, the research question has been to determine the sensitivity of the output of linear models to the alternative weighting schemes.[70] Of specific importance and usefulness is a formula determined by Wilks for the correlation between two additive components formed by combining a common set of independent variables by the application of different sets of weighting coefficients.[71] Given

$$\widehat{Y_v} = v_1x_1 + v_2x_2 + \cdots + v_nx_n$$

and

$$\widehat{Y_w} = w_1x_1 + w_2x_2 + \cdots + w_nx_n$$

as two linear composites based on the weighting coefficients v_i and w_i, and if x_i and w_i are in standardized form, Wilk's formula is

$$r_{\hat{y}_v\hat{y}_w} = 1 - \frac{\dfrac{\delta v^2}{\overline{V}} + \dfrac{\delta w^2}{\overline{W}}}{2nr}$$

where $r_{\hat{y}_v\hat{y}_w}$ is the expected correlation between $\hat{y}_v$ and $\hat{y}_w$, $(\delta_v/\overline{V})$ and $(\delta_w/\overline{W})$ are the coefficients of variation of the sets of v-weights and w-weights, respectively, n is the number of x_i variables combined, and r is the mean correlation among the x_i's. According to the equation, the correlation between predictions resulting from the use of different weighting systems to the same set of independent variables is an increasing function of n and r and a decreasing function of the coefficients of variation. Ashton used the formula to evaluate the sensitivity of multiattribute decision models to alternative specifications of weighting parameters.[72] The results showed that the outputs produced by linear multiattribute models are extremely robust with respect to alternative specifications of the weighting parameters unless the number of cues included in the models is small, the average correlation among the cues is low, and the dispersion of the weights is large relative to their mean.

NOTES

1. P. J. Hoffman, "The Paramorphic Representation of Clinical Judgment," *Psychological Bulletin* (March 1960): 116-131.

2. H. J. Einhorn, "The Use of Nonlinear, Noncompensatory Models in Decision Making," *Psychological Bulletin* (March 1970): 221-230.

3. E. Brunswick, "Thing Constancy as Measured by Correlation Coefficients," *Psychological Review* (January 1940): 69-78.

4. E. Brunswik, *Perception and the Representative Design of Experiments* (Berkeley and Los Angeles: University of California Press, 1956).

5. Ibid.

6. K. R. Hammond, C. J. Hursch, and F. Todd, "Analyzing the Components of Clinical Inference," *Psychological Review* (November 1964): 438-456.

7. K. R. Hammond, "New Directions on Conflict Resolution," *Journal of Social Issues* (July 1965): 44-66.

8. L. R. Beach, "Multiple Regression as a Model for Human Information Utilization," *Organizational Behavior and Human Performance* (August 1967): 276-289.

9. L. W. Dudycha, and J. C. Naylor, "Characteristics of the Human Inference Process in Complex Choice Behavior Situations," *Organizational Behavior and Human Performance* (September 1966): 110-128.

10. G. Hursch, K. R. Hammond, and J. L. Hursch, "Some Methodological Considerations in Multiple Cue Probability Studies," *Psychological Review* (November 1964): 12-60.

11. H. J. Einhorn, "The Use of Nonlinear, Noncompensatory Models in Decision Making," p. 223.

12. L. R. Tucker, "A Suggested Alternative Formulation in the Development by Hursch, Hammond and Hursch, and by Hammond, Hursch, and Todd," *Psychological Review* (November 1964): 528-530.

13. P. Slovic, and S. Lichtenstein, "Comparison of Bayesian and Regression Approaches to the Study of Information Processing in Judgment," *Organizational Behavior and Human Performance* (November 1971): 657.

14. P. J. Hoffman, "The Paramorphic Representation of Clinical Judgment," p. 121.

15. R. B. Darlington, "Multiple Regression in Psychological Research and Practice," *Psychological Bulletin* (Mach 1968): 161-182.

16. R. M. Dawes, "Social Selection Based on Multi-Dimensional Criteria," *Journal of Abnormal and Social Psychology* (October 1964): 104-109.

17. H. J. Einhorn, "The Use of Nonlinear, Noncompensatory Models in Decision Making."

18. L. R. Goldberg, "Five Models of Clinical Judgment: An Empirical Comparison between Linear and Nonlinear Representations of the Human Inference Process," *Organizational Behavior and Human Performance* (July 1971): 458-479.

19. Ibid., pp. 470-471.

20. L. R. Goldberg, "Simple Models or Simple Processes? Some Research on Clinical Judgments," *American Psychologist* (July 1968): 488.

21. Ibid.

22. P. J. Hoffman, "The Paramorphic Representation of Clinical Judgment."

23. R. M. Dawes and B. Corrigan, "Linear Models in Decision Making," *Psychological Bulletin* (February 1974): 105.

24. P. J. Hoffman, P. Slovic, and L. G. Rorer, "An Analysis-of-Variance Model for the Assessment of Configural Cue Utilization of Clinical Judgment," *Psychological Bulletin* (May 1968): 338-349.

25. W. L. Hays, *Statistics* (New York: Holt, Rinehart and Winston, 1973).

26. Hoffman, Slovic, and Rorer, "An Analysis-of-Variance Model."

27. W. T. Federer, *Experimental Design* (New York: Macmillan, 1955); W. G. Cochran and G. M. Fox, *Experimental Designs* (New York: Wiley, 1957).

28. Cochran and Fox, *Experimental Designs*.

29. Hoffman, Slovic, and Rorer, "An Analysis-of-Variance Model," p. 340.

30. P. E. Green and V. Rao, *Applied Multidimensional Scaling* (New York: Holt, Rinehart and Winston, 1972).

31. P. E. Green and F. J. Carmove, "Multidimensional Scaling: An Introduction and Comparison of Nonmetric Unfolding Techniques," *Journal of Marketing Research* (Autumn 1969): 330-341.

32. F. W. Young, "TORSCA-9: An IBM 360175 FORTRAN IV Program for Nonmetric Multidimensional Scaling," *Journal of Marketing Research* (1968): 319-320.

33. J. D. Caroll and J. J. Chang, "Analysis of Individual Differences in Multidimensional Scaling via N-Way Generalization of 'Eckart-Young' Decomposition," *Psychometrika* (September 1970): 238-319.

34. A. Gooding, "Quantification of Investors' Perceptions of Common Stocks: Risk and Return Dimensions," *Journal of Finance* (December 1975): 1301-1316.

35. A. Belkaoui and A. Cousineau, "Accounting Information, Nonaccounting Information and Common Stock Perception," *Journal of Business* (July 1977): 334-342.

36. R. Libby, "Bankers' and Auditors' Perceptions of the Message Communicated by the Audit Report," *Journal of Accounting Research* (Spring 9182): 189-209.

37. P. E. Green and A. Mahareshwari, "Common Stock Perception and Preference: An Application of Multidimensional Scaling," *Journal of Business* (October 1969): 439-457.

38. A. Belkaoui, "The Interprofessional Linguistic Communication of Accounting Concepts: An Experiment in Sociolinguistics," *Journal of Accounting Research* (Autumn 1980): 362-374.

39. J. Pratt, "Post-Cognitive Structure: Its Determinants and Relationship to Perceived Information Use and Predictive Accuracy," *Journal of Accounting Research* (Spring 1982): 189-209.

40. K. E. Bailey, III, J. H. Bylinsku, and M. D. Shields, "Effect of Audit Report Wording Changes on the Perceived Message," *Journal of Accounting Research* (Autumn 1983): 355-370.

41. R. N. Shepard, "Representation of Structure in Similarity Data: Problems and Prospects," *Psychometrika* (December 1974): 373-417.

42. J. D. Carroll and P. Aralie, "Multidimensional Scaling," *Annual Review of Psychology* (1980): 607-649.

43. R. N. Shepard and P. Aralie, "Additive Clustering: Representation of Similarities as Combinations of Discrete Overlapping Properties," *Psychological Review* (March 1979): 87-123.

44. P. Aralie and J. D. Carroll, "MAPCLUS: A Mathematical Programming Approach to Fitting the ADCLUS Model," *Psychometrika* (November 1980): 211-235.

45. Shepard, "Representation of Structure in Similarity Data: Problems and Prospects."

46. P. R. Watkins, "Multidimensional Scaling Measurement and Accounting Research," *Journal of Accounting Research* (Spring 1984): 406-411.

47. D. H. Krantz and A. Tversky, "Conjoint Measurement Analysis of Composition Rules in Psychology," *Psychological Bulletin* (March 1971): 151.

48. Ibid.

49. F. H. Barron, "Axiomatic Conjoint Measurement," *Decision Sciences* (July 1977): 548-559.

50. P. E. Green and V. R. Rao, "Conjoint Measurement for Quantifying Judgmental Data, "*Journal of Marketing Research* (August 1971): 355-363.

51. A. Newell, "Judgment and Its Representation: An Introduction," in B. Kleinmuntz, ed., *Formal Representation of Human Judgment* (New York: Wiley, 1968).

52. R. M. Dawes, "A Case Study of Graduate Admissions: Application of Three Principles of Decision Making," *American Psychologist* (February 1971): 180-188.

53. L. R. Goldberg, "Man versus Model of Man: A Rationale, Plus Some Evidence, for a Method of Improving on Clinical Inferences," *Psychological Bulletin* (June 1970): 422-432.

54. L. G. Rorer, "A Circuitous Route to Bootstrapping Selection Procedures," *Oregon Research Institute Research Bulletin* 12, no. 9 (1972).

55. Colin Camerer, "General Conditions for the Successes of Bootstrapping Models," *Organizational Behavior and Human Performance* (January 1981): 411-422.

56. Ibid.

57. P. E. Meehl, *Clinical vs. Statistical Prediction: A Theoretical Analysis and a Review of the Evidence* (Minneapolis: University of Minnesota Press, 1954).

58. R. R. Holt, "Clinical and Statistical Prediction: A Reformulation and Some New Data," *Journal of Abnormal and Social Psychology* (January 1958): 1-12.

59. Jack Sawyer, "Measurement *and* Prediction, Clinical *and* Statistical," *Psychological Bulletin* (September 1966): 178-200.

60. R. M. Dawes and B. Corrigan, "Linear Models in Decision Making," *Psychological Bulletin* (February 1974): 95-106; H. J. Einhorn, R. M. Hogarth, and E. Klempner, "Quality of Group Judgment," *Psychological Bulletin* (January 1977): 158-172.

61. R. M. Dawes, "An Inequality Concerning Correlation of Composites versus Composite of Correlations," *Oregon Research Institute Methodological Note* 1, no. 1 (1970).

62. Robert Libby and Roger K. Blashfield, "Performance of a Composite as a Function of the Number of Judges," *Organizational Behavior and Human Performance* (April 1978): 121-129.

63. H. Wainer, "Estimating Coefficients in Linear Models: It Don't Make No Nevermind," *Psychological Bulletin* (March 1976): 213-217.

64. P. Cattin, "A Predictive-Validity-Based Procedure for Choosing between Regression and Equal Weights," *Organizational Behavior and Human Performance* (August 1978): 93-102; R. B. Darlingon, "Multiple Regression in Psychological Research Practice," *Psychological Bulletin* (March 1968): 161-182.

65. R. J. Wherry, "A New Formula for Predicting the Shrinkage of the Multiple Correlation Coefficient," *Annals of Mathematical Statistics* (November 1931): 440-457.

66. Robert H. Ashton, "Sensitivity of Multiattribute Decision Models to Alternative Specifications of Weighting Parameters," *Journal of Business Research* (September 1980): 341-359.

67. Einhorn and Hogarth, "Unit Weighting Schemes for Decision Making."

68. R. L. Cooke and T. R. Stewart, "A Comparison of Seven Methods for Obtaining Subjective Descriptions of Judgmental Policy," *Organizational Behavior and Human Performance* (February 1975): 31-45.

69. P. Slovic and S. Lichtenstein, "Comparison of Bayesian and Regression Approaches to the Study of Information Processing in Judgment," *Organizational Behavior and Human Performance* (November 1971): 684.

70. V. Srinivasan, "A Theoretical Comparison of the Predictive Power of the Multiple Regression and Equal Weighting Procedures" (Unpublished manuscript, Stanford University, 1977).

71. S. S. Wilks, "Weighting Systems for Linear Functions of Correlated Variables When There Is No Dependent Variable," *Psychometrika* (March 1938): 23-40.

72. Ashton, "Sensitivity of Multiattribute Decision Models," pp. 341-359.

APPENDIX TO CHAPTER 1
LENS STUDIES A BUSINESS CONTEXT

The objective of this chapter is to review the main studies using the main studies using the lens model for investigating accounting and auditing matters. The studies are organized under headings that characterize the main research questions: bankruptcy prediction, bond ratings prediction, materiality decision, internal control evaluation, internal audit evaluation, analytical review evaluation, common stock recommendation, risk perception, managerial accounting, and other issues.

BANKRUPTCY PREDICTION

Bankruptcy prediction models based on accounting and financial information abound in the accounting and finance literature. Jones provides an excellent critical review of these studies.[1] These mechanical models represent in the context of this book the left side of the Brunswik lens model. Of more interest, however, are the attempts made to investigate the right side of the Brunswik model in the context of bankruptcy prediction, namely attempts to examine the ability of various types of users to predict bankruptcy or going concern problems. Those human information processing studies as they relate to bankruptcy predictions have been conducted by Libby,[2] Casey,[3] Zimmer,[4] Abdel-Khalik and El-Sheshai,[5] Moriarity,[6] Kida,[7] Casey and Selling,[8] Casey,[9] Houghton,[10] Belkaoui,[11] Chalos,[12] Chalos and Pickard,[13] Casey,[14] and Houghton and Sengupta.[15] These studies used cases constructed by sampling real-world examples, where the outcome on bankruptcy or nonbankruptcy is known. They relied on the judgment of subjects who were predominantly commercial loan officers, but also accounting students, practicing accountants, audit partners, and MBA students. These studies were basically interested in judgment accuracy as measured by the correspondence between predictions and outcomes. They also examined judgmental consistency, consensus, predictability, stability, speed, bootstrapping, performance of a "composite judge" formed by computing the average response across all subjects for each firm, effect of the disclosure of priors, calibration, decision time, information overload, task predictability or data diagnosticity, group or committee performance versus individual performance, and the impact of information choice on achievement and its use. The results are summarized in Exhibit Appendix.1.1. Those results after some replications in some cases point to:

- A highly linear decision form of the bankruptcy models based on subject's judgments.
- High to moderate levels of accuracy, consistency, consensus, stability, and predictability.
- A superior performance of the composite judge.
- A mostly superior performance of the mechanical models.
- Choice of cues is crucial while the weighting is of lesser consequence as a change in one selection and processing strategies increased accuracy. This can be tied to findings by Dawes and Corrigan that indicate the "whole trick is to decide what variables to look at."
- Diagnostic data improved accuracy, calibration, and decision time.
- Information load had an impact on accuracy and decision time.
- Disclosure of priors affected accuracy.
- Committee and group decision performance was higher than individual performance.
- Format affected accuracy as accuracy was higher with the disclosure of schematic faces as opposed to financial balances or ratios.

In addition, other studies used the bankruptcy prediction context to provide more evidence on bootstrapping behavior. Bootstrapping, or the replacement of a decision maker by his or her model, was found in psychological studies to result in superior performance when the loss in accuracy caused by the subject's lack of perfect test-retest reliability is greater than the increase in accuracy gained by the existence of correct nonlinear or nonadditive utilization of the information which is not accounted for by the linear-additive model. To test the generality of the bootstrapping behavior observed in psychology, Libby investigated the phenomenon in a more realistic setting where the decision makers were 43 professional loan officers asked to predict business failure from five ratio financial profiles.[16] Unlike the findings in the psychological study, the findings in Libby's study showed that the judges in 26 out of 43 cases significantly outperformed their linear models. The difference between these results and those of other studies, or "judge versus model of judge," were attributed to the greater amount of task expertise of the subjects, the better definition and reliability of the criteria, and the higher skewness of the cue distributions. Goldberg asserted that since predictions from multiple regression models of human judges themselves and have proven to be robust in at least five studies, Libby's contrary findings need to be scrutinized.[17] The scrutiny paid off with the finding that the distributions of the values for four of the five cues were quite skewed and in need of rescaling by a simple normalizing transformation, and therefore the major finding from past studies still remains: linear regression models of clinical judges can be more accurate diagnostic predictors than the humans who are modeled.[18] Needless to say, Libby was not satisfied with Goldberg's reanalysis of his data, his identification of the business failure prediction case as a nonlinear task requiring a nonlinear model, and his findings that a nonlinear model of a judge similar to a logarithmic model outperforms the judges themselves.[19] Zimmer replicated and extended Libby's study with a group of 30 Australian bank loan officers and found evidence of the superiority of the models of judges over judges.[20]

BOND RATINGS PREDICTION

Bond ratings prediction models based on accounting and financial information abound in the accounting and finance literature. Belkaoui provides a review of these studies.[21] In the context of the Brunswik model various attempts were also made to examine the ability of various types of users to predict bond ratings decisions. The human information processing studies as they relate to bond ratings prediction have been conducted by Stock and Watson,[22] Lewis et al.,[23] Kessler and Ashton,[24] Belkaoui,[25] Danos et al.,[26] and Ashton and Kessler.[27]

Exhibit Appendix 1.1
Summary of Bankruptcy Prediction Studies

Study	Type of Decision Maker	Task	Cues	Modeling Technique	Variables of Interest	Results
Libby (1975a)	43 commercial loan officers	Classify five ratio profiles into fail or not-fail	1. Net income/total assets 2. Current assets/total assets 3. Cash/total assets 4. Current assets/current liabilities 5. Current assets/sales	Discriminant analysis, 60 real cases	Consistency Consensus Composite judge Accuracy	High (80%) High (80%) More accurate than average judge 74% for individuals-85% for model
Libby (1975b)	43 commercial team officers	Classify five ratio profiles into fail or not-fail	1. Net income/total assets 2. Current assets/total assets 3. Cash/total assets 4. Current assets/current liabilities 5. Current assets/sales	Discriminant analysis, 60 real cases	Decision rule form Predictability Stability	Highly linear High (88%) Stable over one week and response thresholds

(Continued)

Exhibit Appendix 1.1 Continued

Study	Type of Decision Maker	Task	Cues	Modeling Technique	Variables of Interest	Results
Moriarity (1979)	A. 277 intro- ductory accounting students	A. To predict the failure of 22 dis- count retail firms, half of which had failed, based on four pre- sentations of data	Financial informa- tion in one of four ways		Format accuracy	Subjects were more accurate using the schematic faces as opposed to financial balances or ratios
			a. Schematic faces with no explana- tion of what they meant other than that they represented financial characteristics of firms			
	B. 20 practi- cing accountants	B. To predict the failure of 11 discount retail firms	b. Schematic faces with explana- tions		Information about cue attributes	No effect
			c. Selected key financial statement balances		Speed	Faces produced faster responses
			d. Dunn and Bradstreet Key Business Ratios			

Study	Type of Decision Maker	Task	Cues	Modeling Technique	Variables of Interest	Results
Kida (1979)	27 audit partners	To predict whether 40 firms (20 failed; 20 non-failed) would experience going-concern problems within one year of a particular financial statement date	1. Net income/ total assets 2. Net worth/ total debt 3. Quick assets/ current liabilities 4. Sales/total assets 5. Cash/total assets	Discriminant analysis, 40 real cases	Decision risk form Accuracy Bootstrapping Consensus	Highly linear 33.22% The models were more accurate than the auditors 75.5%
Casey (1980)	46 loan officers	Classify six ratio profiles for a three-year period into fail or not-fail (not told about priors)	1. Net income/ total assets 2. Current assets/ total assets 3. Cash/total assets 4. Current assets/ current liabilities 5. Current assets/ sales	Discriminant analysis, 30 real cases	Decision rule form Accuracy Consensus Composite judge	Highly linear 56.7% 80% 60%

(Continued)

Exhibit Appendix 1.1 Continued

Study	Type of Decision Maker	Task	Cues	Modeling Technique	Variables of Interest	Results
Zimmer (1980)	40 loan officers and part-time accounting students	Classify five ratio profiles for a three year period into fail or not fail (told about priors)	1. Quick asset ratio 2. Earnings before interest 3. Ordinary dividends to ordinary earnings 4. Total debt to gross cash flow 5. Long-term debt equity	Discriminant analysis, 42 real cases	Decision rule form Predictability Composite Judge Consensus Accuracy	Highly linear 90% 86% 72% 77% for bankers 88% for model
Abdel-Khalik and El-Sheshai (1980)	28 commercial lending officers	To buy up to or maximum of eight cues with which to discriminate between firms that failed or did not fail Most frequently purchased cues were: 1. Earning trend 2. Current ratio 3. Cash flow to total debt 4. Trend of cash flow to total debt	Discriminant analysis, 32 real cases	Human mechanical Accuracy Cue Usage Predictability	A change in processing strategy increased accuracy by 5% Change in selection increased accuracy by 23.1% On average 3.5 cues bought in the first round and 1.5 cues in the second 84%

Study	Type of Decision Maker	Task	Cues	Modeling Technique	Variables of Interest	Results
Houghton and Sengupta (1984)	45 participants from banks	To classify firms as fail or not fail	Ratios used in Zimmer (1980) and Houghton (1984), and different proportions of the failure/non-failure split in the information set		Individual accuracy	Higher for the bankers provided with the set containing the low proportion of failures
Houghton (1984)	30 loan officers	Classify ten firms (five bankrupted, five nonbankrupt) into fail or not-fail	A. <u>Cues</u> 1. Earnings before interest and taxes/total assets 2. Quick assets/quick liabilities 3. Ordinary dividends/ordinary earnings 4. Total debt/gross cash flow 5. Long-term debt/equity		Accuracy	79% with priors and new data 59.8% with no priors and old data

(Continue

Exhibit Appendix 1.1 Continued

Study	Type of Decision Maker	Task	Cues	Modeling Technique	Variables of Interest	Results
Belkaoui (1984)	30 loan officers	Classify ten firms (five bankrupt and five nonbank-rupt) into fail or not-fail	A. Ratios 1. Net income/total assets			Improved with the addition of redundant cues up to a point
			2. Cash/total assets		Calibration	The addition of redundant information led to lower calibration, greater over-confidence, resolution
			3. Current assets/ total assets		Accuracy	
			4. Current assets/ current liabil-ities			
			5. Net assets/ current liabili-ties		Decision Time	The addition of redundant information increased the decision time
			6. Total liabili-ties/owner's equity			
			B. Task Predictability Diagnostic versus redundant ratios			

Study	Type of Decision Maker	Task	Cues	Modeling Technique	Variables of Interest	Results
Casey (1980)	122 bank loan officers	To predict which of ten sample firms (five bankrupt, five non-bankrupt) will declare bankruptcy within a subsequent three year period	Treatment I: The five ratios used in Libby (1975) Treatment II: The above ratios plus the financial statements without notes. Treatment III: As in treatment II plus the notes.		Predict accuracy	Information overload had an effect on predictive accuracy and the amount of time spent on the task
Casey (1983)	107 commercial loan officers	To make a judgment of failure or non-failure and an assessment of the probability of failure	1. Total liability/ owners' equity 2. Current assets/ current liabilities 3. Cash/total assets 4. Current assets/ total assets	Discriminant analysis, 49 firms	Accuracy	96% for model 82% for banker Unaffected by the disclosure of the priors

(Continued)

Exhibit Appendix 1.1 Continued

Study	Type of Decision Maker	Task	Cues	Modeling Technique	Variables of Interest	Results
Chalos (1985)	52 commercial loan officers	To provide: a. Subjective judgments of financial distress b. Posterior probabilities of loan default given base rate	1. Net income/ total assets 2. Total debt/ net value 3. Current assets/ current liabilities 4. Working capital/ total assets 5. Net income/ total assets 6. Net sales/ current assets 7. Industry norms 8. Total assets 9. Trend data	Discriminant analysis, 72 real cases	Classification accuracy Likelihood ratios	87% for the model 79% for individuals 98% for interacting committee 92% for statistical group performance Differences between the committees and the individuals

Study	Type of Decision Maker	Task	Cues	Modeling Technique	Variables of Interest	Results
		c. Loan review action	5. Net income/sales 6. Cash/total assets 7. Working capital/sales 8. Quick ratio		Models of committee process	Additional information-processing efficiencies: fewer and less costly loan action errors than the individuals
Chalos and Pickard (1985)	43 students	a. To select two or four areas of their choice b. To classify the companies as financially distressed, a default prior or nondistressed--a distressed--a non default firm	In addition to the cues used in Chalos (1985): - Industry Quantile for: 1. Net income/total assets 2. Total debt/net worth 3. Working capital/sales 4. Acid ratio	Discriminant analysis, 72 real cases	Cue choice Decision consistency Cue weighing	87% for model 75.9% for individuals 81.28% for groups Group performed as well as their "bootstrapped" judgment models. The individuals did not Individual and group decision models outperformed the mechanical model

(Continued)

Exhibit Appendix 1.1 Continued

Study	Type of Decision Maker	Task	Cues	Modeling Technique	Variables of Interest	Results
			- Trend for:			
			1. Net income/ total assets			
			2. Waking capital/sales			
			3. Acid ratio			
Casey (1986)	71 Second year MBA students	To make dichotomous predictions of bankrupt/non-bankrupt for each of 30 disguised (15 bankrupt and 15 nonbankrupt) real-life companies	A. Ratios One to seven ratios	Analysis of variance	Accuracy	Related to task predictability
			B. Task Predictability Low or high		Effect of prior	Not significant but the interaction effect with task predictability was significant
			C. Priors Either specified or not		Confidence	Over confidence

Kessler and Ashton investigated the effectiveness of different types of feedback for improving an individual's performance in a bond rating task using financial ratios.[28] Three types of feedback were investigated in psychology, namely *outcome feedback*, which consists of revealing the correct answer to the subject subsequent to his or her prediction, *cognitive feedback*, which consists of revealing periodic information about the subject's prediction strategy, and *task properties feedback*, which consists of revealing periodic information about statistical properties of the task. A combination of the last two types of feedback is known as the lens model feedback. While the outcome feedback was generally found to be ineffective in psychology, the task properties and lens model feedback were found to be effective.[29] As a result, Kessler and Ashton chose not to investigate the outcome feedback in favor of the following types of feedback.

Feedback Type A was a form of cognitive feedback containing summary measures of performance- the number and percent of ratings that were correct, and the number and percent that were off by one rating category. Feedback Type B involved a more detailed form of cognitive feedback. It included the correlations between each one and the subject's ratings. Type C included information about task properties, that is, the correlations between each cue and the actual ratings assigned by Moody's, in addition to the summary performance measures. Finally, Type D included the correlational information of both Types B and C, in addition to the summary measures of Type A.[30]

Sixty-nine MBA students were asked in four experimental sessions to predict the ratings of 34 bond issues with rating Aaa, Aa, A, Baa, Ba, and B based on a 3 ratio profile and a feedback type A, B, C, D. Two performance measures were used: (1) the one formulated by Tucker,[31]

$$r_a = G R_s R_e + C\sqrt{1 - R^2_e}\sqrt{1 - R^2_s}$$

where r_a is the correlation between actual criterion values and the subject predictions of these values, G is the correlation between the optimal least-square predictions from a model of the environment and a model of the subject, $R_s(R_e)$ is the multiple correlation coefficient of the subject's (environmental) model, and C is the correlation between the residuals of the environmental and subject regression models; and (2) the mean absolute error (MAE).

$$MAE = \frac{\sum_{i=1}^{n} |Y_{ei} - Y_{si}|}{n}$$

Where Y_{ei} is the actual Moody's rating for case I, Y_{si} is the individual's prediction for case I, and n is the number of cases.

The results of the bond rating task show insignificant results of the effects of the time cognitive feedback on both r_a and MAE, significant results of the task properties feedback on both r_a and MAE, and significant results of the lens model feedback on r_a. In brief, the task properties feedback appeared to be the preferable feedback form in the context of bond ratings prediction.

The experiment was used by Ashton and Kessler to report on the performance of six performance measures and to report "judge versus model" results using all six measures.[32] The six measures used were the sample correlation between the individual's predictions and the actual criterion values (GOR), the mean squared error (MSE), the mean absolute error (MAE), the number of correct predictions, the number of predictions that are correct or off by one rating category, and the number of predictions that correctly discriminate between the top four Moody's categories and the bottom two. The results showed that the degree of consistency across the six measures was mixed for both the feedback and the "judge versus model of judge" dimensions of performance.

Those findings are similar to those obtained by Belkaoui in an experiment where second-year MBA students predicted the bond ratings of 60 actual companies on the basis of the actual values of nine financial information cues.[33] The ratios were the same as those used in another mechanical bond ratings model study.[34] The first issue examined related to the usefulness of the financial information in terms of the accuracy of the subjects' predictions and cue usage. The study also examined several issues arising from the use of multiple regression for estimating the weights subjects attach to the financial information in predicting the bond ratings- namely the predictive and convergent validity of the derived regression coefficients as estimates of cognitive weights. The results of the study showed: first, inconsistent results on prediction achievement as measured by the hit rate, the number of ratings correct within each rating category, and the number of ratings correct within a revised rating category based on a reduction of the number of categories; second, high whole-sample goodness of fit and individual differences in one usage; third, high split-sample cross-validity; and fourth, a good degree of convergent validity or self-insight.

Danos et al. examined the issue of how bond raters' credit evaluations are affected by management forecasted data.[35] Because bond raters are expert users, they will use judgment schemata in which cues trigger a stereotype or causal attribution, and they will draw upon more sharply defined schemata than nonexperienced judges.[36] Therefore, if given confirming or disconfirming information in addition to conventional financial information, the bond raters are hypothesized to display more differentiation of confirming and disconfirming forecasts, be more sensitive to rating class, display more confidence in their rating evaluations than the control group of students. The experiment using bond raters and undergraduate students supported all the hypotheses, confirming at the same time the belief that the bond rating environment fosters the development of sharply defined knowledge structures which bond raters share.

Finally, Lewis et al. investigated the ability of municipal analysts to predict municipal bond rating changes and explored some possible sources of prediction errors.[37] Like Abdel-Khalik and El-Sheshai in the context of bankruptcy,[38] Lewis et al. were interested in both information choice and information use in the context of bond ratings. They used six prediction strategies resulting from cross two information selection strategies with three information processing strategies. The information selection was either by human subjects or by a statistical model. The information use strategies were (1) processing by human subjects, (2) processing by statistical models which attempt to capture the underlying processes of the subjects, and (3) processing by the best statistical model of the environment. Consequently, analysts were given a menu from which they chose the information they needed for predictions of municipal bond rating changes. Then the prediction was accomplished by analysts using either their self-selected information or information selected by the statistical model. The results from an experimental sample were consistent with Abdel-Khalik and El-Sheshai's conclusion that information choice and not information processing was the major cause of the analysts' prediction or classification errors. However, using a validation sample the analysts performed as well as statistical models. Previous research results on the issue were reinterpreted in light of the new findings.

We interpret the above results as indicating that analysts use relatively stable models that have similar success across samples. In contrast, statistical models, which are often used as benchmarks against which human performance is evaluated, can be situation specific. This mixture may lead researchers to underestimate the relative performance of the analysts in behavioral predictive ability studies. After adjusting for the situation-specific advantage of statistical models, our results show fairly even performance by models and man in selecting and using data to predict bond rating changes.[39]

MATERIALITY DECISION

The importance of materiality in accounting is highlighted in the following statement from a discussion memorandum on the subject by the Financial Accounting Standards Board (FASB).

The concept of materiality pervades the financial accounting and reporting process. It influences decisions regarding the collection, classification, measurement, and summarization of the data concerning the results of an enterprise's economic activities. It also bears on the decisions concerning the presentation of that data and the related disclosures in the financial statements.[40]

Its importance in auditing is evident by its use as a major determinant or the scope of the audit (and the extent of audit tests) and its important place in the auditor's opinion. The measuring of the phrase "present fairly . . . in conformity with generally accepted accounting principles" in the independent auditor's standard opinion, incorporates the concept of materiality. Statement on Auditing Standards (SAS) No. 5 explains that, with respect to materiality, this phrase means: "The financial statements reflect the underlying events and transactions in a manner that presents the financial position, results of operations, and changes in financial position stated within a range of acceptable limits, that is, limits that are reasonable and practicable to attain in financial statements."[41] There is, however, no generalized standard or set of standards for materiality. The decision is left up to the individual making the decision. The position of the FASB is summarized as follows:

Individual judgments are required to assess materiality in the absence of authoritative criteria or to decide that minimum quantitative criteria are not appropriate in particular situations. The essence of the materiality concept is clear. The omission or misstatement of an item in a financial report is material if, in light of the surrounding circumstances, the magnitude of the item is such that it is probable that the judgment of a reasonable person relying upon the report would have been changed or influenced by the inclusion or correction of the item.[42]

There is definitely a need to provide some guidance to the profession by modeling the materiality decisions of users, producers, and auditors using this type of experiment.

Among the researchers who have examined the judgment processes involved in reaching materiality decisions are Boatsman and Robertson,[43] Hofstedt and Hughes,[44] Moriarity and Barron,[45] Ward,[46] Mayper,[47] Messier,[48] Holstrum and Messier,[49] Firth,[50] Ricchiute,[51] and Schultz and Reckers.[52] These studies used materiality decision cases to elicit a judgment evaluation by users, producers, and auditors. Lens type of issues were examined. A summary of the characteristics of these studies is shown in Exhibit Appendix 1.2. The main results are as follows:

- An additive (linear) model is appropriate for modeling materiality judgments although there is some evidence of some configural (nonlinear) processing in some cases.
- The factors found to be most important in the materiality decision included the percentage effect on income, effect on earning trend, and effects on total assets in some cases.

Exhibit Appendix 1.2

Summary of Disclosure Studies

Study	Type of Decision Maker	Task	Cues	Modeling Technique	Variables of Interest	Results
Boatsman and Roberston (1974)	18 CPA and 15 securities analysts	To sort the set of 30 hypothe- tical cases into three dis- closure sets	Eight materiality factors	Discriminant analysis, 30 simulated cases	Decision rule form	Highly linear
					Predictability	High (63%)
					Subject differences	No difference between the judgmental processes of CPAs and securi- ties analysts
Ward (1976)	24 CPA, partners and managers	Indicate perceived functional relationship between size of audit error and expected loss of auditor; rank 24 materiality factors	24 materiality factors	Q-Sort	Cue usage	% of net income explained 73% of total predictive power
					Consensus	Statistically significant agreement in rankings of materiality factors; half of the subjects specified either logistic or exponential relationships

Study	Type of Decision Maker	Task	Cues	Modeling Technique	Variables of Interest	Results
Moriarity and Barron (1976)	15 audit partners	Rank materiality of error in estimate of depreciable life	Levels of income, asset size and earnings	Conjoint measurement and ANOVA	Decision rule form	11 subjects classified as additive or newly additive and four subjects classified as configural
					Cue usage	Net income most important earnings trend
Hofsted and Hughes (1977)	19 MBA students	To decide whether the loss from a write-down of a subsidiary should be disclosed as an extraordinary item	Three materiality factors	ANOVA	Decision rule form	Highly linear
					Predictability	High (74%)
					Cue usage	Relative income effect most important
					Consensus	Low
					Self-insight	Low

(Continued)

Exhibit Appendix 1.2 Continued

Study	Type of Decision Maker	Task	Cues	Modeling Technique	Variables of Interest	Results
Moriarity and Barron (1979)	Five audit partners	To estimate pre-audit materiality	Five financial cues	Conjoint analysis	Consensus	Low
					Cue usage	Income effect must important
Firth (1979)	150 Individuals from five different backgrounds	To decide whether an extraordinary item should be disclosed	30 case situations	ANOVA and discriminant analysis	Disclosure judgement	Differs among groups
					Cue usage	Differs among groups. Percentage of profits before extraordinary items effect most important.
					Predictability	Differs among subjects (a low of 57% to a high of 96%)
Schultz and Reckers (1981)	64 partners	To assess the probability of the necessity of a footnote disclosure	Two contingency cases	ANOVA	Shift factor	Not significant
					Communication mode	Significant
					Authoritative capacity	Significant
					Materiality	Significant

Study	Type of Decision Maker	Task	Cues	Modeling Technique	Variables of Interest	Results
Mayper (1982)	38 practicing auditors	To evaluate the materiality of 12 internal accounting control weakness	Twelve internal accounting control weaknesses	ANOVA	Consensus	A great amount of variability (.45)
					Experience	Did not affect consensus
Messier (1983)	29 audit partners	To determine the materiality of a write-down and the probability of a separate disclosure	Five financial variables: 1) net income, 2) earnings trend, 3) total assets, 4) total inventories, 5) current ratio	ANOVA	Cue Usage	Net income most important followed by earnings trend
					Consensus	Moderately high but contained some variability
					Self-insight	High
					Stability	High
					Experience and firm type	Related only to consensus
Ricchiute (1984)	60 senior accountants and managers	Probability that a final audit adjustment would be required	Two cases, one with moderate level of materiality and one with low level of materiality	ANOVA	Task presentation mode	Significant
					Materiality level	Significant

- There were differences between users, preparers, and auditors with respect to materiality thresholds. On the average across all studies, the materiality thresholds of auditors tended to be between those of preparers and users, but the variance among auditors was significant.
- There is significant difference in audit decisions when task information is communicated across three alternative models of presentation: visual, auditory, and visual/auditory. Materiality level was found to act as a moderating variable.

INTERNAL CONTROL EVALUATION

The second standard of fieldwork, the mandated requirement of communication of material weaknesses, and the Foreign Corrupt Practices Act recognize the importance of internal control evaluation for external auditing. As a result, there emerged a need for evaluation by auditing professionals of internal control judgments. Various descriptive laboratory studies applied the lens model methodologies to examine the characteristics of internal control judgments. These human information processing studies as they relate to internal control evaluation have been conducted by Ashton,[53] Ashton and Brown,[54] Ashton and Kramer,[55] Gaumnitz et al.,[56] Joyce,[57] Mock and Turner,[58] Reckers and Taylor,[59] Weber,[60] Srinidhi and Vasarhelyi,[61] Trotman et al.,[62] Trotman and Yetton,[63] Hamilton and Wright,[64] and Hall et al.[65]

These studies used internal control cases to elicit a judgment evaluation by auditors in general and students and professors in some cases. The studies were basically interested in investigating whether auditors given the same set of facts would be able to make consistent decisions in the evaluation of internal control. A summary of characteristics of the studies is given in Exhibit Appendix 1.3. The results showed high consensus and agreement among auditors in some studies and opposite results in others. Gaumnitz et al. tried to reconcile these differences and required their subjects to specify both internal control strength ad audit hour estimates.[66] Their results showed that if auditors make an explicit judgment of the internal control strength, and then provide audit hour estimates, good agreement is reached in both internal control evaluation and audit hour judgments. It showed that auditor decisions may be improved in terms of consensus by dividing them into different stages and providing linkages between the stages to guide the decision-making process. Accordingly, Srinidhi and Vasarhelyi identified three stages in evaluating internal controls which can also be linked using reliability concepts.[67] These stages were identification, evaluation, and interpretation. They asked their subjects to make their evaluation decisions under two conditions: (1) when auditors make judgments, given all the relevant information about the internal control system, and (2) when the decision stages are separated and auditors judge singly on substantive test restrictions, given the internal control strength. Their results reconcile the earlier discrepant findings by indicating that auditors will disagree on how to aggregate audit evidence, but once an aggregation rule is established, high consensus will follow. They concluded hat this "indicates the need for decision aids that normatively provide a consistent decision rule."[68]

Finally, a study y Weber on internal control evaluation focused on the question of free recall by experienced electronic data processing (EDP) auditors and accounting students.[69] The experimental task required subjects to write down as many of the controls as they could remember after they heard a list of 50 computer controls from five categories. The experts remember the controls in clusters conforming to the five categories of controls. The results present evidence of the impact of expertise on the organization of memory.

INTERNAL AUDIT EVALUATION

Lens model investigating the judgments of external auditors evaluating internal audits of corporations included experiments by Gibbs and Schroeder,[70] Brown,[71] Schneider,[72] and Abdel-Khalik et al.[73]

SAS No. 9, "The Effects of an Internal Audit Function on the Scope of the Independent Auditor's Examination," requires the independent auditor to evaluate the competence, objectivity, and performance of internal auditors to determine of the degree of reliance to be placed upon the work of internal audit staff.

Exhibit Appendix 1.3
Summary of Internal Control Studies

Study	Type of Decision Maker	Task	Cues	Modeling Technique	Variables of Interest	Results
Ashton (1974a,b)	63 auditors	Rate payroll internal control	Six indicators of payroll internal control	ANOVA (1/2 fractional replication of a 2^6 factorial design)	Decision rule form	Highly linear
					Predictability	86.4% of the variance
					Cue usage	Focus on separation of duties
					Self insight	$r = .89$
					Consistency	High ($\bar{r} = .81$)
					Consensus	High ($\bar{r} = .8$)
Joyce (1976)	35 auditors	Plan ------ of five categories of audit work	Five internal control and related accounting cues	ANOVA (1/2 factorial and complete) replication of a 2^5 factorial design	Decision rule form	Highly linear
					Predictability	High (78%)
					Cue usage	Focus on separation of duties
					Consistency	High
					Consensus	High ($\bar{r} = .863$)
					Self-Insight	Low ($\bar{r} = .39$) Low self insight and overestimation of less important cues ($r = .53$)

Exhibit Appendix 1.3 Continued

Study	Type of Decision Maker	Task	Cues	Modeling Technique	Variables of Interest	Results
Mock and Turner (1979)	71 Seniors and two supervisors	Adjust planned sample size for four specific auditing procedures based on improvement in internal controls	Extremely thorough case materials	ANOVA	Cue usage	Significant effect of changes in control
Reckers and Taylor (1979)	30 practicing auditors, 40 auditing professors	Rate payroll internal control	Payroll questionnaire	ANOVA	Consensus	Low: sample sizes for "strong" controls varied less than for fair controls Low ($\bar{r}$ = 0.1554) for auditors Low ($\bar{r}$ = 0.128) for professors
Weber (1978)	40 auditors	Estimate the dollar error in working papers, rate their confidence, assess the sensitivity of the dollar error, and estimate the man hours still required. Then revise the audit plan given new evidence	Case study and simulation decision aid was used by one of the two groups	Multiple regression	Consistency	Low ($\bar{r}$ = 0.1554) for auditors Low ($\bar{r}$ = 0.128) for professors
					Effects of simulation aid	Better accuracy, more confidence, less time and high level of satisfaction
					Extent of the audit plan	Increased with experience Decreased with risk taking propensity
					Consensus	Low consensus on error sensitivity of the possible dollar error ($\bar{r}$ = .78)

Study	Type of Decision Maker	Task	Cues	Modeling Technique	Variables of Interest	Results
Ashton and Kramer (1980)	30 undergraduate auditing students	Rate payroll internal control	Six indicators of payroll internal control	ANOVA (1/2 fractional) replication of a 2^6 factorial design)	Decision rule form Focus on separation of duties	Highly linear High 66% $r = .77$ Different from results obtained with auditors $\bar{r} = 0.66$
Ashton and Brown (1980)	31 auditors	Rate payroll internal control	Eight indicators of internal control	ANOVA (1/2 fractional) of 28 design plus 32 repeat cases	Decision rule form Predictability Cue usage Consistency Consensus Self-insight Sequence of cues Number of cues	Highly linear High, 71.3% Focus on separation of duties High ($\bar{r} = .91$) High ($\bar{r} = .67$) High ($\bar{r} = .86$) Not significant The addition of this cue had better effect

Exhibit Appendix 1.3 Continued

Study	Type of Decision Maker	Task	Cues	Modeling Technique	Variables of Interest	Results
Gaumnitz et al. (1982)	35 auditors	To make explicit judgments on the quality of internal control over accounts receivables and to estimate the number of hours required to assess the propriety and collectibility of accounts receivable	20 specific audit situations	ANOVA	Consensus	high ($\bar{r}$ = .704) for internal control High ($\bar{r}$ = .617) for the audit ---- estimates
					Internal control evaluation and audit program planning task	Increase relationship between the two judgments
Hamilton and Wright (1982)	78 auditors and students	Rate payroll internal control	Five internal control indicators	ANOVA (2^5 factorial)	Decision rule form	Highly linear
					Cue usage	Focus on separation of duties
					Consensus	High ($\bar{r}$ = .71)
					Self-insight	High
					Experience	Significant

Study	Type of Decision Maker	Task	Cues	Modeling Technique	Variables of Interest	Results
Trotman, Yetton and Zimmer (1983)	105 accounting majors	Evaluate the internal control system	32 audit checklists		Consensus	Higher for groups ($\bar{r}$ = .79) than for individuals ($\bar{r}$ = .56)
					Self-insight	Higher for groups ($\bar{r}$ = .69) than for individuals ($\bar{r}$ = .58)
					Group size	Three member groups outperformed two member groups
Trotman and Yetton (1985)	51 audit seniors and 24 managers	To evaluate whether the controls designed to achieve a payroll objective	Completed payroll internal control questionnaires	Factorial design	Consensus	Higher for the interacting groups than composite groups r = .70 for individuals and .79 for the review process

(Continued)

Exhibit 2.3 (Continued)

Study	Type of Decision Maker	Task	Cues	Modeling Technique	Variables of Interest	Results
Srinidhi and Vasarhelyi (1986)	77 auditors	To evaluate the purchase trans-action cycle and make a judgment at the evalua-tion stage and a judgment at the interpreta-tion stage	Description of the procedures and related controls in the purchase trans-action cycle, with the component reliabilities of four major proce-dures and controls at two levels of reliability	2^4 factorial design	Consensus	$\bar{r}$ = .5758 when component reliabilities are provided $\bar{r}$ = .9294 when system reliability is provided

The objective of Gibbs and Schroeder's study is to evaluate the judgment on internal auditor competence.[74] However, SAS No. 9 does not provide a description of the important criteria used by external auditors in arriving at judgments on internal audit evaluation. Therefore, in a first stage called a component development stage, Gibbs and Schroeder surveyed CPAS and internal auditors to develop a list of competence criteria by which internal audit departments should be evaluated. In a second stage called a component screening stage, they used a delphi method to reduce the list to the following five variables: the existence of a continuing education program, the adequacy of the educational background of the internal audit staff, the internal audit staff's knowledge of new trends and techniques in auditing, and the quantity and quality of internal audit department supervision. The third stage, called the model development stage, required 146 subjects from CPA firms to state a judgment of the internal audit department competence based on one of two levels of the five criteria identified in stage two. The final lens model developed indicated that knowledge of company operations, processes, and procedures and the quantity and quality of supervision are the most important factors, of those studied, affecting an external auditor's judgment of internal audit competence.

Rather than focusing on one factor, competency, Brown focused on some of the factors which might be considered important by independent auditors in evaluating the reliability of an internal audit function and the degree to which consistent use is made of those factors across auditors.[75] The subjects from "Big Eight" firms used one of two levels of six characteristics of internal audit functions to make a judgment of the degree of reliability to be placed on the internal audit function for each of 48 different scenarios. The 48 cases were composed of 32 principal cases followed by 16 repeat ones. Analysis of variance techniques were used to evaluate consistency objectives, namely consensus, insight, and stability. The results showed two factors to be most important: independence and previous audit work. Another interesting result was that, contrary to other studies, less experienced auditors had greater insight than more experienced auditors. Brown's model explained 79% of the total judgment variance, with interactions accounting for only 5% of this explained variation. In addition, he found a high level of consensus across auditors- the average correlation between ratings of all pairs of auditors was .70.

Finally, Schneider used conjoint measurement to derive models of 18 auditors' judgments of overall internal auditing strength, which were based on case profiles constructed using the three criteria suggested by SAS No. 9-competence, objectivity, and work.[76] Additive models were found to be appropriate for most of the auditors. Work was viewed as the most important factor, followed by competence and then objectivity.

Abdel-Khalik et al. investigated the effects of different EDP internal audit techniques and the administrative level to which the managers of the internal audit department report on the external auditor's evaluation of the internal control system.[77] The three EDP audit techniques examined were the integrated text facility, test data, and generalized audit software. The judgments made by seniors and mangers in CPA firms showed that the three EDP techniques were equally important and that the administrative level to which the head of the internal audit department reports was clearly a dominant factor. In addition, intrajudge consistency was high while interjudge consistency was moderate.

Colbert examined the assessment of inherent risk, a judgment that normatively affects the scope of work performed on audit engagement.[78] Auditors presented with four risk factors of a case were asked to make inherent risk assessments. The results pointed to the importance of one inherent risk factor: quality of personnel.

ANALYTICAL REVIEW EVALUATION

The importance of analytical review procedures as an aspect of the audit process was first established by SAS No. 1, Section 320, which states: "The evidential matter required by the third standard [of fieldwork] is obtained through two general classes of auditing procedures: (a) tests of details of transactions and balances, and (b) analytical review procedures applied to financial information."[79] This statement was further interpreted by SAS No. 23, which defines analytical review procedures as "substantive tests of financial information made by a study and comparison of relationships among data" and provides the basic premise that relationships among data may reasonably by expected by the auditor to exist and continue, and roles of the analytical review procedures vary depending on the auditor's objectives.[80] To gain further knowledge of the judgment behind the nature and extent of analytical review procedures, studies were conducted by Biggs and Wild,[81] Holder,[82] and Blocher et al.[83] Holder asked 35 senior accountants to examine a complete audit case, devise and execute a program of analytical review procedures, and identify audit risk areas.[84] The participants selected a wide range of analytical procedures. The most extensively used included inventory turnover, gross margin rates, accounts receivable, and aging analysis. The procedures were classified as either liquidity, reasonableness of individual elements, probability/capital maintenance, or operational and financial structure.

Blocher et al. examined the judgment of auditors concerning (1) the nature and extent of analytical review procedures that are planned in the audit program and (2) the nature of analytical review procedures applied by the auditor during the interim fieldwork for payroll expense and how they may be affected by the scope of tests of details in the prior year's audit program and the checklist of suggested analytical review procedures.[85] Forty-four auditors from a single large audit firm were asked to examine experimental cases adapted from the actual audit working papers of a medium-sized audit engagement and to complete a limited analytical review to identify, if any, the payroll expense accounts for which they feel further audit work is necessary. The results showed considerable variability of auditor judgment concerning the actual usage of analytical review procedures. In addition, the results show a tendency for the auditors to plan an audit approach with greater emphasis on analytical review relative to tests of details when presented with a low-scope audit program for the prior year's audit and the planning of more analytical review by auditors receiving the checklist of suggested analytical review procedures.

Kinney and Ueker had 154 auditors perform an analytical review of the gross profit for a small manufacturing firm after providing them with audited information about the components of the firm's gross profit and the gross profit percentage for two prior years.[86] Their task was to specify a noninvestigation region for the gross profit percentage. The main concern in the study was that the noninvestigation region established by auditors would be inappropriately affected by the opportunity to observe the client's unaudited book values with a bias toward the direction of the client's unaudited book value. One group of auditors was presented with a low unaudited book value and another with a high unaudited book value. The results confirmed the bias in the direction of the unaudited book values, with the added dimension that the auditors receiving the high book values were less influenced by the unaudited data than the auditors receiving the low book value.

Given the importance and implications of Kinney and Uecker's findings, Biggs and Wild conducted two similar experiments to determine the extent to which their results could be obtained with different subjects and a slightly modified task environment.[87] The first experiment required 121 practicing auditors to generate expected values and noninvestigation intervals given variations in the amount of audited information available and the presence or absence of unaudited information. The findings indicated that the auditors' judgments were biased in the direction of the unaudited information and the bias was moderated wen additional audited information was available. The second experiment required auditors to extrapolate intuitively an expected value for an account, given six different time-series patterns. The motivation for the second experiment refers to the evidence in psychology indicating that most individuals lack the ability to make accurate extrapolations. More specifically, these studies indicate the considerable difficulty individuals experience when dealing with quantitative data in an intuitive fashion,[88] the use of heuristic strategies that result in "nonoptimal" outcomes as prescribed by normative theory,[89] and the deficiencies in the ability of individuals to extrapolate from a relatively simple time series.[90] The auditors in Biggs and Wild's second experiment made accurate extrapolations for those time series that are more likely to be encountered in practice. The accuracy was higher for increasing trends than decreasing trends and for linear and logarithmic patterns than exponential patterns.

While all the studies reviewed so far have relied on regression or ANOVA methodologies to model judgment processes involved in the practice of accounting and auditing, a paramorphic technique. Saaty's analytic hierarchy process may be used to construct dominance scales of attributes that drive preferences for certain items over others.[91] To demonstrate the analytic hierarchy process, Arrington et al. investigated the preferences for various analytical review procedures of a sample of expert auditors.[92] They argued that the method is applicable to any number of auditing processes in which qualitative, nonmetric methods influence the quality of professional judgments. It can be used to determine both what attributes are important to subjects in forming their predictions and what independent variables subjects perceive as representative of those attributes.

COMMON STOCK RECOMMENDATION

Common stock recommendation and/or perception was also examined using the lens model to develop judgmental models of either stockbrokers or MBA students. To date, these models have been examined in studies conducted by Slovic,[93] Slovic et al.,[94] Belkaoui and Cousineau,[95] Wright,[96] and Ebert and Kruse.[97] A summary of the characteristics of these studies is shown in Exhibit Appendix 1.4. The main results are as follows:

- An additive (linear) model is appropriate for modeling common stock recommendation and perception although there is evidence of some configural (non-linear) processing in two studies.

Exhibit Appendix 1.4
Summary of Stock Recommendation Studies

Study	Type of Decision Maker	Task	Cues	Modeling Technique	Variables of Interest	Results
Slovic (1969)	Two young stockholders	To make a recommendation of stocks on a nine point scale	11 market and accounting cues	ANOVA	Decision rule form	Highly linear
					Predictability	High ($\bar{r}$ = .82)
					Consensus	Low ($\bar{r}$ = .32)
Slovic et al. (1972)	13 stockholders five MBA students	To estimate capital appreciation on a 9 point scale	Eight out of 11 market and accounting cues	ANOVA	Decision rule form	Highly linear
					Predictability	High
					Cue usage	EPS trend most important
					Consensus	Low
					Self-insight	Low and over-estimation of minor cues
					Prior experience	Significant
Belkaoui and Cousineau	50 MBA students	To state similarity ratings of each of the pairs of six stocks	Stock name, accounting and nonaccounting information	MDS Technique	Cue usage	Growth and ris
					Information	Stock name, accounting and nonaccounting information were useful

Study	Type of Decision Maker	Task	Cues	Modeling Technique	Variables of Interest	Results
Wright (1977)	39 second-year MBA students	To estimate ex-post price changes for 60 companies	Five accounting and market indicators	Regression, 60 real cases	Decision rule form	Partly nonlinear
					Predictability	High ($\bar{R}$ = .76 and .67)
						Low ($\bar{r}$ = .16 and .2)
					Accuracy	
					Consensus	Low
Ebert and Kruse (1978)	Five security analysts	To estimate the returns of 35 securities	22 information cues plus five repeat cases	Regression	Consistency	High
					Models of man	Average model of man outperformed average man
					Composite judge	More accurate than four out of five analysts

(Continued)

Exhibit Appendix 1.4 Continued

Study	Type of Decision Maker	Task	Cues	Modeling Technique	Variables of Interest	Results
Wright (1979)	35 first-year and 12 second-year MBA students	To estimate ex-post price changes for 60 companies	Four accounting and market indicators	Regression, 60 real cases	Decision rule form	Partly nonlinear
					Predictability	Median ($\bar{R}$ = .53 and .62)
					Accuracy	Low ($\bar{r}$ = .2 and .31)
					Consensus	Low ($\bar{r}$ = .38 and .54)
					Composite judge	More accurate than average judge
					Prior experience	2nd-year students more predictable, accurate and ----------

- The factors found to be important in the stock recommendation and perception decisions included earnings per share (EPS) trend, stock name, and accounting and nonaccounting information growth and risk.
- The consensus, accuracy, and self-insight of subjects were low, attesting to the difficulty of the decision itself and the need for better cues.
- Models of judges and composite judges were again proven to be superior to judges.

RISK PERCEPTION

Traditionally, the concept of risk was examined using market-data-based measures of risk, especially ex-post beta. The question remains to determine the ability of ex-post beta to reflect ex-ante risk accurately. The dilemma is raised as follows: "Through risk is a concept relevant before the occasion (i.e., ex-ante), it essentially must be measured in actual empirical work after the occasion (i.e., ex-post)."[98] Because assets are allocated on the basis of ex-ante risk and return, the examination of ex-ante measures is necessary for an evaluation of the efficiency of the investment process. The fact that risk perception may be used as a proxy for ex-ante risk motivated various studies examining the risk perceptions o financial analysis.

McDonald and Stehle examined how institutional investors perceive risk.[99] They asked 225 financial analysts to assess the risk of a sample of stocks, using their own definition of risk and their familiarity with each company and stock. The hypothesis was that historical beta and nonmarket risk substantially "explain" perceived risk, as judged by portfolio managers and analysts. The results were that beta and nonmarket risk were significantly related to perceived risk and perceived risk was lower as investors' own assessments of their familiarity with a company and its stock increase, provided beta and nonmarket risk are accounted for. McDonald and Stehle's study could be criticized for two reasons: its failure to specify the setting (individual or portfolio basis) in which the stock's risk should be assessed and the fact that risk perceptions could be regressed against other data sets than those considered by McDonald and Stehle. Accordingly, Farrelly and Reichenstein asked 209 portfolio managers and financial analysts to assess the risk of a sample of stocks as if each stock was to be added to a diverse portfolio.[100] The risk perceptions were then regressed against several publicly available measures of risk. The results provided evidence that the dispersion of analysts' forecasts appear to be measures that are more inclusive than systematic risk, and subjective measures of risk appear to conform more closely to analysts' risk perceptions and securities' expected return than do objective measures. In a follow-up study, Farrelly et al. used the risk assessment of 25 companies to investigate the issue of whether financial reports appear to convey, at least in an implicit fashion, information on risk.[101] The analysts were only provided the company names. The average risk perceptions were regressed against seven accounting measures of risk and explained 79% of the variations. In addition, the reasonableness of rising analysts' risk perceptions as a proxy for market risk was supported. One important caveat is admitted:

The present research is also only an *indirect* test of the relevance of accounting information in that only the company names, and no accounting data were supplied to the respondents. A desirable follow-up study would have respondents assess risk on the bases of accounting risk measures only- that is, without the names of companies. This would provide a direct test of the relevance of accounting information in assessing risk.[102]

Mear and Firth asked 38 financial analysts to provide risk and return judgments on 30 equity securities.[103] Their purpose was to provide more evidence on the self-insight ability of financial analysts, given the fact that related research indicates only limited self-insight. They used three alternative methods of measuring self-insight: the correlation between the objective and subjective weight indications of financial analysts, the ability of subjective weight models to reproduce actual judgments, and the correlation between the predicted outputs of the subjective weight model and the individual's optimal regression model. In general, the results indicate that the analysts were able to express the cue usage and importance in a manner which was consistent with the models and outputs of their judgment policies.

Mear and Firth conducted a similar experiment to test the relevance of accounting information and other market-related information in a risk assessment task.[104] Thirty-eight financial analysts were required to provide an assessment of the risk contribution of an individual security to a well-diversified client portfolio on the basis of cues that included accounting-based ratios, systematic risk, and variance of returns. The results provide significant support for the notion that publicly available information does convey some information relevant for security risk assessment.

MANAGERIAL ACCOUNTING

Managerial accounting issues were examined using the lens framework in three studies.

Harrell investigated two assumptions of Anthony's[105] conceptual framework in management planning and control: "(1) that middle-level managers' management control decisions are influenced strongly by the organizational goals emphasized by their senior managers and (2) that middle-level managers accurately can incorporate a specified importance of organizational goals into their management control decision."[106] Harrell asked 75 air force officers to rate the overall performance of 32 hypothetical pilot training wings on a scale from one (highly unsatisfactory) to eight (highly satisfactory) based on one of two levels of five primary goals that the pilot training wing wished to achieve. The levels were either satisfactory or unsatisfactory.

A pretest/post-test design with five groups of 15 individuals was used.[107] In the pretest, groups 2, 3, 4, and 5 were given a policy statement indicating the relative importance of the five goals. In addition, groups 3, 4, and 5 were given either consonant, dissonant, or random feedback after each of the 32 cases indicating the rating their immediate supervisor had given to each hypothetical wing. No significant differences were observed in the decisions made by the five groups during the pretest, indicating that the random selection and assignment procedures were successful. The post-test results showed different decisions between groups 1 and 2, indicating that the information in the policy statement did influence the subjects' decision-making behavior. Subjects in group 2 made decisions that were the same as those indicated by the policy-statement-based scoring model for 21 of the 32 cases. However, the same subjects placed different relative weights vis-à-vis the scoring model for three of the five cues. The results of the feedback cases showed that the subjects were influenced strongly by the feedback, which verified Anthony's first assumption. The second assumption was not supported by the results, leading Harrell to suggest that the problem is primarily cognitive and not motivational. He concludes as follows:

This outcome logically leads to the conclusion that the subjects were unable to accurately incorporate five weighted organizational goals into their decision making processes. Such a conclusion suggests that managers sometimes may make decisions that are not consistent with their organization's goals because of the information processing difficulties they experience when they attempt to incorporate multiple-weighted criteria into their decisions. If this is the case, then more attention should be given to the information processing limitations of managers when management control systems are designed.[108]

Ashton examined the performance of decision makers, their models, and composite predictions in a budgeting task.[109] Thirteen Time, Inc. employees were asked to make 42 predictions of the actual number of annual advertising pages appearing in *Time* magazine over a 14-year period based on five cues. The environmental predictability was .944. The accuracy of the subjects ranged from a low of .607 to a high of .916. While matching is typically higher than consistency in lens model studies, in this study median consistency (.96) was greater than median matching (.89), indicating that the subjects were less successful at acquiring knowledge than at applying it. In general, the models of people outperformed the individuals, the composite of the best three individuals, the composite of the three individuals actually responsible for such predictions, and the composite of all 13 individuals in the study. Ashton concludes as follows:

Since these are sophisticated decision makers who presumably can understand and appreciate these results, they should be willing to accept the prescription of replacing the procedure currently employed (i.e., consensus predictions by the magazine's publisher, advertising director, and business manager) with the model based on the cues actually used by the human decision makers.[110]

OTHER STUDIES

Various other lens studies have been reported.

- Schultz and Gustavson's study was aimed at mathematically modeling the decision processes of actuaries who price accountants' professional liability insurance.[111]
- Libby studied the effects on loan decision behavior of disclosing an uncertainty in the footnotes of the financial statements, and of adding the auditor's "subject to" uncertainty qualification to the footnote disclosure.[112]
- Danos and Imhoff studied the factors affecting reasonableness judgments in the auditor's review of financial forecasts.[113]
  A summary of the characteristics of these studies is shown in Exhibit Appendix 1.5.

CONCLUSION

The studies reviewed here witness the ability of the lens model to explain a large proportion of judgment variance in a wide variety of accounting and auditing issues and to provide relevant information on cue usage, accuracy of judgments, self-insight, consensus, consistency, and relative importance of individuals, models of individuals, composites of individuals, and mechanical models. One exception is Schepanski's finding that, despite generating high correlations, the linear model may not be an appropriate representation of information processing behavior of lenders in credit evaluation.[114] Chapter 6 will provide an alternative to the lens model.

Exhibit Appendix 1.5

Study	Type of Decision Maker	Task	Cues	Modeling Technique	Variables of Interest	Results
Schultz and Gustavson (1978)	Five actuaries	To assess the risk of litigation against CPA firm	Five character- istics of practice and clients	ANOVA	Cue usage Consensus Self-insight	All cue weights were significant Low ($\bar{r}$ = .12) High
Libby (1979)	34 commercial loan officers	To evaluate a \$2 million term loan request from a medium- sized company	Varying degrees of uncertainty disclosures	ANOVA	Cue usage Heuristics	Uncertainty dis- closure, supple- mental report was significant, whereas types of auditor report had no effect Subjects esti- mated the most likely outcome and then treated it as certain
Danos and Imhoff (1982)	42 auditors	To register a reasonableness judgment on a forecasting case	Five variables of importance to forecast accuracy	ANOVA	Decision rule form Self-insight Cue usage	Highly linear, r = .80 High Track record of management in forecasting income was the most important

NOTES

1. Frederick L. Jones, "Current Techniques in Bankruptcy Prediction," *Journal of Accounting Literature 6* (1987): 131-164.

2. Robert Libby, "Accounting Ratios and the Prediction of Failure: Some Behavioral Evidence," *Journal of Accounting Research* (Spring 1975): 151-161; "The Use of Stimulated Decision Makers in Information Evaluation," *Accounting Review* (July 1975): 475-489.

3. C. J. Casey, "The Usefulness of Accounting Ratios for Subjects' Predictions of Corporate Failure: Replications and Extensions," *Journal of Accounting Research* (Autumn 1980): 603-613.

4. I. Zimmer, "A Lens Study of the Prediction of Corporate Failure by Bank Loan Officers," *Journal of Accounting Research* (Autumn 1980): 629-636.

5. A. R. Abdel-Khalik and K. El-Sheshai, "Information Choice and Utilization in an Experiment on Default Prediction," *Journal of Accounting Research* (Autumn 1980): 325-342.

6. S. Moriarity, "Communicating Financial Information through Multidimensional Graphics," *Journal of Accounting Research* (Spring 1979): 205-224.

7. T. Kida, "An Investigation into Auditors' Continuity and Related Qualification Judgments," *Journal of Accounting Research* (Autumn 1980): 506-523.

8. Cornelius J. Casey and Thomas I. Selling, "The Effect of Task Predictability and Prior Disclosure on Judgment Quality and Confidence," *Accounting Review* (April 1986): 302-317.

9. C. J. Casey, "Prior Probability Disclosure and Loan Officers' Judgments: Some Evidence of the Impact," *Journal of Accounting Research* (Spring 1983): 300-307.

10. K. A. Houghton, "Accounting Data and the Prediction of Business Failure: The Setting of Priors and the Age of Data," *Journal of Accounting Research* (Spring 1984): 361-368.

11. Ahmed Belkaoui, "The Effect of Diagnostic and Redundant Information on Loan Officers' Predictions," *Accounting and Business Research* (Summer 1984): 249-256.

12. Peter Cahlos, "Financial Distress: A Comparative Study of Individual, Model, and Committee Assessments," *Journal of Accounting Research* (Autumn 1985): 527-543.

13. Peter Chalos and Sue Pickard, "Information Choice and Cue Usage: An Experiment in Group Information Processing," *Journal of Applied Psychology* 70, no. 4 (1985): 634-641.

14. Cornelius J. Casey, Jr., "Variations in Accounting Information Load: The Effects on Loan Officers' Predictions of Bankruptcy," *Accounting Review* (January 1980): 36-49.

15. Keith A. Houghton and Ratna Sengupta, "The Effect of Prior Probability Disclosure and Information Set Construction on Bankers' Ability to Predict Failure," *Journal of Accounting Research* (Autumn 1984): 768-775.

16. Robert Libby, "Man versus Model of Man: Some Conflicting Evidence," *Organizational Behavior and Human Performance* (June 1976): 1-12.

17. Lewis R. Goldberg, "Man Versus Model of Man: Just How Conflicting Is the Evidence?" *Organizational Behavior and Human Performance* (June 1976): 13-22.

18. Lewis R. Goldberg, "Man versus Model of Man: A Rationale, Plus some Evidence, for a Method of Improving on Clinical Inferences," *Psychological Bulletin* (June 1970): 422-432.

19. Robert Libby, "Man versus Model of Man: The Need for a Nonlinear Model," *Organizational Behavior and Human Performance* (June 1976): 23-26.

20. Ian Zimmer, "A Comparison of the Prediction Accuracy of Loan Officers and Their Linear-Additive Models," *Organizational Behavior and Human Performance* (February 1981): 69-74.

21. Ahmed Belkaoui, *Industrial Bonds and the Rating Process* (Westport, Conn.: Greenwood Press, 1983).

22. Duane Stock and Collin J. Watson, "Human Judgment Accuracy, Multidimensional Graphics, and Human versus Models," *Journal of Accounting Research* (Spring 1984): 192-206.

23. Barry L. Lewis, James M. Pattern, and Sharon L. Green, "The Effects of Information Choice and Information Use on

Analysts' Predictions of Municipal Bond Rating Changes," *Accounting Review* (April 1988): 270-282.

24. Lawrence Kessler, and Robert H. Ashton, "Feedback and Prediction Achievement in Financial Analysis," *Journal of Accounting Research* (Spring 1981): 146-162.

25. Ahmed Belkaoui, "Financial Information and the Prediction of Bond Ratings: Some Behavioral Evidence" (Working paper, University of Ottawa, July 1979).

26. Paul Danos, Doris L. Holt, and Eugene A. Imhoff, Jr., "Bond Raters' Use of Management Financial Forecasts: An Experiment in Expert Judgment," *Accounting Review* (October 1984): 547-573.

27. Robert H. Ashton and Lawrence Kessler, "Consistency among Alternative Performance Measures in an Applied Judgment Setting," *Acta Psychologica* 65 (1987): 211-225.

28. Kessler and Ashton, "Feedback and Prediction Achievement in Financial Analysis."

29. D. O. Steinmann, "The Effects of Cognitive Feedback and Task Complexity in Multiple-Cue Probability Learning," *Organizational Behavior and Human Performance* (April 1976): 168-179.

30. Kessler and Ashton, "Feedback and Prediction Achievement in Financial Analysis," p. 151.

31. R. Tucker, "A Suggested Alternative Formulation in the Developments by Hursch, Hammond, and Hursch, and by Hammond, Hursch, and Todd," *Psychological Review* (November 1964): 528-530.

32. Ashton and Kessler, "Consistency among Alternative Performance Measures," pp. 211-225.

33. Belkaoui, "Financial Information and the Prediction of Bond Ratings."

34. Ahmed Belkaoui, "Industrial Bond Rating: A Discriminant Analysis Approach," *Financial Management* (Spring 1978): 93-107.

35. Danos, Holt, and Imoff, Jr., "Bond Raters' Use of Management Financial Forecasts."

36. J. S. Carroll, "Causal Attribution in Expert Parole Decisions," *Journal of Personality and Social Psychology* (December 1978): 1501-1511; R. H. Phelps and J. Shanteau, "Livestock Judges: How Much Information Can an Expert Use?" *Organizational Behavior and Human Performance* (April 1978): 209-215; H. Einhorn, "Synthesis: Accounting and Behavioral Science," in supplement to *Journal of Accounting Research* (1976): 196-206.

37. Lewis, Patton, and Green, "The Effects of Information Choice and Information Use."

38. Abdel-Khalik and El-Sheshai, "Information Choice and Utilization in an Experiment on Default Prediction."

39. Lewis, Patton, and Green, "The Effects of Information Choice and Information Use."

40. Financial Accounting Standards Board, Discussion Memorandum, *Criteria for Determining Materiality* (Stamford, Conn.: FASB, May 1980), p. 3.

41. American Institute of Certified Public Accountants, *Statement on Auditing Standards* No. 5 (New York: American Institute of Certified Public Accountants, 1981), par. 411.04.

42. Financial Accounting Standards Board, *Criteria for Determining Materiality*, p. 132.

43. J. R. Boatsman and J.C. Robertson, "Policy-Capturing on Selected Materiality Judgments," *Accounting Review* (April 1974): 342-352.

44. T. R. Hofstedt and G. D. Hughes, "An Experimental Study of the Judgment Element in Disclosure Decisions," *Accounting Review* (April 1977): 379-395.

45. S. Moriarity and F. H. Barron, "Modeling the Materiality Judgments of Audit Partners," *Journal of Accounting Research* (Autumn 1976): 320-341; "Judgment Based Definition of Materiality," in supplement to *Journal of Accounting Research* (1979): 114-135.

46. B. H. Ward, "An Investigation of the Materiality Construct in Auditing," *Journal of Accounting Research* (Spring 1976): 138-152.

47. Alan G. Mayper, "Consensus of Auditor's Materiality Judgments of Internal Accounting Control Weaknesses," *Journal of Accounting Research* (Autumn 1982): 773-783.

48. William F. Messier, Jr., "The Effect of Experience and Firm Type on Materiality/Disclosure Judgments," *Journal of Accounting Research* (Autumn 1983): 611-618; "An Analysis of Expert Judgment in the Materiality/Disclosure Decision," *SE Aids Proceedings* (1981): 117-119.

49. G. L. Holstrum and W. F. Messier, Jr., "A Review of Integration of Empirical Research on Materiality," *Auditing: A Journal of Theory and Practice* (Autumn 1982): 45-63.

50. M. Firth, "Consensus Views and Judgment Modes in Materiality Decisions," *Accounting, Organizations and Society* 4, no. 4 (1979): 283-295.

51. David N. Ricchiute, "An Empirical Assessment of the Impact of Alternative Task Presentation Modes on Decision Making Research in Auditing," *Journal of Accounting Research* (Spring 1984): 341-353.

52. J. J. Schultz, Jr. and P. M. J. Reckers, "The Impact of Group Processing on Selected Audit Disclosure Decisions," *Journal of Accounting Research* (Autumn 1981): 482-501.

53. R. H. Ashton, "An Experimental Study of Internal Control Judgments," *Journal of Accounting Research* (Spring 1974): 143-157; "Cue Utilization and Expert Judgments: A Comparison of Independent Auditors with Other Judges," *Journal of Applied Psychology* (August 1974): 437-444.

54. R. H. Ashton and P. R. Brown, "Descriptive Modeling of Auditors' Internal Control Judgments: Replication and Extension," *Journal of Accounting Research* (Spring 1980): 269-277.

55. R. H. Ashton and S. S. Kramer, "Students as Surrogates in Behavioral Accounting Research: Some Evidence," *Journal of Accounting Research* (Spring 1980): 1-15.

56. B. R. Gaumnitz, T. R. Nunamaker, J. J. Surdick, and M. F. Thomas, "Auditor Consensus in Internal Control Evaluation and Audit Program Planning," *Journal of Accounting Research* (1982): 745-755.

57. E. J. Joyce, "Expert Judgment in Audit Program Planning," in supplement to *Journal of Accounting Research* (1976): 29-60.

58. T. J. Mock and J. L. Turner, "The Effects of Changes in Internal Controls on Audit Programs," in T. H. Burns, ed., *Behavioral Experiments in Accounting* (Columbus: Ohio State University, 1979), 2:277-302.

59. P. M. J. Reckers and M. E. Taylor, "Consistency in Auditors' Evaluations of Internal Accounting Controls," *Journal of Accounting, Auditing and Finance* (Fall 1979): 42-55.

60. R. Weber, "Auditors Decision Making on Overall System Reliability: Accuracy, Consensus and the Usefulness of a Simulated Decision Aid," *Journal of Accounting Research* (Autumn 1978): 368-388.

61. B. N. Srinidhi and M. A. Vasarhelyi, "Auditor Judgment Concerning Establishment of Substantive Tests Based on Internal Control Reliability," *Auditing: A Journal of Practice and Theory* (Spring 1986): 64-76.

62. K. T. Trotman and P. W. Yetton, and I. Zimmer, "Individual and Group Judgments of Internal Control Systems," *Journal of Accounting Research* (Spring 1983): 286-292.

63. K. T. Trotman and P. W. Yetton, "The Effects of the Review Process on Auditor Judgments," *Journal of Accounting Research* (Spring 1985): 256-267.

64. R. E. Hamilton and W. F. Wright, "Auditor Consensus in Internal Control Evaluation and Audit Program Planning," *Journal of Accounting Research* (Autumn 1982): 756-765.

65. C. Hall, P. W. Yetton, and I. Zimmer, "The Assessment of Payroll Internal Control Systems and Auditors' Experience, Tolerance of Ambiguity, and Dogmatism," *Australian Journal of Management* (June 1982): 49-60.

66. Gaumnitz, Nunamaker, Surdick, and Thomas, "Auditor Consensus in Internal Control Evaluation and Audit Program Planning."

67. Srinidhi and Vasarhelyi, "Auditor Judgment Concerning Establishment of Substantive Tests."

68. Ibid., p. 75.

69. R. Weber, "Some Characteristics of the Free Recall of Computer Controls by EDP Auditors," *Journal of Accounting Research* (Spring 1980): 214-241.

70. Thomas E. Gibbs and Richard G. Schroeder, "Evaluating the Competence of Internal Audit Departments," in *Symposium on Auditing Research III* (Urbana-Champaign: Department of Accountancy, University of Illinois, 1979), pp. 207-225.

71. Paul R. Brown, "Independent Auditor Judgment in the Evaluation of Internal Audit Functions," *Journal of Accounting Research* (Autumn 1983): 444-455.

72. Arnold Schneider, "Modeling External Auditors' Evaluations of Internal Auditing," *Journal of Accounting Research* (Autumn 1984): 657-678.

73. A. R. Abdel-Khalik, Doug Snowball, and John H. Wragge, "The Effects of Certain Internal Audit Variables on the Planning of External Audit Programs," *Accounting Review* (April 1983): 215-227.

74. Gibbs and Schroeder, " Evaluating the Competence of Internal Audit Departments," pp. 207-225.

75. Brown, "Independent Auditor Judgment in the Evaluation of Internal Audit Function," pp. 444-455.

76. Schneider, "Modeling External Auditors' Evaluations of Internal Auditing," pp. 657-671.

77. Abdel-Khalik, Snowball, Wragge, "The Effects of Certain Internal Audit Variables on the Planning of External Audit Programs," pp. 215-222.

78. Janet L. Colbert, "Inherent Risk: An Investigation of Auditors' Judgments," *Accounting, Organizations and Society* (January 1988): 111-121.

79. American Institute of Certified Public Accountants, Statement on Auditing Standards No. 1, *Codification of Auditing Standards and Procedures* (New York: American Institute of Certified Public Accountants, 1978), p. 34.

80. American Institute of Certified Public Accountants, Statement on Auditing Standards No. 23, *Analytical Review*

Procedures (New York: American Institute of Certified Public Accountants, 1978), p. 1.

81. Stanley F. Biggs and John J. Wild, "An Investigation of Auditor Judgment in Analytical Review," *Accounting Review* (October 1985): 607-633.

82. W. Holder, "Analytical Review Procedures in Planning the Audit: An Application Study," *Auditing: A Journal of Practice and Theory* (Spring 1983): 100-107.

83. E. Blocher, R. Esposito, and J. Willingham, "Auditors' Analytical Review Judgments for Payroll Expense," *Auditing: A Journal of Practice and Theory* (Fall 1983): 75-91.

84. Holder, "Analytical Review Procedures in Planning the Audit."

85. Blocher, Esposito, and Willingham, "Auditor's Analytical Review Judgments for Payroll Expense."

86. W. R. Kinney and W. C. Uecker, "Mitigating the Consequences of Anchoring in Auditor Judgments," *Accounting Review*, (January 1982): 55-69.

87. Biggs and Wild, "An Investigation of Auditor Judgment in Analytical Review."

88. C. R. Peterson and L. R. Beach, "Man as an Intuitive Statistician," *Psychological Bulletin* (July 1967): 29-46; A. Tversky and D. Kahneman, "The Belief in the Law of Small Numbers," *Psychological Bulletin* (August 1971): 105-110; A. Tversky and D. Kahneman, "Availability: A Heuristic for Judging Frequency and Probability," *Cognitive Psychology* (September 1973): 207-232; G. DeZeeuw and W. A. Wagenaar, "Are Subjective Probabilities Probabilities?" in C. A. S. Stael VonHolstein, ed., *The Concept of Probability in Psychological Experiments* (Dordrecht, Neth.: Reidel Publishing Company, 1974).

89. R. M. Hogarth and S. Makridadis, "Forecasting and Planning: An Evaluation," *Management Science* (February 1981): 115-138.

90. W. A. Wagenaar and S. Sagaria, "Misperception of Exponential Growth," *Perception and Psychographics* (December 1975): 416-422; W. A Wagenaar and H. Timmers, "Intuitive

Prediction of Growth," in D. F. Burkhardt and W. H. Ittelson, eds., *Environmental Assessments of Socio-Economic Systems* (New York: Plenum, 1978), pp. 103-122; W. A. Wagenaar and H. Timmers, "The Pond-and-Duckweed Problem: Three Experiments on the Misperception of Growth," *Acta Psychologica* (may 1979): 239-251.

91. T. L. Saaty, *The Analytic Hierarchy Process* (New York: McGraw-Hill, 1980).

92. C. Edward Arrington, William Hillison, and Robert E. Jensen, "An Application of Analytical Hierarchy Process to Model Expert Judgments on Analytical Review Procedures," *Journal of Accounting Research* (Spring 1984): 298-312.

93. P. Slovic, "Analyzing the Expert Judge: A Descriptive Study of a Stockbroker's Decision Process," *Journal of Applied Psychology* (August 1969): 255-263.

94. P. Slovic, D. Fleissner, and W. S. Bauman, "Analyzing the Use of Information in Investment Decision Making: A Methodological Proposal," *Journal of Business* (April 1972): 283-301.

95. Ahmed Belkaoui and Alain Cousineau, "Accounting Information, Nonaccounting Information and Common Stock Perception," *Journal of Business* (July 1977): 334-342.

96. W. F. Wright, "Properties of Judgments in a Financial Setting," *Organizational Behavior and Human Performance* (February 1979): 73-85; "Cognitive Information Processing Models: An Empirical Study," *Accounting Review* (July 1977): 676-689.

97. R. J. Ebert and T. E. Kruse, "Bootstrapping the Security Analyst," *Journal of Applied Psychology* (February 1978): 110-119.

98. E. H. Bowman, "Risk Seeking by Troubled Firms," *Sloan Management Review* (Summer 1982): 33-42.

99. John G. McDonald and Richard E. Stehle, "How Do Institutional Investors Perceive Risk?" *Journal of Portfolio Management* (Fall 1975): 11-16.

100. Gail E. Farrelly and William R. Reichenstein, "Risk Perceptions of Institutional Investors," *Journal of Portfolio Management* (Summer 1984): 5-12.

101. Gail E. Farrelly, Kenneth R. Ferris, and William R. Reichenstein, "Perceived Risk, Market Risk, and Accounting Determined Risk Measures," *Accounting Review* (April 1985): 278-288.

102. Ibid., p. 287.

103. Ross Mear and Michael Firth, "Cue Usage and Self-Insight of Financial Analysts," *Accounting Review* (January 1987): 176-182.

104. Ross Mear and Michael Firth, "Risk Perceptions of Financial Analysts and the Use of Market and Accounting Data," *Accounting and Business Research* (Forthcoming).

105. Robert A. Anthony, *Planning and Control Systems: A Framework for Analysis* (Cambridge, Mass.: Harvard University Press, 1965).

106. Adrian M. Harrell, "The Decision-Making Behavior of Air Force Officers and the Management Control Process," *Accounting Review* (October 1977): 833-841.

107. D. T. Campbell and J. T. Stanley, *Experimental and Quasi-Experimental Designs for Research* (Chicago: Rand McNally College Publishing Company, 1963).

108. Harrell, "The Decision-Making Behavior of Air Force Officers," p. 840.

109. Alison Hubbard Ashton, "An Empirical Study of Budget Related Predictions of Corporate Executives," *Journal of Accounting Research* (Autumn 1982): 440-449.

110. Ibid., p. 448.

111. J. J. Schultz and S. G. Gustavson, "Actuaries' Perceptions of Variables Affecting the Independent Auditors' Legal Liabilities," *Accounting Review* (July 1978): 626-641.

112. R. Libby, "The Impact of Uncertainty Reporting on Loan Decision," in supplement to *Journal of Accounting Research* (1979): 35-57.

113. P. Danos and E. A. Imhoff, Jr., "Auditor Review of Financial Forecasts: An Analysis of Factors Affecting Reasonableness Judgments," *Accounting Review* (January 1982): 39-54.

114. A. Schepanski, "Tests of Theories of Information Processing Behavior in Credit Judgment," *Accounting Review* (July 1983): 581-599.

CHAPTER 2
EXPECTED UTILITY MODEL AND THE SUBJECTIVE EXPECTED UTILITY PARADIGM

Models of risky choice are used either to predict or describe how individuals make risky choices. These models rely generally on expectation models where the objective function of individuals is assumed to be the maximization of a mathematical expectation. This chapter describes the expectation models or expected utility models in general and the subjective expected utility (SEU) model in particular as SEU is the most popular research paradigm in the risky choice literature. Because the SEU model has not been proven to be a good descriptor of decision making and because its assumptions have been found to be easily violated, other risky choice models have been proposed in the literature and will also be covered in this chapter. Accounting research has also provided some evidence on the axioms of the SEU model and the relevance of the model in both accounting and in auditing. Therefore, a final objective of this chapter is to cover the situation in accounting.

EXPECTED UTILITY MODELS

Expected utility models focus on choices among risky projects whose outcomes may be either single or multidimensional. If n outcome vectors can be denoted by $\bar{x}_i$ and n probabilities by p_i such that

$$\sum_{i=1}^{n} p_i = 1$$

then an expected utility model is one which predicts or prescribes that people maximizes

$$\sum_{i=1}^{n} F(p_i)U(\bar{x}_i)$$

If the probabilities are expected to be subjective the model is known as an SEU model. The SEU for a particular act is determined by the total of the products of probability and utility for each combination of act and event. The next step is to choose the act that maximizes the SEU.

Other expectation models exist depending on how the probabilities and outcomes are defined:

- If the outcomes are defined in terms of value (like money) and the probabilities are defined as objective probabilities, the expectation model is an expected value model.
- If the outcomes are defined in terms of utility and the probabilities are objective, the expectation model is an expected utility model.
- If the outcomes are values and the probabilities are subjective, the expectation model is a subjective expected value model.
- If the outcomes are utility and the probabilities are subjective, the expectation model is an SEU model.

In fact, variants of the expected utility models differ on how utilities are measured, what types of probability transformation $F(.)$ are allowed, and how the outcomes $\overline{x}_i$ are measured. If $v(x)$ denotes an interval scaled utility measure constructed under uncertainty and $u(x)$ denotes one constructed in lotteries, the nine variants of the expected utility model are:[1]

1. Expected monetary value: $\Sigma p_i \Sigma x_i$
2. Bernoullian expected utility:[2] $\Sigma p_i v(x_i)$
3. Von Neumann-Morgenstern expected utility:[3] $\Sigma p_i u(x_i)$
4. Certainty equivalent theory:[4] $\Sigma(p_i)x_i$
5. Subjective expected utility:[5] $\Sigma(p_i)v(x_i)$
6. Subjective expected utility:[6] $\Sigma(p_i)u(x_i)$
7. Weighted monetary value: $\Sigma w(p_i)x_i$
8. Prospect theory:[7] $\Sigma w(p_i)v(x_i)$
9. Subjectively weighted utility:[8] $\Sigma w(p_i)u(x_i)$

SUBJECTIVE EXPECTED UTILITY (SEU) MODEL
Purposes of the SEU Model

The most generally accepted expectation model rests on the maximization of SEU. SEU is a theory of decision that rests on certain axioms. Acceptance of the axioms makes SEU a rational or normative theory of decision making. Rejection of the axioms defeats the SEU maximization model. As a result, four essentially different purposes of the SEU model by be distinguished:

1. The SEU model may be used *descriptively* to model the decision process underlying risky choice.
2. The SEU model may be viewed as *predictive* or *positivistic*. The validity of the assumptions are not important as long as the model has good predictive accuracy compared to other models. The assumptions are viewed as "plausible provisional assumptions"[9] and "the relevant question to ask about the 'assumptions' of a theory is not whether they are descriptively 'realistic' for they never are, but whether they are sufficiently good approximations for the purpose in hand. This question can be answered only by seeing whether the theory works, which means whether it yields sufficiently accurate predictions."[10]
3. The SEU model may be viewed as *postdictive*.
4. The SEU model may be viewed as a *rational* or *normative* theory of decision.

The proponents of each of these views interpret empirical evidence on SEU differently. The descriptive and normative views favor evidence on the axioms while the predictive and postdictive view favors evidence on real world behavior.

Basic Axioms of the SEU Model

There are slightly different axioms and axiom systems underlying slightly different versions of SEU.[11] Becker and McClintock described a typical system including five axioms: (1) *Transitivity*- if A is preferred to B and B is preferred to C, then A should be preferred to C; (2) *Comparability* or *Decidability*- in comparing two outcomes, individuals should be able to decide either that they prefer one to the other or are indifferent between them; (3) *Dominance*- if for every possible state of nature, act A produces at least as desirable an outcome as act B, then act B should not be preferred to act A; (4) *Irrelevance* (of identical outcomes)- in the process of making a choice between two possible acts, the outcomes that are not related to the choice should not influence the choice. Then if for some event two acts lead to the same outcome, they should not affect the decision. This axiom has also been called the *sure-thing principle*; (5) *independence* (of utility and probability)-

the individual's beliefs about the probability of the occurrence of a given outcome should not be affected by the extent of desire for or against the outcome.[12]

If an individual accepts these five axioms, then the following three consequences follow: the probabilities exist in a ratio scale (0 to 1); the utilities exist on an interval scale (0 to 100 with, for example, a score of 60 having twice as much utility as a score of 30); and the maximization of SEU is the optimal choice criterion.

Should the axioms be accepted? In what follows, research findings on these axioms are presented that cast doubts on the normative status of the SEU model.

TESTING THE AXIOMS OF THE SEU MODEL
Transitivity of Preferences

Examination of an individual's preferences pointed to a violation of the transitivity axiom in cases involving the intransitivity of indifference and in cases involving multidimensional alternatives. In an example of the multidimensional alternative case, Tversky examined the conditions under which the transitivity axiom may be violated.[13] He noted that "the purpose of the following studies was to create experimental situations in which individuals would reveal consistent patterns of intrasensitive choices. The experiments are not addressed to the question of whether human preferences are, in general, transitive, but rather to the question of whether reliable intrasensitivities can be produced, and under what conditions."[14] The transitivity axiom has both a deterministic and stochastic form: in the deterministic case it states that AB and BC implies AC; in the stochastic form it posits that the probability that AB, denoted P(AB) is at least ½ and P(BC)≥1/2. Violations of this weak stochastic transitivity cannot be due to random error or inconsistency alone. In two separate experiments, one dealing with gambles, the other with college applicant decisions, Tversky provided evidence of systematic and predictable violations of weak stochastic transitivity.[15] The first experiment investigated preferences between sample gambles. The five two-outcome gambles were of the form (x,p,o,), where one receives a payoff of $x if a chance event p occurs and nothing if p does not occur. The values of p, *displayed in nonnumerical form*, were 7/24, 8/24, 9/24, 10/24, and 11/24 for gambles a, b, c, d, and e, respectively; the corresponding values of x were $5.00, $4.75, $4.50, $4.25, and $4.00. Because of the nonnumerical form of the probabilities no exact calculation of expected values was possible. In addition, the gambles were constructed so that the expected value increased with probability and decreased with payoff. It was hypothesized that at least some subjects would ignore small probability differences and chose between adjacent gambles (e.g., A and B, B and C, etc.) on the basis of payoffs, but for gambles lying far apart on the chain (e.g., A and E), on the basis of the probability p or the expected value (EV) of the gamble, which increased monotonically in p. As expected, the majority of the participants violated transitivity in the expected direction and in the expected location. The second experiment, structured as the first one, called for the selection of college applicants focusing on preference between profiles rather than gambles. Intransitive preferences were also exhibited in the second experiment;. The subjects were surprised by their own intransitivity at the postexperimental debriefing. Four possible explanations are provided for the violation of transitivity: (1) transitivity is viewed as a logical principle whose violation represents an error of judgment or reasoning; (2) intransitivities can be attributed to a change in taste that took place between choices; (3) most decisions are made sequentially-thus, having chosen y over x and then z over y, one is typically committed to z and may not even compare it with x, which has already been eliminated; and (4) the eliminated alternative is no longer available so there is no way of finding out whether our preferences are transitive or not.[16] Tversky warns about the consequences of the intransitivity of preferences as follows:

Transitivity, however, is one of the basic and the most compelling principles of rational behavior. For if one violates transitivity, it is a well known conclusion that he is acting, in effect, as a "money-pump." Suppose an individual prefers y to x, z to y, and x to z. It is reasonable to assume that he is willing to pay some amount of money to replace y by z and still a third amount to replace z by x. Thus, he ends up with the alternative he started with but with less money.[17]

Irrelevance of Identical Outcomes

The irrelevance of identical outcomes axiom or sure-thing principle was first tested by Ellsberg.[18] The problem presented an individual with two decision situations, each involving a pair of gambles as shown in Exhibit 2.1. The probabilities are drawn from an opaque bad containing 90 balls; 30 are red and the remaining 60 are black or yellow in unknown proportions. On ball is drawn at random from the bag . Ellsberg's subjects chose act 1 in situation A reasoning that there are at least 60 balls that are either red or black. Notice, however, that in each situation acts have common axioms in the case of a yellow ball. Following the sure-thing principle in making the choice between two acts, the outcomes from a yellow ball should not influence the choice. Therefore , a choice of act 1 in situation A calls for a choice of act 3 in situation B. Alternatively, a choice of act 2 in situation A calls for a choice of act 4 in situation B. Therefore, Ellsberg's students violated the irrelevance of identical outcomes axioms. Ellsserg did, however, argue that some of the probabilities involved in Ellsberg's paradox are ambiguous, which brings us to the next experiment.

The irrelevance of identical outcomes axion was also tested by Allais, resulting in what is known as the Allais paradox.[19] The problem presented to the subjects is shown in Exhibit 3.2. Allias' subjects chose gamble 1 over gamble 2 in situation A, reasoning that there is a 100% chance of winning $1,000,000, and chose gamble 4 over gamble 3, reasoning that the probabilities of winning are almost similar and the payoff is larger in gamble 4. If, however, the problem was represented as in Exhibit 3.3, assuming that there are 100 probability points of each gamble available to be drawn at random, then the gambles in each situation appear identical and the payoffs attached to balls 12 to 100 should not affect the choice. In such a case the sure-thing principle calls for a choice of either gamble 1 and gamble 3 or gamble 2 and gamble 4. Therefore, Allais' subjects violated the irrelevance of identical outcomes axioms.

Exhibit 2.1
Ellsberg's Test of the Sure-Thing

	Red	Black	Yellow
Situation A			
Act 1: Bet on red	$10	Nothing	Nothing
Act 2: Bet on black	Nothing	$10	Nothing
Situation B			
Act 3: Bet on red or yellow	$10	Nothing	$10
Act 4: Bet on black or yellow	Nothing	$10	$10
Probabilities	30/90	60/90	

Exhibit 2.2
Allais' Test of the Sure-Thing Principle

Situation A

	Probability of Winning	Amount to Win
Gamble 1	100%	$1,000,000
Gamble 2	10%	5,000,000
	89%	1,000,000
	1%	Nothing

Situation B

Gamble 3	11%	$1,000,000
	89%	Nothing
Gamble 4	10%	$5,000,000
	90%	Nothing

Exhibit 2.3
Representation of the Allias Problem

	Ball Numbers		
	1	2-11	12-100
Situation A			
Gamble 1	$1,000,000	$1,000,000	$1,000,000
Gamble 2	Nothing	$5,000,000	$1,000,000
Situation B			
Gamble 3	$1,000,000	$1,000,000	Nothing
Gamble 4	Nothing	$5,000,000	Nothing

gamble available to be drawn at random, then the gambles in each situation appear identical and the payoffs attached to balls 12 to 100 should not affect the choice. In such a case the sure-thing principle calls for a choice of either gamble 1 and gamble 3 or gamble 2 and gamble 4.

Given the serious implications of these findings for the normative status of SEU, another study was undertaken by MacCrimmon.[20] Business executives were presented the following four gambles after being given arguments for conforming and conflicting with the axiom.

A: 500% return with p=.10, bankruptcy with p=.01, and 5% return with p=.89
B:5% return for sure
A':500% return with p=.10 and bankruptcy with p=.90
B': 5% return with p=.11 and bankruptcy with p=.89.

In this test, 40% of the subjects violated the sure-thing principle. During a postexperimental interview, MacCrimmon found that his managers viewed their choices and ratings as mistakes, leading him to conclude that the normative status of SEU was not violated. MacCrimmon's conclusions were questioned by Slovic and Tversky, who noted that the subjects may have been influenced to conform to the axiom.[21] Their one study asked the question: Do reasonable people, who understand the competing arguments, accept the sure-thing principle? Their results supported the violation of the axiom.

Dominance

Dominance or admissibility as an axiom was tested by MacCrimmon.[22] The subjects were asked to rank a number of alternative wagers from the one they preferred most to the one they preferred least. The three pairs of wagers used to test dominance were:

(a_1) Win $1,200 if the Gross National Product for 1964 is $610 billion; lose $400 otherwise.
(b_1) Win $1,200 if the Gross National Product for 1964 is over $600 billion; lose $400 otherwise.
(a_2) Win $1,200 if Goldwater receives the Republican nomination for president in 1964; lose $400 otherwise.
(b_2) Win $1,200 if Goldwater or Rockefeller receives the Republican nomination for president in 1964; lose $400 otherwise.

(a₃) Win $1,200 if the price of Syntex on the American Stock Exchange is at least twice its current price by the end of the year; lose $400 otherwise.
(b₃) Win $1,200 if the price of Syntex on the American Stock Exchange is higher than its current price by the end of this year; lose $400 otherwise.

In each case the b alternative dominates the a alternative. Of the 37 subjects who completed the experiment, 12 violated it at least once, and five out of 12 had multiple violations. During the postexperiment interview, almost all the subjects who had violated the postulate revised their decisions.

Independence of Utility and Probability

The axiom asserts that decision makers' beliefs should be independent of their tastes and was also tested by MacCrimmon.[23] The subjects were asked to rank, from most preferred to least preferred, all bets on a page containing either eight or 12 bets. An example of the type of quadruple and reward condition used is:

1. Win $1,200 if a fair coin falls heads up; lose $400 otherwise.
2. Win $1,200 if the gold outflow exceeds the gold inflow in the U.S. tis year; lose $400 otherwise.
3. Win $1,200 if Britain enters the Common Market this year; lose $400 otherwise.
4. Win $1,200 if the price of the Stock System on the American Stock Exchange at the end of this year will be at least twice its current price; lose $400 otherwise.

The axiom was violated by the majority of the subjects, indicating strong dependence between tastes and beliefs. During the postexperiment interview, however, almost all of the violations were attributed to mistakes the complexity of the experiment. The several forms that the violation may take are shown in Exhibit 3.4.[24] Graph 1 describes the independence between utilities and subjective probabilities as stated by the axiom. Graphs 2 and 3 show that individuals may overestimate the probability of desirable events and underestimate the probability of undesirable events. A situation of "partial optimism" is generated when the level of assessed probability is a function of the sign, but not the magnitude of the utilities.

Exhibit 2.4
Possible Dependencies of Subjective Probability on Utility

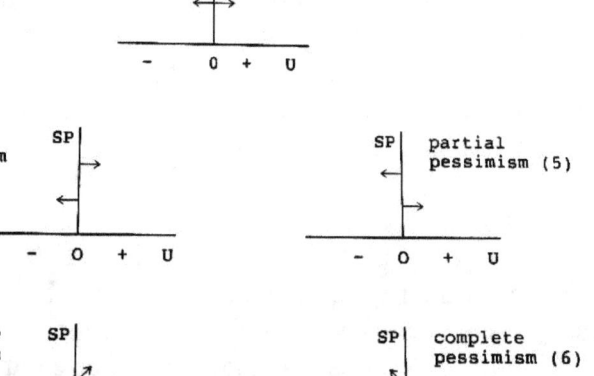

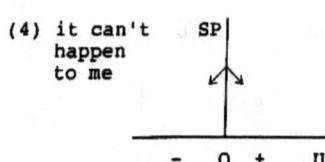

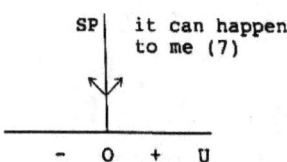

Arrows indicate changes in the subjective probability of an event as the event becomes more desirable (+) or more undesirable (−).

A situation of "complete optimism" is generated when the relationship between utilities and subjective probabilities is more or less continuous over the entire range of utilities. Graphs 5 and 6 show the cases of partial and complete pessimism. They are the converse of partial and complete optimism.

DOES SUBJECTIVE EXPECTED UTILITY THEORY DESCRIBE DECISION MAKING?

Subjective expected utility maximization or subjective expected value maximization is assumed to predict the choices made by individuals. In the studies investigating this hypothesis, subjects were asked to make choices between gambles which were then compared to those predicted by the SEU model. If the theory worked, subjects given two gambles having the same expected values should be indifferent between the two. However, Edwards in a series of experiments showed that two-thirds of his subjects had definite preferences between pairs of gambles that had equivalent expected values.[25] Even when the concept was carefully explained to the subjects, Lichtenstein, Slovic, and Zinc found that expected value was irrelevant as a guide to choice.[26] To check on some of the reasons behind the failure of the model, Lichtenstein and Slovic asked their subjects to evaluate gambles using either a choice procedure or a bidding procedure.[27] In the choice procedure the subjects indicate which pair of gambles they prefer, while under the bidding procedure they name an amount of money at which they would be indifferent between playing a specified single gamble or having that amount of money. The results of the two procedures for the same subject were not correlated. The subjects tended to prefer the gambles containing a higher probability of winning when choosing between gambles, and gave higher bids for gambles containing the large amounts to win, which is inconsistent with the SEU model's specification that all choices should be made by maximizing SEU.

While the above studies and others presented evidence contradicting the SEU or the Expected Value (EV) models, various other studies found support for the models. Examples of studies finding support for the models include those by Coombs, Bezembinder, and Goode,[28] Tversky,[29] Wallsten,[30] Miller and Lanzetta,[31] Mosteller and Nogee,[32] Myers, Reilly, and Taub,[33] Myers, Suydam, and Gambino,[34] Royden, Suppes, and Walsh,[35] and Suydam.[36] It is appropriate to not that studies that support SEU theory are based on experiments that are simpler than those that refute SEU theory. A resultant argument, if correct, restricts the applicability of the model. As Rapoport and Wallsten state:

Moreover, if correct, the argument severely restricts the applicability of SEU theory to a very narrow, unacceptable class of experimental tasks. It seems then that the conflicting evidence pertaining to SEU theory is presently irreconcilable. Consequently, the basic experimental question should not be whether to accept or reject SEU theory as a whole, but rather to systemically discover the conditions under which it is or is not valid.[37]

The failure of the SEU models may in fact be due to inabilities of subjects in structuring the decision problem. If the structure is wrong then SEU will automatically fail. The structuring of a problem representation is itself a clinical art rather than a science. Fischhoff states: "Regarding the validation of particular assessment techniques we know . . . next to nothing about eliciting the structure of problems from decision makers."[38] Decision aids may, of course, be used to help decision makers structure the decision problem.[39] The danger is that these aids, derived from decision theory, may have no relations whatsoever to real-world problems. One solution calls for the development of "prototypical decision analytic structures."[40]

Prototypical decision analytic structures . . . are developed to meet the substantive characteristics of a given problem, but are at the same time general enough to apply similar problems. . . .

Today decision analysis books have chapters such as simple decisions under uncertainty and multi-attribute evaluation problems. I am looking forward to chapters such as "sitting industrial facilities, pollution control management" and "contingency planning."[41]

These developments are important in view of the notion that the process of problem representation may be more important than the subsequent SEU computation. The way knowledge is elicited affects decision makers' estimates, judgment, and choices. Engaging in decision analysis without a good assessment of knowledge may lead the decision maker to have unwarranted confidence in the stated problem representation. As Fischhoff notes: "Decision Analysis is oriented to picking the apparent best alternative rather than to assessing the adequacy of our knowledge. It may encourage us to act where ignorance dictates hesitation or continued information gathering."[42]

OTHER RISKY CHOICE MODELS
Higher Moments Model
The most important criticism of the SEU model is the argument that individuals base their risk-taking decisions to a certain extent on the dispersion of a gamble's possible outcome. The gamble may be viewed as a probability distribution over the possible monetary outcomes. While expectation models of risky choice have focused on the first moment of the probability distribution outcomes, i.e., the means, other higher moments have been ignored, namely the second moment (variance), the third moment (skewness), and the fourth moment (Kurtosis). An argument for a focus on the variance is the belief that a person's "utility for risk" can be expressed in terms of his or her preference for variance.

The first experimental study of variance preferences concluded that they were less important than probability preferences.[43] Later studies, however, presented evidence indicating that variance has rather strong effects[44] and some preferences for skewness.[45] Slovic and Lichtenstein warned, however, that because the variance of the gamble is invariably confounded with the gamble's probabilities and payoffs, behaviors interpreted by studies as indicating variance preference are subject to alternative interpretations.[46]

For example, consider the choice between the following gambles:

A.	.5 wins $1	B.	.5 wins $2
	.5 loses $1		.5 loses $2
	(variance = 1.00)		(variance = 4.00)

While the choice of gamble A over gamble B could be attributed to a preference for minimizing variance, it could be explained alternatively as a desire to maximize EU or to minimize the maximum possible los. Similarly, while the choice of gamble B could be due to a desire to maximize variance, it could just as well be interpreted as our attempt to maximize the potential gain.[47]

To untangle the effects of variance from the effects of other aspects of the payoff distribution, Slovic and Lichtenstein managed to manipulate the variance without changing the particular probabilities and payoffs explicitly displayed to the subjects. The device used involves a stimulus called a "duplex gamble." It consists of two disks, one used to determine winning and one used to determine loss. The subject can win and not lose, lose and not win, both win and lose, or neither win nor lose. It is different from the standard two-outcomes gamble where the subjects either win or lose. Exhibit 3.5 shows a parallel duplex and standard gamble. They are parallel because they have the same stated probabilities and payoffs. The duplex gamble has, however, less variance. In three experiments, Slovic and Lichentstein asked subjects to evaluate the attractiveness of parallel standard and duplex gambles after manipulating the sizes of the variances, the differences between variances, and the response mode. The subjects were required to choose between gambles or to state a price for which they would sell a ticket that would enable them to play each gamble. The results indicated that variance is at best a minor determinant of gambling decisions.

These results were supported by Payne and Braunstein.[48] Unlike Slovic and Lichenstein, who held the payoffs and probabilities constant across pairs of parallel standard and duplex gambles, Payne and Braunstein presented their subjects with different values of payoffs and probabilities for pairs of duplex gambles with equal variance. Exhibit 3.6 shows an example of a pair of duplex gambles with equal variance. Payne and Braunstein hypothesized that if subjects choose between these gambles on the basis of the underlying distributions, no consistent preferences would be expected.

Exhibit 2.5
Parllel Duplex and Standard Gambles

Win $2

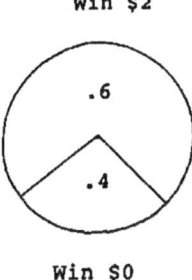

.6

.4

Win $0

Lose $2

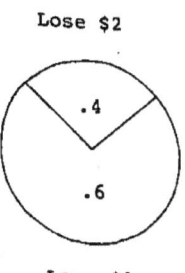

.4

.6

Lose $0

Expected Value = $ .40
Variance   = $1.92

Standard Gamble

Win $2

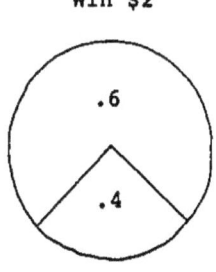

.6

.4

Lose $2

Expected Value = $ .40
Variance   = $3.84

Exhibit 2.6
Pair of Duplex Gambles Equivalent in Variance

Duplex Gamble No. 1

Win $.40

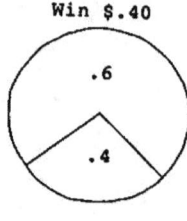

Win $0

Lose $.40

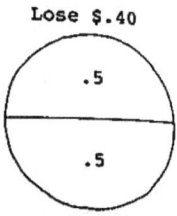

Lose $0

Expected Value = $.0784
Variance   = $.04

Duplex Gamble No. 2

Win $.40

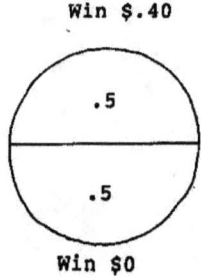

Win $0

Lose $.40

Lose $0

Expected Value = $.0784
Variance   = $.04

However, if choices are based on the explicit stated values on the risk dimensions, preferences should be related to these dimensions.[49] The results showed that the preferences among these gambles were related to the relationships among the displayed probabilities, again indicating that choices were not influenced by variance.

Expected Regret Ratio

The risky choice situation can be characterized by the following payoff matrix:

	P	1-P
α	a	b
β	c	d

The subject is asked to choose between the two alternatives or gambles, α or β, given two states of nature with probabilities P and 1-P respectively. The cells a, b, c, and d represent the payoffs available to the subject. In most SEU studies the strength of preference for one gamble versus the other has been measured by the probability $p(\alpha\beta)$ (that α is chosen rather than β) and the subject's direct rating of his or her strength of preference for α over β (or vice-versa). Most SEU studies have relied on the difference in expected value for the two gambles as the index to account for the different preference strength found as a function of variation in payoff and state-of-nature probabilities. Let x=a-c and y=d-b. When x and y are positive, the difference in the expected value of the two gambles, D, is equal to

$$D(\alpha\beta) = P_x - (1-P)y$$

Various studies show that preference strength increases with D.[50]

Another proposed index is called the expected regret ratio (R)[51] or the "expected loss ratio."[52] The proposition is that as in the case of D, the greater the R for a pair of gambles, the greater will be the preference strength. The expected regret ratio may be computed as:

Various studies have shown that both D and R predict preference strength, with R appearing to be superior.

Lee, however, argued that in this type of research both D and R have been strongly confounded and gave formulas for the construction of sets of gamble pairs unconfounded (orthogonal) in D and R.[53] Hence, for given values of $D(\alpha\beta)$, $R(\alpha\beta)$, and D, we can compute

$$x = \frac{D(\alpha\beta)R(\alpha\beta)}{L[2R(\alpha\beta) - 1]}$$

and

$$y = \frac{D(\alpha\beta)[1 - R(\alpha\beta)]}{(1 - P)[2R(\alpha\beta) - 1]}$$

Using gambles where D and R were unconfounded, he ran two experiments on the effects of expected value difference (D) and expected regret ratio (R) in the strength of preference between the gambles.[54] The results showed that D can affect preference strength when R is controlled and vice-versa. In addition, it was found that there are strong determinants of preference strength other than D and R that need to be accounted for in the future.

Risk Dimension Models

The lack of consistent results in studies of the descriptive validities of the SEU model or the preference for higher moments in general and variances in particular may be due to the use of gambles whose probabilities and payoffs were highly, if not completely, confounded. What this means is that subjects' preferences may be explained not by recourse to notions of probability and variance preferences but, alternatively, by strategies that focus on the basic risk dimensions of the gamble. In fact, various studies have suggested that the preferences for some of the risk dimensions may better explain risky choice behavior.[55] Coombs and Pruitt's study found some probability preferences, but was based on the idea that a person has an ideal probability of winning and that, when other variables such as expected value are controlled, choices among bets are determined by the similarity of each bet's probability of winning to the person's ideal.[56] Their results suffer, however, from the confounding inherent in the two-outcome gambles.

A study that investigates the risk dimension model and escapes the confounding limitations was conducted by Slovic and Lichenstein.[57] They viewed gambles as multidimensional stimuli along four basic risk dimensions: probability of winning (P_W), amount to win ($\$_W$), probability of losing (P_L), and amount to lose ($\$_L$). The influence of these basic risk dimensions was investigated with particular emphasis on two ideas. The first idea is the notion of "importance beliefs," which means that individuals rely more on some basic risk dimensions than others because they believe that these particular dimensions are more important for their particular decisions. A person with little money and fear of losing it will rely more on the amount to lose ($\$_L$) in making a gambling decision. The second idea is the notion of information processing. Individuals with strong beliefs about the relative importance of various risk dimensions will focus on these beliefs and neglect others because of their limited information processing capabilities.

To test these ideas, two experiments were conducted by Slovic and Lichtenstein in which subjects judged the attractiveness of the same duplex gambles under different instructions. Subjects in a rating group rated the attractiveness (or unattractiveness) of each gamble on a 10-point scale. Subjects in a bidding group relied on one of three bidding techniques. The first bidding technique required the subjects to state the largest amount of money they would be willing to pay in order to play a bet if it was attractive, and the smallest amount they would like to receive in order to play a bet if it was unattractive. The second bidding technique required the subjects to state the least amount of money for which they would sell a ticket that enables them to play attractive gambles. For unattractive gambles, they stated the highest amount of money they would pay the experiments in order not to play the gamble. The third bidding technique required the subjects to state a fair price for a gamble without knowing whether they or the experiments owned the right to play it. The human information processing model of the individuals making the risky choice was formulated as

$$A(G) = U + W_1P_W + W_2\$_W + W_3P_L + W_4\$_L$$

Where $A(G)$ is the attractiveness of a gamble and the W's are weights reflecting the relative importance of each risk dimension. This model has its advantages: it "combines, in additive fashion, variables such as P_W and $\$_W$ or P_L and $\$_L$, which are usually thought to combine multiplicatively. In addition, it assumes that the import of probabilities and payoffs is a linear function of their objective values."[58] Using analysis of variance, Slovic and Lichenstein found that an average of about 75% of the total response variation in $A(G)$ was accounted for by the simple weighted combinations of the four risk dimensions. The results showed that most of the subjects' responses were overwhelmingly determined b one or two of the risk dimensions and were unresponsive to large changes in the values of the less important factors. Approximately two thirds of the subjects were influenced more by P_W than P_L in the rating group with an average correlation of .48 between P_W and attractiveness in the bidding group. The bidding group found the amount to lose, P_L, to be the most important with an average correlation of -0.50 between $\$_L$ and bids. These results support the usefulness of the risk dimension model in explaining risky choice behavior. They were supported by other studies.[59]

Prospect Theory

SEU's most formidable contemporary competitor as a descriptive theory of choice is the *prospect theory* introduced by Kahneman and Tversky on the basis of a series of experimental observations.[60] They argued that choices among risky projects exhibit several pervasive effects that are inconsistent with the basic tenets of utility theory. Four effects observable in the process of choosing among bets were introduced:

1. *Certainty effect*: "people outweigh outcomes that are considered certain, relative to outcomes which are merely probable."[61]
2. *Reflection effect*: "the reflection of prospects around 0 reverses the preference order."[62]
3. *Aversion to probabilistic insurance*: while expected utility theory implies that probabilistic insurance is superior to regular insurance, respondents did not like it.
4. *Isolation effect*: "in order to simplify choices between alternatives, people often disregard components that the alternatives share, and focus on the components that distinguish them."[63]

Prospect theory includes two phases in the choice process: an early phase of editing and a subsequent phase of evaluation. "The editing phase consists of preliminary analysis of the offered prospects, which often yields a simpler representation of these prospects. In the second phase, the edited prospects are evaluated and the prospect of highest value is chosen."[64]

Six major editing operations are proposed:
1. *Coding*: people normally perceive outcomes as gains and losses relative to some neutral reference point, rather than final states of wealth or welfare.
2. *Combination*: prospects are sometimes simplified by combining the probabilities associated with identical outcomes.
3. *Segregation*: some prospects include a riskless component that is segregated from the risky component in the editing phase.
4. *Cancellation*: involves the discarding of common constituents of options, such as common outcome-probability combinations.
5. *Simplification*: refers to the simplification of prospects by rounding probabilities or outcomes and discarding extremely unlikely outcomes.
6. *Detection of dominance*: involves the scanning of offered prospects to detect dominated alternatives, which are rejected without further evaluation.

In addition, Kahneman and Tversky argue that the subjective valuation of the possible outcomes of a decision depends on a person's reference point or frame of reference, where the frame of a decision is simply the decision maker's concept of the decision problem or structure.[65] The *framing effect* refers to the tendency of people to maintain psychological accounts.

To describe the framing and evaluation of compound outcomes, we use the notion of a psychological account, defined as an outcome frame, which specifies (i) the set of elementary outcomes that are evaluated jointly and the manner in which they are combined, and (ii) a reference outcome that is considered neutral or normal.[66]

For example, the possible outcomes of a gamble can be framed either as gains or losses relative to the status quo or as asset positions that incorporate initial wealth. While invariance requires that changes in the description of outcomes should not alter the preference order, evidence on framing effects shows a violation of this requirement. As a result, Kahneman and Tversky presented an analysis that implied that an individual's subjective state can be improved by framing negative incomes as costs rather than as losses.[67] Such manipulation can explain a paradoxical form of behavior known as the dead-loss effect. Thaler gives the example of a man who develops tennis elbow soon after paying the membership fee in a tennis club and continues to play in spite of the pain to avoid wasting his investment.[68] Kahneman and Tversky explain the man's behavior as follows:

Assuming that the individual would not play if he had not paid the membership fee, the question arises: How can playing in agony improve the individual's lot? Playing in pain, we suggest, maintains the evaluation of the membership fee as a cost. If the individual were to stop playing, he would be forced to recognize the fee as a dead-loss, which may be more aversive than playing in pain.[69]

Preference Reversals

In the Slovic and Lichtenstein study covered earlier in this chapter, the results showed that the subjects' bidding responses to gambles were markedly different from their ratings of the attractiveness of the same gambles.[70] The former response related to the amount that could be lost or won, the latter to the probability of losing or winning. A response mode effect was obtained in two other experiments by Lichtenstein and Slovic.[71] Subjects were presented with gambles where they could win either a medium amount of money with a high probability (P) or a large amount of money with a low probability ($). Both students and gamblers in a casino playing for high stakes showed a preference reversal phenomenon: the tended to prefer (P) when asked to make a choice and they bid higher amounts for ($) when asked to make a bid. This preference reversal phenomenon is important as it violates almost all theories of preference, including expected utility theory. It was observed in various studies.[72] After increasing motivation by raising the face value of the payoffs and creating differences in expected value between P and $ bets in a pair, Grether and Plott still found a substantial proportion of reversals, leading them to conclude that "even when the subjects are exposed to strong incentives for making motivated, rational decisions, the phenomenon of preference reversal does not vanish."[73] After imposing more controls, giving a description of the expected value concept, and even showing the expected values of all gambles, Reilly found some evidence of the preference reversal phenomenon as a persistent behavioral phenomenon in situations where economic theory is generally applied.[74] Slovic and Lichtenstein, however, reviewed all these preference reversal studies and interpreted the findings as reflecting different information processing strategies induced by the different response modes.[75] In choice questions and in the ratings of attractiveness of gambles, subjects seem to focus on probabilities; in bidding questions, subjects seem to focus on dollar amounts. They suggested three paths for research:

- Continue subjecting preference reversal studies to more scrutiny.
- Modify utility theory in order to accommodate as many of the behavioral anomalies as possible without abandoning the theory altogether.
- Accept the reality of preference reversals and related information processing phenomena and explore their implications for important social and economic behaviors.

THE SITUATION IN ACCOUNTING
Testing the Axioms of the SEU Model in Accounting

As stated earlier, if a decision maker rejects one or more of the axioms of the SEU model applied in accounting, then SEU maximization does not necessarily follow. One of the axioms most often violated by decision makers is the independence axiom. It has two major sets of implications-the irrelevance of identical outcomes and risk versus uncertainty. Ashton investigated the former using 83 MBA students.[76] A hypothetical investment decision was used where three independent variables were manipulated: the probability distribution over the potential payoffs (.10, .89, .01), the amount of the desirable payoff (45% or 45% return while the level of the certain payoff was held constant at 9% return), and the amount of the undesirable payoff or loss (bankruptcy or 1% return). The hypothetical decision situation was similar to that used by MacCrimmon.[77] The choices made by the subjects showed a surprisingly high degree of conformity to the axiom. Following their choices, the subjects were presented with two arguments, one in favor of the choices prescribed by the axiom and the other in opposition to the choices prescribed by the axiom. Of those who initially conformed to the axiom, 14% decided to make violating changes after reading the arguments. The subjects who initially conformed to the axiom rated the violating argument as more compelling than the conforming argument, a phenomenon which was also observed in the other experimental studies of the independence axiom in psychology. Ashton used the written explanations of the choice made by the students to argue that the vast majority of the subjects relied upon a single expected value (expected return) criterion. A follow-up experiment (involving 32 MBA students) in which the task dimensions of expected value and maximum payoff were disentangled, provides more support for the first findings that subjects used an expected value maximization strategy in making their choices that conformed to those prescribed by the independence axiom. In the accounting study, fewer violations of the independence axiom were found in the investment decision-making task involving graduate students.

Another study by Allison H. Ashton investigated whether 439 audit partners and managers of "Big Eight" public accounting firms violated the irrelevance axiom (the Allais paradox), first using the abstract Allais problem and then in two adaptations of the problem to auditing contexts.[78] One context involved three problems on bidding on two municipal audits. The second context involved three problems on audit opinion concerning technically unresolved matter. One of each of the three problems on bidding and on opinion had the same probability as the original Allais problem. The results showed that more violations occurred in response to the original Allais problem than in response to the similar problems crouched in auditing-related contexts. The violation rate in the opinion context was significantly less than the violation rate in the original Allais problem, but the violation rate in the municipal context is not significantly different from that in the original Allais problem. There were more violations for the three municipality bidding problems than the three opinion problems.

Both accounting studies point to the role of "experience" and "realism" as factors contributing to the lower level of violations than those observed in psychology. Expert auditors seem to be less likely to violate the axiom when exposed to familiar problems than when exposed to abstract problems.

SEU Maximization in Accounting

Studies by Ronen,[79] Hirsch,[80] and Snowball and Brown[81] examined a sequencing effect contrary to the SEU model where individual decision makers would be indifferent between events with equal point probability (expected values) but different sequences of marginal probabilities.

In Ronen's experiment the hypothesis was that in a two-stage process, despite the identical objective joint probability for each action, subjects would choose the action with the higher probability of first-stage success because of some form of discounting of probabilities.[82] Twenty-two graduate business school students were presented with two sets of two bags A and B, each containing specific proportions of different colors of marbles. The subjects were required to choose set A or set B in such a way that one could sequentially pick a blue marble from the first bag, followed by a red marble from the second bag. In 16 out of 20 trials, the joint probability of picking a blue marble followed by a red marble was identical for set A and set B and the first-stage probabilities of drawing a blue marble from bag 1 differed between the two sets. A sequence effect resulting from a discounting strategy was found as a majority of the subjects preferred those sets in which there was a higher probability of picking a blue (winning) marble from the first bag. So, rather than being indifferent between actions of the same expected utility, the subjects were affected by the way the probabilities were presented. A replication using 96 management-program participants in a two-act decision where the joint probabilities were unequal showed a preference for the act with the higher initial probability but the lower overall expected value. In addition, this preference was found not to hold for small differences between first-stage probabilities.

Hirsch extended Ronen's findings of a sequence effect by using both a chance task and a business task, manipulating more independent variables, and examining the effect of a personality variable.[83] The subjects in the manufacturing task were asked to decide between specialty products which were identical in terms of the probabilities of successful production in each of two production departments and in terms of their joint probabilities of success. Three independent variables were manipulated with (1) four levels for the joint probabilities of the alternative choices, (2) two levels for the magnitudes of the joint probabilities, and (3) three levels of the difference between the initial probabilities of the alternative choices. For both tasks the sequence effect (in terms of a preference for higher initial probabilities) existed at all levels of the other variables. In addition, the sequence effect was stronger at lower levels of joint probability differences, higher levels of joint probability magnitudes, and higher levels of initial-probability differences. These results were stronger in the chance task than the business task. The responses in the business task showed that subjects who scored as internals on an locus-of-control scale were significantly more prone to the sequence effects than externals, who were almost unanimously expected value maximizers.

Snowball and Brown used an estate trust investment context to investigate bank trust officers' use of disaggregated probabilities.[84] They noted that the choice sets in Ronen's and Hirsch's experiments were constructed in such a way that if the joint probability of A exceeded B, the first-stage probability of B exceeded A, which automatically sets a deviation from expected values as a sequence effect. The manipulation included four levels of both first-stage and second-stage probability differences and three levels of joint probability differences. The task was set up to be capable of distinguishing between four types of choice models: maximization of joint probability (expected value), maximization of first-stage probability, maximization of second-stage probability, and minimization of joint probability. The results showed that nearly two thirds of the responses supported the maximization of expected value, while 18.5% of the responses supported the maximization of first-stage probability (the sequence effect) and 11% supported the maximization of second-stage probability. In addition, normative behavior was associated with larger joint probability differences while suboptimal strategies were associated with larger firms or second-stage probability differences (a higher disposition toward risk).

Greer hypothesized that there exists a basic conflict between utility theory and actual risk tolerance decision processes, namely that intuitive decisions made by business executives will be inconsistent with decisions prescribed by expected utility models derived, in part, from estimates supplied by the same executives.[85] Business executives were asked to choose between 20 pairs of hypothetical capital investments structured as standard lottery type gambles with an opportunity to receive either X_0 with certainty or a 50% chance of X_1 or X_2. Expected utility models for each subject were constructed using the following model:

$$U(\bar{x}, \sigma_x) = \frac{\frac{A}{C}\bar{x} - Z(p_i)\frac{A}{C}\sigma_x}{F_{min}}$$

Where

$\overline{X}$ = the expected payoff associated with the project in question
σ = the standard deviation of that project
A = the dollar size of the firm's entire earning-asset package
c = the capital required for the project in question
F_{min} = some minimally acceptable level of total net cash flow from operations
P_t = the maximum probability the firm is willing to tolerate of having actual total net cash flows from operations dip below F_{min} in a given reporting period
$Z (p_t)$ = the standard normal deviation associated with the tolerable probability, p_t.

The values of F_{min} and A were derived from published sources and the value of p, was inferred from questioning the executives.

The utility functions obtained were used to remake the risk/no-risk decisions for all investments which were accepted by each firm. The choices made by the executives were found to be inconsistent with those made by the expected utility models. Greer concludes:

This is a classic case of actual behavior conflicting with a pre-activity statement of what behavior would be. It suggests that utility theory may not be acceptable to real-world decision makers because, when they actually sit down to make a decision they are not willing to take the amount of risk they said they *would* take before they sat down.[86]

He also suggested that the minimum possible outcome may be an important factor in the subjects' decisions.

This seems to indicate that the *minimum possible* outcome associated with a risky project is an important factor in real-world decision processes- that firms operate almost in according with a MAXIMIN rule of some sort or that decision makers are under great pressure to avoid any chance of a project outcome lower than some specified minimum.[87]

In Greer's study the utility of an investment opportunity is an increasing function of the expected value of that opportunity and a decreasing function of the risk of the opportunity. The standard deviation of payoffs was used as a measure of risk. Hoskins disagreed and showed that the semivariance of outcomes rather than the standard deviations in the choices made by the expected utility models were more consistent with the subjects' actual choices.[88] Greer and Skekel retorted that the decision makers were, in fact, using a curvilinear linked utility function.[89] Fischburn argued that Greer's mean-standard-deviation utility tradeoff model is incompatible with the expected utility model of von Neumann and Morgenstern except when the firm's utility function is linear in returns.[90] He also examined the extent to which the choices made by the subjects could be explained by expected utility models based on four types of u function, namely, a linear function, a quadratic function, a two-piece linear function, and a general increasing function. The general function was found to account for almost all the decisions, which indicated good support for the correspondence between intuitive decisions and those prescribed by expected utility models. Greer remained unconvinced.[91]

SEU Maximization in Auditing

Lewis examined expert judgment in auditing within an expected utility framework.[92] Under such a framework he argued that there are two sufficient conditions for consensus. "First, different auditors would have to arrive at the same probability distribution over the specified set of states. Second, auditors would have to possess homogenous utilities for the outcomes or consequences of their decisions."[93] Of these two conditions, homogeneous probability distributions over states of nature and homogeneous utilities for outcomes or consequences of decisions, Lewis chose to investigate the latter. The context chosen was of a product liability suit against a client. The subjects ranked the desirability of two consequences associated with three outcomes. The three outcomes, derived from FASB statement No. 5, pertain to the following disclosure rules based on the probability that future events will confirm the existence of a liability at the balance sheet date: accrual of a liability if it is probable that a liability has been incurred; disclosure in notes to the financial statements if it is reasonably possible that a liability has been incurred; and no disclosure if the probability is remote that a liability has been incurred. The two consequences included a favorable or unfavorable disposition of the lawsuit: client liable or client not liable. In addition, the materiality of the contingent loss from the lawsuit was manipulated to yield low and high materiality conditions.

Seventy auditors with at least five years of experience from four big eight audit firms participated in the experiment. Homogeneity was measured as the average pairwise correlation of the utility measures among all auditors in each case. The results showed that different firms have different loss functions and that partners from different firms have different abilities or desires to transfer those functions to staff members. In addition, the level of homogeneity utilities tend to be higher in highly material situations, especially among members of the same firm. Lewis gave his reasons for expecting that utilities may differ across individuals from different accounting firms:

Although "Big 8" firms have obvious similarities, they differ in several important dimensions. It is known, for example, that insurance costs differ significantly across firms. Such differences would logically affect the perceived significance of potential lawsuits. Differences in total revenues (size) could also affect the impact of undesirable outcomes. The desire to develop or maintain distinct reputations or personalities might also be a source of firm differences. Such firm differences, if significant, would lead us to expect greater homogeneity among members of the same firms than among members of different firms.[94]

In an investigation of the materiality construct in auditing, Ward provided some results on the specification of auditors' loss functions.[95] Each of the subjects, eight partners and 16 managers in public accounting firms, were presented with six different monotonically increasing functional forms: linear, bounded linear, modified exponential, step, logistic, and exponential, where the x-axis represented the magnitude of an overstatement of net income resulting from a type of error in reporting receivables and the y-axis represented the expected loss to the auditor. The subjects were asked to select the form which best expressed their perception of the relationship between the negative consequences to the auditor (should the error go undetected) and the magnitude of the overstatement. The results showed that 12 out of 24 subjects felt that either the logistic or exponential relationship was most descriptive, and more than 6% of the auditors thought that the potential expected loss would "level off" at some point. Six auditors found the loss functions for income overstatement effects and income understatement to be symmetrical. The same six, plus another six, found the threshold amounts for the expected loss to be equal for over- and underestimates. The mean overstatement threshold was, however, 70% smaller than the mean understatement threshold. In addition, 17 auditors placed dollar values on the amount of expected loss. Ward also asked the subjects to rank the importance of 24 factors in making materiality judgments, including elements of legal, technical, professional, personal, and environmental influences on the auditor.[96] A Q-sorted method was chosen for ordering the items into five piles. The results showed little agreement among auditors as to their cognitive beliefs about the materiality construct (Kendall's $W = .386$, $p \geq .01$).

Newton tested whether the decision reached concerning the materiality of an item is influenced by the degree of uncertainty about the final resolution of the issue and the CPA's willingness to accept the risk of an incorrect decision.[97] The technique of cardinal utility curve analysis was used to investigate the materiality decisions of 19 partners of COA firms. The subjects were asked to respond to three decision cases, each involving three different amounts. Case 1 was a standard gamble used to very broadly measure the subject's attitude toward risk, in which the subjects were given three separate situations and asked what probability of winning a given gamble would be needed to make them indifferent between the sure receipt of a given sum of money and the gamble. Case 2 involved the value of marketable securities whose value had declined permanently and management refused to write down the investment. The subjects specified a materiality amount at which they would qualify the audit report. Then, after being told that the permanence of the decline was probabilistic, the subjects were presented with several dollar value declines and asked for the minimum probability that the decline would be permanent, which would justify issuance of a qualified opinion. Case 3 involved a situation in which a contingent liability arose from the damages of a lawsuit which the company fully expected to lose. The subjects were first asked for the minimum amount of damages arising from the lawsuit which would influence them to issue a qualified audit report. Then, after being told that the loss would be one of three amounts, the subjects were asked to state the minimum probability that the damages would be reduced to each amount that would be necessary for them not to qualify the report.

Sixteen out of nineteen subjects were classified as risk averse in Case 1 (standard gamble), while the results were mixed for Cases 2 and 3. Some subjects indicated that they would qualify the opinions without regard to the probability, although most seemed to use the probabilities in their judgments. Few subjects (10 in Case 2 and seven in Case 3) exhibited invariance of probabilities over different dollar amounts, a result Newton viewed as a violation of utility theory. Libby, in his analysis of Newton's results, noted however, that the behavior observed does conform with a model constrained by absolute aversion to risk of all losses in excess of some cut-off.[98]

CONCLUSION

Much remains to be done in accounting research with respect to testing the axioms of the SEU model in accounting and auditing contexts, testing the SEU maximization hypothesis, and examining the relevance of the other risky choice models identified in the psychological literature.

NOTES

1. Paul J. Schoemaker, "The Expected Utility Model: Its Variants, Purposes, Evidence and Limitations," *Journal of Economic Literature* (June 1982): 529-563.

2. Daniel Bernoulli, "Specimen Theorial Novae De Mensura Sortis," in *Commentarri Acadmiae Scientiarium Imperialis Petropolitanae 1738, Tomus V,* pp. 195-197. Translated by Louise Sommer as "Expositions of a New Theory or the Measurement of Risk," *Econometrica* (January 1954): 23-26.

3. John von Neumann and Oscar Morgenstern, *Theory of Games and Economic Behavior*, 2nd ed. (Princeton, N.J.: Princeton University Press, 1947).

4. Hans Schneeweis, "Probability and Utility Dual Concepts in Decision Theory," in Guenter Menges, ed., *Information, Inference and Decision* (Dordrecht, Netherlands: D. Reidel, 1974), pp. 113-144; Jagdish Handa, "Risk, Probabilities and a New Theory of Cardinal Utility," *Journal of Political Economy* (February 1977): 97-122; Bruno de Finetti, "La Prevision: Ses Lois Logiques, Ses Sources Subjectives," *Annales de l'Institut Poincare 7* (1937): 1-68.

5. W. Edwards, "The Prediction of Decisions among Bets," *Journal of Experimental Psychology* (September 1955): 201-214.

6. Frank P. Ramsey, *The Foundations of Statistics* (New York: Harcourt Brace, 1931); Leonard J. Savage, *The Foundations of Statistics* (New York: Wiley, 1954); John Quiggin, "A Theory of Anticipated Utility" (Unpublished manuscript, Canberra City, Australia, Bureau of Agricultural Economics, 1980).

7. D. Kahneman and A. Tversky, "Prospect Theory: An Analysis of Decision under Risk," *Econometrica* (March 1979): 263-291.

8. Uday S. Karmarkar, "Subjectively Weighted Utility: A Descriptive Extension of the Expected Utility Model," *Organizational Behavior and Human Performance* (February 1978): 61-72.

9. E. F. Fama and M. H. Miller, *The Theory of Finance* (Chicago: Dryden, 1972).

10. M. Friedman, "The Methodology of Positive Economics," in M. Friedman, ed., *Essays in Positive Economics* (Chicago: University Chicago Press, 1953), pp. 3-43.

11. K. R. MacCrimmon and S. Larsson, "Utility Theory: Axioms Versus 'Paradoxes.'" Forthcoming in M. Allais and O. Hagen, eds., *Rational Decisions under Uncertainty*, special volume of *Theory and Decision*.

12. G. M. Becker and C. G. McClintock, "Value: Behavioral Decision Theory," *Annual Review of Psychology* (1967): 239-286.

13. Amos Tversky, "Intransivity of Preferences," *Psychological Review* (January 1969): 31-48.

14. Ibid., pp. 32-33.

15. Ibid., pp. 31-48.

16. Ibid., p. 45.

17. Ibid., p. 45.

18. D. Ellsberg, "Risk, Ambiguity, and the Savage Axioms," *Quarterly Journal of Economics* (November 1961): 643-665.

19. M. Allais, "Le Comportement de l'Homme Rationnel Devant le Risque: Critique des Postulates et Axioms de l'Ecole Americaine," *Econometrica* (October 1953): 503-546.

20. K. R. MacCrimmon, "Descriptive and Normative Implications of the Decision-Theory Postulates," in K. Borch and J. Mossini, eds., *Risk and Uncertainty* (New York: Macmillan, 1968), pp. 3-23.

21. P. Slovic and A. Tversky, "Who Accepts Savage's Axioms?" *Behavioral Science* (November 1974): 368-373.

22. MacCrimmon, "Descriptive and Normative Implications of the Decision-Theory Postulates," pp. 3-73.

23. Ibid., pp. 3-23.

24. P. Slovic, "Value as a Determiner of Subjective Probability," *IEEE Transactions as Human Factors in Electronics* (March 1966): 22-28.

25. Edwards, "The Prediction of Decisions among Bets," pp. 201-214.

26. S. Lichtenstein, P. Slovic, and D. Zink, "Effect of Instructions in Expected Value on Optimality of Gambling Decisions," *Journal of Experimental Psychology* (February 1969): 236-240.

27. S. Lichtenstein, and P. Slovic, "Reversals of Reference between Bids and Choices in Gambling Decisions," *Journal of Experimental Psychology* (July 1971): 46-55.

28. C. H. Coombs, T. G. Bezendinger, and F. M. Goode, "Testing Expectation Theories of Decision Making without Measuring Utility or Subjective Probability," *Journal of Mathematical Psychology* (February 1967): 72-103.

29. A. Tversky, "Additivity, Utility, and Subjective Probability," *Journal of Mathematical Psychology* (June 1967): 175-202; "Utility Theory and Additivity Analysis of Risky Choices," *Journal of Experimental Psychology* (September 1967): 27-36.

30. T. S. Wallsten, "Subjectively Expected Utility Theory and Subjects' Probability Estimates: Use of Measurement-Free Techniques," *Journal of Experimental Psychology* (April 1971): 31-40.

31. L. Miller and J. T. Lanzetta, "Choice among Four-Alternative Gambles as a Function of Monetary Level of Play," *Psychological Reports* (December 1962): 869-894.

32. F. Mosteller and P. Nogee, "An Experimental Measurement of Utility," *Journal of Experimental Psychology* (October 1961): 357-404.

33. J. L. Myers, R. E. Reilly, and H. A. Taub, "Differential Cost, Gain, and Relative Frequency of Reward in a Sequential Choice Situation," *Journal of Experimental Psychology* (October 1961): 357-360.

34. J. L. Myers, M. M. Suydam, and B. Gambino, "Contingent Gains and Losses in a Risk-Taking Situation," *Journal of Mathematical Psychology* (July 1965): 363-370.

35. H. L. Royden, P. Suppes, and K. Walsh, "A Model for the Experimental Measurement of the Utility of Gambling," *Behavioral Science* (January 1959): 11-18.

36. M. M. Suydam, "Effects of Cost and Gain Ratios, and the Probability of Outcome on Ratings of Alternative Choices," *Journal of Mathematical Psychology* (February 1965): 171-179.

37. A. Rapaport and T.S. Wallsten, "Individual Decision Behavior," *Annual Review of Psychology* (1972): 131-176.

38. B. Fischoff, "Decision Analysis- Clinical Art of Clinical Science?" In L. Sjoberg, T. Tyszka, and J. A. Wise, ed., *Human Decision Making* (Forthcorming).

39. Ibid.

40. D. W. von Winterfeldt, "Structuring Decision Problems for Decision Analysis," *Acta Psychologica* (March 1980): 71-93.

41. Ibid., p. 72.

42. Fischhoff, "Decision Analysis- Clinical Art or Clinical Science," p. 78.

43. W. Edwards, "Variance Preferences in Gambling," *American Journal of Psychology* (September 1954): 441-452.

44. D. Davidson and J. Marschak, "Experimental Tests of a Stochastic Decision Theory," in C. W. Chuchan, ed., *Measurement: Definitions and Theories* (New York: Wiley, 1959); L. W. Littig, "Effects of Skill and Chance Orientations on Probability Preferences," *Psychological Reports* (February 1962): 67-70; S. Lichtenstein, "Bases for Preferences among Three-Outcome Bets," *Journal of Experimental Psychology* 69 (1965): 162-169; H. L. Royden, P. Suppes, and K. Walsh, "A Model for the Experimental Measurement of the Utility of Gambling," *Behavior Science* 4 (1959): 11-18; H. C. Van Der Meer, "Decision Making: The Influence of Probability Preference, Variance Preference and Expected Value on Strategy in Gambling," *Acta Psychologica* (October 1963): 231-259; C. H. Coombs and D. G. Pruitt, "Components of Risk in Decision Making: Probability and Variance Preferences," *Journal of Experimental Psychology* (November 1960): 265-277.

45. Coombs and Pruitt, "Components of Risk in Decision Making."

46. P. Slovic and S. Lichtenstein, "Importance of Variance Preferences in Gambling Decisions," *Journal of Experimental Psychology* (December 1968): 646-654.

47. Ibid., p. 647.

48. J. W. Payne and M. L. Braunstein, "Preferences among Gambles with Equal Underlying Distributions," *Journal of Experimental Psychology* (January 1971): 13-18.

49. Ibid., p. 13.

50. F. Mosteller and P. Nogee, "An Experimental Measurement of Utility," *Journal of Political Economy* (October 1951): 371-404; Myers, Reilly, and Taub, "Differential Cost, Gain and Relative Frequency of Reward"; Myers, Suydam, and Gambino, "Contingent

Gains and Losses in a Risk-Taking Situation"; Suydam, "Effects of Cost and Gain Ratios."

51. W. Lee, "Preference Strength, Expected Value Difference, and Expected Regret Ratio," *Psychological Bulletin* (March 1971): 162-169.

52. Suydam, "Effects of Cost and Gain Ratios"; W. Edwards, "Reward Probability, Amount, and Information as Determiners of Sequential Two-Alternative Decisions," *Journal of Experimental Psychology* (September 1956): 177-188.

53. Lee, "Preference Strength, Expected Value Difference, and Expected Regret Ratio."

54. W. Lee, "The Effects of Expected Value Difference and Expected Regret Ratio on Preference Strength," *American Journal of Psychology* (June 1971): 194-204.

55. Payne and Braunstein, "Preferences among Gambles with Equal Underlying Distributions"; P. Slovic, "The Relative Influence of Probabilities and Payoffs upon Perceived Risk of a Gamble," *Psychonomic Science* (October 1967): 223-224; Slovice and Lichtenstein, "Importance of Variance Preferences in Gambling Decisions."

56. Coombs and Pruitt, "Components of Risk in Decision Making."

57. P. Slovic and S. Lichenstein, "Relative Importance of Probabilities and Payoffs in Risk Taking," *Journal of Experimental Psychology Monograph* (November 1968): 1-18.

58. Ibid., p. 7.

59. Slovic, "The Relative Influence of Probabilities and Payoffs upon Perceived Risk of a Gamble"; Lichtenstein and Slovic, "Reversals of Preference between Bids and Choices in Gambling Decisions"; S. Lichtenstein and P. Slovic, "Response-Induced Reversals of Preference in Gambling: An Extended Replication in Las Vegas," *Journal of Experimental Psychology* (November 1973): 16-20; H. R. Lindman "Inconsistent Preferences among Gambles," *Journal of Experimental Psychology* (August 1971): 390-397.

60. Kahneman and Tversky, "Prospect Theory: An Analysis of Decision Under Risk."

61. Ibid., p. 265.

62. Ibid., p. 268.

63. Ibid., p. 271.

64. Ibid., p. 274.

65. D. Kahneman and A. Tversky, "The Framing of Decisions and the Psychology of Choice," *Science* 211 (1981): 453-458.

66. Ibid., p. 456.

67. D. Kahneman and A. Tversky, "Choices, Values, and Frames," *American Psychologist* 35 (1984): 341-350.

68. R. Thaler, "Towards a Positive Theory of Consumer Choice," *Journal of Economic Behavior and Organization* 1 (1980): 39-60.

69. Kahneman and Tversky, "Choices, Values and Frames," p. 349.

70. Slovic and Lichtenstein, "Relative Importance of Probabilities and Payoffs in Risk Taking."

71. Lichtenstein and Slovic, "Reversals of Preference between Bids and Choices in Gambling Decisions"; Lichtenstein and Slovic, "Response-Induced Reversals of Preference in Gambling."

72. Werner W. Pommerehne, Friedrich Schneider, and Peter Zweifel, "Economic Theory of Choice and the Preference Reversal Phenomenon: A Reexamination," *American Economic Review* (June 1982): 576-584; Robert J. Reilly, "Preference Reversal: Further Evidence and Some Suggested Modifications in Experimental Design," *American Economic Review* (June 1982): 576-584.

73. David M. Grether and Charles R. Plott, "Economic Theory of Choice and the Preference Reversal Phenomenon," *American Economic Review* (September 1979): 623-638.

74. Reilly, "Preference Reversal: Further Evidence and Some Suggested Modifications in Experimental Design."

75. P. Slovic and S. Lichtenstein, "Preference Reversals: A Broader Perspective," *American Economic Review* (March 1983): 596-605.

76. R. H. Ashton, "Behavioral Assumptions of Normative Decision Theory: An Experimental Test of the Independence Axiom

in an Accounting/Business Context," in Thomas J. Burns, ed., *Behavioral Experiments in Accounting* (Columbus: College of Administrative Science, Ohio State University, 1979), 2:175-204.

77. MacCrimmon, "Descriptive and Normative Implications of the Decision-Theory Postulates."

78. Allison Hubbard Ashton, "The Descriptive Validity of Normative Decision Theory in Auditing Contexts," *Journal of Accounting Research* (Autumn 1982): 415-428.

79. J. Ronen, "Some Effects of Sequential Aggregation in Accounting on Decision Making," *Journal of Accounting Research* (Autumn 1971): 307-332.

80. M. L. Hirsch, "Disaggregated Probabilistic Accounting Information: The Effect of Sequential Events on Expected Value Maximization Decisions," *Journal of Accounting Research* (Autumn 1978): 254-269.

81. D. Snowball and C. Brown, "Decision Making Involving Sequential Events: Some Effects of Disaggregated Data and Dispositions toward Risk," *Decision Sciences* (October 1979): 527-546.

82. Ronen, "Some Effects of Sequential Aggregation in Accounting on Decision Making."

83. Hirsch, "Disaggregated Probabilistic Accounting Information."

84. Snowball and Brown, "Decision Making Involving Sequential Events."

85. Willis R. Greer, Jr., "Theory versus Practice in Risk Analysis: An Empirical Study," *Accounting Review* (July 1974): 496-505.

86. Ibid., p. 501.

87. Ibid., p. 502.

88. C. G. Hoskins, "Theory versus Practice in Risk Analysis: An Empirical Study: A Comment," *Accounting Review* (October 1975): 835-838.

89. Willis R. Greer, Jr. and Ted D. Skekel, "Theory versus Practice in Risk Analysis: A Reply," *Accounting Review* (October 1975): 839-843.

90. P. C. Fishburn, "Theory versus Practice in Risk Analysis: An Empirical Study: A Comment," *Accounting Review* (July 1967): 657-662.

91. Greer, Willis R., Jr., "Theory versus Practice in Risk Analysis: An Empirical Study: A Reply," *Accounting Review* (July 1976): 663.

92. B. L. Lewis, "Expert Judgment in Auditing: An Expected Utility Approach," *Journal of Accounting Research* (Autumn 1980): 594-602.

93. Ibid., p. 595.

94. Ibid.

95. B. H. Ward, "An Investigation of Auditors' Perceptions of the Severity of Error in Audited Financial Statements," in *Symposium on Auditing Research* (Urbana: University of Illinois Press, 1974), pp. 23-39; "An Investigation of the Materiality Construct in Auditing," *Journal of Accounting Research* (Spring 1976): 138-152.

96. Ibid.

97. Lauren K. Newton, "The Risk Factor in Materiality Decisions," *Accounting Review* (January 1977): 97-108.

98. R. Libby, *Accounting and Human Information Processing: Theory and Applications* (Englewood Cliffs, N.J.: Prentice-Hall, 1981), p. 170.

CHAPTER 3
PROBABILITY ELICITATION AND REVISION

Various tasks in accounting and auditing call for the quantification of subjective evidence in the form of prior probability distributions (PPDs) and for the use of the Bayesian inference model for a revision of these PPDs. As a result, this chapter presents probability elicitation and revision as studied and evaluated in psychology as applied in accounting research and practice.

ELICITATION PROBLEM
Elicitation Techniques

Subjective probability has been defined as a measure of the confidence that a particular individual has in the truth of a particular proposition.[1] In psychological research there is a need for subjective probability and various probability elicitation methods have been used resulting in different probability assessments. Based on a classification scheme suggested by Savage,[2] Chesley classified the elicitation approaches in terms of three dimensions: first, a directness of the assessment dimension (either (1) direct question, (2) inference from decisions, or (3) a hybrid of direct and infer); second, a dimension which distinguishes between self-elicitation and elicitation from an interview; and third, a dimension which distinguishes between responses made in terms of probabilities and those made in terms of the value or independent variable scale.[3] This scheme resulted in the following list of elicitation techniques:[4]

A. *Direct methods*
  1. Magnitude or direct estimation
  2. Ratio or odds estimation
  3. Equating sense distances
  4. Graphical
  5. Probability density function estimation
  6. Hypothetical future samples
  7. Equivalent prior sample
  8. Distribution parameter estimation
B. *Infer Methods*
  1. Betting
C. *Hybrid methods*
  1. Lottery
  2. Bid or bet choice.

These methods differ in terms of the question mode posed to the subjects. The direct methods may be defined as follows:

1. *The magnitude or direct estimation* asks "what is the probability that x equals, is less than, or is equal to y where y is specified?"
2. *The ratio or odds estimation method*, which involves estimating the ratio of two probabilities rather than the probabilities themselves, asks "what are the odds in favor of outcome x versus outcome y?"
3. *The equating senses distance method* involves the equating of sense distance in finding equally likely points.
4. *The graphical or diagrammatic representation method* asks the subject to draw histograms, smooth curves, or graphs of common probability functions which represent the probability distribution of the parameter of interest.
5. *The probability density function estimation method* asks about relative areas, i. e., the probability of x falling in the interval y_1-y_2, y_2-y_3 . . . etc., where the values of y are specified.
6. *The hypothetical future samples method* asks subjects to state the change in their estimate of a parameter of interest after seeing the results of hypothetical samples drawn at random independently.
7. *The equivalent prior sample method* asks the subjects to specify the number of successes and the sample size such that the subjective probability is equivalent to having observed r successes in a sample size of n.
8. *The distribution parameter estimation* asks for a direct specification of the parameters of the distribution, such as the mean and variance for the normal probability function.

The infer or indirect method involves asking subjects to formulate their bets and infer probabilities from their choices among gambles. The hybrid methods involve asking subjects what their actions would be if faced with a given situation. Examples include lottery and bid or bet choice.

What makes a "good" probability assessor can be evaluated in terms of "substantive" goodness, which refers to knowledge which the assessor has concerning the subject matter of concern, and "normative" goodness, which refers to the ability of the assessor to express their opinions in probabilistic form.[5] This question of what makes a good probability assessor is important given the limited information processing capacity of humans and our difficult appreciation of fundamental statistical concepts, including distribution, independence and randomness, and measures of central tendency and dispersion.[6] The responses of the assessor need to be accurate, consistent across elicitation methods, and a result of a good understanding of the methods. One way of checking on the consistency of subjective estimates is to ask for assessments elicited by various elicitation techniques, then ask the subjects to indicate the estimate they prefer. This reconciliation process may suffer, however, from primacy versus recency differences and a tendency of the subjects to "split the difference."[7]

Elicitation Research in Accounting

Various experiments conducted either in an abstract or financial context have investigated the assessment of subjective probabilities in accounting.

Chesley asked undergraduate industrial engineering students and undergraduate accounting students to assess subjective probabilities and subjective likelihoods using two elicitation methods: the direct magnitude method, which calls for direct estimates of the amount of the variable at particular points on the probability scale, and the successive subdivision method, which calls for repeated estimates of the amount of the variable that will bisect certain specified intervals of the probability scale.[8] The results involving these variables and five probability distributions for a drill press manufacturing process showed a better performance when using the direct magnitude method than when using the successive subdivision method, even after reconciliation and repeated elicitations. Using the same task but with a different group of student subjects, Chesley was able to replicate the superior performance of the direct magnitude method over the successive subdivision method using any of the data modes, probabilities, and odds.[9] The next project by Chesley called for a comparison of the performance resulting from the use of five elicitation methods to elicit dependent and independent variables.[10] The five methods involved odds, bids, lotteries, the direct magnitude method, and the "line-chart" method. These methods were described as follows:

The odds method asked for a ratio representing the cumulative odds for the specified independent variable amount. The bid method asked for the maximum bid a subject would be willing to make for a one-dollar payoff if the actual independent was less than or equal to the specified amount of the variable. The one dollar amount was used to help avoid strategies caused by risk preferences or state desirabilities and to make the bid inference as easy as possible for the subject. With a one-dollar payoff, the bid should equal the cumulative probability if no risk aversion is present. The lottery method asked for the number of lottery tickets out of one hundred in the lottery the subject would require to be indifferent between the lottery and decision situation where the same payoff would occur if the independent variable were less than or equal to the specified level. . . . The line-chart method was similar to the direct magnitude method, in that both asked cumulative probabilities for the specified amounts of independent variables. However, if permitted subjects to draw arrows from the line of specified amounts to the line of cumulative probabilities positioned parallel to it. This approach simplifies the explanation to the subject and permits a pictorial view of the relations.[11]

The results on the elicitation of the dependent variable by the five methods did not show any performance difference between them. However, the elicitation of the independent variable showed the direct magnitude method to be slightly superior to the line-chart method. In addition, the line-chart method was found to be better for the estimation of the dependent variables than the independent variables.

Finally, Chesley investigated the relationship between numerical probabilities and several words and phrases that are used to communicate probabilistic events.[12] The task required subjects to substitute probabilities for words and words for probabilities. The results were disappointing as they revealed a lack of consensus across subjects concerning the probabilities that were considered equivalent to words and vice-versa. Not short of excuses, Chesley concluded that the students in undergraduate auditing classes used as subjects "do not appear to have developed a refined and commonly understood language for accurately communicating uncertainty between themselves."[13]

Elicitation Research in Auditing

Auditors rely on evidence regarding the fairness of the financial statements reported by their clients before formulating audit opinions. The evidence is either of the objective type, resulting from either the auditor's past experience with and knowledge about the client or a study and evaluation of management integrity, strength of internal control system, and the like. The Bayesian approach enables auditors to combine both the objective or sampling evidence and the subjective or nonsampling evidence. Hence, the auditor forms a belief about the population to be sampled in the form of a prior probability distribution to express the auditor's total assurance about a population. The crucial step for this procedure to be effective rests on a proper and satisfactory elicitation of the auditor's PPDs. As a result, studies of probability elicitation techniques in auditing focused on the consistency of the elicited prior probability distributions using the same elicitation technique and among elicitation techniques used by the same auditor. Corless reported consistencies between the practice method of the cumulative distribution function and the probability of error intervals method of the probability density function.[14] Felix, focusing on the equivalent prior sample method and the fractile method of the cumulative distribution function, found small differences which can be attributed to the oral training he provided his students.[15] A replication by Crosby failed to detect any differences in the measures of central tendency of prior probability distributions generated by the cumulative distribution function and the probability of error intervals method.[16] It is interesting to not, however, that when Crosby examined the effects of using different elicitation techniques on a subsequent audit decision, that of attribute sample size selection, he found that the use of different techniques can lead to differences in sample sizes if the prior is used as an input to a Bayesian model.[17]

Solomon investigated the probability assessment of audit teams using the cumulative distribution function[18] following the observation that in other decision contexts the team probability density function has been found superior to those assessed by individuals.[19] Solomon found evidence of superior audit team vis-à-vis individual auditor performance. Solomon et al. found the cumulative distribution function to be feasible for prior probability distributions (PPDs).[20] They concluded that: "The resulting PPDs exhibited several desirable characteristics including a sensitivity to the internal control environment and, therefore, provide preliminary evidence that it is possible for auditors to assess their subjective beliefs about the audit values of accounting populations as PPDs."[21]

In another study, however, Solomon et al. raised questions about auditors' use of the equivalent prior sample method (EQPS) in the substantive testing context given the presence of a disturbing degree of variability in the prior probability distribution means, and even greater variability in specified prior probability distribution dispersion.[22] Abdolmohammadi provided training to his auditor subjects in the use of four major probability assessment techniques: the cumulative distribution function (CDF), the probability density function (PDF), the equivalent prior sample information (EPS), and the hypothetical future samples (HFS).[23] When asked to specify which method is easiest to use, the auditors revealed that PDF and HFS were considered the easiest and CDF and EPS were viewed as the most difficult to use. Another study by Shields et al. tested for the accuracy of the PDF and CDF methods and found PDF to be a more accurate elicitation technique.[24] Abdolmohammadi and Berger extended the results by studying the accuracy of four elicitation techniques (i.e., CDF, PDF, EPS and HFS) for an account balance estimation task in auditing.[25] As with other previous studies the PDF was found to outperform the CDF, EPS and HFS in the account balance estimation task.

Finally, Abdolmohammadi used three evaluation criteria, acceptability, accuracy, and concordance to compare prior probability assessment techniques in auditing, namely the cumulative distributive function, the probability density function, the equivalent prior sample information, and the hypothetical future samples.[26] The three criteria were defined as follows:[27]

1. The *acceptability* criterion- a technique will be called the most appropriate if subjects considered it the easiest to use.

2. The *accuracy* criterion- a technique will be called the most appropriate if, by using it, subjects create the closed distribution to the 'true' compliance error rate.
3. The *concordance* criterion- a technique will be called the most appropriate if, by using it, subjects create the highest degree of agreement among themselves.

After a training session, 73 auditors participated in a task of compliance error quantification in an audit study. The results showed that the probability density function was the most appropriate and the equivalent prior sample information was the least appropriate elicitation technique for use in practical audit situations while the two others were in the middle.

As it appears from the above review, the research results in auditing on the four elicitation techniques examined (CDF, PDF, EPS, and HFS) are far from conclusive, and further investigation is needed. In addition, other elicitation techniques (Ets) remain to be given serious consideration in auditing. Examples include the odds or ratio estimation, the distribution parameter estimation, the graphical or diagrammatic representation, and the (most) likely, maximum, and minimum value estimation, as well as the infer and indirect methods identified earlier.

The training methods used were those suggested by Winkler, which call for a mixture of written and oral training with a written questionnaire and provision for some feedback to decision makers from the researcher. Other training methods that could be used include Spetzler and von Holstein's precoding-encoding feedback approach,[28] Hogarth's traditional reading exercise and audiovisual approach,[29] and Chesley's programmed approach.[30] Not only were these found to be time-consuming and complex when compared to Winkler's approach, but at least in the programmed approach there is evidence of possible cheating, reduced motivation, and disinterest fatigue.[31] The need for a balanced training approach was formulated as follows: "Hence, a great need exists for further research to find a balanced training approach. Such an approach should provide auditors with coverage of subjective probabilities and ETs using the least amount of technical jargon, tailored to auditing problems, and the minimum possible time period."[32]

Felix went one step further by suggesting nontechnical training material that would provide "self-insight" to auditors using elicitation techniques and yet would not overwhelm the relatively modest statistical knowledge of the auditor.[33]

EVALUATION OF THE GOODNESS OF SUBJECTIVE PROBABILITIES
Goodness Criteria

The goodness of subjective probabilities may be evaluated on the basis of either a *coherence* criterion or a *calibration* criterion.

The coherence criterion investigates whether subjective probabilities obey the probability axioms. Examples include research to investigate whether an individual's probability estimates sum to 1.0[34] or whether individual estimates of the probabilities of compound events are consistent with their estimates of the probabilities of the underlying events.[35] The evidence is mixed, neither supporting the hypothesis that the probability axioms are followed nor the hypothesis that they are not followed. In accounting research, the coherence issue has not been examined in spite of the research on elicitation techniques.

The calibration criterions is a more popular method for the evaluation of the goodness of subjective probabilities.[36] A judge is considered well-calibrated if, over the long run, for all propositions assigned a given probability, the proportion that is true is equal to the probability assigned. In general, the calibration of individuals is evaluated by determining their probability assessments, and then determining the proportion that is true for each case examined. Individuals who are not calibrated are said to be their underconfident or confident. Three direct measures of the validity of probability assessments are possible: over- or underconfidence, calibration, and resolution.[37]

Over/underconfidence may be measured as

$$\frac{1}{N}\sum_{t=1}^{T} n_t(r_t - c_t)$$

where N is the total number of responses, n_t is the number of times the response r_t was used, c_t is the proportion correct for all items assigned probability r_t, and T is the total number of different response categories.

Calibration may be measured as

$$\frac{1}{N}\sum_{t=1}^{T} n_t(n - c_t)^2$$

A perfectly calibrated person would score 0 on this measure.

Resolution may be measured as

$$\frac{1}{N}\sum_{t=1}^{T} n_t(n - C)^2$$

were C is the overall percentage correct. The higher the resolution score the better. The term *knowledge* refers to another measure of probabilistic performance introduced by Murphy.[38] It is measured as
$C(1-C)$

Knowledge refers to the subject's ability to pick the correct alternative. Finally, Murphy showed that calibration, resolution, and knowledge form a partition of the Brier score, an overall measure of the adequacy of performance in a probabilistic task, such as the smaller the score the better.[39] The Brier score is as follows:
Brier Score = Knowledge + Calibration – Resolution

$$\text{Brier Score} = C(1\text{-}C) + \frac{1}{N}\sum_{t=1}^{T} n_t(r_t - c_t)^2 - \frac{1}{N}\sum_{t=1}^{T} n_t(c_t - C)^2$$

The Brier score is used as a scoring rule; in other words, it is a means of attaching to a probability distribution and the event which obtains a reward or penalty, which, in effect, informs the assessor of the "goodness" of his or her probabilistic prediction.[40]

Other scoring rules exist[41] and the evidence on their effectiveness for the improvement of assessment is either mixed[42] or favorable.[43] To achieve the objectives of the scoring rules, which are to encourage assessors to take care of their assessments and to report only their "true" beliefs, the following assumptions have to be made about the idea properties of an assessor:[44]

1. He never violates the postulates of coherence. Following Savage . . . "This person is idealized; unlike you and me, he never makes mistakes, never gives thirteen pence for a shilling, or makes a combination of bets that he is sure to lose no matter what happens."
2. He fully understands both the methods used to obtain his probability assessments and the methods used to encourage careful assessments. That is, he understands the alternatives open to him and the implications of each alternative.
3. He has a utility function which is linear with respect to money in the relevant range (that is, the range of monetary amounts used in conjunction with the assessment procedure). Furthermore, he chooses his responses in such a way as to maximize his expected utility.

Evidence seems to show that two of these assumptions are not correct: coherence is problematic and elicitation techniques and scoring rules are perceived to be difficult subjects. In addition, Hogarth identifies a number of flaws in the use of scoring rules:[45]

- They show the existence of a one "time" underlying probability distribution within an assessor.
- They take no account of the cost of the assessment procedure to the assessor.
- They are found to be insensitive in the sense that differences in expected scores attributable to different stated probabilities are not always that large.

Given these limitations, Hogarth suggests task feedback as more effective than outcome feedback for learning in a probabilistic environment.[46]

In addition to coherence and calibration, the psychological literature has advocated the use of composite assessments, namely the behavioral and mathematical ones.[47]

The behavioral approaches allow the assessors either to interact and discuss their differences in order to reach a consensus which, unfortunately, may be subject to the "risky shift" phenomenon,[48] or to independently alter their assessments after receiving a feedback on the other individuals' assessments.

The mathematical approaches include, in general, "opinion pool" methods in which subjects' assessments are combined via some arithmetical weighting scheme. Various weighting schemes have been proposed with very little difference.[49] Winkler provided an alternative to the "opinion pool"; he termed this the "natural conjugate" approach.[50] Under this method, each subject's opinion is considered "sample evidence" which can be represented by a natural conjugate prior to the distribution of interest. Successive applications of the Bayes' theorem is used to combine the individual natural conjugate priors to form the group assessment.

Evidence in Accounting

In addition to calibration and scoring rules, accounting researchers have relied on another measure termed extremeness. It refers to the assignment of higher probabilities near the actual population value and lower probabilities elsewhere. Solomon used both calibration and extremeness.[51] His results showed that the team-assessed probabilities were more extreme than those assessed by individuals and were more severely miscalibrated. In addition, underconfidence served to predominate, especially for audit teams. Solomon used calibration to study a Chi-square goodness of fit on differences between expected and observed probability values for the interquantile range (i.e., values in the .25 to .75 fractiles) and surprise indices (i.e., values in the .01, .10, .90, and .99 fractiles). Using similar meaning of the goodness of the prior probability distribution both Solomon et al.[52] and Tomassini et al. presented evidence of miscalibration. In fact, although the general calibration studies presented evidence of overconfidence by auditors.[54] In a context other than auditing, Belkaoui hypothesized that redundant accounting information added to diagnostic information will lead to overconfidence by loan officers in their predictions of bankruptcy.[55] This result using the Brier score showed that the addition of redundant information to diagnostic information led to a greater overconfidence and resolution, lower calibration, and an overall better performance in the probabilistic task presented to loan officers. This finding was supported by three types of evidence. First, Oskamp found that as the amount of information about a case increased, the confidence of subjects increased dramatically and entirely out of proportion to actual correctness.[56] Second, Einhorn et al. stated that the belief that one has made use of many cues in forming one's judgment coupled with the attentional effort spent on cues that are not marginally predictive can lead to overconfidence.[57] Finally, it is maintained that in intuitive judgment, people tend to have great confidence in predictions based on redundant input variables.[58]

Two major problems are associated with the use of meaning of goodness or prior probability distributions used in elicitation techniques audit studies, namely the need for standard conjugate prior probability distributions and the need for "time" values and observed" frequency distributions.[59] The use of compensatory methodology could, however, compensate for the lack of time value. For example, Scott provided a formulation of a scoring rule that can be used for probabilistic reporting and can be interpreted as the auditor's loss function:[60]

The "score" obtained by the auditor who reports a whole probability distribution is determined by the "goodness" of the reported probabilities in relation to the stated realization that actually happens. If the scoring rule is strictly proper (SPSR), then the auditor's expected score is maximized only by reporting the probability distribution he actually believes. Subject to the ability of scoring rules to capture essentially all of the auditor's loss structure, this provides a vehicle for public confidence in the probabilistic statements since each user knows the auditor is motivated to be "honest" despite the fact that with probabilistic reporting it would not, in general, be possible to check up on the reported probabilities to determine if they were "right" or "wrong" in the usual way.[61]

To compensate for the lack of time values, Newman and Tomassini suggested simulating account balance distributions to achieve a frequency distribution to compare to the elicited subjective distribution.[62] Goodness-of-fit statistics, such as the Chi-square and Kolmogorov-Smirnov test, are then used to compare the elicited and observed distribution. Newman and Tomassini made the suggestion after finding poor sensitivity of interquartile range and surprise indices.

THE REVISION OF PROBABILITIES
Conservatism

The revision of probability in light of new evidence is accomplished by the Bayes' theorem. For discrete hypotheses, the Bayes' theorem states that

$$P\left(\frac{H_i}{D}\right) = \frac{P\left(\frac{D}{H_i}\right)P(H_i)}{P(D)} = \frac{P\left(\frac{D}{H_i}\right)P(H_i)}{\Sigma_i P\left(\frac{D}{H_i}\right)P(H_i)}$$

In this theorem, $P(H_i)$ is the prior probability that H_i is true. Given the acquisition of new evidence, D, the credibility of H_i is increased. Therefore, $P(H_i/D)$, the posterior probability of H_i, is the probability of H_i given that one could observe the new evidence D. Similarly, $P(D/H_i)$ is the conditional probability of observing D given that H_i is true. $P(D/H_i)$, by expressing the degree to which one's posterior probability, $P(H_i/D)$, should differ from the prior probability $P(H_i)$, is a measure of the diagnosticity of the datum D. Therefore, if $P(H_i)$ and $P(D/H_i)$ are known, $P(H_i/D)$ may be easily computed using the Bayes' theorem.

In general, $P(D)$ is eliminated in Bayesian revision studies by restating Bayes' theorem in its odds-likelihood ratio form. If an alternative hypothesis $P(H_i)$ is considered, then

$$P\left(\frac{H_i}{D}\right) = \frac{P\left(\frac{D}{H_i}\right)P(H_i)}{P(D)}$$

Therefore,

$$\frac{P(\frac{H_i}{D})}{P(\frac{H_i}{D})} = \frac{P(\frac{D}{H_i})}{P(\frac{D}{H_i})} \cdot \frac{P(H_i)}{P(H_j)}$$

or

$$\Omega_1 = LR \cdot \Omega_0$$

where Ω_1 is the posterior odds in favor of H_i over H_j, Ω_0 is the prior odds, and LR is the likelihood ratio. The prior odds are also called the *base rate*. The new form of the Bayes theorem is more practical as people find it easier to estimate likelihood ratios.

Early research in the Bayesian revision studies consisted of the elicitation of individuals' subjective likelihood ratios (SLR) after providing them with stated prior and new evidence, and comparing the SLR with the assessed posteriors in order to investigate the question of whether probabilities are revised in accordance with the normative model. Another method consists of a comparison of SLR with optimal Bayesian likelihood ratios (BLR). Finally, to supplement direct comparisons of Bayesian probabilities and subjective estimates, Peterson, Schneider, and Miller suggested a measure of the degree to which performance is optimal, termed the accuracy ratio:

AR=SLLR/BLLR

Where SLLR is the log likelihood ratio inferred from the subject's probability estimates and BLLR is the optimal (Bayesian) log likelihood ratio.[63] Logs are used because the optimal responses become linear with the amount of evidence favoring one hypothesis over the other. The usefulness of the accuracy ratio is expressed as follows: "The accuracy ratio can be computed for each datum, or it can serve as a summary measure across many responses made to a variety of data. In the latter case, it is the slope of the regression line relating SLLR's to BLLR's, and is thus similar to a beta weight in the correlation model."[64]

A value of 1.0 for the accuracy ratio is indicative of optimal revision. A less than 1.0 value is indicative of "conservative" revision compared to that prescribed by the Bayes' theorem. Finally, a greater than 1.0 value is indicative of extreme revision compared to that prescribed by the Bayes' theorem.[65] In fact, the primary finding in the Bayesian revision studies is conservatism in the sense that upon receipt of new evidence, the subjects revised their posterior probability estimates in the same direction as the optimal model, but the revision is typically too small, as if the data are less diagnostic than they truly are.[66] In addition, the subjects in some studies have been found to require from two to nine data observations to revise their opinions as much as Bayes' theorem would indicate for one observation.[67] Slovic and Lichtenstein's review reported that the extent of conservatism depended on some task determinants.[68] Hence, response mode (direct estimation methods, indirect estimation methods, intermittent responding, or nominal vs. probability responses), payoffs to motivate the subjects, the level of the diagnostically of the new data, the manipulation of prior probabilities, the sequence length, the order of the evidence, and inertia following disconfirming evidence affected the extent of conservatism.

Three competing explanations of the "laws of conservatism" were identified, namely misperception, misaggregation, and anticraft hypotheses.[69]

Misperception is a source of conservatism because subjects may misunderstand the data given the hypothesis, $P(D/H_i)$. As a result, their estimates of the posterior probabilities $P(H_i/D)$ end up biased in the same way as their estimate of $P(D/H_i)$[70] A typical kind of misperception error may result from rare events, in which case subjects underestimate the informativeness of the rare events and are found to be more conservative.[71]

Misaggregation is a second source of conservatism because subjects experience great difficulty in aggregating or putting together various pieces of information to produce a single response. A source of support for the misaggregation hypothesis came from the finding that subjects tended to perform better in the first trial of a sequence. Another source of support for the misaggregation hypothesis came from man-machine system studies, known as research on "probabilistic information processing" systems.[72] Basically, in a situation where subjects estimate $P(D/H)$ separately for each datum and the machine produced the corresponding posterior probabilities in a Bayes' theorem, the results were less conservative than when subjects were asked to aggregate the data into a $P(H/D)$ estimate. In fact, while Edwards et al. found the probabilistic information system was superior to unaided inference in that it favored the hypothesis that was eventually agreed upon much earlier in the data sequence,[73] Kaplan and Newman found it inferior to ideal performance, shown when Bayes' theorem was used to aggregate objective priors and likelihoods compared to the use of the Bayes' theorem to aggregate subjective priors and likelihoods.[74] While the evidence on the probabilistic information (PIP) system is mixed, its usefulness outside the laboratory is seriously questioned. The evidence reviewed here appears to favor a PIP system, at least in a laboratory simulated military decision making context. However, there are some problems with diagnostic tasks in the real world that have not been studied extensively in a "laboratory PIP" system, so applying PIP systems elsewhere should be done with caution. There are problems in the real world of defining an exhaustive set of mutually exclusive hypotheses, of determining whether or not conditional dependencies exist among the data (either in pairs or higher orders), of determining the reliability of the sources of the data, and of the nonstationarity of the data sources.[75]

Anticraft is a third source of conservatism because conservatism may simply be due to a "response bias." For example, Duscharme found that subjects are capable- and optimal- when dealing with responses when the odds range from 1:10 to 10:1, but are conservative when forced, either by the accumulation of data or by the addition of a very diagnostic datum, to go outside that range.[76]

Generalizability of the Conservatism Result

Can the conservatism result be generalized? Do people indeed accept the axioms of the Bayes' theorem and are the conservatism studies based on realistic tasks? The answer to both conditions is negative.

First, the Bayes' theorem as a normative theory of opinion revision rests on four axioms:

1. A probability is a number which lies between zero and one, and the probability of a sure event is one.
2. The sum of the probabilities of an exhaustive set of mutually exclusive events is equal to one.
3. The probability of either of two mutually exclusive events occurring is equal to the sum of their individual probabilities.
4. The probability of *both* event X and even Y occurring is equal to the probability of event X multiplied by the probability of event Y *given* that event X has occurred.

While no evidence exists on the first axiom, research findings exist on the acceptability of the others. The research findings on the second axiom are inconclusive, reporting that the sum of the subjects' assessed probabilities were either greater than unity[77] or less than unity.[78] Research findings on the third axiom show a tendency to underestimate these probabilities.[79] Research findings on the fourth axiom are contradictory, showing either close approximation of the axiom to related assessments[80] or a tendency to slightly overestimate the probabilities involved.[81] From these findings there is obviously a need for more research to assess the normative acceptability of the Bayes' theorem.

In addition, the typical book-bag and poker-chip task used in Bayesian revision studies is outwardly simple and unrealistic. In fact, Ducharme and Peterson investigated conservatism in a more realistic situation than the book-bag and poker-chip task.[82] They used a hypothesis set consisting of the population of male heights and the population of female heights and asked their subjects to decide which population was being sampled on the basis of the data contained in random sampled heights from that population. Their results showed a level of conservatism half as great as with the typical book-bag and poker-chip task. Carrying the argument one step further, Winkler and Murphy argued that the typical book-bag and poker-chip task differs from the real world in four respects:[83]

- First, the inference tasks are not realistic because in most laboratory tasks, samples of data are conditionally independent.
- Second, in most book-bag and poker-chip based experiments, the data generators (the book-bags) are stationary.
- Third, real-world data may be unreliable and, therefore, less diagnostic.
- Fourth, real-world data may be relatively undiagnostic while the book-bag and poker-chip tasks rely on highly diagnostic data.

In addition, while the typical book-bag and poker-chip task involves single-stage inference, multistate or cascaded inference involves a series of single-stage inferences in which the output (i.e., an inference) from one stage is used as an input in the next stage. The problem is stated as follows:

While you always know with certainty what your data are in a single-stage inference, in multi-stage inference your data are often the result of previous probabilistic inferences. Thus, succeeding stages of inference are based on probabilities of events, rather than the certain knowledge that an event occurred.[84]

The multistage inference studies showed, in fact, that their inferences are less conservative than those made in noncascaded settings.[85]

Evidence in Accounting

In accounting, three studies have examined the phenomenon of probability revision.

The first study by Dickhaut examined the impact of alternative information structures on probability revisions, or more specifically, the ability of individuals to adjust their personal probabilities when they receive just one accounting report as against receiving both accounting reports.[86] Two groups of subjects, an undergraduate student group and businessmen in an executive development course were asked to observe the profit figure(s) generated by a single information system (one profit figure based on historical cost) or a joint information system (one profit figure based on historical cost and one based on current cost) and to estimate the probability that the observation came from T_1 (businesses whose stock price increased during the year) or T_2 (those whose stock price decreased). They were also asked to participate in a similar abstract task, a cubes/algebraic identities task. The mean absolute difference between the subjects' revisions and the corresponding Bayesian revisions over 100 experimental trials were used as the performance measure. The results showed a better performance with the single information system, a significant three-factor interaction among subjects, tasks, and information systems.

The second study by Kennedy investigated Bayesian revision as it affects the usefulness of four financial ratios in the prediction of bankruptcy.[87] Twenty-four experienced loan officers and credit analysts from commercial banks were asked to consider the case of 12 business firms, half of which actually failed to assess a prior probability of bankruptcy on the basis of the knowledge of the industry in which they operated. Then the subjects were asked to revise their probabilities based on four financial ratios and asset size. The impact of each cue or ratio was computed as the difference between the likelihood ratio and 1.00. In addition, the accuracy of the direction of the impact was examined. The results showed the five cues having significant impacts on the probability-of-bankruptcy assessment. The accuracy of the direction of the impact was significant only half the time.

The third study by Wright investigated the accuracy of subjective probabilities for a financial variable.[88] Eleven graduate students were presented with priors of β_i, a security's systematic risk from five classes. They were then asked to revise the β_i based on cues including one for each of the three levels of two financial variables (the standard deviation of income available for common stockholders divided by the book value of stockholders' equity at the beginning of the year and a financial structure variable for debt relative to stockholders' equity) and one for each of the nine pairwise combinations to those levels or joint cues. As a result, 75 posterior probabilities were obtained for each subject. The absolute difference between the median probability estimate for the group and the relative frequency probability was used as a measure of accuracy of subjects for each of the 75 assessments. The results showed a fairly accurate performance, especially when using the single cues. The absolute difference between subjects' and environmental probabilities over the 75 assessments was used as a measure of the accuracy of individual assessors. The results showed a less accurate performance than in the aggregate analysis.

Evidence in Auditing

While, as suggested earlier, various auditing studies have investigated the feasibility and effectiveness of using elicitation techniques to quantify subjective evidence in the form of prior probability distribution,[89] other auditing studies have advocated the use of the Bayesian inference model for prior probability distribution revisions and opinion formulation.[90] As a result, some empirical studies in auditing have examined the conservatism phenomenon.

Crosby was first concerned by the effects of using different elicitation techniques on a subsequent auditing decision, that of sample size selection.[91] In addition to responding to the questioning modes of two alternative PPD elicitation techniques, his subjects were asked to make sample-size decisions on judgmental and classical statistical bases. Following the suggestions of various researchers[92] to use a Beta distribution to model the auditor's prior over possible error, Crosby used a beta-binomial model of the Bayesian process to compute Bayesian sample sizes and compare them to judgmental sample sizes selected by auditors on the basis of their beliefs, regardless of whether their priors were elicited using the CDF or EPS technique, a finding consistent with conservatism.

Corless asked audit seniors to participate in two attribute sampling tasks and compared subjects' judgmental compliance error revisions with the corresponding Bayesian revisions.[93] His results showed that the Bayesian evaluation of audit evidence reflected a greater degree of assurance that the amount of error is immaterial than did the intuitive evaluation of this same evidence. He concluded:

This suggests that auditors may be able to use smaller sample sizes by employing Bayesian techniques whenever the sampling evidence indicates that the amount of error is immaterial. However, when the sampling evidence indicates that the amount of error is material, it is concluded that auditors should use statistical techniques.[94]

This line of research was continued by Abdolmohammadi, who examined the efficiency of the Bayesian approach in compliance testing over the classical approach.[95] His results were supportive of the Bayesian approach. The subjects using the Bayesian approach selected smaller sample sizes than those using the classical approach for the same level of confidence (95%). The results on conservatism and excessive revision were, however, mixed. He concluded:

It Is important to not that, consistent with previous conceptual work, the study reported in this paper indicates that, by using both nonsampling and sampling evidence in assessing and revising compliance error rates, the auditor can improve audit efficiency using the Bayesian model. To get this benefit, however, the auditor has to pay for the costs of assessing and revising PPDs. A future study could investigate the level of the cost involved and whether it exceeds the benefits provided. *A priori*, it is suggested that the cost should be minimal in the automation of the Bayesian approach is quite feasible. The use of high speed computers for this purpose would free the auditor from many of the difficult judgmental revision tasks, while at the same time it would cut the time and the cost of the revision task. However, the cost of training auditors for PPD assessment, and also the time and the cost of actual PPD assessment, should be investigated in future studies.[96]

BELIEF UPDATING
The Contrast-Inertia Model

The updating of beliefs has been examined in various contexts, including probability inference,[97] decision theory,[98] economics,[99] impression formation,[100] social cognition,[101] jury decision making,[102] communication and persuasion,[103] attitude change,[104] causal inference,[105] and psychophysics.[106] It is a sequential process where new information is received and integrated to be a continuously evolving impression.[107] To reconcile the conflicting results on belief updating, Einhorn and Hogarth proposed a model of belief updating based on the following three general principles: a beliefs change via a sequential anchoring-and-adjustment process, evidence is encoded as being either positive (for) or negative (against) with respects to the hypothesis, and adjustments to new information reflect conflicts between forces of adaptation and intertia.[108] The resulting model is termed the contrast-inertia model of belief and its two forms, the discount and accretion models, are expressed as:

$S_B = S_{k-1} - W_k S(a)_k$

For the discount model and

$S_k = S_{k-1} + r_k S(b)_k$

For the accretion model, where

S_k = degree of belief in some hypothesis or attitude after evaluating k pieces of evidence ($0 \leq S_k \leq 1$).

S_{k-1} = anchor or prior opinion before evaluating the kth piece of evidence $(0 \leq S_{k-1} \leq 1)$.

$S(a_k)$ = subjective evaluation of the kth piece of evidence when this is negative $(0 \leq S(a_k) \leq 1)$.

$S(b_k)$ = subjective evaluation of the kth piece of evidence when this is positive $(0 \leq S(b_k) \leq 1)$.

W_k = the adjustment weight for negative evidence.

r_k = the adjustment weight for positive evidence.

The two equations model the anchoring-adjustment process and highlight the notion that evidence is encoded as either positive or negative before being integrated with the anchor. The model is then operationalized by the following assumptions:

$$W_k = \alpha S_{k-1}$$
$$r_k = \beta(1 - S_{k-1})$$

where α and β are constants of proportionality.

These two assumptions create a "contrast" or "surprise" effect in the model which implies that the same negative evidence will induce greater discounting when prior opinion is high as opposed to low, and the same positive evidence will have more impact on belief when prior opinion is low as opposed to high. The contrast effect is obtained by making the adjustment weight for negative evidence equal to the anchor, and the adjustment weight for positive evidence equal to the complement of the anchor.

α and β represent sensitivity toward negative and positive evidence. Depending on the values of α and β, four different types may be identified: the insensitive ($\beta=0$; $\alpha=0$), the advocate ($\beta=1; \alpha=0$), the highly sensitive ($\beta=1$; $\alpha=1$), and the skeptic ($\beta=0$; $\alpha=1$). These are shown in Exhibit 4.1.

To model the consideration that task demands can influence the updating process, thereby inducing serial effects, the following assumptions were made:

$$w_k = \alpha^\theta S_{k-1}$$

$$r_k = \beta^\lambda (1 - S_{k-1})$$

where θ and λ are both functions of k.

Exhibit 3.1

Different Types in the "Contrast-Inertia" Model

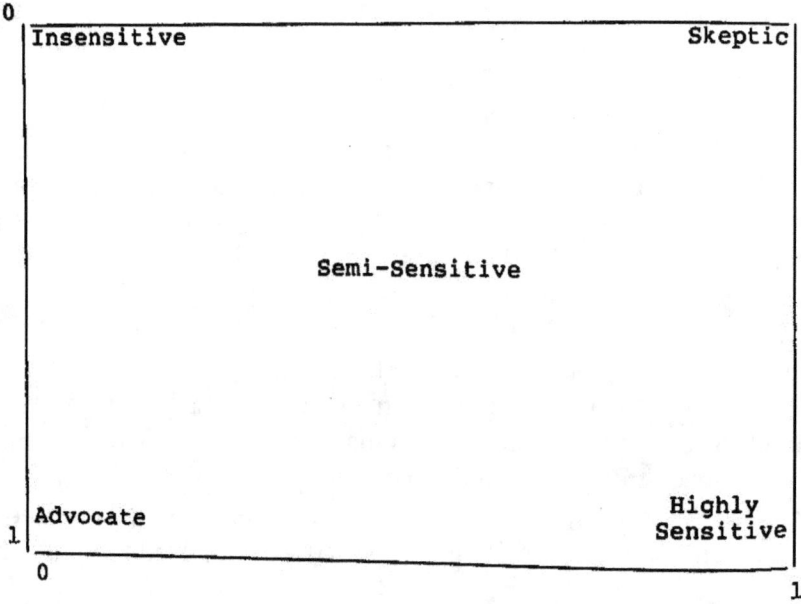

All these assumptions are integrated in the original equations of the contrast-inertia model of belief to yield the final discount and accretion models:

$S_k = S_{k-1} - \alpha^\theta S_{k-1} S(a_k)$

for the discount model and

$S_k = S_{k-1} - \beta^\lambda (1 - S_{k-1}) S(b_k)$

for the accretion model .

The contrast-inertia model specifies that the degree of belief held after seeing k pieces of evidence is a complex function of initial opinion, the particular sequences of pieces of positive and negative information encountered, levels of sensitivity to negative and positive evidence, and serial position effects induced by task demand. The model clarifies phenomena concerning the shape of "opinion curves," effects of discrediting information, conditions under which beliefs might be expected to converge or diverge over time, and order effects in sequential judgment. Einhorn and Hogarth tested the model by concentrating on the qualitative predictions concerning order effects. Different assumptions made about the adjustment weight process in other formulations are: (1) a *constant weight model* where the adjustment weight is a constant that depends neither on the anchor nor on the evaluation of evidence, (2) a *weight proportional to scale value* model where the size of the adjustment weight for a specific piece of evidence is proportional to the strength of the evidence, (3) *an assimilation model* where, as in the contrast-inertia model, the adjustment weight is hypothesized to be a function of the anchor, (4) *the crystallized hypothesis* where as one processes information there is a growing tendency for early judgments to become "crystalized" and, therefore, increasingly resistant to change,[109] and (5) the *grain size effect model* where people are assumed to sequentially average the information received across time.[110] Depending on the type of evidence the order effect predictions of the different models are shown in Exhibit 4.2.

Unlike these alternative formulations the contrast-inertia model of belief predicts recency effects with the sequential processing of mixed evidence and no order effects for consistent evidence.

Exhibit 3.2
Order Effect Predictions of Different Models

Models	Types of Evidence		
	Consistent		Mixed
	Discount	Accretion	
1. Constant Weight	No Effect	No Effect	No Effect
2. Weight Proportional to Scale Value	No Effect	No Effect	No Effect
3. Weight as Function of Anchor:			
a. Assimilation	No Effect	No Effect	Primacy
b. Contrast Inertia	No Effect	No Effect	Primacy
4. Crystallization Hypothesis	Primacy	Primacy	Primacy
5. "Grain Size" Effect	Recency	Recency	Recency
6. Bayesian	No Effect	No Effect	No Effect

The contrast or surprise effect, which is determined by the adjustment weight, is greater for positive evidence when the anchor is small and for negative evidence when the anchor is large.

Einhorn and Hogarth conducted seven experiments to test the contrast-inertia model. The results showed the absence of order effects in the sequential processing of consistent evidence (i.e., all positive or all negative) and the presence of recency effects for mixed evidence.

Evidence in Accounting

The contrast-inertia model has definite implications in auditing, where information is needed about the order effects of auditing evidence and the impact of sequential versus simultaneous evaluation of the evidence.

The model was investigated using auditing tasks. The first study by Ashton and Ashton tested the absence of order effects for consistent evidence (positive and negative) and the presence of recency with mixed evidence.[111] They asked their subjects to perform updating tasks in an auditing environment. The results conformed to the contrast-inertia model with no order effects for consistent evidence and recency for mixed evidence. The second study by Messier, Knechel, and Tubbs also investigated the contrast-inertia model using both step-by-step and end-of-sequence response modes in task involving consistent and mixed evidence.[112] Their results were mixed. In the test of the accretion model using two pieces of evidence they found no order effects in the end-of-sequence response mode, but a small recency effect for step-by-step. In the test of the discount model, however, no order effects were observed with either response model. In the case of mixed evidence using four pieces of information, they found recency results with both response models. However, with two pieces of evidence, recency occurred in the step-by-step procedure and no order effect for end-of-sequences. Needless to say, more work is needed in the updating of belief in auditing and accounting.

CONCLUSION

This chapter considered probability elicitation and revision. Probability elicitation techniques and their application in accounting and auditing were examined before considering the attempts made at evaluating the goodness of these subjective probabilities. The revision of probability using the Bayes' theorem and the general phenomenon of conservatism were discussed in terms of the empirical results in psychology, accounting, and auditing. A belief updating model, the contrast-inertia model, was finally presented as an attempt to integrate the diverse results in this area of research.

NOTES

1. L. J. Savage, *The Foundations of Statistics*, 2nd ed. (New York: Dover Publications, 1979), p. 3.

2. Ibid., p. 27.

3. G. R. Chesley, "Elicitation of Subjective Probabilities: A Review," *Accounting Review* (April 1975): 327.

4. Ibid., p. 328.

5. R. L. Winkler and A. H. Murphy, "Evaluation of Subjective Precipitation Probability Forecasts," in *Proceedings of the First National Conference on Statistical Meteorology* (Boston: American Meteorological Society, 1968), pp. 148-157.

6. Robin M. Hogarth, "Cognitive Processes and the Assessment of the Subjective Probability Distributions," *Journal of the American Statistical Association* (June 1975): 271-289.

7. R. L. Winkler, "The Assessment of Prior Distributions in Bayesian Analysis," *Journal of the American Statistical Association* (September 1967): 776-800.

8. G. R. Chesley, "The Elicitation of Subjective Probabilities: A Laboratory Study in an Accounting Context," *Journal of Accounting Research* (Spring 1976): 27-48.

9. G. R. Chesley, "Subjective Probability Elicitation: The Effect of Congruity of Datum and Response Mode on Performance," *Journal of Accounting Research* (Spring 1977): 1-11.

10. G. R. Chesley, "Subjective Probability Elicitation: A Performance Comparison," *Journal of Accounting Research* (Autumn 1978): 225-241.

11. Ibid., pp. 227-228.

12. G. R. Chesley, "Procedures for the Communication of Uncertainty in Auditor's Working Papers," in T. H. Burns, ed., *Behavioral Experiments in Accounting* (Columbus: Ohio State University, 1979), 2:115-149.

13. Ibid., p. 141.

14. John C. Corless, "Assessing Prior Distributions for Applying Bayesian Statistics in Auditing," *Accounting Review* (July 1972): 556-566.

15. William L. Felix, Jr., "Evidence on Alternative Means of Assessing Prior Probability Distributions for Audit Decision Making," *Accounting Review* (October 1976): 800-807.

16. Michael A. Crosby, "Bayesian Statistics in Auditing: A Comparison of Probability Elicitation Techniques," *Accounting Review* (April 1981): 355-365.

17. Michael A. Crosby, "Implications of Prior Probability Elicitation on Auditor Sample Size Decisions," *Journal of Accounting Research* (Autumn 1980): 585-593.

18. Ira Solomon, "Probability Assessment by Individual Auditors and Audit Teams: An Empirical Investigation," *Journal of Accounting Research* (Autumn 1982): 689-710.

19. B. H. Beach, "Expert Judgment about Uncertainty: Bayesian Decision Making in Realistic Settings," *Organizational Behavior and Human Performance* (August 1975): 10-69.

20. Ira Solomon, Jack L. Krogstad, Marshall B. Romney, and Lawrence A. Tomassini, "Auditors' Prior Probability Distributions for Account Balances," *Accounting, Organizations and Society* (February 1982): 27-41.

21. Ibid., p. 38.

22. Ira Solomon, Lawrence A. Tomassini, Marshal B. Romney, and Jack L. Krogstad, "Probability Elicitation in Auditing: Additional Evidence on the Equivalent Prior Sample Method," *Advances in Accounting* 1 (1984): 267-290.

23. Mohammad J. Abdolmohammadi, "Bayesian Inference in Substantive Testing: An Ease-of-Use Criterion," *Advances in Accounting* 2 (1985): 275-289.

24. N. D. Shields, Ira Solomon, and W. S. Waller, "Effects of Question Framing on the Accuracy of Auditors' Uncertainty Judgments" (Paper presented at the American Accounting Association National Meeting in Toronto, 1984).

25. Mohammad J. Abdolmohammadi and Paul D. Berger, "A Test of the Accuracy of Probability Assessment Techniques in Auditing," *Contemporary Accounting Research* (Fall 1986): 149-165.

26. Mohammad J. Abdolmohammadi, "Bayesian Inference in Auditing: Evidence on the Most Appropriate Assessment Techniques," *Accounting and Bayesian Research* (Fall 1987): 291-300.

27. Ibid., p. 294.

28. C. S. Spetzler and C. A. S. Stael von Holstein, "Probability Encoding in Decision Analysis," *Management Science* (November 1975): 340-358.

29. R. M. Hogarth, "Training Probability Assessors: An Experimental Paradigm for the Basic Statistical Concepts," INSEAD Research Paper Series (Fontainebleau, France: 1974).

30. G. R. Chesley, "Design and Evaluation of Training Programs for Individual Subjective Probability Assessors" (Working paper, Dalhousie University, 1981).

31. Ibid.

32. Mohammad J. Abdolmohammadi, "Bayesian Inference Research in Auditing: Some Methodological Suggestions," *Contemporary Accounting Research* (Fall 1985): 88.

33. Felix, Jr., "Evidence on Alternative Means of Assessing Prior Probability Distributions."

34. C. R. Peterson and L. R. Beach, "Man as an Intuitive Statistician," *Psychological Bulletin* (January 1967): 29-46.

35. M. Bar-Hillel, "On the Subjective Probability of Compound Events," *Organizational Behavior and Human Performance* (June 1973): 396-406.

36. S. Lichtenstein, B. Fischhoff, and L. D. Phillips, "Calibration of Probabilities: The State of the Art," in H. Jungermann and G. deZeeuw, eds., *Decision Making and Change in Human Affairs* (Dordrecht, Neth.: Reidel, 1977), pp. 275-324.

37. S. Lichtenstein, B. Fischhoff, "Do Those Who Know More Also Know About How Much They Know?" *Organizational Behavior and Human Performance* (December 1977): 159-183.

38. A. H. Murphy, "A New Vector of the Probability Score," *Journal of Applied Meteorology* 12 (1973): 595-600; A. H. Murphy, "A Sample Skill Score for Probability Forecasts," *Monthly Weather Review* 102 (1974): 48-55.

39. Ibid.

40. G. W. Brier, "Verification of Forecasts Expressed in Terms of Probability," *Monthly Weather Review* 75 (1950): 1-3.

41. C. A. S. Stael von Holstein, "Probabilistic Forecasting: An Experiment Related to the Stock Market," *Organizational Behavior and Human Performance* (August 1972): 139-158.

42. R. M. Hogarth, "Cognitive Processes and the Assessment of Subjective Probability Distribution," *Journal of the American Statistical Association* (June 1975): 271-289.

43. Lichtenstein, Fischhoff, and Phillips, "Calibration of Probabilities: The State of the Art."

44. R. L. Winkler, "The Quantification of Judgment: Some Methodological Suggestions," *Journal of the American Statistical Association* (December 1967): 776-800.

45. Hogarth, "Cognitive Processes and the Assessment of Subjective Probability Distributions," p. 280.

46. Ibid.

47. Winkler and Murphy, "Evaluation of Subjective Precipitation Probability Forecasts."

48. N. Kogan and M. A. Wallach, "Risk Taking as a Function of the Situation, the Person, and the Group," in *New Directions in Psychology III* (New York: Holt, Rinehart and Winston, 1967).

49. Hogarth, "Cognitive Processes and the Assessment of Subjective Probability Distributions."

50. R. L. Winkler, " The Consensus of Subjective Probability Distributions," *Management Science* (October 1968): 61-75.

51. Solomon, "Probability Assessments by Individual Auditor and Audit Teams."

52. Solomon, Krogstad, Romney, and Tomassini, "Auditors' Prior Probability Distributions for Account Balances."

53. L. A. Tomassini, Ira Solomon, M. B. Romney, and J. L. Krogstad, "Calibration of Auditors' Probabilistic Judgments: Some Empirical Evidence," *Organizational Behavior and Human Performance* (February 1982): 391-406.

54. Ibid.

55. Ahmed Belkaoui, "The Effects of Diagnostic and Redundant Information on Loan Officers' Predictions," *Accounting and Business Research* (Summer 1984): 249-256.

56. S. Oskamp, "Overconfidence in Case-Study Judgments," *Journal of Consulting Psychology* 29 (1965): 261-265.

57. H. J. Einhorn, D. N. Kleinmuntz, and B. Kleinmuntz, "Linear Regression and Process-Tracing Models of Judgment," *Psychological Review* (1979): 465-485

58. D. Ryback, "Confidence and Accuracy as a Function of Experience in Judgment Making in the Absence of Systematic Feedback," *Perceptual and Motor Skills* 24 (1967): 331-334; A. Tversky and D. Kahneman, "Judgment under Uncertainty: Heuristics and Biases," *Science* 185 (1974): 1124-1131.

59. Abdolmohammadi, "Bayesian Inference Research in Auditing: Some Methodological Suggestions."

60. William R. Scott, "Scoring Rules for Probabilistic Reporting," *Journal of Accounting Research* (Spring 1979): 156-178.

61. Ibid., pp. 174-175.

62. D. P. Newman and L. A. Tomassini, "Calibration of Subjective Probability Assessments: A Methodological Perspective," in S. Moriarity and Edward Joyce, eds., *Decision Making and Accounting: Current Research* (Norman: College of Business Administration, University of Oklahoma, 1984), pp. 90-100.

63. C. R. Peterson, R. J. Schneider, and A. J. Miller, "Sample Size and the Revision of Subjective Probabilities," *Journal of Experimental Psychology* (May 1965): 522-527.

64. P. Slovic and S. Lichtenstein, "Comparison of Bayesian and Regression Approaches to the Study of Information Processing in Judgment," *Organizational Behavior and Human Performance* (November 1971): 649-744.

65. L. D. Phillips and W. Edwards, "Conservatism in a Simple Probability Inference Task," *Journal of Experimental Psychology* (September 1966): 346-354.

66. G. F. Pitz and L. Downing, "Optimality of the Decision Making as a Function: Payoffs and Instructions," *Journal of Experimental Psychology* (April 1967): 549-555; G. F. Pitz, L. Downing, and H. Reinhold, "Sequential Effects in the Revision of Subjective Probabilities," *Canadian Journal of Psychology* (October 1967): 381-393; W. Edwards and L. D. Phillips, "Man as a Transducer for Probabilities in Bayesian Command and Control Systems," in M. W. Shelly and G. L. Bryan, eds., *Human Judgments and Optimality* (New York: Wiley, 1964).

67. D. H. Gustafson, "Evaluation of Probabilistic Information Processing in Medical Decision Making," *Organizational Behavior and Human Performance* (February 1969): 20-34.

68. Slovic and Lichtenstein, "Comparison of Bayesian and Regression Approaches to the Study of Information Processing in Judgment."

69. W. Edwards, "Conservatism in Human Information Processing," in B. Kleinmuntz, ed., *Formal Representation of Human Judgment* (New York: Wiley, 1968).

70. C. R. Peterson, W. M. Ducharme, and W. Edwards, "Sampling and Probability Revisions," *Journal of Experimental Psychology* (February 1968): 236-243.

71. A. Rapaport and T. S. Wallsten, "Individual Decision Behavior," *Annual Review of Psychology* (1972): 131-176.

72. W. Edwards, L. D. Phillips, W. L. Hayes, and B. G. Goodman, "Probabilistic Information Processing Systems: Design

and Evaluation," *IEEE Transactions on Systems Science and Cybernetics* (September 1968): 248-265.

73. Ibid.

74. R. J. Kaplan and J. R. Newman, "Studies in Probabilistic Information Processing," *IEEE Transactions in Human Factors in Electronics*, HFE 7 (1966): 49-63.

75. Beach, "Expert Judgment About Uncertainty: Bayesian Decision Making in Realistic Settings."

76. W. M. Ducharme, "A Response Bias Explanation of Conservative Human Inference," *Journal of Experimental Psychology* (July 1970): 66-74.

77. L. D. Phillips, W. L. Hayes, and W. Edwards, "Conservatism in Complex Probabilistic Inference," *IEEE Transactions in Human Factors in Electronics* 7 (1966): 7-18; D. F. Marks and J. K. Clarkson, "An Explanation of Conversatism in the Book-Bag and Poker-Chips Situation," *Acta Psychologica* 36 (1972): 145-160.

78. F. Aberoni, "Contribution to the Study of Subjective Probability," *Journal of General Psychology* 66 (1972): 261-264.

79. S. Barclay and L. R. Beach, "Combinatorial Properties of Personal Probabilities," *Organizational Behavior and Human Performance* (August 1972): 176-183.

80. Peterson, Schneider, and Miller, "Sample Size and the Revision of Subjective Probability."

81. Barclay and Beach, "Combinatorial Properties of Personal Probabilities;" Peterson, Schneider, and Miller, "Sample Size and the Revision of Subjective Probability."

82. W. M. Ducharme and C. R. Peterson, "Intuitive Inference About Normally Distributed Populations," *Journal of Experimental Psychology* (October 1968): 269-275.

83. R. L. Winkler and A. H. Murphy, "Experiments in the Laboratory and the Real World," *Organizational Behavior and Human Performance* 10 (1973): 252-270.

84. J. H. Steiger and C. F. Gettys, "Best-Guess Errors in Multi-Stage Inference," *Journal of Experimental Psychology* (January 1972): 1-7.

85. I. Yossef and C. R. Peterson, "Intuitive Cascaded Inference," *Organizational Behavior and Human Performance* (December 1973): 349-358.

86. John W. Dickhaut, "Alternative Information Structures and Probability Revisions," *Accounting Review* (January 1973): 61-79.

87. Henry A. Kennedy, "A Behavioral Study of the Usefulness of Four Financial Ratios," *Journal of Accounting Research* (Spring 1975): 97-116.

88. W. F. Wright, "Accuracy of Subjective Probabilities for a Financial Variable," in T. H. Burns, ed., *Behavioral Experiments in Accounting* (Columbus: Ohio State University, 1979), 2:1-13.

89. Abdolmohammadi, "Bayesian Inference Research in Auditing: Some Methodological Suggestions."

90. J. G. Birnberg, "Bayesian Statistics: A Review," *Journal of Accounting Research* (Spring 1964): 10-59; W. H. Kraft, Jr., "Statistical Sampling for Auditors: A New Look," *Journal of Accountancy* (August 1968): 49-56; J. E. Sorensen, "Bayesian Analysis in Auditing," *Accounting Review* (July 1969): 555-561; J. A. Tracy, "Bayesian Statistical Confidence Intervals for Auditors," *Journal of Accountancy* (July 1969): 41-47; J. A. Tracy, "Bayesian Statistical Methods in Auditing," *Accounting Review* (January 1969): 90-98; R. S. Kaplan, "A Stochastic Model for Auditing," *Journal of Accounting Research* (Spring 1973): 38-46; W. R. Scott, "A Bayesian Approach to Asset Valuation and Audit Size," *Journal of Accounting Research* (Autumn 1973): 304-330; W. R. Kinney, Jr., "A Decision Theory Approach to the Sampling Problem in Auditing," *Journal of Accounting Research* (Spring 1975): 134-142.

91. Michael A. Crosby, "Implications of Prior Probability Elicitation on Auditor Sample Size Decisions," *Journal of Accounting Research* (Autumn 1980): 585-593.

92. E. Blocher, "A Multivariate Variables Extension of Bayesian Statistical Sampling Methods for Auditors," *AIDS Proceedings* (October 1977): 13-15; E. Blocher and J. C. Robertson, "Bayesian Sampling Procedures for Auditors: Computer Assisted Instruction," *Accounting Review* (April 1976): 359-363; Corless, "Assessing Prior Distributions for Applying Bayesian Statistics in

Auditing"; W. L. Felix, Jr., "Evidence on Alternative Means of Assessing Probability Distributions for Audit Decision Making," *Accounting Review* (October 1976): 800-807; J. W. Gentry, C. Caldwell, and G. Holtman, "An Expanded Interactive Approach to Bayesian Sampling Procedures for Auditors," *AIDS Proceedings* (October 1977): 10-12; D. R. Nichols and R. C. Baker, "Testing the Consistency of Auditors' Prior Distributions and Sampling Results," *Abacus* (December 1977): 91-104.

93. Corless, "Assessing Prior Distributions for Applying Bayesian Statistics in Auditing."

94. Ibid., p. 566.

95. Mohammad J. Abdolmohammadi, "Efficiency of the Bayesian Approach in Compliance Testing: Some Empirical Evidence," *Auditing: A Journal of Practice and Theory* (Spring 1986): 1-11.

96. Ibid., pp. 13-14.

97. Peterson and Beach, "Man as an Intuitive Statistician"; Edwards, "Conservatism in Human Information Processing"; Slovic and Lichtenstein, "Comparison of Bayesian and Regression Approaches to the Study of Information Processing in Judgment'" Hogarth, "Cognitive Processes and the Assessment of Subjective Probability Distributions"; B. Fischhoff, and R. Beyth-Maron, "Hypothesis Evaluation from a Bayesian Perspective," *Psychological Review* 90 (1983): 239-260; D. A. Schum, "Current Developments in Cascaded Inference," in T. W. Wallsten, ed., *Cognitive Processes in Choice and Decision Behavior* (Hillsdale, N.J.: Erlbaum 1980).

98. H. A. Raiffa and R. Schlaifer, *Applied Statistical Decision Theory* (Cambridge, Mass.: MIT Press, 1961); R. L. Winkler, *Introduction to Bayesian Inference and Decision* (New York: Holt, Rinehart and Winston, 1986).

99. C. F. Camerer, "Do Biases in Probability Judgments Matter in Markets? Experimental Evidence." *American Economic Review* (in press).

100. M. Fischbein and I. Azzeri, *Belief, Attitude, Intention and Behavior- An Introduction to Theory and Research* (Reading, Mass.: Addison-Wesley, 1975).

101. R. Nisbett and L. Ross, *Human Inference: Strategies and Shortcomings of Human Judgment* (Englewood Cliffs, N. J.: Prentice-Hall, 1980); R. Hastie, "Social Inference," *Annual Review of Psychology* (1983): 511-542.

102. D. A. Schum and A. W. Martin, "Formal and Empirical Research on Cascaded Inference in Jurisprudence," *Law and Society Review* 17 (1982): 105-151; J. H. Davis, "Order in the Courtroom," in D. J. Miller, D. G. Blackman, and A. J. *Chapman*, eds., *Perspectives in Psychology and Law* (New York: Wiley, 1984); N. Pennington and R. Hastie, "Explaining the Evidence: Further Tests of the Story Model for Juror Decision Making" (Unpublished manuscript, University of Chicago, March 1987).

103. C. I. Hovland, I. L. Jarvis, and H. H. Kelly, *Community and Persuasion: Psychological Studies of Opinion Change* (New Haven: Yale University Press, 1953).

104. H. D. Triandis, *Attitude and Attitude Change* (New York: Wiley, 1971); J. Cooper and R. T. Croyle, "Attitudes and Attitude Change," *Annual Review of Psychology* (1984): 395-426.

105. E. E. Jones, "The Rocky Road from Acts to Dispositions," *American Psychologist* 34 (1979): 104-117; H. J. Einhorn and R. M. Hogarth, "Judging Probable Cause," *Psychological Bulletin* 99 (1986): 3-19.

106. D. M. Green and J. A. Swets, *Signal Detection Theory and Psychophysics* (New York: Wiley, 1966).

107. N. H. Anderson, *Foundations of Information Integration Theory* (New York: Academic Press, 1981).

108. H. J. Einhorn and R. M. Hogarth, "Adaptation and Inertia in Belief Updating: The Contrast-Inertia Model" (Working paper, University of Chicago, October 1987).

109. Anderson, *Foundations of Information Integration Theory.*

110. L. L. Lopes, *Averaging Rules and Adjustment Process: The Role of Averaging in Inference* (University of Wisconsin,

Department of Psychology, Wisconsin Information Processing Center, 1981).

111. A. H. Ashton and R. H. Ashton, "Sequential Belief Revision by Auditors: Tests of a New Model" (Unpublished manuscript, Fuqua School of Business, Duke University, 1987).

112. W. F. Messier, Jr., W. R. Knechel, and R. M. Tubbs, "Recency and Response Mode Effects in the Auditor's Belief Revision Process" (Unpublished manuscript, Fisher School of Accounting, University of Florida, Gainesville, March 1987).

CHAPTER 4
HEURISTICS AND BIASES

Research in behavioral decision theory suggests that individuals seem to employ heuristics and biases in order to reduce complete cognitive processes to simpler judgmental obligations which are more manageable. Research in behavioral accounting has tried to verify the existence of these heuristics and biases in accounting and auditing settings. To date, this type of research has examined the following heuristics: representativeness, availability, confirmation bias, anchoring and adjustment, the conjunction fallacy, hindsight bias, illusory correlation, and the Weber-Fechner Law. Accordingly, this chapter will review the findings on these heuristics both in psychology and accounting and identify the heuristics which remain to be tested in accounting.

REPRESENTATIVENESS
Evidence in Psychology

A frequent heuristic in probability assessment appears to be representativeness. "A person who follows this heuristic evaluates the probability of an uncertain event, or a sample, by the degree to which it is: (i) similar in essential properties to its parent population; and (ii) reflects the salient features of the process by which it is generated."[1] According to this heuristic a person will estimate the probability that subject A belongs to class B by the extent to which A resembles B. This heuristic, where class membership is assessed by the degree of its similarity to a stereotypical class member, has been found to lead to the following systematic biases in probability estimation:[2]

- Insensitivity to prior probability or base rate.
- Insensitivity to the impact of sample size on the variance of the sampling distribution.
- Misperception of the likelihood of different sequences resulting from a random process.
- Insensitivity to the predictability of data.

The neglect of the base rate was investigated a number of times, varying base rates, problem content, information order, and response mode.[3] The results confirmed the findings that base rates were ignored. When other experiments used within subject experimental designs rather than between subjects, the findings showed that base rates were not ignored, in the sense that the subjects modified their judgments in the appropriate direction as the base rate was changed.[4]

Where the base rate was neglected, it was attributed to the fact that people lacked good schemata for working with probabilistic information[5] and the "abstract, pallid, and remote" nature of the base rate contrasted to the generally "concrete, vivid, and salient" character of individuating information.[6]

In fact, three situations characterize the base rate fallacy case:[7]

- People tend to rely on the base rate in making their judgments when case-specific evidence doesn't suggest a hypothesis (i.e., is not diagnostic and therefore not informative).[8]
- People ignore the base rate when case-specific evidence strongly favors a particular hypothesis (i.e., is not diagnostic and therefore not informative).[9]
- People rely on the base rates when the experimental case working or format make them appear causal[10] or specific.[11] This naturally follows from the findings that different framings of short cases will provide different results[12] and the suggestion by Tversky and Kahneman[13] that in the preliminary analysis of a decision problem, the decision maker frames the effective acts, contingencies, and outcomes: "Framing is controlled by the manner in which the choice problem is presented as well as by norms, habits and expectancies of the decision maker."[14]

Evidence in Accounting

Swieringa et al. conducted several experiments aimed at investigating the representativeness in accounting.[15] The first set of experiments investigated the psychological findings of insensitivity to the prior rate or base rate by subjects making probabilistic judgments. Two contexts were used. The first, identical to the one used by Tversky and Kahneman, involved the probability of a person being a lawyer or an engineer in cases where the base rates were 70% or 30%. The second involved the probability of the strength of the internal controls of a given company in cases where the base rates were 70% and 30%. In both cases, the students did not ignore the base rates, contrary to both the representativeness heuristic and Tversky and Kahneman's results.

The results of this experiment also suggest that people do not respond differently when they are given no evidence that when they are given worthless evidence. When our subjects were not given a company description, they properly relied on the prior probabilities in making their probability judgments. They also relied on the prior probabilities in making these judgments when they were given a company description. Subjects did not tend to associate distinct stereotypes with companies that have or do not have excellent internal controls. Lacking well-delineated stereotypes, subjects tended to rely on the prior probabilities in making their probability judgments.[16]

The second set of experiments by Swieringa et al. investigated the psychological findings of insensitivity to sample size by subjects making probabilistic judgments. Two contexts were used. The first was identical to the one used by Tversky and Kahneman and the second was a similar accounting problem. The subjects made many choices that were consistent with the representativeness heuristic. The next experiment investigated the tendency for judgments of posterior probabilities to be influenced by sample proportions. Two cases were used- balls and urns, and accounts/notes receivables. The subject performed better than Tversky and Kahneman's subjects but experienced great difficulty in the statement of correct posterior odds.

The final experiment investigated the suggestion by Tversky and Kahneman that input correlation tends to increase the confidence people have in the resulting predictions, which contradicts the statistics or correlation that higher accuracy results from independent input variables. Using grade-point predictions, Swieringa et al. confirmed Tversky and Kahneman's findings. They also found that consistency among input variables and not correlation among these variables, tends to result in greater confidence.

Gibbons replicated the Swieringa et al. experiments using 71 audit partners and staff from public accounting firms.[17] Using the same problems devised by Swieringa et al. he found evidence of insensitivity to prior probability in one of two cases, or insensitivity to sample size and a tendency for judgments to be strongly affected by the consistency of cases not properly sensitive to the intercorrelations.

Joyce and Biddle conducted a series of experiments to assess the neglect of base rates and the insensitivity to reliability and predictability.[18] Normative statistical principles require that base rates be used in probabilistic assessment and that the extremeness of predictions be mitigated by the predictability of information and the reliability of its source.

The first experiment investigated the impact of the false positive rate and the base rate in probabilistic judgments. Subjects were asked to estimate the probability that a key manager who received a "fraud" test signal is actually involved in fraudulent activities. Two false positive rates of 1% and 20% were used as well as two base rates of 1% and 10% . The positive hit rate was held at 80%. The subjects reacted to the base rates in conformance with normative principles. They did not, however, consider the false positive rate relevant in their probability estimates.

The next three experiments were based on consecutive manipulations of the stated base rates of fraud, the sample sizes on which these base rates were established, and the nature of the individuating data representing "fraud" in some cases and "no fraud" in others. The results of all these experiments showed that to a certain extent the base rates affected the auditors' probability assessments.

Base rates make a difference, yet they are not appropriately combined with individuating data. This appears to be a robust phenomenon, observed across different base rate manipulation, individuating information, and subjects. The explanation for the phenomenon most consistent with prior research seems to be that base rates are not fully appreciated in probabilistic inference, and this lack of appreciation becomes more critical when base rates are low.[19]

The last two experiments reported on the reliability of data. The last experiments required subjects to estimate the probability that an account receivable will be collected by the client in one case where the customer information was provided by the client and in another case where it was provided by an independent credit agency.

The base rates of collection were the same to allow for an investigation of the impact of reliability on probabilistic assessments. No difference was found.

In the experiment, two measures- probability assessments and decisions on the provision for uncollectibles- are consistent with the representativeness heuristic. To the extent that the individuating data were provided by sources that are differently reliable, as the auditing literature suggests, this finding is troublesome. Auditors may be insufficiently sensitive to the reliability of data.[20]

Because the findings may be due to the probability that the independent credit agency and client's credit manager are not differentially reliable a second experiment was conducted with these differences: in one case the base rate of collection was manipulated (either 25% or 75%) and a within-subject manipulation was added requiring subjects to respond to both sources of information. While the impact of the change in the base rate was not significant, the reliability of the source of the individuating data was significant using the within-subject design.

The finding may have important implications for auditors since the audit environment is more like a between-subjects design than a within-subject design. That is, the auditor typically obtains information from only one data source a a time. It may be the case that auditors are insufficiently sensitive to reliability under these conditions. One possible remedy- one which we are now exploring- is to have the auditor explicitly consider how he(she) might respond if a particular piece of information came from other, differentially reliable sources. By explicitly considering other sources, auditors may attend more to reliability. The evidence accumulated in this experiment on the sensitivity of subjects to base rates is less encouraging. Neither judgment made by the subjects was significantly different across base rate conditions.[21]

The most important findings from Joyce and Biddle's experiments relate to the fact that auditors underweighted base rates relative to a normative standard (Bayes' theorem) but auditors appeared to be more sensitive to base rates than other subject groups. A replication of their experiments by Holt showed that it is the framing of Joyce and Biddle's experimental problem that drives their results rather than the attributes of auditors or auditing context.[22]

Uecker and Kinney examined the extent to which practicing CPAs may employ two heuristics, representativeness and protectiveness.[23] They hypothesized that if auditors used the representativeness heuristic in their subjective evaluation of the sample outcome, they would base their evaluation of the sample outcome primarily upon the sample error rate, given that it is most representative of the population characteristic of interest, i.e., the population error rate; also, if auditors followed the protectiveness heuristic, they would select the items that maximize the dollar value audited by preferring a large sample outcome to a smaller one, even if the smaller sample had a lower error rate.[24] The auditors in the experiment were presented with five pairs of sample results involving various sample sizes and sample error rates, and were asked to choose the member of a pair that provides better evidence that the error rate in the population is 5% or less. For each pair, the sample results were selected so that one outcome provided adequate evidence that the population error rate is less than the critical rate at a 95% level of confidence, while the other outcome provided inadequate evidence at a 90% level of confidence. For three pairs, used to test the representativeness heuristic, the better sample outcome was the one with the larger error rate. For two pairs, used to test the protectiveness heuristic, the better evidence that the population error rate is less than 5% is based on the smaller sample. Therefore, subjects relying on the representativeness heuristic would opt for the smaller sample error rates given that these rates are more representative of the population characteristic of interest, while those relying on the protectiveness heuristic would opt for the outcomes based on large sample sizes. The results showed that only a minority of the auditors consistently employed either the representativeness or protectiveness heuristic.

The smaller number of CPAs who consistently based their choices on sample size or sample error rate and the variation in frequency of error from case to case indicate that the CPAs were employing a more complex model of information processing than is suggested by the literature on heuristics in information processing. The desire for some minimum sample size before choosing on the basis of sample error rate is consistent with a lexicographic model of choice in which sample sizes the dominant attribute. . . The superiority of the CPAs performance and the evidence of lexicographic ordering indicates that the use of simple heuristics may not be as persuasive as research by Kahneman and Tversky suggests.[25]

Johnson also examined the use of a "representativeness" heuristic in judgmental predictions of corporate bankruptcy.[26] He examined the relationship between sample evidence "representativeness" and base rate neglect with the hypothesis that probability judgments that are insensitive to the base rate when the sample is highly representative of the target population will not exhibit this bias where the sample is not representative of the target population. This result provided evidence that the probability judgments were governed by similarity assessments (a result consistent with the subject use of representativeness), base rate probability had little effect on subjects' bankruptcy judgments, and the tendency to ignore base rate information in probability judgment task is directly influenced by the degree of assessed similarity ("representativeness") of the corporate financial data. Johnson makes the following interesting speculation:

Intuition suggests that some stereotypes are strongly held, detailed descriptions of the population while others are at best vague, tentative organizing principles. We can speculate that the representativeness is likely to be used, and base rate information ignored, in prediction contexts where the population and hypotheses under consideration can be characterized in terms of stereotypic numbers, the stereotypes are well defined, and the sample information provides evidence about relevant attributes of the stereotype. The particular accounting and auditing probability judgment problems which fit this remains to be identified.[27]

AVAILABILITY
Evidence in Psychology

Availability of information is argued to be an important clue that people use in making judgments. It has been considered as a bias whereby people make a probabilistic judgment on an event by the ease with which similar events are recalled. "A person is said to employ the availability heuristic whenever he estimates frequency or probability of the case with which instances or complications can be brought to mind."[28] That is, frequent events are easier to recall than infrequent ones, making availability a valid cue for the assessment of frequency and probability. Availability is also influenced by factors unrelated to likelihood, such as familiarity, recency, and emotional saliency and imaginability. Lichtenstein et al. asked their subjects to compare the frequency of occurrence of pairs of lethal events and found that they overestimated the relative frequency of diseases or causes of death that are much publicized.[29] What seems apparent is that emphasis on some aspects in the environment affects judgment by making it easier to recall instances and estimate their frequency.

Ross and Sicoly postulated that an egocentric bias in availability of information in memory could produce biased attribution of responsibility for a joint product because of significant processes that may be operating to increase the availability of one's own contributions: selective encoding and storage of information, differential retrieval, informational disparities, and motivational influences.[30] Three experiments confirmed the prevalence of self-centered biases in availability and judgments of responsibility.

In everyday life the egocentric tendencies may be overlooked when joint endeavors do not require explicit allocations of responsibility. If allocations are stated distinctly, however, there is a potential for discussion, and individuals are unlikely to realize that their differences in judgment could arise from honest evaluations that are differentially available.[31]

Evidence in Accounting

Libby examined the role of availability in the generation of hypotheses in analytical review.[32] More specifically, he examined the role of prior knowledge of financial statement errors in the generation of initial diagnostic hypotheses in preliminary analytical review, with the assumption that financial statement error hypotheses are influenced by their expected frequency of occurrence and their recency of occurrence. In addition, two hypotheses were used to test the transaction cycle organization of memory whereby an inherited hypothesis or the generation of a hypothesis increases the likelihood that subsequent hypotheses are generated from the same cycle. The influence of perceived frequency is taken from findings in psychology that frequency of experience affects ease of retrieval.[33] The influence of recency is taken from the findings of a strong recency effect of the length of the intervening period as the free recall of a variety of stimuli.[34] The experiment where a group of experienced auditors performed a diagnostic task regarding the detection of material financial statement errors through preliminary analytical review showed that: perceived error frequencies are closely associated with the frequency with which individual error hypotheses are generated: recency of experience was also associated with the generation of hypothetical errors; error types could not be cued to specific transaction cycles using initial hypotheses; and there is a clustering of generated errors by transaction cycles.

CONFIRMATION BIAS

It is an accepted normative view of scientific inference that disconfirmation and testing of alternative hypotheses have major roles. More particularly, Popper's philosophy of science centers around the concept of disconfirmation or refutation.[35] He maintained that hypotheses can only be disconfirmed by evidence and never confirmed. Platt also argued that successive generations of alternative hypotheses should be disconfirmed- a strategy he labels "strong inference."[36]

Karl Popper asserted that the purpose of science is not the verification but the falsification of theories.[37] The falsification can be achieved by deductive logic. If one adopts a *rationalist* view of humanity, then deductive logic is a necessary and natural part of human thought.[38] The *behaviorist* view would argue that the use of logical knowledge depends on whether or not the appropriate reinforcement contingencies have been applied.[39]

People are generally presented with conditional relationships between propositions that may be represented as "if p, then q," where p is the antecedent and q is the consequent. A typical deductive reasoning problem is to entertain alternative hypotheses with respect to the truth or the falsity of the rule. Given p, q, p' (not p) and q' (not q), the problem of deciding whether the rule "if p, then q" is true or false becomes a deductive reasoning problem. The selection may be accomplished using either a verification of falsification principle, depending on the degree of weight[40] and as follows:

- A subject with no insight will select the options that verify the rule. That is, they will choose p or p and q.
- A subject with partial insight will appreciate the need to select potential falsifiers, but only choose options that could only verify. p' will be considered irrelevant because it should neither verify nor falsify. All other options will be chose (i.e., p, q, and q') because they could either verify, falsify, or both.
- A subject with complete insight will select only the options that could falsify. That is, p and q' will be chosen.

Which strategies will be used has been the subject of experiments using either abstract or thematic problems, with the evidence showing only 10% of the subjects capable of solving the problem using the falsification principle.[41] The results were consistent with undergraduates as well as more sophisticated subjects (e.g., Ph.D. psychologists and statisticians)[42] and with abstract as well as thematic tasks.[43]

Which of these three strategies will be used by the accountant? The auditor's concern is mainly with verification- the examination of financial data for the purpose of judging the faithfulness with which they portray events and conditions. Mautz and Sharaf emphatically state the focus on verification:

In the business world, the act of verification is the trade of auditors, both internal and external. This philosophical truth about the necessity of verification is so well accepted that the business world has adopted a general practice of submitting such propositions to a verification process before they are given any serious consideration for many purposes. This verification consideration takes many forms; sometimes it is the continuous examination of procedures and data performed by an internal audit staff, sometimes the annual examination of an independent auditor, sometimes the investigation of an Internal Revenue Agent. Whatever the form, the importance and fact of verification are well accepted.[44]

Therefore, while deductive logic dictates the use of falsification in a deductive reasoning task, the emphasis on verification in auditing will lead the auditors to rely on a verification principle.

Belkaoui examined the use of logical knowledge in deductive reasoning by students and auditors.[45] An abstract and two thematic tasks were used and subjects were asked to test the truth or falsity of an implication rule. The results in the abstract test verified the dominance of the verification principle rather than the falsification principle for both students and auditors. No thematic effect was observed as the use of thematic effects showed a worsening of the falsification principle. In addition, the strong results on the dominance of the verification principle were found to be independent of the level of education, affiliation with a given accounting firm, position in the firm, years of experience as an auditor, years of application with the firm, or age of the subjects. While there are strong evidence both in accounting and psychology for this "confirmation bias," Klayman and Ha showed that many phenomena labeled confirmation bias are better understood in terms of a general "positive test strategy."[46] In addition, confirmation bias has meant different things to different researchers. Examples include the findings that people pay undue attention to the frequency of occurrence of two events, while underweighting instances in which one event occurs without the other,[47] the findings that people tend to discredit or interpret information counter to a hypothesis they hold,[48] and the findings that people may conduct "biased" tests that pose little risk of producing disconfirming results.[49]

ANCHORING AND ADJUSTMENT
Evidence in Psychology

In many situations, people make estimates by thinking of an internal value or "anchor" that is suggested by the formulation of the task or as a result of partial computation, and then make some adjustment to it to yield the final answer. This heuristic has been termed "anchoring and adjustment." For example, if a purchasing agent is asked to estimate next year's purchases he may start with last year's purchases before making some adjustments to them to reflect new environmental conditions. Therefore, people starting from different anchors end up with different answers. In addition, this heuristic has been found to lead to the following systematic biases in probability estimation.[50]

- Insufficient adjustment.
- Biases in the evaluation of conjunctive and disjunctive events. "The chain-like structure of conjunctions leads to overestimation, the funnel-like structure of disjunctions leads to underestimation."[51]
- Anchoring in the assessment of subjective probability distributions.

Slovic also found evidence of anchoring in the subjective valuation of gambles.[52] Subjects finding a gamble basically attractive use the amount to win as an anchor, then adjust it downward to take into account the less-than-perfect chance of winning and the possibility of losing a small amount. The adjustment was insufficient and Slovic pointed out that it may be the reason why people *price* gambles inconsistently with straight choices between pairs of gambles where a monetary response is not required.

The anchoring heuristic was also observed in an experiment by Albert and Raiffa.[53] They asked subjects to give the first and 99th percentile values for various quantities of items. It amounted to asking the subjects to estimate the 98% confidence intervals for the population value of the various quantities. The evidence showed that, on average, the subject's 98% confidence intervals included the true value only 40-50% of the time.

Evidence in Accounting

Joyce and Biddle investigated the anchoring-adjustment heuristic in three audit-related experiments.[54] The first experiment tested for the bias of insufficient adjustment for an anchor. In experiment A the subject were supplied with an irrelevant anchor (either 10 or 200) and were asked to estimate the number of Big Eight clients for 1,000 that have significant executive-level management fraud. The results showed that the high anchor group had higher estimates than the low anchor group. In experiment B the threshold for significant executive-level management fraud was fixed and four anchors (1, 10, 200, and 300 of 1,000) were provided.

The results were again consistent with anchoring and adjustment heuristic. In addition, the magnitude of the anchoring effect did not seem to increase monotonically with the size of the anchor. This is consistent with research in psychographics showing nonmonotone anchoring effects.[55]

The second experiment examined adjustment from an anchor. Subjects were asked to indicate the extensiveness of the substantive tests they would perform to detect a particular audit error. An experimental group of subjects made a rating given strong internal control first then given weaker internal control. The control group made a rating for the weaker case. The idea was to have the experimental group develop an anchor in the strong internal control case and make insufficient adjustment in the weaker control case. Therefore, the mean rating in the weaker case would be stronger for the experimental group than for the control group following the anchoring and adjustment heuristic. The findings were not supportive. A follow-up experiment required the subjects to respond to three internal control cases: the strong case, followed by the weaker case, while a weak-then-strong sequence was used for other subjects. Again, the results did not support the anchoring and adjustment heuristic but a contingent adjustment strategy. In other words, subjects overadjusted when controls became weak and underadjusted when controls became stronger.

The third set of experiments was designed to test for anchoring and adjustment in conjunctive events (success requires all elementary events) and disjunctive events (failure results if at least one elementary event does not occur). In the first experiment, subjects were required to state the probability of successful product introduction and to express an opinion on the financial statements, given the probabilities of either five conjunctive events or three of the five conjunctive events. The probabilities estimated by both groups were overstated, confirming anchoring on individual-event probabilities. The adjustments would not be concluded to be insufficient since it is not known what the subjects assumed about event independence. In the second experiment some subjects received the five- and three-event conjunctive formulation, while the others received disjunctive formulation. Basically, the complements of the probability of the elementary events in the conjunctive case were used and subjects were told that *any one* of the five (or three) events would prevent successful introduction of the new product line. The anchoring phenomenon suggests that the probability of success estimate should be lower in the disjunctive and conjunctive cases were not significantly different.

Kinney and Uecker reported the results of an experiment involving two audit tasks to investigate auditors' use of the anchoring and adjustment heuristic.[56] The first task involved auditors' judgments when using "limited information" in analytical review. The hypothesis was that auditors assessing the reasonableness of current unaudited values. The second task involved auditors' evaluations of compliance sample outcomes using either a fractile assessment or a risk (probability) assessment method. The hypothesis is that auditors using the fractile assessment will understate the achieved upper precision built for the population error rate while those using the risk assessment method will overstate the achieved risk that the population error rate exceeds the maximum allowable rate. In the fractile assessment case the auditors responded to the following statement: "Based on a sample of 40 invoices with no errors, I believe that there is only 1 chance that in 20 that the time population rate is "greater than ___ percent." In the risk assessment case the statement read as follows: "Based upon a sample of 40 invoices with no errors, I believe that there is a ___ (between 100% and 0%) chance that the true population error rate is greater than 8%." The results confirmed the speculations in the sense that the judgments of the auditors were biased consistently with their use of the anchoring and adjustment heuristic. In addition, the number and percentage of type II error was higher with the fractile assessment method while the number and percentage of type I error was greater with the risk assessment method. As a result of these findings the Sampling Standards Task Force decided to revise the proposed SAS to exclude the suggestion of the fractile assessment method. Note that anchoring is still in effect. Kinney and Uecker conclude as follows: "Use of the risk assessment method will not, of course, eliminate the anchoring effect in auditors' judgmental evaluations of sample results. It merely avoids some of the more severe consequences of anchoring, i.e., excessive type II error risk."[57]

Butler suggested that there are at least two other anchors that could explain Kinney and Uecker's findings.[58] First, given that information provided in the task is more likely to be used than information to be retrieved from memory,[59] auditors may have anchored on 8%, prominently used by Kinney and Uecker as a tolerable error rate. Second, auditors may use some interval expectations as anchor, based on experience and institutional guidance on what to expect. As a result, Butler conducted the experiments to determine the anchor used by experienced auditors in their judgmental evaluation of a compliance test sample and a substantive test of details sample.[60] The results indicated the existence of an anchoring behavior in the judgmental evaluation of audit samples, by starting at a low level of risk of .05 or .10. One consequence is stated as follows:

This internal anchor may be the result of evaluating a number of samples that have low risk, with the result that the auditors tend to expect low risk in samples to such an extent that the sample result does not have much impact. By having a bias toward low risk assessments, the auditor may be unconsciously increasing the risk of incorrectly accepting an account balance.[61]

THE CONJUNCTION FALLACY IN PROBABILITY JUDGMENT
Evidence in Psychology

The conjunction rule, a qualitative law of probability, specifies that the probability of a conjunction, $P(A\&B)$, cannot exceed the probabilities of its constituents, $P(A)$ and $P(B)$, because the extension (or the possibility set) of the conjunction is included in the extension of its constituents. In other words

$P(A\&B) \leq \min [P(A), P(B)]$

But intuitive judgments of probability are generally not extensional. People instead use a limited number of heuristics. The natural assessments of representativeness and availability do not conform to the extensional logic of probability theory. "In particular, a conjunction can be more representative than one of its constituents, and instances of a specific category can be easier to retrieve than instances of a more inclusive category."[62]

One would expect, therefore, that representativeness and availability will make a conjunction appear more probable than one of its constituents. Indeed, Tversky and Kahneman present convincing evidence that people often violate the conjunction rule of probability theory when assessing the joint probability of two events.[63] They showed that both sophisticated and naïve people, in many different substantive problems, often judge the conjunction of events to be larger than one of its components ("single violation") or as large as both of its components ("double violation"). Their experimental task included the following components:

A   = the judged probability of an event A given model M
J   = the judged probability of an event B given model M
A&J = the judged probability of the conjunction of A and J given model M

The violations to the conjunction rule were B<J<A or B<A<J.

For example, they gave their subjects the following task: "Bill is 24 years old. He is intelligent, but unimaginative, compulsive, and generally lifeless. In school he was strong in mathematics. Please rank order the following statements by the degree to which Bill resembles the identical member of that class."

- Bill is a physician, who plays poker for a hobby.
- Bill is an architect.
- Bill is an accountant. (A)
- Bill plays jazz for a hobby. (J)
- Bill surfs for a hobby.
- Bill is a reporter.
- Bill is an accountant who plays jazz for a hobby. (A&J)
- Bill climbs mountains for a hobby.

The risk included (1) a model M (the description of Bill), (2) an event A similar to the description (Bill is an accountant), (3) a dissimilar event J (Bill plays jazz for a hobby), and (4) the conjunction of the two events (event A and J: Bill is an accountant who plays jazz for a hobby). The subjects ranked the conjunctive event (A&J) as more probable than one of its constituents in this task as well as for other tasks in a variety of contexts using a number of different methods.

One explanation of this phenomenon may be derived from Tversky's feature-matching model, which suggests:[64]

S(a,b)=J(A&B) - J(A-B) - J(B-A)

Where

$\theta, \alpha, \beta \geq 0$

A&B = the features that are common to both A and B

A-B = the features that belong to A but not to B

B-A = the features that belong to B but not to A

J = an interval scale measure of feature salience

S = an interval scale measure of similarity

The model stipulates that the addition of a common feature to the stimuli produces an increase in their judged similarity and probability while the addition of a distinctive feature to either of the two produces a decrease in their judged similarity and probability. In the Tversky and Kahneman experiments the addition of event A with common features to the prototypical outcome of the description and event J with distinctive features led the subjects to rank conjunctive event (A&J) as more probable than J but not more than A. Einhorn provides a more formal representation of the conjunction fallacy.[65] More examinations of judgments of event conjunctions were provided in various studies.[66]

Evidence in Accounting

Frederick and Libby examined the role of expertise and auditors' judgments of conjunctive events.[67] The hypothesis is that auditors and novices will have a different behavior although they may both behave in a fashion which violates the conjunction rule. It is suggested that auditors have two types of knowledge: knowledge of the double-entry generating process which results in the occurrence of certain pairs of account errors and knowledge of the association of internal control weakness with particular errors. Students are assumed to have only the former type of knowledge.

The task presented to the subjects was analogous to Tversky and Kahneman's[68] and Beyth-Maron's,[69] and required reliance on auditing knowledge. It relied on the relations between control weaknesses and the accounts affected and the relations among accounts in the double-entry accounting system. Half of the subjects were provided with the following first scenario (M_1):

Open Company has engaged your office to perform the current year audit. While this is the twenty-second year that the office has had Open Company as an audit client, this is your first year on the engagement. However, you know from reviewing prior year work papers, and the systems of internal accounting and control have been relied upon in past audits. The current year documentation, review and update of the internal accounting and control systems (of Open Company) has disclosed that: (1) due to heavy personnel attrition, independent operations of sales, billings and accounts receivable departments could not be achieved; (2) no regular aging of accounts receivables was performed; (3) there was no independent mathematical check of sales invoices for accuracy of pricing, quantities and extensions.[70]

This scenario was designed to be representative of a system most prone to produce sales amounts recording errors (S) which affect the balances in net accounts sales revenue and accounts receivable (A).

The other half of the subjects were provided with the following scenario (M_2):

The current year documentation review and update of the internal accounting and control systems (of Open Company) has disclosed that: (1) due to heavy personnel attrition, independent operation of cash receipts function and accounts receivable record keeping could not be achieved; (2) no regular follow-up of overdue accounts was performed; (3) there was no independent comparison of the cash deposit slips with the initial cash control record.[71]

This second scenario was designed to be representative of a system most prone to produce cash receipts recording errors (C) which affect the balances in accounts receivable and cash (A).

In the first scenario, A and S share common features and their conjunctions should be judged more likely than both constituents. In the second scenario, A and C share common features and again their conjunction should be judged more likely than both constituents.

The instructions following both scenarios asked the participants to:

Please rank order the following by the probabilities that they will be among the consequences of the above internal control weaknesses [use 1 for the most probable consequences and 7 for the least probable].

___ [second constituent event]

___ quantity of goods shipped does not agree with quantity ordered.

___ [first constituent event] and [second constituent]

___ [second constituent event used in other treatment]

___ cost of goods sold expense balance as recorded is not correct and goods are shipped to fictitious customers.

___ [first constituent event]

___ trade notes receivable balance as recorded is not correct.[72]

Two treatments were used with each scenario. In the first treatment the first constituent event was A, "net accounts receivable balance as recorded is incorrect," and the second constituent event was S, "sales amounts are recorded incorrectly." The second constituent event forming the conjunction in treatment 2 was event C, "cash receipts are recorded incorrectly." Basically, the subjects in treatment 1 evaluated the accounts receivable and sales conjunction and those in treatment 2 evaluated the accounts receivable and cash conjunction. Both students as novices and auditors as experts were asked to complete the tasks. The results showed that both auditors and students behaved in a way which violates the conjunction rule and the audit and accounting knowledge of the subjects determined their behavior. Belkaoui investigated the presence of the conjunction fallacy in the judgmental predictions of corporate bankruptcy.[73] In addition, the extent to which subjects' probability judgments are consistent with the use of the conjunction fallacy was investigated in terms of the degree of assessed similarity ("representativeness") of the corporate financial data, the variations in the base rate, and the type of audits. Subjects presented with selected ratios and financial statements of five bankrupt and five nonbankrupt firms were required to do the following:

Please rank in order the following items by the probability that they will be among the consequences of the above financial statements within a three year period from the last year for which data are provided. Use 1 for the *most* probable consequence and 7 for the *least* probable consequence.

___ Loss of purchase discount from supplier.
___ Loss of major customer.
___ Employee strike.
___ Firm is filing for bankruptcy.
___ Accounts receivable factored.
___ Firm is filing for bankruptcy and loss of major customer.
___ Money lost on a fixed price contract.

The results of three experiments showed that the extent to which subjects' probability judgments were consistent with the use of a conjunction fallacy rule depended on the degree of assessed similarity ("representativeness") of the corporate financial data, but not on the variations of the base rate and types of audits.

HINDSIGHT BIAS
Evidence in Psychology

The hindsight bias or hindsight illusions were studied by Fischhoff[74] and Fischhoff and Byeth.[75] Basically, hindsight bias stipulates that subjects who have a knowledge that an outcome has occurred give that outcome a higher prior probability of occurrence than subjects that do not have any knowledge of the outcome. Fischhoff explains as follows:

In hindsight, people consistently exaggerate what could have been anticipated in foresight. They not only tend to view what has happened as inevitable, but also to view it as having appeared "relatively inevitable" before it happened. People believe that others should have been able to anticipate events much better than was actually the case. They even misremember their own predictions so as to exaggerate in hindsight what they know in foresight.[76]

In addition, subjects seem to be unaware of the influence of outcome knowledge on assessed probabilities. As stated by Fischhoff: "Making sense out of what he is told about the past seems so natural and effortless a response that one may be unaware that outcome knowledge has had any effect at all on him."[77]

Hindsight bias was observed in experiments by Fischhoff[78] employing psychotherapy cases, by Slovic and Fischoff[79] employing the outcomes of scientific experiments, and by Fischhoff and Beyth,[80] Fischhoff,[81] and Wood[82] employing general knowledge events. It was also observed in a number of medical settings involving judgments by nurses,[83] patients,[84] surgeons,[85] and physicians.[86]

Various arguments were provided to explain the hindsight bias. First, that outcome knowledge restructures memory.[87] Hogarth, for example states:

The knowledge that an event has occurred seems to restructure one's memory. Our memory of the past is not a memory of the uncertainties of the past, rather it is a reconstruction of past events in terms of what actually occurred. Furthermore, that past is structured in a way that makes some kind of coherent sense to the individual, for example, concerning the relationship between what actually happened and *particular* (but not all) antecedent events.[88]

Second, it stems from the difference between foresight and hindsight, with the first requiring more powers of imagination.

Prediction requires considerable powers of imagination and both the ability and willingness to entertain several hypotheses simultaneously. Keeping one's options open is not a tidy exercise and can induce considerable anxiety.

Postdiction or hindsight, on the other hand, requires little imagination and is an invitation to impose a causal structure on a sequence of past events. Furthermore, subjectively there is less uncertainty than in prediction problems concerning the events the 'caused' what happened. One can believe any claim that seems plausible since it was seen to precede the event.[89]

Third, hindsight bias results from the limited availability of causal scenarios for alternative outcomes vis-à-vis scenarios for the reported outcome.[90]

Fourth, hindsight bias is a result of the individual's "fluency of diagnostic thinking."[91] In other words, outcome information make possible the generation of a coherent story and what follows in terms of forward inference (i.e., prediction of outcomes) involves less uncertainty, given the reduction in the multiplicity of causation.

Fifth, hindsight bias is a result of motivating factors given that subjects, eager to preserve their self-images and how they are perceived by others, may be motivated to act as if they always knew what was going to occur.[92]

The hindsight bias raises a number of important issues with regard to judgments of the apparent failures (and successes) of others, distortions in memory, overcoming bias, and learning from experiences.[93]

- With regard to judging others, hindsight makes it easier to judge the mistakes of others without considering that at the time a decision was made, It might have been quite reasonable.
- Distortions in memory result from hindsight bias. We may fail to blame people who make the wrong decision but get away with it.
- Fischhoff was able to "debias" distortions in memory caused by the knowledge of outcomes by giving the subject knowledge of the true outcomes following the false information provided earlier. That created a stimulus capable of overcoming hindsight bias.
- The hindsight bias raises questions concerning the ability of people to learn from experience and to make predictions.[94]

Evidence in Accounting

Brown and Solomon examined the potential effects of outcome information on evaluations of managerial decisions.[95] Based on cognitive considerations surrounding the hindsight bias they developed hypotheses about a baseline effect of outcome information and attenuation of that effect by (1) the evaluator's prior involvement with the evaluatee's decision process and (2) the extent to which reported outcomes imply evaluatee responsibility for anticipating such outcomes. Faced with a capital budgeting project, subjects were asked to assume the role of assistant controller and to indicate how strongly they believed that the capital budgeting committee's approval of the project was a significant judgmental error. The results confirmed the hypotheses of a hindsight bias attenuated by some contextual factors.

Buchman examined the effect of hindsight on predicting bankruptcy with accounting information.[96] His results supported a first hypothesis of hindsight bias but could not support a surprise hypothesis when subjects were provided with a qualified opinion. Unlike the psychological findings of Arkes et al., the subjects exhibited greater hindsight where there should have been less surprise.[97] The explanations for this result include:

One is that a 'subject to' qualification contains little information (or indicated by some prior research . . .) prior to bankruptcy, but given that the firm has declared bankruptcy there may be a higher "anchoring point" caused by the bankruptcy knowledge in conjunction with the qualified opinion followed by insufficient adjustment. Alternatively, the subjects may not have a higher anchoring point, but seeing the qualified opinion inhibits their adjustment more than for those subjects receiving an unqualified opinion. Further research will have to investigate these findings.[98]

ILLUSORY CORRELATION AND CONTINGENCY JUDGMENTS

Illusory correlation refers to the belief that two variables covary when, in fact, they do not. Chapman defined it as "the report by observers of a correlation between two classes of events which, in reality, (a) are not correlated, (b) are correlated to a a lesser extent than reported, or (c) are correlated in the opposite direction from that which is reported.[99] In fact, Chapman and Chapman provided subjects with information concerning hypothetical mental patients which included a clinical diagnosis and a drawing of a person made by the patient.[100] The drawings and symptom statements were combined in such a way that "each drawing occurred as often with one statement as another."[101] Therefore, no relationship existed between drawings and symptom statements. The subjects were then asked to estimate the frequency with which each diagnosis (e.g., suspiciousness or paranoia) had been accompanied by various features of the drawings (e.g., peculiar eyes). The results showed that the subjects markedly overestimated the frequency of occurrence of pairs commonly believed to exist by society, such as suspiciousness and peculiar. Similar results in illusory correlations were provided by Chapman and Chapman,[102] Golding and Rorer,[103] and Starr and Katkin.[104]

Illusory correlation studies point to the tendencies of finding nonexistent relationships.[105] Studies of contingency judgments, however, point to sensitivity to certain relationships and not to others. If X_1 and X_2 represent two events like the presence or absence of cloud seeding, and Y_1 and Y_2 represent two other events like the presence or absence of rain, then a contingency exists between X (cloud seeding) and Y (rain) to the extent the probability of Y_1 given A_1 differs from the probability of Y_1 given X_2 (see Exhibit 4.1). A contingency exists between X and Y to the extent that a/a+b differs from c/c+d. In contingency studies, subjects are generally asked to make a judgment J about the degree to which the variables X and Y covary. The normative or objective covariation, N, is measured by organizing the data in a 2 x 2 joint frequency rule as in Exhibit 4.1 and applying one of the following correct data-integration rules:

N_1 (difference in diagonals) = [a+d] − [b+c]

N_2 (delta coefficient) = [a/(a+b)] − [c/(c+d)]

N_3 (contingency coefficient) = $[X^2/(n+X^2)]^{1/2}$

N_4 (lambda coefficient) = [max (a,c) + max (b,d) − max a+b, c+d)]/ [n − max (a+b, c+d)]

N_5 (phi coefficient) = $[ad-bc]/[(a+c)(b+d)(a+b)(c+d)]^{1/2}$

The correlation between J, the judgment about the degree to which the variables X and Y covary, and the data integration rule N_i is a measure of accuracy. The results of experiments point to the following:

- Subjects fail to appreciate that all the four frequencies in the table in Exhibit 4.1 are required.[106]
- Subjects make errors in estimating cell frequencies when factors unrelated to frequency influence the availability of data retrieved from memory or produced by imagination.[107]
- Subjects concentrate on the number of positive confirmatory data of a cell *a* and occasionally cell *d*, and ignore or underestimate the number of disconfirmatory data.[108]
- Studies of manipulative task difficulty indicate that the covariation judgment accuracy decreases as establishing a data set becomes more difficult.[109]

Waller and Felix examined auditors' covariation judgments.[110] Their objective was to determine whether auditors' covariation judgments are prone to the inaccuracies observed in psychological studies.

Exhibit 4.1
2 x 2 Joint Frequency Table

	Presence of Y	Absence of Y
Presence of X	a	b
Absence of X	c	d

Two complementary experiments were conducted to examine the rules by which auditors integrate joint frequency data when making covariation judgments and whether their judgments are affected by context, prior expectations, and amount of auditing experience. Their findings suggest that auditors rely on available bivariate data when judging covariations between task variables and use data-integration rules that are sensitive to the objective covariation level, but often overstated or understated this level. The following research issues were also identified:

First, overstatements and/or understatements of the objective covariation level were repeatedly observed in both experiments. Overstatements/ understatements may have efficiency and effectiveness implications for auditors in their identification of variables that are useful for inference making. Future research might use alternative response scales to determine whether these apparent errors represent misperceptions or merely response biases. Second, in light of the internal consistency observed in Experiment 1, future research might examine the cognitive processes by which expectations are mapped onto joint frequency estimates vs. covariation judgments. Third, consistent with most psychological studies, this study focused on auditor's covariation judgments for binary variables. Future research might use task variables with interval or ratio scales, which are typically encountered in judgmental analytical review. Finally, this study abstracted from possible errors in auditors' covariation judgments due to faulty data. Future research should examine the factors that potentially cause errors in auditors' frequency and joint frequency estimates.[111]

WEBER-FECHNER LAW

The Weber-Fechner law suggests that a just noticeable difference is uniquely related to the standard for which it was established. More explicitly, given a standard S and a just noticeable difference ΔS, then

$\Delta S/S = K$ for all S

where

K = constant

In other words, the change in intensity of a stimulus that is necessary before it can be detected is a constant function of the amount of stimuli present. To measure the just noticeable difference the method used is the method of constant stimulus differences.

Under this method, subjects are presented with a standard, followed by a series of changes above and below the standard. The subjects are then asked to judge the pairs of stimuli. For the responses, three curves are drawn representing the relative frequency of judgments of larger, equal, and smaller for the different magnitudes of the comparison stimulus.

Accordingly, Rose et al. made the hypothesis that people do respond to data stimuli as a sense stimuli and these stimuli obey the Weber-Fechner law.[112] They asked the subjects to judge whether a stock should sell for more than, less than, or the same as a series of copairons stocks, based on comparison of earnings-per-share (EPS) figures. The results showed that judgments of numerical stimuli could be represented by Weber-Fechner's law. In effect, the Weber ratios ranged from 6.6% to 7.0% of the standard stimulus across two experiments and two standards.

Dickhaut and Eggleton continued this line of research on the Weber-Fechner law of examining comparative judgments of numerical information, especially accounting information.[113] Unlike the study by Rose et al., they manipulated the stated setting in which judgments were made, the sequence of data presentation, and the format in which standards and comparison stimuli were presented. The results showed that the subjects' perceptions of the data were consistent with Weber-Fechner's law. Examination of individual plots raised serious doubts about a similarity of the psychophysical process of comparing physical stimuli and the process of comparing numerical stimuli. A second experiment was conducted followed by a questionnaire designed to elicit heuristics the subjects used in making similarity judgments. The results suggested that subjects used single decision rules, formulated either early in the task or possibility before the task was undertaken, applied inconsistently and defined as percentage functions of the expectations.

Magee and Dickhaut examined whether alternative compensation plans and the nature of the decision task conditions the choice of heuristics.[114] Individuals' decision-making abilities in a cost control setting were examined in an attempt to assess the effect of the compensation plan on these decisions. Based on an earlier study by Magee,[115] the identified the heuristic to be used for each compensation plan. The results showed that alternative compensation plans condition the choice of heuristics. In addition, a questionnaire to elicit heuristics yielded results which were found to be related to differences in costs to the firm that would result from the different compensation plans. In short, alteration of the decision environment (specifically the compensation plan) influences the choice of heuristics and, ultimately, the costs incurred by an operating department.[116]

OTHER HEURISTICS

Various other heuristics have been extensively examined in psychology but not in accounting. There is a need for more accounting research to examine these untested heuristics in accounting. They include the following:

1. Selective perception
2. Frequency
3. Concrete information
4. Data presentation
5. Inconsistency
6. Conservatism
7. Nonlinear extrapolation
8. Law of small numbers
9. Habit/"rules of thumb"
10. "best-guess' strategy
11. complexity in the decision environment
12. emotional stress in the decision environment
13. social pressures in the decision environment
14. consistency of information sources
15. question format
16. scale effects
17. wishful thinking
18. outcome irrelevant learning structures
19. misperceptions of chance fluctuations (gambler's fallacy)
20. success/failure attributions
21. logical fallacies in recall (see Exhibit 4.2).

CONCLUSION

While this chapter identified various experiments attempting to replicate in accounting psychological research on heuristics and biases that individuals use to reduce complex cognitive processes to simpler judgmental operations, it also showed that a lot remains to be done. Some remaining tasks are explaining some differences in findings between psychological research and behavioral accounting research and investigating in an accounting or auditing setting, various untested and interesting heuristics and biases examined in psychology but not in accounting.

Exhibit 4.2
Biases in Information Processing

Bias/source of bias		Description	Example
INFORMATION	Availability	– Ease with which specific instances can be recalled from memory affects judgements of frequency.	– Frequency of well-publicized events are over-estimated (e.g. deaths due to homicide, cancer); frequency of less well-publicized events are under-estimated (e.g. deaths due to asthma and diabetes).
		– Chance 'availability' of particular 'cues' in the immediate environment affects judgement.	– Problem-solving can be hindered/facilitated by cues perceived by chance in a particular setting (hints set up cognitive 'direction').
	Selective perception	– People structure problems on the basis of their own experience.	– The same problem can be seen by a marketing manager as a marketing problem, as a financial problem by a finance manager, etc.
		– Anticipations of what one expects to see bias what one does see.	– Identification of incongruent objects, e.g. playing cards with red spades, are either inaccurately reported or cause discomfort.
		– People seek information consistent with their own views/hypotheses.	– Interviewers seek information about candidates consistent with first impressions rather than information that could refute those impressions.
		– People downplay/disregard conflicting evidence.	– In forming impressions, people will under-weight information that does not yield to a consistent profile.
	Frequency	– Cue used to judge strength of predictive relationships is observed frequency rather than observed relative frequency. Information on 'non-occurrences' of an event is often unavailable and frequently ignored when available.	– When considering relative performance (of, say, two persons), the absolute number of successes is given greater weight than the relative number of successes to trials, i.e., successes and failures (the denominator is ignored). Note, however, that the number of failures is frequently unobservable.

(Continued)

Exhibit 4.2 Continued

ACQUISITION		
Concrete information (ignoring base-rate, or prior information)	– *Concrete* information (i.e. vivid, or based on experience/incidents) dominates *abstract* information (e.g. summaries, statistical base-rates, etc.).	– When purchasing a car, the positive or negative experience of a *single* person you know, is liable to weigh more heavily in judgement than available and more valid statistical information, e.g. in *Consumer Reports*.
Illusory correlation	– Belief that two variables covary when in fact they do not (Possibly related to 'Frequency' above).	– Selection of an inappropriate variable to make a prediction.
Data presentation	– Order effects (primacy/recency).	– Sometimes the first items in a sequential presentation assume undue importance (primacy), sometimes the last items (recency).
	– Mode of presentation.	– Sequential vs. intact data displays can affect what people are able to access. Contrast, for example, complete unit-price shopping vs. own sequential information search.
	– Mixture of types of information, e.g. qualitative and quantitative.	– Concentration on quantitative data, exclusion of qualitative, or vice versa.
	– Logical data displays.	– Apparently complete 'logical' data displays can blind people to critical omissions.
	– Context effects on perceived variability	– Assessments of variability, of say a series of numbers, is affected by the absolute size (e.g. mean level) of the numbers.
PROCESSING OF INFORMATION		
Inconsistency	– Inability to apply a consistent judgemental strategy over a repetitive set of cases.	– Judgements involving selection, e.g. personnel/graduate school admissions.
Conservatism	– Failure to revise opinion on receipt of new information to the same extent as Bayes' theorem. (Note this may be counterbalanced by the 'best-guess' strategy and produce near optimal performance in the presence of unreliable data sources).	– Opinion revision in many applied settings, e.g. military, business, medicine, law.

Bias/source of bias	Description	Example
Non-linear extrapolation	– Inability to extrapolate growth processes (e.g. exponential) and tendency to underestimate joint probabilities of several events.	– Gross underestimation of outcomes of exponentially increasing processes and overestimation of joint probabilities of several events.
'Heuristics' used to reduce mental effort:		
– Habit/'rules of thumb'	– Choosing an alternative because it has previously been satisfactory.	– Consumer shopping; 'rules of thumb' adopted in certain professions.
– Anchoring and adjustment	– Prediction made by anchoring on a clue or value and then adjusting to allow for the circumstances of the present case.	– Making a sales forecast by taking last year's sales and adding, say, 5%.
– Representativeness	– Judgements of likelihood of an event by estimating degree of *similarity* to the class of events of which it is supposed to be an exemplar.	– Stereotyping, e.g. imagining that someone is a lawyer because he exhibits characteristics typical of a lawyer.
– Law of *small* numbers	– Characteristics of small samples are deemed to be representative of the populations from which they are drawn.	– Interpretation of data, too much weight given to small sample results (which are quite likely to be atypical).
– Justifiability	– A 'processing' rule can be used if the individual finds a rationale to 'justify' it.	– When provided with an apparently rational argument, people may follow the ensuing rule even if it is inappropriate.
– Regression bias	– Extreme values of a variable are used to predict extreme values of the next observation of the variable (thus failing to allow for regression to the mean).	– Following observation of bad performance by an employee, a manager could attribute subsequent improvement to his intervention (e.g. warning to the employee). However, regression effects would imply that improvement (performance closer to the mean level), is highly likely *without* intervention.

(Continued)

Exhibit 4.2 Continued

OF	'Best-guess' strategy	– Under conditions involving several sources of uncertainty, simplification is made by ignoring some uncertainties and basing judgement on the 'most likely' hypothesis. (Note, people simplify by ignoring uncertainty.) More generally, tendency to discount uncertainty.	– Ignoring the fact that information sources are unreliable.
PROCESSING	*The decision environment:* Complexity	– Complexity induced by time pressure, information overload, distractions leads to reduced consistency of judgement.	– In decisions taken under time pressure, information processing may be quite superficial.
	Emotional stress	– Emotional stress reduces the care with which people select and process information.	– Panic judgements.
	Social pressures	– Social pressures, e.g. of a group, cause people to distort their judgements.	– The majority in a group can unduly influence the judgement of minority members.
	Information sources: Consistency of information sources	– Consistency of information sources can lead to increases in confidence in judgement but not to increased predictive accuracy.	– People often like to have more information, even though it is redundant with what they already have.
	Data presentation: See items under the *Acquisition* section.		
OUTPUT	*Response mode:* Question format	– The way a person is required or chooses to make a judgement can affect the outcome.	– Preferences for risky prospects have been found to be inconsistent with the prices for which people are willing to sell them.
	Scale effects	– The scale on which responses are recorded can affect responses.	– Estimates of probabilities can vary when estimated directly on a scale from zero to one, or when 'odds' or even 'log-odds' are used.

	Bias/source of bias	Description	Example
OUTPUT	Wishful thinking	– People's preferences for outcomes of events affect their assessment of the events.	– People sometimes assess the probability of outcomes they desire higher than their state of knowledge justifies.
	Illusion of control	– Activity concerning an uncertain outcome can by itself induce in a person feelings of control over the uncertain event.	– Activities such as planning, or even the making of forecasts, can induce feelings of control over the uncertain future.
FEEDBACK	Outcome irrelevant learning structures	– Outcomes observed yield inaccurate or incomplete information concerning predictive relationships. This can lead, inter alia, to unrealistic confidence in one's own judgement.	– In personnel selection you can learn how good your judgement is concerning candidates selected; but you usually have no information concerning subsequent performance of rejected candidates.
	Misperception of chance fluctuations (e.g. gambler's fallacy)	– Observation of an unexpected number of similar chance outcomes leads to the expectation that the probability of the appearance of an event not recently seen increases.	– So-called 'gambler's fallacy'—after observing, say, 9 successive Reds in roulette, people tend to believe that Black is more likely on the next throw.
	Success/failure attributions	– Tendency to attribute success to one's skill, and failure to chance (This is also related to the 'Illusion of control'—see above).	– Successes in one's job, e.g. making a difficult sale, are attributed to one's skill; failures to 'bad luck.'
	Logical fallacies in recall	– Inability to recall details of an event leads to 'logical' reconstruction which can be inaccurate.	– Eyewitness testimony.
	Hindsight bias	– In retrospect, people are not 'surprised' about what has happened in the past. They can easily find plausible explanations.	– The 'Monday morning quarterback' phenomenon.

Source: Robin Hogarth, *Judgment and Choice*, pp. 166–170. Copyright © 1980 by John Wiley & Sons, Ltd. Reprinted by permission of John Wiley & Sons, Ltd.

NOTES

1. D. Kahneman and A. Tversky, "Subjective Probability: A Judgment of Representativeness," *Cognitive Psychology* (July 1972): 431.

2. Ibid., pp. 430-454; D. Kahneman and A. Tversky, "On the Psychology of Prediction," *Psychological Review* (July 1973): 237-251; A. Tversky and D. Kahneman, "Judgment under Uncertainty: Heuristics and Biases," *Science* (September 1974): 1124-1131.

3. M. Bar-Hillel, "The Base Rate Fallacy in Probability Judgments," *Acta Psychologica* (October 1980): pp. 211-233; D. Lyon and P. Slovic, "Dominance of Accuracy Information and Neglect of Base Rates in Probability Estimation," *Acta Psychologica* (January 1976): 287-298.

4. N. E. Airs and M. Maris, "Base-Rates Do Influence Social Judgments (But Not Optimally)" (Working paper, University of Michigan, 1978); B. Fischhoff, P. Slovic, and S. Lichtenstein, "Subjective Sensitivity Analysis," *Organizational Behavior and Human Performance* (1979): 339-359; D. M. Grether, "Bayes Rule as a Descriptive Model: The Representativeness Heuristic" (Working paper, California Institute of Technology, 1979); M. Mavis and I. Dovalina, "Base-Rates Can Affect Individual Predictions" (Working paper, University of Michigan, 1978).

5. R. E. Nisbett, R. Crandall, and H. Reed, "Popular Induction: Information is Not Necessarily Informative," in J. S. Carroll and J. W. Payne, eds., *Cognitive and Social Behavior* (New York: Lawrence Erlbaum Associates, 1976).

6. R. E. Nisbett and E. Borgida, "Attribution and the Psychology of Prediction," *Journal of Personality and Social Psychology* (November 1975): 932-943.

7. D. Holt, "Evidence Integration in the Formation of Risk Assessments by Auditors and Bank Lending Officers" (Unpublished dissertation, University of Michigan, January 1984).

8. Fischhoff and M. Bar-Hillel, "Diagnosticity and the Base-Rate Effect," *Memory and Cognition* (July 1984): 402-410.

9. Ibid.

10. A. Tversky and D. Kahneman, "Evidential Impact on Base Rates," in D. Kahneman, P. Slovic, and A. Tversky, eds., *Judgment under Uncertainty: Heuristics and Biases* (New York: Cambridge University Press, 1982), pp. 153-160.

11. Bar-Hillel, "The Base Rate Fallacy in Probability Judgments."

12. P. Slovic, B. Fischhoff, and S. Lichtenstein, "Response Mode, Framing, and Information-Processing Effects in Risk Assessments," in R. Hogarth, ed., *New Directions for Methodology of Social and Behavioral Science: Question Framing and Response Consistency*, no. 11, (San Fransisco: Jossey-Bass, 1982), pp. 22-36.

13. A. Tversky and D. Kahneman, "Rational Choice and the Framing of Decisions," *Journal of Business* (October 1986).

14. Ibid., pp. 8251-8278.

15. Robert Swieringa, Michael Gibbins, Lars Larsson, and Janet Lawson Sweeny, "Experiments in the Heuristics of Human Information Processing," supplement to *Journal of Accounting Research* (1976): 159-187.

16. Ibid., p. 168.

17. M. Gibbins, "Human Inference, Heuristics and Auditors' Judgment Processes," in *CICA Auditing Research Symposium* (Toronto: Canadian Institute of Certified Public Accountants, 1977).

18. Edward J. Joyce and Gary C. Biddle, "Are Auditors' Judgments Sufficiently Regressive?" *Journal of Accounting Research* (Autumn 1981): 323-349.

19. Ibid., p. 339.

20. Ibid., p. 341.

21. Ibid., p. 346.

22. D. L. Holt, "Auditors and Base Rates Revisited," *Accounting Organizations and Society* (November 1987): 571-578.

23. Wilfred C. Uecker and William R. Kinney, Jr., "Judgmental Evaluation of Sample Results: A Study of the Type and Seventy of Errors Made by Practicing CPAs," *Accounting, Organizations and Society* (June 1977): 269-275.

24. Ibid.

25. Ibid.

26. W. Bruce Johnson, "Representatives' in Judgmental Predictions of Corporate Bankruptcy," *Accounting Review* (January 1983): 78-97.

27. Ibid., p. 94.

28. A. Tversky and D. Kahneman, "Availability: A Heuristic for Judging Frequency and Probability," *Cognitive Psychology* 5 (1973): 208.

29. S. Lichtenstein, P. Slovic, B. Fischhoff, M. Layman, and B. Combs, "Perceived Frequency of Lethal Events," *Decision Research Report* 78-2 (Eugene, Ore.: Decision Research, a Branch of Perceptronics, Inc., 1978).

30. Michael Ross and Fiore Sicoly, "Egocentric Biases in Availability and Attributions," *Journal of Personality and Social Psychology* 37 (1979): 322-336.

31. Ibid., p. 336.

32. Robert Libby, "Availability and the Generation of Hypotheses in Analytical Review," *Journal of Accounting Research* (Autumn 1985): 648-667.

33. D. Kahneman and A. Tversky, "Variants of Uncertainty," *Cognition* (April 1982): 143-157; W. C. Howell, "Representation of Frequency in Memory," *Psychological Bulletin* (July 1973): 44-53; T. O. Nelson, "Repetition and Depth of Processing," *Journal of Verbal Learning and Verbal Behavior* (April 1977): 151-172.

34. A. D. Baddeley, *The Psychology of Memory* (New York: Basic Books, 1976); R. L. Klatzky, *Human Memory: Structure and Processes* (San Fransisco: W. H. Freeman and Co., 1980).

35. K. R. Popper, *Conjectures and Refutations* (New York: Basic Books, 1962).

36. J. R. Platt, "Strong Inference," *Science* 146 (1964): 347-353.

37. K. R. Popper, *The Logic of Scientific Discovery* (London: Hutchinson, 1959).

38. R. J. Fahnagne, ed., *Reasoning: Representation and Process* (New York: Wiley, 1975); R. Revlin and R. E. Mayer, *Human Reasoning* (New York: Wiley, 1987).

39. B. F. Skinner, *Beyond Freedom and Dignity* (London: Basic Books, 1963).

40. P. N. Johnson-Laird and P. C. Wason, eds., *Thinking: Readings in Cognitive Science* (New York: Cambridge University Press, 1977).

41. J. S. Evans and B. T. Evans, *The Psychology of Deductive Reasoning* (London: Routledge and Kegan Paul, 1982).

42. R. M. Dawes, "The Mind, the Model and the Task," in F. Restel, R. M. Sliffrin, N. J. Castellan, H. R. Lindman, and D. B. Risoni, eds., *Cognitive Theory*, vol. 1 (Hillsdale, N.J.: Erlbaum, 1975); R. A. Griggs and S. E. Ravesdell, "Scientists and the Selection Task" (Unpublished manuscript, Department of Psychology, University of Florida, Gainesville, 1985); R. A. Griggs and J. R. Cox, "The Elusive Thematic-Materials Effects in Wason's Selection Task," *British Journal of Psychology* 73 (1982): 407-420.

43. B. Fischhoff and R. Beyth-Maron, "Hypothesis Evaluation from a Bayesian Perspective," *Psychological Review* (June 1983): 239-260; P. C. Vanduyne, "Necessity and Contingency in Reasoning," *Acta Psychologica* (May 1976): 85-101.

44. R. K. Mautz and H. A. Sharaf, *The Philosophy of Auditing,* American Accounting Association Monograph No. 6 (Evanston, Ill: American Accounting Association, 1961).

45. A. Belkaoui, "Auditing and the Use of Logical Knowledge in Deductive Reasoning: An Experiment" (Unpublished manuscript, University of Illinois at Chicago, 1987).

46. Joshua Klayman and Young-Won Ha, "Confirmation, Disconfirmation and Information in Hypothesis Testing" (Working paper, Graduate School of Business, University of Chicago, Center for Decision Research, February 1986).

47. H. R. Arkes and A. R. Harkness, "Estimates of Contingency between Two Dichotomous Variables," *Journal of Experimental Psychology* (October, 1983): 117-135.

48. C. Lord, L. Ross, and M. Legger, "Biased Assimilation and Attitude Polarization: The Effect of Prior Theories on Subsequently Considered Evidence," *Journal of Personality and Social Psychology* (March 1979): 2098-2109.

49. M. Snyder, "Seek and Ye Shall Find: Testing Hypotheses about Other People," in E. T. Higgins, C. P. Heiman, and M. P.

Zamma, eds., *Social Cognition: The Ontario Symposium on Personality and Social Psychology* (Hillsdale, N. J.: Erlbaum, 1981).

50. A. Tversky and D. Kahneman, "Judgment under Uncertainty: Heuristics and Biases," *Science* (September 1974): 1124-1131.

51. Ibid.

52. P. Slovic, "From Shakespeare to Simon: Speculations and Some Evidence About Man's Ability to Process Information," in *Research Monograph* (Oregon Research Institute, April 1972).

53. M. Albert and H. Raiffa, "A Progress Report on the Training of Probability Assessors" (Unpublished Manuscript, Harvard University, Graduate School of Business Administration, 1968).

54. Edward J. Joyce and Gary C. Biddle, "Anchoring and Adjustment in Probabilistic Inference in Auditing," *Journal of Accounting Research* (Spring 1981): 120-145.

55. H. Helson and H. Masters, "A Study of the Inflection-Points in the Locus of Adaptation-Levels as a Function of Anchor-Stimuli," *American Journal of Psychology* (October 1966): 400-408; V. Sarris, "Adaptation-Level Theory: Two Critical Experiments on Helson's Weighed Average Model," *American Psychologist* (1967): 331-344.

56. William R. Kinney, Jr. and Wilfred C. Uecker, "Mitigating the Consequences of Anchoring in Auditors' Judgments," *Accounting Review* (January 1982): 55-69.

57. Ibid., p. 69.

58. Stephen A. Butler "Anchoring in the judgmental Evaluation of Audit Samples," *Accounting Review* (January 1986): 101-111.

59. Slovic, "From Shakespeare to Simon."

60. Butler, "Anchoring in the Judgmental Evaluation of Audit Samples."

61. Ibid., p. 109.

62. A. Tversky and D. Kahneman, "Extensional versus Intuitive Reasoning: The Conjunction Fallacy in Probability Judgment," *Psychological Review* (October 1983): 295.

63. Ibid., pp. 293-315.

64. A. Tversky, "Features of Similarity," *Psychological Review* (February 1977): 327-352.

65. H. J. Einhorn, "A Model of the Conjunction Fallacy" (Working paper, Center for Decision Research, University of Chicago, June 1985).

66. Frank J. Yates and Bruce W. Carlson, "Conjunction Errors: Evidence for Multiple Judgment Procedures, Including 'Signed Summation,'" *Organizational Behavior and Human Decision Processes* 37 (1986): 230-253; Dean M. Morier and Eugene Borgida, "The Conjunction Fallacy: A Task Specific Phenomenon?" *Personality and Social Psychology Bulletin* (June 1984): 243-252; John Uddo, Robert P. Abelson, and Paget H. Gross, "Conjunctive Explanations: When Two Reasons Are Better Than One," *Journal of Personality and Social Psychology* (March 1984): 933-943; A. Locksley and C. Stangor, "Why vs. How Often: Causal Reasoning and the Incidence of Judgmental Bias," *Journal of Experimental Social Psychology* (October 1984): 430-455.

67. David M. Frederick and Robert Libby, "Expertise and Auditors' Judgments of Conjunctive Events," *Journal of Accounting Research* (Autumn 1986): 270-290.

68. Tversky and Kahneman, "Extensional Versus Intuitive Reasoning: The Conjunction Fallacy."

69. R. Beyth-Maron, "The Subjective Probability of Conjunctions," in *Decision Research Report,* No. 81-12 (Eugene, Ore.: Decision Research, 1981).

70. Frederick and Libby, "Expertise and Auditors' Judgments of Conjunctive Events," p. 276.

71. Ibid., p. 277.

72. Ibid., p. 281.

73. Ahmed Belkaoui, "Conjunction Errors in Judgmental Predictions of Corporate Bankruptcy" (Unpublished manuscript, University of Illinois at Chicago, 1988).

74. B. Fischhoff, "Hindsight ≠ Foresight: The Effect of Outcome Knowledge on Judgment under Uncertainty," *Journal of Experimental Psychology: Human Perception and Performance* (May 1975): 288-299; "Perceived Informativeness of Facts,"

Journal of Experimental Psychology: Human Perception and Performance (May 1977): 349-358.

75. B. Fischhoff and R. Beyth, "I Knew It Would Happen: Remembered Probabilities of Once-Future Things," *Organizational Behavior and Human Performance* (February 1975): 1-16.

76. B. Fischhoff, "Debasing," in D. Kahneman, P. Slovic, and A. Tversky, eds., *Judgment under Uncertainty: Heuristics and Biases* (New York: Cambridge University Press, 1982), p. 428.

77. Fischhoff, "Hindisght ≠ Foresight," p. 298.

78. Fischhoff, "Hindsight ≠ Foresight."

79. P. Slovic and B. Fischhoff, "On the Psychology of Experimental Surprises," *Journal of Experimental Psychology: Human Perception and Performance* (November 1977): 544-551.

80. Fischhoff and Beyth, "I Knew It Would Happen."

81. Fischhoff, "Perceived Informativeness of Facts."

82. G. Wood, "The Know-It-All-Along Effect," *Journal of Experimental Psychology: Human Perception and Performance* (May 1978): 345-353.

83. T. Mitchell and L. Kalb, "Effects of Outcome Knowledge and Outcome Valence on Supervisors' Evaluation," *Journal of Applied Psychology* (October 1981): 604-612.

84. D. Pennington, D. Rutter, K. McKenna, and I. Morley, "Estimating the Outcome of a Pregnancy Test: Women's Judgments in Foresight and Hindsight," *British Journal of Social and Clinical Psychology* (November 1980): 317-323.

85. D. Detmer, D. Fryback, and K. Gassner, "Heuristics and Biases in Medical Decision-Making," *Journal of Medical Education* 53 (1978): 682-683.

86. H. Arkes, R. Wortmann, P. Saville, and A. Harkness, "Hindsight Bias among Physicians Weighing the Likelihood of Diagnoses," *Journal of Applied Psychology* (October 1981): 252-254.

87. R. Hogarth, *Judgment and Choice: The Psychology of Decisions* (New York: Wiley, 1980).

88. Ibid,. p. 102.

89. Ibid., p. 102.

90. R. Nisbett and L. Ross, *Human Inference: Strategies and Shortcomings of Social Judgment* (Englewood Cliffs, N. J.: Prentice-Hall, 1980).

91. H. Einhorn and R. Hogarth, "Behavioral Decision Theory: Process of Judgment and Choice, *Journal of Accounting Research* (Spring 1981): 32-41.

92. M. Ross and F. Sicoly, "Egocentric Biases in Availability and Attribution," in D. Kahneman, P. Slovic, and A. Tversky, eds., *Judgment under Uncertainty: Heuristics and Biases* (New York: Cambridge University Press, 1982), pp. 179-189.

93. Hogarth, *Judgment and Choice: The Psychology of Decisions*, p. 103.

94. Fischhoff, "Debasing."

95. Clifton E. Brown and Ira Solomon, "Effects of Outcome Information on Evaluation of Managerial Decisions," *Accounting Review* (July 1987): 564-577.

96. Thomas H. Buchman, "An Effect of Hindsight on Predicting Bankruptcy with Accounting Information," *Accounting, Organizations and Society* (August 1983): 267-285.

97. Arkes, Wortmann, Saville, and Harkness, "Hindsight Bias among Physicians Weighing the Likelihood of Diagnoses."

98. Buchman, "An Effect of Hindsight on Predicting Bankruptcy with Accounting Information," p. 274.

99. L. J. Chapman, "Illusory Correlation in Observational Report," *Journal of Verbal Learning and Verbal Behavior* (February 1967): 151.

100. L. J. Chapman and J. P. Chapman, "Genesis of Popular but Erroneous Psychodiagnostic Signs," *Journal of Abnormal Psychology* (June 1967): 193-204.

101. Ibid., p. 196.

102. L. J. Chapman and J. P. Chapman, "Illusory Correlation as an Obstacle to the Use of Valid Psychodiagnostics Signs," *Journal of Abnormal Psychology* (June 1969): 271-280.

103. S. L. Golding and L. G. Rorer, "Illusory Correlations and Subjective Judgment," *Journal of Abnormal Psychology* (June 1978): 249-260.

104. J. Starr and E. S. Katkin, "The Clinician as an Aberrant Actuary: Illusory Correlation and the Incomplete Sentences Blank," *Journal of Abnormal Psychology* (December 1969): 670-675.

105. H. M. Jenkins and W. C. Ward, "Judgment of Contingency between Responses and Outcomes," *Psychological Monographs: General and Applied*, no. 594 (1965); J. Smedsbund, "The Concept of Correlation in Adults," *Scandinavian Journal of Psychology* (Third Quarter, 1963): 165-173; J. Smedsbund, "Note on Learning, Contingency, and Clinical Experience," *Scandinavian Journal of Psychology* (Fourth Quarter, 1966): 265-266; W. C. Ward and H. M. Jenkins, "The Display of Information and the Judgment of Contingency," *Canadian Journal of Psychology* (September 1965): 231-241.

106. Nisbett and Ross, *Human Inference: Strategies and Shortcomings of Social Judgments.*

107. Chapman, "Illusory Correlation in Observational Report"'" Tversky and Kahneman, "Availability: A Heuristic for Judging Frequency and Probability"'" R. Schweder, "Likeness and Likelihood in Everyday Thought: Magical Thinking in Judgments about Personality," *Current Anthropology* (December 1977): 637-658.

108. Chapman and Chapman, "Genesis of Popular but Erroneous Psychodiagnostic Observations"; "Illusory Correlation as an Obstacle to the Use of Valid Psychodiagnostic Signs."

109. Ward and Jenkins, "The Display of Information and the Judgment of Contingency"; H. Arkes and A. Harkness, "Estimates of Contingency between Two Dichotomous Variables," *Journal of Experimental Psychology: General* (March 1983): 117-135; H. Skaklee and M. Mins, "Sources of Error in Judging Event Covariations: Effects of Memory Demands," *Journal of Experimental Psychology: Learning: Memory and Cognition* (May 1982): 208-292.

110. William S. Waller and William L. Felix, Jr., "Auditors' Covariation Judgments," *Accounting Review* (April 1987): 275-292.

111. Ibid., p. 290.

112. J. Rose, W. Beacer, S. Becker and G. Sorter, "Toward an Empirical Measure of Materiality," supplement to *Journal of Accounting Research* (Spring 1970): 138-148.

113. John W. Dickhaut and Ian R. C. Eggleton, " An Examination of the Process Underlying Comparative Judgments of Numerica Stimuli," *Journal of Accounting Research* (Spring 1975): 38-72.

114. Robert P. Magee and John W. Dickhaut, "Effects of Compensation Plans on Heurisitcs in Cost Variance Investigations," *Journal of Accounting Research* (Autumn 1978): 294-314.

115. Robert P. Magee, "A Simulation Analysis of Alternative Cost Variance Investigation Models," *Accounting Review* (July 1976): 529-544.

116. Magee and Dickhaut, "Effects of Compensation Plans on Heuristics in Cost Variance Investigations," p. 307.

APPENDIX TO CHAPTER 4
BEHAVIORAL ISSUES IN CONTROL

INTRODUCTION

Control of individual processes and activities in a given period involves mostly (a) a clinical judgment on whether or not to investigate a variance between actual performance and standard performance and (b) actions that reduce and/or correct the problems created by management's attempts to manipulate or normalize accounting data destined for internal or external decision making.

Studies have not been very conclusive in evaluating the accuracy of clinical judgment as an ex ante skill; the results show the correlation between judgment and some standard criterion to be low. In spite of these results, control continues to be practiced without any challenge to the validity of the clinical judgment it is generally based on. This chapter examines the possible threats to the validity of control judgments.

With regard to the manipulation of data, control may be exercised to limit the consequences of both slack budgeting and income smoothing. This chapter elaborates on the nature and causes of these managerial tricks of influencing data.

BASE RATE ISSUES IN CONTROL

The most important information used in any judgment in general and in a control judgment in particular is the *base rate*, which is the probability of the occurrence of an event. Not only is its determination difficult, but evidence shows that people tend to ignore the base rate and focus on positive hits.

Task Structure of Control

The structure of tasks, proposed initially in the accounting literature by H. Bierman and his associates, considers control situations characterized by a *two-state*, two-action problem with these states:
S_1 in control,
S_2 out of control,

and these possible actions:
A_1 = Investigate the variance,
A_2 = Do not investigate the variance.[1]

The structure of tasks, proposed in the psychological literature by H. J. Einhorn and R. M. Hogarth to consider judgments, actions, and outcome feedback and as a criterion for the evaluation of the accuracy of the judgment, is as follows:

1. Denote by x an evaluative judgment and by x_c, a cutoff point such that if

   $x \leq x_c$, investigate the variance,

   $x \geq x_c$, do not investigate the variance.

2. Consider also the existence of a criterion, y, used to evaluate the accuracy of the judgment x and y_c, a cutoff point, such that if

   $y \geq y_c$, S_1 is assumed,

   $y \leq y_c$, S_2 is assumed.[2]

   Two assumptions are necessary at this stage for an application of the items in accounting. First, x_c and y_c are part of the standards set in the budgeting procedure, and x and y are observed outcomes of the process to be controlled.

   The combination of the structure of tables in performance evaluation is shown in Exhibit Appendix 4.1.1. The interrelations between the judgment x and the criterion y result in four quadrants:

   Quadrant 1 denotes the false negative rate:

   $p(y \geq y_c / x < x_c) = fn$,

   Quadrant II denotes the positive hit rate:

   $p(y \geq y_c / x \geq x_c) = ph$,

   Quadrant III denotes the false positive rate:

   $p(y < y_c / x < x_c) = fp$

   Quadrant IV denotes the negative hit rate:

   $p(y < y_c / x < x_c) = nh$.

   This is obtained by denoting the correct predictions as positive and negative hits and the two types of errors as false positive $(y < y_c / x \geq x_c)$ and false negative $(y > y_c / x < x_c)$.

   Other relevant information includes:

a. The base rate: $p(y \geq y_c) = br$, the unconditional probability of exceeding the criterion

b. The selection ratio: $p(x \geq x_c) = 0$

   This structure of tasks, as depicted in Exhibit Appendix 4.1.1, shows three factors affecting the positive hit rate:

Exhibit Appendix 4.1
Action-Outcome Combination that Result from Using Judgment
Whether or Not to Investigate a Given Variance

y(Performance)		
S_1	**I**	**II**
Unfavorable Variance Resulted from Controllable Causes or Process in Control	False Negative Hits	Positive Hits
y_c		
S_2	**IV**	**III**
Unfavorable Variance Resulted from Noncontrollable Causes or Process out of Control	Negative Hits	False Positive Hits
		x
	x_c	
	Do not Investigate	Investigate (judgement)
	$x < x_c$	$x > x_c$

1. the correlation between x and y as measured by P_{xy};
2. the selection ratio θ, and
3. the base rate, br.

Evidence of the effects of these three factors on the positive hit rate is also provided by H. C. Taylor and T. T. Russell.[3]

This structure of tasks may also be used to determine the number of positive hits and false positives resulting from making predictions in selection tasks in general and performance evaluation in particular. Hence let:

N = Number of total decisions to be made, or the total number of variances to be investigated.

P_{xy} = Correlation between prediction and outcomes.

N_P = Number of positive hits = N x $p(y \geq y_c, x \geq x_c)$.

N_f = Number of false positives = N x $p(y < y_c, x \geq x_c)$.

From these definitions it can be show, after replacing the joint probabilities by conditional probabilities multiplied by their respective marginal probabilities, that

$N_P = N$ x $p(y \geq y_c / x \geq x_c) p(x \geq x_c) = Nph0$,

$N_f = N$ x $p(y < y_c / x \geq x_c) p(x \geq x_c) = Nfp0$,

and since ph=1-fp

N, =Nph0

NI=M(1-ph)0

Einhorn maintained that if N_p/N_f is used by people to evaluate the feedback effect of outcomes, the positive hit rate determines the sig of the feedback. With ph>0.5, $N_P > N_f$. If people evaluate the same feedback by the difference $N_p - N_f$, then $N_p - N_f - N0$ (2ph-1) and $N_p > N_f$ if ph>0.5.[4]

The Determination of the Base Rate

In accounting literature, Bierman and his associates were the first use the normative structure of tasks in performance evaluation and introduced the costs and benefits of an investigation in the investigation decision.[5] Given a particular observation on a given activity, the actual base rate, $P_a(y \geq y_c)$, given that the system is in control, is determined. Assuming the cost of the investigation to be the amount c, the cost of correction to be M, and the present value of the savings obtainable from an investigation when the activity is out of control to be L – M, an investigation is signaled if $P_a(y \geq y_c)$ <1- C/(L-M). This normative accounting control model rests therefore on a proper estimation of the actual base rate, $P_a(y \geq y_c)$. But can the actual base rate be estimated? From the known, nor can it be estimated by past data.

The base rate can be expressed as a function of the positive hit rate, the false negative rate, and the selection ratio. From Exhibit Appendix 4.1.1, it may be stated that

$P(y \geq y_c) = p(y \geq y_c / x \geq x_c)p(x \geq x_c) + p(y \geq y_c / x < x_c)p(x < x_c)$

In other words, the base rate = positive hit rate x selection ration + false negative rate (1-selection ratio). Therefore, the computation of the base rate depends on the availability of (1) of the positive hit rate, (2) the selection ratio, and (3) the false negative rate. It may be argued that both the positive hit rate and the selection ratio may be available, but the false negative rate may not be. For example, in a control context the selection ratio may be estimated from past records. It corresponds to the proportion of variances getting investigated as opposed to not getting investigated. Similarly, the positive hit rate may be easily estimated. It corresponds to the proportion of "successes" of those variances that have been investigated. The problem is that the determination of the false negative rate. It corresponds to those variance that have not been investigated; therefore, it would be difficult to estimate how many of those variances not investigated would have been due to the controllable causes. The base rate may then be difficult to estimate given the difficulty of estimating the false negative rate.

Ignorance of the Base Rate

Both singular and distributional information are usually available to people when they judge the probability of an event. *Singular information*, or *case data*, refers to evidence on the case under consideration. *Distributional information*, or *base-rate data*, refers to the probability of the occurrence of the event in general. For example, the number of defective items in a sample provides singular information about the probability of the system being in control, and the base-rate *frequency* of the process being in control constitutes distributional information. Research has shown that intuitive judgments are generally influenced by singular evidence and a general neglect of base rates. This ignorance of the base rate was confirmed in a number of replications, varying base rates, problem content, information order, and response mode and using simple experimental tasks and complex realistic problems.[6] More recently, however, A. Tversky and D. Kahneman have shown that base-rate information that is given a casual interpretation affects judgment.[7] The evidence in the accounting literature is mired. Swieringa and associates and M. Gibbins, replicating and extending some of Tversky and Kahneman's work, reported that their subjects, students and practicing auditors did systematically react to base rates.[8] However, E. J. Joyce G. C. Biddle, using between-subject design rather than within-subject design, found that the auditor's probability judgments were slightly regressed toward the base rate.[9] The magnitude of the regression was, however, considered low.

Focus on Positive Hits

Various experiments have shown that people fail to show an intuitive appreciation of correlation or contingency when judging the relations between events on the basis of a serial correlation. Most of these studies show that the judgments are not based on a comparison of conditional probabilities.[10] More explicitly, J. Smedslund showed that people with no statistical training have no adequate concept of a correlation and tend to depend exclusively on the frequency of positive confirming cases.[11] Similarly, H. M. Jenkins and W. C. Ward found also a lack of appreciation on the concept of correlation.[12] Their subjects made judgments of control that bore no relationship to the concept of statistical control. They seemed to perceive a contingency only when favorable events occurred. In a second experiment Jenkins and Ward found that the type of information display may affect the perception of a contingency.[13] However, their results, in general, support the earlier findings that statistically naïve subjects lack an abstract concept of contingency that is isomorphic with the statistical concept and tend to rely on rules involving the frequency of positive favorable events.

Thus, using the terminology of Exhibit Appendix 4.1, these findings imply that people judge the strength of relationships by the frequency of positive hits and disregard the other three informations, namely, the negative hit rate, the false positive hit rate, and the false negative hit rate.[14]

HEURISTIC AND BIAS IN CONTROL JUDGMENTS
Representativeness

Representativeness refers to the heuristic used by people when they judge the probability of an event by its degree of similarity (representativeness) to the category of which it is perceived to be an example. "A person who follows this heuristic evaluates the probability of an uncertain event, or a sample, by the degree to which it is: (i) similar in essential properties to its parent population; and (ii) reflects the salient feature of the process by which it is generated." It is a mental process or strategy of stereotyping by degree of similarity, for example, imagining that someone is an accountant because he exhibits characteristics typical of an accountant. Consequently, people often fail to give enough credence to the possibility of "surprising" or "unusual events." Representativeness may lead to several systematic biases in probability estimation, including (1) insensitivity to prior probabilities, (2) disregard for the impact of sample size on the variance of the sampling distribution, misperception of the likelihood of different sequences resulting from a random process, and (4) insensitivity to the predictability of data, which results in unwarranted confidence in judgment and misconception of regression toward the mean (for example, that extreme values predictor variables are likely to produce less extreme outcomes).[15]

Availability

Availability refers to the heuristic used by people when they assess the probability of an event by the case with which it comes to mind. "A person is said to employ the availability heuristic whenever he estimates frequency or probability by the case with which instances or associations can be brought to mind."[16] It is a mental process, a strategy related to the case of recollecting specific examples or instances from memory that affects judgments of frequency. As an example, the frequency of well-publicized events like death from terrorism is overestimated, but the frequency of less well-publicized events like death from hunger in America is underestimated. Instances of frequent events are recalled more easily than instances of less frequent events. The availability heuristic depends on familiarity, salience, recency of occurrence, imaginability, or the effectiveness of a search net.

Adjustment and Anchoring

Adjustment and *anchoring* refer to the heuristic used by people when they make estimates by starting from an initial value (anchoring) and then adjusting the values to yield the final answer.[17] For example, this heuristic may lead cost analysts to make a cost forecast by taking last year's costs and adding, say, 10 percent. Last year's cost is taken as an anchor and adjustments are made according to changes in conditions foreseen by the cost analyst. Adjustment and anchoring imply that availability is necessary. Robin Hogarth stated:

That is, predictions are made by reference to cases that are available [and] adjustments made concerning the particular case to be predicted relative to the cases. Furthermore, availability and adjustment and anchoring are heuristics that both depend heavily upon the initial point in the judgment process: the information that is available and which forms the anchor.[18]

Adjustment and anchoring are more standard procedures in managerial accounting decisions and especially in budget behavior and performance evaluation.[19]

Hindsight Bias

Hindsight bias means that the knowledge that an event has happened increases its perceived prior probability of occurrence, and the knowledge that an event has not occurred decreases its perceived prior probability of occurrence.[20] In retrospect, people are not "surprised" about a past event. They can easily explain it. A good example is the "Monday morning quarterback phenomena." In addition, people do not realize the impact of outcome knowledge on probability assessment. B. Fischhoff noted that "making sense out of what one is told about the past seems so natural and effortless a response that one may be unaware that outcome knowledge has had any effect at all on him."[21] What may result from the hindsight bias is the observed overconfidence in probability assessments. The presence of hindsight bias raises the following important issues.

1. The judgment of the apparent failures or successes of others may be colored by the hindsight bias.
2. Hindsight bias implies distortion in memory.
3. Overcoming the bias is important to force people to realize the real significance of events.
4. Learning from experience is not evident.[22]

Calibration of Judgments

A probability expresses a degree of belief that an individual associates with a statement whose truth has not been ascertained. When the truth or the falsity of the statement can be verified, the adequacy of probability may be assessed. One way of assessing the adequacy of the probability is to look at the calibration of the confidence statements that reflect the amount of knowledge of the topic area contained in the probability assessments. A judge is considered well calibrated if in the long run, for all propositions assigned a given probability, the proportion that is true is equal to the probability assigned. In general, the calibration of individuals is evaluated by determining their probability assessments, verifying the related statements, and then determining the proportion that is true overall. Individuals who are not calibrated will be underconfident or overconfident. A survey of the growing literature on calibration has been provided by S. Lichtenstein, B. Fischhoff, and L. D. Phillips.[23] The main evidence from the existing research is that people tend to be overconfident. The effect was found to be robust. The calibration of probability is independent of several examined factors, namely, subjects' intelligence, subjects' expertise in the subject matter of 0.50 and 1.00. It was, however, found to depend on item difficulty. Subjects tend to be overconfident with hard items and underconfident with easy items.

Ignoring and Disconfirming Information

It is an accepted normative view of scientific inference that disconfirmation and testing of alternative hypotheses have major roles. More particularly, K. R. Popper's philosophy of science is based on the concept of disconfirmation or refutation.[24] He maintained that hypotheses can be disconfirmed only by evidence and can never be confirmed. J. R. Platt also argued that successive generations of alternative hypotheses should be disconfirmed- a strategy he labeled "strong inference."[25] The findings in psychological research, however, show that people have difficulty using "disconfirming information." C. R. Mynatt and associates, M. E. Doherty and associates, and P. C. Wason provided evidence of the tendency for people to look only for confirmatory evidence.[26]

Effect on Judgment Fallibility on Control

Control involves a clinical judgment about whether to investigate a given variance. The evidence reviewed shows a general fallibility of judgments. Why should one worry about the fallibility of judgments in control? D. Von Winterfield and W. Edwards argued that, in most real-world decision problems, material errors have a minor impact on the expected gain.[27] A suboptimal choice does not seriously hurt the decision maker as long as the alternative selected is not grossly away from the opimum.[28] However, there are situations in which the fallibility of judgment in performance evaluation might make a difference. For example, cost accountants must decide the probability that the process is out of control and should be corrected versus having the process in control and not being corrected. Let us also assume that the utilities to the person investigated are such that the correction of the variance is better if the probability of the process out of control is ≥ 0.35, as shown in Exhibit Appendix 4.2. If cost accountants estimate the probability, or in their judgment they should have estimated it, to be 0.30, they would advise for the correction of the variance and create a loss of utility applied to the person investigated. D. G. Fryback has shown similar real-life utility functions.[29]

THE "PELZ EFFECT" AND CONTROL

Exhibit Appendix 4.2
Loss of Utility due in Fallability Judgment in a Performance Evaluation Sample

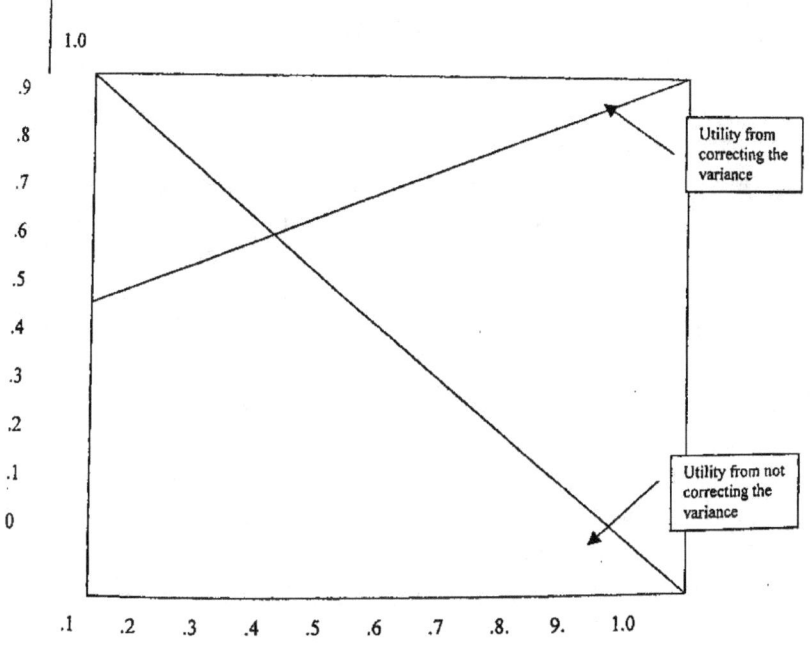

Researchers of superior-subordinate communication have studied the effects of a superior's upward influence in the organizational hierarchy on his or her relationship with subordinates. The best-known result of this line of research is the so-called Pelz effect. In his seminal study, D. Pelz reported the existence of a positive association between a supervisor's upward hierarchical influence and a subordinate's satisfaction with the performance of the supervisor, provided the superior also exhibited "supportive" leadership style in interactions with the employee.[30] As Pelz noted, "If the supervisor has *little* power or influence, then neither his helpful behavior nor his restraining behavior will have much concrete effect on employees."[31] L. W. Wager also explored the effects of supervisors' hierarchical influence and of leadership style on the fulfillment of their supervisory role obligations toward others lower in the organization.[32] He found results similar to Pelz's. He also observed that a supportive style of leadership was a more powerful variable than hierarchical influence in contributing to the fulfillment of supervisory-role obligations and that the magnitude of the moderating effect of influence varies markedly with organizational status of the respondent. As Wager noted, *"The more organizationally marginal the status occupied by subordinates, the greater will be the pervasiveness of the effect of a supervisor's influence on his style of leadership as it bears on fulfillment of his supervisory role."*[33]

CONCLUSIONS

This chapter examined both the judgment fallibility in control and the attempts by managers to manipulate accounting data. Both phenomena need to be controlled to secure a "healthy" behavioral atmosphere within the organization. With regard to the manipulation of data, control may need to at least correct some of the consequences of slack budgeting and income smoothing. With regard to the fallibility of judgment, negative behavioral effects may have resulted in the implementation of control in corporations. To alleviate the situation, controllers may have to exhibit appropriate caution concerning their judgment ability in performance evaluation, especially in view of the evidence of the use of heuristics and bias in judgment.

NOTES

1. H. Bierman, Jr., L. E. Fourakeer, and R. K. jJaedicke, "A Use of Probability and Statistics in Performance Evaluation," *The Accounting Review* (July 1961): 409-17.

2. H. J. Einhorn and R. M. Hogarth, "Confidence in Judgment: Persistence of the Illusion of Validity," *Psychological Review* 85 (1978): 395-416.

3. H. C. Taylor and T. T. Russell, "The Relationship of Validity Coefficients to the Practical Effectiveness of Tests in Selection: Discussion and Tables," *Journal of Applied Psychology* 23 (1939): 565-78.

4. H. J. Einhorn, "Learning from Experience and Suboptimal Rules in Decision Making," in *Cognitive Processes in Choice and Decision Behavior*, ed. T. Wallsten (Hillsdale, NJ: Erlbaum, 1980).

5. Bierman, Fourakeer, and Jaedicke, "Use of Probability and Statistics in Performance Evaluation," 409-17.

6. I. Ajzen, "Intuitive Theories of Events and the Effects of Base-Rate Information on Prediction," *Journal of Personality and Social Psychology* 101 (197): 377-83; M. Hammerton, "A Case of Radical Probability Estimation," *Journal of Experimental Psychology* 101 (1973): 252-54; D. Kahneman and A. Tversky, "On the Psychology of Prediction ," *Psychological Review* 80 (1973), 237-251; D. Lyon and P. Slovic, "Dominance of Accuracy Information and Neglect of Base Rates in Probability Estimation," *Acta Psychologica* 9 (1976): 287-98; R. E. Nisbett and E. Borida, "Attribution and the Psychology of Prediction," *Journal of Personality and Social Psychology* 11 (1975): 932-43; R. E. Nisbett, E. Borgida, E. Crandall, and H. Reed, "Popular Induction: Information Is Not Necessarily Informative," in *Cognition and Social Behavior*, ed. J. S. Carroll and T. W. Payne (Hillsdale, NJ: Erlbaum, 1976).

7. A. Tversky and D. Kahneman, "Causal Schemata in Judgments under Uncertainty," in *Progress in Social Psychology*, ed. M. Fishbein (Hillsdale, NJ: Erlbaum, 1977).

8. R. Swieringa, M. Gibbons, L. Larson, and J L. Sweeny, "Experiments in the Heuristics of Human Information Processing," *Studies on Human Information Processing in Accounting*, Supplement to the *Journal of Accounting Research* 91976): 207-32; M. Gibbins, "Human Inference, Heuristics, and Auditor's Judgment Processes," *CICA Audit Research Symposium* (Toronto: Canadian Institute of Chartered Accountants, 1977).

9. E.J. Joyve and G. C. Biddle, "Are Auditors' Judgments Sufficiently Regressive?" (Manuscript, University of Chicago, October 1979).

10. J. Smedslund, "The Concept of Correlation in Adults," *Scandinavian Journal of Psychology* 4 (1963): 165-73; E.D. Neimark and E.H. Shuford, "Comparison of Predictions and Estimates in a Probability Learning Situation," *Journal of Experimental Psychology* 57 (1959): 254-58.

11. Smedlund, "Concept of Correlation in Adults," 165-73.

12. H. M. Jenkins and W. C. Ward, "The Judgment of Contingency between Responses and Outcomes," *Psychological Monographs* 79 (1965): 16-25.

13. Ibid.

14. D. Kahneman and A. Tversky, "Subjective Probability: A Judgment of Representativeness," *Cognitive Psychology* (July 3, 1972): 430-54.

15. Robert Libby, *Accounting and Human Information Processing: Theory and Applications* (Englewood Cliffs, NJ: Prentice-Hall, 1981), 58.

16. A. Tversky and D. Kahneman, "Availability: A Heuristic for Judging Frequency and Probability," *Cognitive Psychology* (September 1973): 207-32.

17. A. Tversky and D. Kahneman, "Judgment under Uncertainty: Heuristics and Biases," *Science* (September 1974): 1124-31.

18. Robin Hogarth, *Judgment and Choice* (New York: Wiley, 1980), 47.

19. Ahmed Belkaoui, "Judgment-Related Issues in Performance Evaluation," *Journal of Business Finance and Accounting* (Winter 1982): 489-500.

20. B. Fischhoff, "Perceived Informativeness of Facts," *Journal of Experimental Psychology: Human Perception and Performance* (May 1977): 349-58; B. Fisschoff and R. Beyth, "I Knew It Would Happen'- Remembered Probabilities of Once-Future Things," *Organizational Behavior and Human Performance* (February 1975): 1-16.

21. B. Fischhoff, "Hindsight/Foresight: The Effect of Outcome Knowledge on Judgment under Uncertainty," *Journal of Experimental Psychology: Human Perception and Performance* (May 1975): 288-99.

22. Hogarth, *Judgment Choice*, 103.

23. S. Lichenstein, B. Fischhoff, and L.D. Philips, "Calibration of Probabilities: The State of the Art," in *Decision Making and Change in Human Affairs*, ed. H. Jungeman and G. de Zeew (Amsterdam: Reidel, 1977), 325-30.

24. K. R. Popper, *The Logic of Scientific Discovery* (London: Hutchinson, 1959); idem, *Conjectures and Refutations* (New York: Basic Books, 1962).

25. J. R. Platt, "Strong Influence," *Science* 146 (1964): 347-53.

26. C. R. Mynatt, M. E. Doherty, and R. D. Tweeny, "Confirmation Bias in a Simulated Research Environment: An Experimental Study of Scientific Influence," *Quarterly Journal of Experimental Psychology* 29 (1977): 85-95; M. E. Doherty, C. R. Mynatt, R. D. Tweeny, and M. Schiavo, "Pseudodiagnosticity," *Acta Psychologica*, in press; P. C. Wason, "On the Failure to Eliminate Hypotheses in a Conceptual Task," *Quarterly Journal of Experimental Psychology* 12 (1960): 15-25; idem, "Reasoning about a Rule," *Quarterly Journal of Experimental Psychology* 20 (1968): 273-81.

27. D. Von Winterfield and W. Edwards, *Flat Maxima in Linear Optimization Models, in Progress in Social Psychology,* ed. M. Fishhein (Hillsdale, NJ: Erlbaum, 1977).

28. Ibid., 213.

29. D. G. Fryback, *Use of Radiologists' Subjective Probability Estimates in a Medical Decision-Making Problem,* Michigan Mathematical Psychology Program, Report 74-14 (Ann Arbor: University of Michigan, 1974).

30. D. Pelz, "Influence; A Key to Effective Leadership in the First Line Supervision," *Personnel* 29 (1952): 209-71.

31. Ibid. 213.

32. L. W. Wager, "Leadership Style, Influence, and Supervisory Obligations," *Administrative Science Quarterly* 9 (1965): 391-420.

33. Ibid., 418.

CHAPTER 5
COGNITIVE SCIENCE RESEARCH IN A BUSINESS CONTEXT

The lens model of behavior relying on either linear statistical procedures or Bayesian decision theory focuses on what decisions are made rather than how they are made. The understanding of how decisions are made is in the realm of cognitive science, a field composed of elements of cognitive psychology, computer science, philosophy, education, and artificial intelligence.[1] Cognitive science entails four levels of decision-making behavior that build on one another:[2]

1. Identify cues and determine their relative importance through statistical analysis.
2. Identify cues, the sequence in which the cues are utilized, and determine the relative importance of the frequency of their use or process modification accounted for by the cue.
3. Specify general evaluative processes employed and interrelationships between cues.
4. Specify how knowledge representations are modified in order to increase capability.

These levels result from the theoretical work associated with Newell and Simon as set forth in *Human Problem Solving*, including ideas about long-term memory, short-term memory, task environment, knowledge representation, and problem space.[3]

Basically, while long-term memory is assumed to have unlimited storage capacity, relatively high write-time, high retrieval time, and long retention time, short-term memory is assumed to have very limited storage, relatively rapid write-time, short retrieval time, and short retention time. Knowledge is written from short-term memory into long-term memory over time. The decision maker finds himself or herself facing an external factor, the task, and an internal factor, knowledge representation, consisting of the knowledge brought by the decision maker to the problem-solving situation. A problem space containing the needed knowledge is used for the problem solving.

All these concepts, long-term memory, short-term memory, task environment, knowledge representation, and problem space, are assumed in both cognitive science and accounting research to investigate the "what" and "how" of decision making in accounting. Two streams of research have emanated from the application of cognitive science in accounting: one using process tracing to investigate the decision-making process in an accounting or auditing context and one investigating the significance of knowledge structures or schematic structures in accounting and auditing.

PREDECISIONAL BEHAVIOR

In Chapters 1 and 2 we elaborated on the linear models of decision making which treat the decision process as a "black box" and focus on the cues (inputs) and judgments (outputs) and the linear relationship between them. In general, the type of decision task used in studies has the following four common characteristics: "(1) the task was well defined, that is, the subject knew what he/she had to do; (2) the subject was given information of some sort; (3) the information given was perfectly reliable; (4) the range of hypotheses that were considered about the data was considerably restricted by having a particular dependent variable."[4] But in reality people in general as well as accountants face a different type of situation where "(1) the task is ill-defined; (2) information must be searched for- it is not given; (3) data are rarely perfectly reliable; (4) hypothesis formation, as well as hypothesis confirmation/ disconfirmation, occurs within a broad range of possibilities."[5]

The reality of this situation called for an examination of all the stages of predecisional behavior: stages concerned with problem definition, hypothesis formation, and information search. This new type of research was further spurred by the various limitations that have been attributed to the linear model:

- Its application is restricted to highly structured decision setting.
- The standardized regression coefficient is a measure of cue importance only if no correlation exists among the cues, all the relevant cues are incorporated in the model, and the omitted cues are uncorrelated with the cues included.
- Various cues weighting systems seem to adequately replicate the subject's judgment.[6] The issue is still whether the cue coefficients can be psychologically interpreted as measures of cue importance or as a statistical artifact.[7]
- The approach is viewed as having a "black box" orientation that yields minimal insight into the judgment process.[8]

- Its success rests on those structured situations where the relationships between the information cues and the judgment are conditionally monotone; whereby a higher value as a given cue yields a more favorable judgment regardless of the values of the other cues.[9]
- The related concepts- attention and memory- are ignored by the paramorphic linear models.[10]
- The use of regression analysis or variance analysis does not explain the judgment process. As Simon states, "the variance analysis paradigm, designed to test whether particular stimulus variables do or do not have an effect upon response variables, is largely useless for discovering and testing process models to explain what goes on between the appearance of stimulus and performance of response."[11]

Basically, the linear model fails to capture the selective and sequential aspects of cognition.

PROCESS TRACING RESEARCH IN ACCOUNTING

Unlike the lens-based research, the predecisional behavior research was concerned with the cognitive processes used by people solving complex problems given their limited information processing abilities. Insight into how human decision makers solve problems (predecisional behavior) is the focus. It stemmed from Newell and Simon's research viewing problem solving activity as a journey through the problem space- a series of interconnected knowledge states.[12] The problem space is an internal structure- the cognitive representation of the task- consisting of all the relevant information for solving the problem and of the process for transforming and storing information. It is these transformation processes, labeled as operators, that are used to derive new knowledge from old knowledge.[13] To capture the processes used by the decision maker in deriving solutions to a problem, process tracing approaches are used. Three process tracing methods have been used in predecisional behavior research. More specifically, process tracing methods analyze a subject's judgment by reference to verbal protocols,[14] information display boards,[15] and/or eye movements.[16]

Under the verbal protocols procedure, the subject is asked to verbalize or "think aloud" while processing some task. Under the eye movements approach, the subject's eye movements are monitored during the solution process. Under the information display boards approach the subject is asked to search for information on a cardboard sheet with small envelopes arranged in a row and column format.

The verbal protocol procedure is the most frequently used process tracing method. Various approaches have been used. The approach used by Bowman[17] after the procedure outlined by Waterman and Newell[18] included the following representations: (1) the audio tape representation containing the tapes themselves, (2) the lexical representation containing the transcripts, (3) the topic representation containing the topic segments as the units of analysis, (4) the element representation where meanings are extracted from the protocols, (5) the group representation, where combinations of operator elements and input and output knowledge elements are formed, (6) problem behavior graph (PBG), where operator groups form modes and act as a dynamic representation of the processor, and (7) the trace value is the PBG of the model.

What the above procedures imply is that the researcher should collect the reports, make a complete transcript of the verbal reports, break up the protocols with short phrases which will clarify the sequential nature of the observations and create units of analysis, encode the protocols with formal categories, and develop a PBG type of coded summary of decision protocols. Basically, the focus of the approach is in the identification of the elements of each subject's "problem space," which is a model of the individual's cognitive representation of a task. The major uses of protocol analysis are suggested by Payne and Braunstein:[19]

- For exploratory research as the source of data during the early phases of an investigation of decision behavior.
- For supplementing other data as a way of confirming and extending the interpretations of data collected by other methods.
- For testing hypotheses about decision behavior.
- For building and testing computer models of decision behavior.

However, the ultimate purpose of the process tracing approach is the development of a detailed model of a subject's

cognitive rules by deriving such rules from the verbal protocols and expressing them in a computer algorithm. Such a computer model is assumed to have the following features:
(a)   it apparently captures the ongoing problem-solving, since it is based on the person's own report; (b) since the verbal report is usually made on representative stimuli, the natural environment or problem space of the person is preserved; (c) the computer model is a sequential step-by-step set of rules, and since we generally seem to process information sequentially, the model has greater face validity than the regression approach; and (d) the computer model seems configural in that the patterns of information are conditional on one another. This fits our preconceived ideas about how we make analysis judgments.[20]

Financial Analysis

Some studies attempted to model expert financial analysts. Clarkson was the first to use a process tracing approach to construct a model of a bank trust officer's portfolio selection process.[21] Protocols and prior evidence were used to devise and test a computer program. The predictive ability of the models were good and superior to random and naïve single-variable models.

Biggs attempted to determine if the information processing of subjects was consistent with the information processing assumptions of four theoretical models of individual choice behavior.[22] These are (1) additive compensatory,[23] (2) additive difference,[24] (3) conjunctive,[25] and (4) elimination by aspects.[26]

The additive compensatory model implies that the subject will make a judgment as an event by evaluating each of its relevant dimensions and summing the weights to yield a rating.

The additive difference model implies that the subject evaluates one alternative at a time on the basis of its relevant dimensions. If the value of one of the dimensions does not meet a given criterion, the alternative is then eliminated. Another alternative is then evaluated in the same manner. The process of elimination will continue until one alternative is chosen because all of its dimensions exceed their respective criterion levels.

The elimination-by-aspects model is a probabilistic model with noncompensatory and elimination features. It was described as follows:

Suppose that each alternative consists of a set of aspects [or dimensions], and that at every stage of the process, an aspect is selected (from those included in the available alternatives) with probability that is proportional to its weight. The selection of an aspect eliminates all the alternatives that do not involve the selected aspect, and the process continues until a single alternative remains. If a selected aspect is included in all the available alternatives, no alternative is eliminated and a new aspect is selected. Consequently, aspects that are common to all the alternatives under consideration do no affect choice probability.[27]

Biggs asked 11 experienced financial analysts to think aloud while selecting the company with the highest earnings power from a group of five companies. The first step of the verbal protocol analysis examined the protocols in terms of three types of operators: information gathering operators, task structuring operators, and choice process operators. These operators were then used as a basis for inferring the use of the four decision models: additive differences, conjunctive, and elimination by aspects. The results showed that at least one financial analyst relied on all four decision models. All the models led to the same results. In addition, the compensatory model took more time than any other model while the elimination-by-aspects model took less time than any other model. A postexperimental questionnaire used to validate the results was successful in 10 out of 11 subjects.

Biggs' study is very similar to Payne's use of two process tracing techniques, explicit information search and verbal protocols, to examine the information processing strategies subjects used in reaching a decision, given two variations in the complexity of a decision task: number of alternatives and number of decisions.[28] The results showed that when faced with two alternative situations, the subjects relied on search strategies consistent with a compensatory decision process. They searched the same amount of information on each alternative. When faced with a multialternative decision task, the subjects relied on decision strategies designed to eliminate some of the available alternatives as quickly as possible and on the basis of a limited amount of information search and evaluation.

A third study using verbal protocol analysis in financial analysis, by Bowman, examines the differences between expert and novice behavior.[29] Both groups of experts and novices were asked to verbalize during their financial analysis. The protocols were transformed into problem behavior graphs presenting knowledge states as nodes and operators as arrows between nodes. The results showed that while the experts and the novices used similar decision-making processes, the relative frequencies of specific processes were very different. More specifically:

Novices, are characterized by passive, inductive strategy of "collecting data and seeing what happens." Experts, on the other hand, frequently follow up on specific observations. Moreover, experts regularly summarize the results, and formulate hypotheses. Such "reasoning" phases further direct the decision making process. The result is that experts use a much more varied mix of decision making processes. The sequencing of the experts' decision making processes is also much more complex and totally lacks the repetitive character of that of the novices.[30]

In addition, the experts and the novices differed in the three phases of the financial analysis task, namely the examination of information, integration of observations and findings, are reasoning. It is in the reasoning phase that the differences are the most significant.

For novices, reasoning appears to mean deciding *when* to select *what* observed fact as the main "problem." For experts, on the other hand, it is an attempt to develop a "*picture* of what is going on." Experts employ a number of tools in this phase that are rarely used by the novices: (1) Experts *summarize* groups of related findings, thereby eliminating the need to keep track of the individual findings, (2) experts *formulate hypotheses*, and (3) experts use a *list of typical problems*. This list facilitates the analysis in a number of ways; it transfers apart of "reasoning" to "recognition" which is psychologically a much less demanding, and much faster process. It also expresses the analysis process into more generally used and therefore more accessible terms and finally it generates additional leads to further confirmation and evaluation.[31]

The fourth study using protocol analysis in financial analysis is by Stephens.[32] He asked 10 bankers to verbalize during the evaluation of two commercial lending cases. The lending officers spent a lot of time computing and analyzing ratios and trends. They did not make adjustments for differences in inventory or depreciation method.

The fifth study using protocal analysis in financial analysis, by Campbell, was used to collect and analyze data about the usefulness to bank loan officers of four types of financial statement information for smaller, closely held companies: earnings per share, deferred income taxes, capitalized leases, and inflation adjusted information.[33] An item was considered useful if it was used by the subjects in their decision processes. The results were consistent with Stephens' findings of a three-step general structure for loan officer decision processes: determination of information adequacy, quick review of many items, and extended analysis of several items.[34] In addition, the usefulness of capitalized lease information was evident in the analysis of protocols.

The sixth study using protocol analysis in financial analysis is by Bowman, Fishkoff, and Fishkoff.[35] They examined the decision-making processes of 12 financial analysts in the process of screening prospective investments. Unlike the previous study by Bowman, this study relied on a considerably more complex task and the participation of experts instead of students. As in previous studies, these experts are assumed to possess "task specific knowledge" that allows them to recognize many different situations and that they can draw upon as a source of hypotheses and direction.[36] Upon receipt of a package of information, the analysts were asked to think out loud. Subsequent analysis consisted of coding the protocols, identifying the codes, tabulating the code frequencies, defining the protocol episodes, classifying the goals, and development of a process picture or episode summary.

A descriptive model of the process of financial screening was produced. It showed that experts operate with a hierarchy of goals, from operational to tactical to strategic graph. Their information searching strategies differed along the following two dimensions.

The first dimension characterizes what drives the selection of information. "Directed" search describes the case where the expert wants a specific item of information; in a "sequential" search the next item selected is the next one on the page. The second dimension characterizes the ease with which the search is interrupted or halted, in order to achieve a new objective. Analysts using an "active" strategy quickly change objectives, whereas analysts using a "methodical" strategy insist on completing the current goal before starting a new one.[37]

As a result, experts used four information search strategies: active directed, which is high on both search for specific information and interruptability of analysis; active sequential, which is low on search for specific information and high on interruptability of analysis; methodical directed, which is high on search for specific information and low on interruptability of analysis; and methodical sequential, which is low on both dimensions.

The direction of the search relied on three different vehicles: the checklist, the theme, and the conditional checklist. Finally, the study verified the existence of financial templates, "memory structures that accumulate a major part of an analyst's experience."[38]

Auditing

Process Tracing Research in Internal Control Judgments
The lack of consensus in auditor decisions in the evaluation of internal control and the resulting risk of excessive audit costs was shown in the lens-based experiments.[39] These studies, however, did not try to explain the reasons behind the lack of consensus. To fill the gap, Biggs and Mock used verbal protocol analysis to determine how four experienced auditors made different internal control evaluations and audit scope decisions in a relatively complex and comprehensive experimental task.[40] The focus was on the identification of the elements of each subject's "problem space," that is to say, a model of each individual's cognitive representation of the task as introduced in Newell and Simon's theory of human problem solving.[41] The analysis of the subject's protocols was conducted at two levels of detail, a microlevel and a macrolevel.

The microlevel was used to identify four aspects of each subject's task performance: information used, operators used, evaluation criteria used, and the reasoning underlying the final choices. Four operators were used to describe the subject's processes: task structuring, information acquisition, analytical, and action.

The macrolevel was used to identify each subject's episode abstracts and flowcharts. The results showed the importance of "information search" and "evaluation" in each subject's decision process. The strategies used included a directed strategy by one subject, a systematic strategy by two subjects, and a mixed strategy by one subject. Basically, a systemic strategy consists of a thorough and sequential search of information prior to making decisions. A directed strategy, instead, consists of the selection of an audit step followed by a directed search for an evaluation of information relevant to that audit step alone, before proceeding to another audit step. As a result of the use of different strategies, the information acquisition, information evaluation process, decisions made, heuristic used, and alternatives considered differed among the four subjects. This explains the lack of consensus in auditor judgments found in the lens-based studies.

Process Tracing Research in Analytical Review Analytical review has been found to be essentially a judgmental process[42] that affects other audit procedures. Biggs et al. used a process tracing approach to provide some initial descriptive evidence of how auditors perform judgmental analytical review in a complex and realistic task setting and to identify the role of expertise in the judgment process.[43] A comprehensive case was administered to two managers and two senior auditors who performed the task while thinking aloud. Einhorn and Hogarth's framework of the general categories of operations that compose the decision-making process was used.[44] It views decision processes as composed of four interacting phases: information acquisition, information evaluation, action/choice, and feedback. For the information acquisition phase, the results revealed a number of differences in information acquisition between the seniors and managers. The findings were consistent with Chi et al.'s results that physics experts have internal schemata (problem representation in memory) that allow them to identify, from their memory, the type of problem involved and to use these schemata to solve the problem, while the novices, on the other hand, do not seem to have well-developed internal schemata to help them solve problems.[45]

For the information evaluation stage, the protocols from the conditions showed no evidence of probabilistic reasoning.

Managerial Accounting

Shields proposed a framework within which to describe how the amount of information in a performance reports impacts on a manager's report analysis process.[46] Four hypotheses about managers' search patterns when they analyze performance reports are tested. The performance report complexity or information load is defined by the number of responsibility units and the number of performance parameters. The four search patterns examined are the additive difference, the additive linear, elimination by aspects, and the conjunctive model. This follows from the human information processing findings that when individuals perform complex tasks, they rely on search patterns (or heuristics) that keep the information processing requirements within the adaptive limits of the human processor. In this context of Shields' study, the changes in the performance report complexity are assumed to affect the search patterns used by managers in the evaluation of a performance report. Twelve executive MBA graduates were asked to think aloud while analyzing four performance reports in order to estimate the cause of the observed behavior and predict future behavior. The four cases examined differed in terms of the number of responsibility units an the number of performance reports. The data were presented in an information board which contained envelopes which contained information on each performance cue. The information search was measured by the order of card collection. The results showed that the four theory-based hypotheses concerning the impact of information load on the search patterns used by managers in performance evaluation were not empirically supported. Given that studies in psychology and marketing used similar settings to show congruence between the theory and the data, Shields offers the following explanation:

A more interesting attribution to account for the inconsistency between hypotheses and data concerns the goal of the information processing. In this experiment, the managers focused primarily on making an attribution for the reported performance and, to a much lesser extent, on developing an expectancy of future managerial behavior. In contrast, the goal of the information processing in the marketing and psychology studies has been a choice between alternatives. There may be differences between ex ante choice and ex post explanation that may account for the results of this research compared to the hypotheses based on the other research.[47]

Shields suggests, however, that future descriptive modeling of how performance reports are analyzed consider variables such as the format of a report, the effects of the level of aggregation, and the amount of time allotted or available for the report analysis.

In a second study Shields relied on explicit information search to investigate two issues concerning the demand for information in performance reports: the level of convergence among measures of demand and the level of demand consensus.[48] The measures of demand were exante and ex-post subjective importance, frequency of selection, total frequency of selection, order of selection, and average order of selection. The same performance reports as in the first study were used, with nine responsibility units and 13 performance reports. Again, data were presented to the subjects on information boards which contained one envelope with data cards enclosed for each performance cue. The results indicated that there was a moderate but varying level of convergence among the measures of demand and a low but statistically significant level of demand consensus. Two implications are presented:

Predecisional research could be used to identify the source(s) of the less than complete convergence. The sources could be the subjects' problem solving process, inconsistency in the subject's behavior, the specific measurement methods, measurement error, or that demand is a multidimensional construct. . . .

Future research using predecisional research methods could explore the sources and costs of low demand consensus. . . . Future research should also investigate whether the level of demand consensus affects the level of judgment consensus. Finally, if low consensus continues to be found, future research should also investigate how accountants should select information for general purpose reports.[49]

RETROSPECTIVE PROCESS TRACING APPLIED IN ACCOUNTING

As stated earlier, process tracing methods analyze a subject's judgment using verbal protocols, information display boards, and/or eye movements. There are, however, two general process tracing methods relying on verbal protocols: concurrent process tracing and retrospective process tracing. The studies reviewed in the previous reports are made at the exact time the judgment is made. In studies using retrospective process tracing, the verbal reports are made immediately after the evaluation task is completed. Retrospective process tracing has, however, been criticized because: it may not allow access to the subject's neutral processes;[50] it is possible that the subject provides reports by "abstracting inference, search for prototypic examples, and so on,"[51] or by "altering their normal mode of processing in order to be able to give the requested information to the experimenter."[52] In spite of these "interference process," evidence seems to show that the retrospective tracing approach has some validity as needed information may still be in short-term memory after completion of a task.[53] In fact, the conditions under which retrospective process tracing can be accurate are when "influential stimuli are (a) available and (b) plausible causes of the response, and when (c) few or no plausible but noninfluential factors are available."[54]

Given this assessment of the retrospective tracing approach in the psychology literature, the following calls for a multimethod approach for studying human judgment,[55] Larcker and Lessig compared the linear model and the retrospective tracing approach in an experiment requiring subjects to provide either a buy or no-buy decision for 45 stocks described by six information cues.[56] The results indicated that "(1) each method was generally able to replicate subject judgments, but that the retrospective process tracing exhibited superior predictive validity, (2) measures of cue importance from each method were related, and thus exhibited convergent validity, and (3) the linear models were generally reliable."[57]

KNOWLEDGE STRUCTURES IN ACCOUNTING AND AUDITING

The cognitive revolution in social psychology has created strong interest in the knowledge structure in memory in general and how people learn in particular.[58] A central concept called the "schema" is used to refer to the cognitive structure of organized prior knowledge, abstracted from experience with special instances. It has been eloquently defined as follows:

A schema is conceived as a modifiable information structure that represents generic concepts stored in memory. Schemata represent knowledge that we experience- interrelationships between objects, situations, events, and sequences of events that normally occur. In this sense, schemas are prototypes in memory of frequently experienced situations that individuals use to interpret instances of related knowledge. . . . A schema can be thought of as a theory or internal model that is used and tested as individuals instantiate the situations they face. As is the case for a scientific theory, a schema is compared with observations and if it fails to account for certain aspects of these observations, it can either be accepted temporarily, rejected, modified, or replaced. Like a theory, a schema is a source of prediction and enables individuals to make assumptions about events that generally occur in a particular situation, so that the knowledge they infer goes beyond the observations that are available in any one instance. Such prototypical structures play a central role in thinking and understanding, and the reasoning that occurs takes place in the context of these specific networks of knowledge.[59]

The concept of schema refers to the generality in how people process information across social and nonsocial domains and rests on memory issues. These issues pertain to short-term memory vs. long-term memory, episodic memory vs. semantic memory, and declarative knowledge vs. procedural knowledge.[60] The first issue pertains to the organization and limitations of the human memory system, i.e., a limited capacity, short-term memory and an unconstrained, unlimited capacity, long-term memory. While the short-term memory is a "working memory," the long-term memory is a "test" of stored information for use at an unspecified future time.

The second issue pertains to the differences between an episodic memory, consisting of information about autobiographical experiences associated with particular times and places, and semantic memory, consisting of general knowledge of concepts and meanings.[61] Both memories are interdependent and build on each other to form the schemas or knowledge structure used to integrate stimuli into recognizable patterns.

The third issue pertains to the differences between declarative and procedural knowledge, or between content knowledge and the use of that knowledge, or between "knowing that" and "knowing how." Schemas facilitate both.

Waller and Felix used the concepts to propose a model of how the ordinary person learns from experience.

Its thesis is that learning from experience involves the formation and development of generalized cognitive structures that organize experience-based declarative and procedural knowledge in long-term memory. Declarative knowledge is organized by categories, which depend on similarity or class membership relations, and schemata, which depend on spatial and/or temporal relations. Procedural knowledge is organized into production systems, i. e., hierarchies of condition-action pairs.[62]

What the model implies is that schemas are developed through a gradual process of abstracting a domain-specific knowledge on the basis of experience. The differences between the expert and novice's knowledge structure is therefore the result of differences in experience. What is appearing from the research on novices and experts is that larger chunks of information are taken and stored by experts than novices at any point in time for a particular task,[63] pieces of information are better clustered into meaningful categories within a single chunk by experts,[64] and the recall of experts is based on conceptual representations of information while that of the novices is based on functional relationships.[65] The findings in accounting so far parallel those of psychology. More specifically, Weber found that expert auditors clustered internal control cues according to their control categories significantly more than novices did.[66] Frederick and Libby found that expert auditors clustered financial statement errors by transaction cycles.[67]

CONCLUSION

Future research may have to investigate how the experience-based knowledge structures affect auditor judgments. For example, Libby suggested that by failing to consider the task-specific knowledge and its structure in memory brought to a decision setting by the experienced accountant, a highly incomplete picture of accounting decision making will result.[68] Waller and Felix went one step farther by suggesting two lines of research:
(1) descriptive research which examines how and how well the auditor acquires, represents and/or uses experience-based knowledge and (2) prescriptive research which includes the construction of instructional aids that might improve the processes by which the auditor acquires and stores experimental data and exploits any regularities reflected in these data.[69]

NOTES

1. D. G. Bobrow, "Dimensions of Representations," in D. G. Bobrow and A. Collins, eds., *Representation and Understanding* (New York: Academic Press, 1975).

2. J. F. Diclard, "Cognitive Science and Decision Making Research in Accounting," *Accounting, Organizations, and Society* (June 1984): 343-354.

3. A. Newwell and H. A. Simon, *Human Problem Solving* (Englewood Cliffs, N. J.: Prentice-Hall, 1972).

4. H. Einhorn, "Synthesis: Accounting and Behavioral Science," supplement to *Journal of Accounting Research* (1976): 200.

5. Ibid.

6. R. Dawes and B. Corrigan, "Linear Models in Decision Making," *Psychological Bulletin* (February 1974): 95-106; H. Einhorn and R. Hogarth, "Unit Weighting Schemes for Decision Making," *Organizational Behavior and Human Performance* (Spril 1975): 171-192.

7.   N. Schmidt, and R. Levine, "Statistical and Subjective Weights: Some Problems and Proposals," *Organizational Behavior and Human Performance* (October 1977): 15-30.

8.   J. Hayes, "Strategies in Judgment Research," in B. Kleinmuntz, ed., *Journal Representation of Human Judgment* (New York: Wiley, 1968), pp. 251-259; C. Graesser and N. Anderson, "Cognitive Algebra of the Equation: Gift Size = Generosity x Income," *Journal of Experimental Psychology* (October 1974): 692-699.

9.   Dawes and Corrigan, "Linear Models in Decision Making."

10. J. G. Birnberg and M. D. Shields, "The Role of Attention and Memory in Accounting Decisions," *Accounting, Organizations, and Society* (June 1984): 365-382.

11. H. A. Simon, "Discussion: Cognition and Social Behavior," in J. S. Carroll and J. W. Payne, ed., *Cognition and Social Behavior* (Hillsdale, N. J.: Erlbaum, 1976), pp. 253-267.

12. Newell and Simon, *Human Problem Solving.*

13. M. J. Anderson, "Arguments Concerning Representations for Mental Imagery," *Psychological Review* (March 1978): 249-277.

14. A. Newell and H. A. Simon, "Elements of a Theory of Human Problem Solving," *Psychological Review* (May 1968): 151-166; B. Kleinmuntz, "MMPI Decision Rules for the Identification of College Maladjustment: A Digital Computer Approach," *Psychological Monographs* (1963).

15. J. Payne, "Task Complexity and Contingent Processing in Decision Making: An Information Search and Protocol Analysis," *Organizational Behavior and Human Performance* (August 1978): 17-44.

16. J. Russo and L. Rosen, "An Eye Fixation Analysis of Multialternative Choice," *Memory and Cognition* (May 1975): 265-276.

17. M. J. Bowman, "Computer Simulation of Human Decision Making in Accounting: The Analysis of Financial Statements" (Unpublished dissertation, Carnegie Mellon University, 1978).

18. D. A. Waterman and A. Newell, "Protocol Analysis as a Task for Artificial Intelligence," *Artificial Intelligence* (March 1971): 285-318; "Pas II: Interactive Task-Free Version of an Automatic Protocol Analysis System," *IEEE Transactions on Computers* (February 1976): 402-413.

19. J. W. Payne, M. L. Braunstein, and J. S. Carroll, "Exploring Predecisional Behavior: An Alternative Approach to Decision Research," *Organizational Behavior and Human Performance* (October 1978): 17-44.

20. H. J. Einhorn, D. N. Kleinmuntz, and B. Kleinmuntz, "Linear Regression and Process Tracing Models of Judgments," *Psychological Review* (March 1979): 465-485.

21. G. P. E. Clarkson, *Portfolio Selection: A Simulation of Trust Investment* (Englewood Cliffs, N. J.: Prentice-Hall, 1962).

22. S. F. Biggs, "An Empirical Investigation of the Information Processes Underlying Four Models of Choice Behavior," in T. L. Burns, ed., *Behavioral Experiments in Accounting*, vol. 2 (Columbus: College of Administrative Science, Ohio State University, 1979).

23. A. Tverskey, "Intransitivity of References," *Psychological Review* (March 1969): 31-48.

24. Ibid.

25. C. H. Coombs, *A Theory of Data* (New York: Wiley, 1964).

26. R. M. Dawes, "Social Selection Based on Multidimensional Criteria," *Journal of Abnormal and Social Psychology* 68 (1964): 104-109; A. Tversky, "Elimination by Aspects: A Theory of Choice," *Psychological Review* (July 1972): 281-299.

27. Ibid., pp. 284-285.

28. J. W. Payne, "Task Complexity and Contingent Processing in Decision Making," *Organizational Behavior and Human Performance* (August 1976): 366-387.

29. Ibid., p. 327; M. J. Bowman, "The Use of Accounting Information: Expert versus Novice Behavior," in G. R. Ungson and D. N. Braunstein, eds., *Decision Making: An Interdisciplinary Inquiry* (Boston: Kent Publishing Company, 1982), pp. 134-167.

30. M. J. Bowman, "Expert vs. Novice Decision Making in Accounting: A Summary," *Accounting, Organizations, and Society* (December 1982): 325-327.

31. Ibid., p. 376.

32. R. G. Stephens, "Accounting Disclosures for User Decision Processes," in Y. Ijiri and A. B. Whinston, eds., *Quantitative Planning and Control* (New York: Academic Press, 1979), pp. 291-309.

33. Jane. E. Campbell, "An Application of Protocol Analysis to the 'Little GAAP' Controversy," *Accounting, Organizations, and Society* (June 1984): 329-342.

34. R. G. Stephens, *Uses of Financial Information in Bank Lending Decisions* (Ann Arbor, Mich.: UMI Research Press, 1980).

35. M. J. Bowman, P. A. Fischoff, and P. Fishkoff, "How Do Financial Analysts Make Decisions? A Process Model of the Investment Screening Decision," *Accounting, Organizations, and Society* (January 1987): 1-29.

36. A. D. De Groot, *Thought and Choice in Class* (The Hague: Mouton, 1965); M. T. H. Chi, R. Glaser, and E. Rees, "Expertise in Problem Solving," in R. J. Sternberg, ed., *Advances in the Psychology of Human Intelligence*, vol. 1 (Hillsdale, N.J.: Erlbaum, 1982); E. Hayes-Roth, D. A. Waterman, and D. B. Lenat, eds., *Building Expert Systems* (Reading, Mass.: Addison Wesley, 1983).

37. Bowman, Fishkoff, and Fishkoff, "How Do Financial Analysts Make Decisions? A Process Model," p. 25.

38. Ibid., p. 26.

39. T. J. Mock and J. L. Turner, *Internal Accounting Control Evaluation and Auditor Judgment*, Audit Research Monograph No. 3 (New York: AICPA, 1981).

40. S. F. Biggs and T. J. Mock, "An Investigation of Auditor Decision Processes in the Evaluation of Internal Controls and Audit Controls and Audit Scope Decisions," *Journal of Accounting Research* (Spring 1983): 234-255.

41. Newell and Simon, *Human Problem Solving*.

42. S. F. Biggs and J. J. Wild, "A Note on the Practice of Analytical Review," *Auditing: A Journal of Practice and Theory* (Spring 1984): 68-79; R. H. Tabor and J. T. Willis, "Empirical Evidence on the Changing Role of Analytical Review Procedure," *Auditing: A Journal of Practice and Theory* (Spring 1985); 93-109.

43. S. F. Biggs, T. J. Mock, and P. R. Watkins, "Auditor's Use of Analytical Review in Audit Program Design," *Accounting Review* (January 1988): 148-161.

44. H. Einhorn and R. M. Hogarth, "Behavioral Decision Theory: Processes of Judgment and Choice," *Journal of Accounting Research* (Spring 1981): 245-271.

45. M. T. H. Chi, R. Glaser, and E. Rees, "Expertise in Problem Solving," in R. J. Sternberg, ed., *Advances in the Psychology of Human Intelligence*, vol. 1 (Hillsdale, N. J.: Erlbaum, 1982), pp. 2-25.

46. M. D. Shields, "Some Effects of Information Load on Search Patterns Used to Analyze Performance Reports," *Accounting, Organizations and Society* (December 1980): 429-442.

47. Ibid., p. 438.

48. M. D. Shields, "A Predecisional Approach to the Measurement of the Demand for Information in a Performance Report," *Accounting, Organizations, and Society* (June 1984): 355-363.

49. Ibid., pp. 361-362.

50. R. Nisbett and T. Wilson, "Telling More Than We Can Know: Verbal Reports on Mental Processes," *Psychological Review* (May 1977): 231-259.

51. K. Ericsson and H. Simon, "Retrospective Verbal Reports as Data" (Unpublished manuscript, Carnegie-Mellon University, 1978), p. 13.

52. K. Ericson and H. Simon, "Verbal Reports as Data," *Psychological Review* (May 1980): 215-251.

53. Ibid., p. 226.

54. Nisbett and Wilson, "Telling More Than We Can Know," p. 253.

55. R. Olshavsky and F. Acito, "An Information Processing Probe in to Conjoint Analysis," *Decision Sciences* (June 1980): 451-470.

56. D. F. Larcker and V. Parker Lessig, "An Examination of the Linear and Retrospective Process Tracing Approaches to Judgment Modeling," *Accounting Review* (January 1983): 58-77.

57. Ibid., p. 77.

58. A. B. Zajonc, "Cognition and Social Cognition: A Historical Perspective," in L. Festinger, ed., *Four Decades of Social Psychology* (New York: Oxford University Press, 1980).

59. R. Glaser, "Education and Thinking- The Role of Knowledge," *American Psychology* (February 1984): 93-104.

60. W. S. Waller and W. L. Felix, Jr., "Cognition and the Auditor's Formulation Process: A Schematic Model of Interactions between Memory and Current Audit Evidence," in S. Moriarity and E. Joyce, eds., *Decision Making and Accounting: Current Research* (Norman: University of Oklahoma Press, 1984).

61. J. Bransford, *Human Cognition: Learning, Understanding and Remembering* (Belmont, Calif.: Wadsworth, 1979).

62. W. S. Waller and W. L. Felix, Jr., "The Auditor and Learning from Experience: Some Conjectures," *Accounting, Organizations and Society* (June 1984): 390.

63. W. Chase and H. Simon, "Perception in Class," *Cognitive Psychology* 4 (1973): 55-87; H. L. Chisi, G. J. Splich, and J. F. Voss, "Acquisition of Domain- Related Information in Relation to High and Low Domain Knowledge," *Journal of Verbal Learning and Verbal Behavior* 18 (1979): 257-273.

64. A. R. Halpern and H. G. Boner, "Musical Expertise and Melodic Structure in Memory for Musical Notation," *American Journal of Psychology* 95 (1982): 31-50.

65. B. Schneiderman, "Exploratory Experiments in Programmer Behavior," *International Journal of Computer and Information Science* 5 (1976): 123-143; K. B. McKeithen, J. S. Reitman, H. H. Reuter, and S. C. Hirtle, "Knowledge Organization and Skill Differences in Computer Programmers," *Cognitive Psychology* (March 1981): 307-325; B. Adelson, "Problem Solving

and the Development of Abstract Categories in Programming Languages," *Memory and Cognition* 9 (1981): 422-433; B. Adelson, "When novices Surpass Experts: The Difficulty of a Task May Increase with Expertise," *Journal of Experimental Psychology: Learning, Memory, and Cognition* (October 1984): 483-495.

66. R. Weber, "Some Characteristics of the Free Recall of Computer Controls by EDP Auditors," *Journal of Accounting Research* (Spring 1980): 214-241.

67. D. M. Frederick and R. Libby, "Expertise and Auditors' Judgments of Conjunctive Events," *Journal of Accounting Research* (Autumn 1986): 270-290.

68. R. Libby, "Determinants of Performance in Accounting Decisions" (Paper presented at the Accounting Research Convention in Alabama, January 1984 revision).

69. Waller and Felix, Jr., "The Auditor and Learning From Experience," p. 400.

CHAPTER 6
FUNCTIONAL AND DATA FIXATION

Functional fixation, as it is used in accounting, suggests that under certain circumstances a decision maker might be unable to adjust his or her decision process to a change in the accounting process that supplied him or her with input data. Borrowed from the literature of psychology, the phenomenon has been used in a slightly different way by accounting researchers. The purposes of this chapter are, first, to differentiate between the functional-fixation phenomenon as it is understood in psychology and the data-fixation phenomenon as it is used in accounting; second, to examine the results of the various experimental studies in the area; and third, to provide possible theoretical explanations of the phenomenon and to suggest better methodologies for studying the phenomenon in accounting.

NATURE OF FUNCTIONAL FIXATION
Functional Fixation in Psychology

Functional fixation originated as a concept in psychology, arising from an investigation of the impact of past experience on human behavior. In his examination of the relation between stimulus equivalence and reasoning, Maier identified several ways in which past experience can affect the problem-solving process.[1] He viewed past experience as a salient factor in problem solving, in that problem solving can be facilitated by equivalences that exist in immediate problem situations and in past experiences. In addition, the background of past learning is an essential repertoire of behavior that is available for restructuring when it is needed for new situations. Not all psychologists, however, have viewed past experience as a positive factor. Some have been it as an obstacle that prevents protective thinking. Duncker introduced the concept of functional fixation to illustrate the negative role of past experiences.[2] He investigated the hypothesis that an individual's prior use of an object in a function dissimilar to that required in a present problem would serve to inhibit the discovery of an appropriate, novel use for the object. His results supported the functional-fixation hypothesis with regard to several common objects, for example, boxes, pliers, weights, and paper clips. Birch and Rabinowitz criticized Duncker's experiments, showing that an individual can also learn about an object's versatility and therefore display a relatively low degree of fixation even if learning about one function of an object restricts the number of ways in which it is used.[3] A series of experiments by Flavell, Cooper, and Loisell supported this conclusion.[4]

Others who have refined Duncker's experiments nevertheless have supported that functional-fixation hypothesis. Adamson, in his box experiment, gave subjects of the task of attaching three small candles to a screen, at a height of about five feet, using to accomplish the task any of a large number of objects that were lying on the table, namely three pasteboard boxes, five matches, and five thumb-tacks.[5] The solution consisted of putting one candle on each box by melting wax on the box, sticking the candle to the box, and then taking the boxes to the screen. The idea was to have the box to be used as a platform on which to attach the candle, a novel function for boxes. Two groups were used. The experimental one was presented with the objects inside the box, the control group had the objects on the table. "Hence, the boxes had their initial function, that of containing, whereas in their solution function, they had to be used as supports or platforms."[6] The results showed that the control group outperformed the experimental group in terms of both the number of solutions and the time required to reach the solutions. This suggested that the subjects in the experimental group were functionally fixated on using boxes as containers rather than as platforms.

In the two-string experiments, Adamson and Taylor asked their subjects to tie together the free ends of strings hanging from the ceiling.[7] Because the strings were placed so far apart, the problem could be solved only by tying a weight to one string, swinging it like a pendulum, and catching it while holding the other string. The task then could be completed by tying the two strings together. Of the various objects provided to the subjects, only two- an electrical switch and an electrical relay- were sufficiently heavy to serve as weights. Half of the subjects were trained before the experiment to use the switch to complete an electrical circuit, while the other half were trained to use a relay for the same task. The results of the experiment supported the functional-fixation hypothesis for the reason that the subjects trained to use the switch to complete the circuit used the relay to solve the two-string task, while those who had been trained to use the relay to complete the circuit used the switch as a pendulum weight. This fixation phenomenon was reported in a series of other experiments.[8] The degree of fixity also was found to depend on some mediating factors, such as the span of time since the object was previously used,[9] the necessity of using the object in a novel way to solve the problem,[10] hints,[11] and intelligence.[12]

Data Fixation in Accounting

Ijiri, Jaedicke, and Knight viewed the decision process as being characterized by three factors: decision inputs, and decision rules. They then introduced the conditions under which a decision maker cannot adjust his or her decision process to a change in the accounting process. For example, changes in depreciation methods or inventory techniques lead to different profit figures. Ijiri, Jaedicke, and Knight attributed the inability to adjust, if it existed, to the psychological factor of functional fixation.[13] They stated:

Psychologists have found that there appears to be functional fixation in most human behavior in which the person attaches a meaning to a title or object (e.g., manufacturing cost) and is unable to see alternative meanings or uses. People intuitively associate a value with an item through past experience, and often do not recognize that the value of the item depends, in fact, upon the particular moment in time and may be significantly different from what it was in the past. Therefore, when a person is placed in a new situation, he views the object or term as used previously.[14]

To link the psychological concept of functional fixation to accounting, they merely stated the following:

If the outputs from different accounting methods are called by the same name, such as profit, costs, etc., people who do not understand accounting well tend to neglect the fact that alternative methods may have been used to prepare the outputs. In such cases, a change in the accounting process clearly influences the decisions.[15]

This extrapolation of a psychological concept to accounting is welcome if it is interpreted correctly. The literature now recognizes the point that the focus in psychology is on *functions*, whereas Ijiri, Jaedicke, and Knight focuses on *outputs*. If we go back to the example of a change in inventory techniques, functional fixation in psychology implies that the decision makers are accustomed to using the data for one function (such as price decisions) and now fail to see its potential use for another function (such as price decisions) and now fail to see its potential use for another function (for example, price decisions) and now fail to see its potential use for another function (for example, production decisions). As introduced by Ijiri, Jaedicke, and Knight, functional fixation implies that decision makers are fixated on the accounting output (for example, the profit output) and are unable to adjust to see that the change in output is due to the change in inventory techniques. Thus, while psychologists are interested in functional fixation involving functions or objects, accounting research, influenced by Ijiri, Jaedicke, and Knight's extrapolation, is interested in functional fixation involving data. One might assume correctly that most of the interest in psychology has been on functional fixation. The exceptions to this assumption are a psychological data-fixation study by Knight and a mixed data-fixation/functional-fixation study in accounting by Barnes and Webb.[16] Ashton also has recognized the difference between the two views of functional fixation in accounting and psychology.[17] He came to a peculiar conclusion, however, when he stated:

We should recognize that the functional fixation hypothesis in accounting is modified form (or forms) of the hypothesis in psychology. The modified functional hypothesis should be subjected to research in accounting contexts, rather than relying entirely on the original functional fixation research as Ijiri, Jaedicke, Knight, and subsequent researchers appear to have done.[18]

The approach should consider two forms of the functional-fixation hypothesis, one focusing on function and one focusing on output or data. There lies the main difference: in the case of functional fixation, psychologists used objects such as medallions, string, and boxes to solve relatively simple tasks, whereas the data-fixation experiments all used data to solve unstructured problems.

DATA-FIXATION RESEARCH IN ACCOUNTING
Data-Fixation Research Based on the Ijiri-Jaedicke-Knight Paradigm

Functional-fixation research in accounting generally has followed Ijiri, Jaedicke, and Knight's prescriptions, focusing on data rather than function, and has led to a series of data-fixation experiments. Ashton used M. B. A. students to assess the extent to which individual decision makers alter their decision processes after the occurrence of an accounting change, from full-cost to variable-cost data, as evidenced by the effect of this cognitive change on subsequent decisions.[19] Ashton not only discussed the accounting change with the subjects but also mentioned whether it reflected more or less important informational content, and consequently may have dictated a change in the decision behavior of the subjects. This result suggests that a large proportion of subjects in the experimental groups failed to adjust significantly their decision process in response to the accounting change, thereby providing evidence of the existence of functional fixation in accounting. The study was not met with complete approval. First, Libby criticized it for an experimental design that might have become confounded with the effects of the accounting change.[20] He concluded that

serious questions concerning the way in which the conceptual network was operationalized, coupled with methodology deficiencies, question whether any conclusions can be drawn from the results. The major problems relate to the presentation of the accounting change to the subjects, the manipulation of the moderating variables information and importance, and the method of measuring the change in the subject's decision process.[21]

Second, Pearson, a practitioner, simply rejected the study's objectives and results as irrelevant to accounting.[22] These criticisms, as might be expected, motivated further empirical research.

Swieringa, Dyckman, and Hoskin looked into Libby's criticisms and found that subjects tended to adjust their information processing as a result of the accounting change even though the significance of these adjustments differed depending on how they were measured.[23] The amount of information provided was found to influence the subject's adjustments of their information processing. Swieringa, Dyckman, and Hoskin had made two modifications in Ashton's experimental design. One modification was to isolate the effects of the amount and form of the information about the accounting change. The second modification was to have the data received by the control groups be equivalent to the data received by the experimental groups.

A second study by Dyckman, Hoskin, and Swieringa merely replicated the earlier study by Swieringa, Dyckman, and Hoskin with subjects who, on average, were older and had more exposure to accounting and business matters.[24] The students used in the first study were enrolled in an introductory accounting course in a college of agriculture and life science and did not know what direct costing meant. In addition, the second study relied on a cross-sectional approach instead of a time-series approach to analyze the effects of the experimental conditions and demographic variables on the prices set by the subjects for each product. The results of the second study were found to be similar to those of the first one.

In their experiment, Chang and Birnberg provided M.B.A. students with a cost-variance report and a cost standard.[25] The subjects were required to indicate (1) whether they would investigate the production process, and (2) how large a variance would be necessary to justify an investigation. Their results pointed to the existence of a "weak form" of data fixity when a change in the variance amount was introduced. The "weak form" label was used to characterize a slight change in behavior; no change in behavior was evidence of the "strong form" of fixity. Two significant findings were noted by the authors:

First, fixity is not a phenomenon that is unavoidable. Research indicates that once we are aware of its presence, we can take steps to cope with it. The real question becomes one of finding the manner in which it can be reduced and efficient ways of doing so. Second, unfortunately, once alerted to the problem, there is reason to believe that the subject's behavior will continue to reflect elements of past behavior- behavior which should have been forgotten along with the superseded data set. This then suggests two topics for future research. One is how past experience affects the subject's behavior. The other is how to extinguish the older, now unnecessary patterns of behavior.[26]

Abdel-Khalik and Keller used bank investment officers and security analysts in their investigation of functional fixation.[27] They articulated their research problems as follows:

If investors are functionally fixated on the use of reported accounting earnings, then they will tend to ignore other accounting information which is not consistent with accounting numbers. The accounting signal which we chose to be inconsistent with reported earnings is the decision of management to switch the method of inventory valuation from First-in, First-out (FIFO) or from average cost to Last-in, First-out (LIFO) for both accounting and tax purposes.[28]

Because of the higher cash flows that result from change to LIFO in a period of rising prices, the investor using a cash-flow discounted model would value the firm higher, while another relying and fixated on earnings would value it lower. The results of the experiment showed evidence of functional fixation, as the subjects relied on the adjusted net income rather than cash flows in evaluating the securities. One problem with Abdel-Khalik and Keller's study is the fact that the firms that switched to LIFO received qualified audit opinions, while those on FIFO obtained unqualified opinions. This could explain why the LIFO firms generally were viewed as having lower expected returns.

Bloom, Elgers, and Murray extended the Ashton study by examining both individual and group decisions in response to a fully disclosed, cosmetic change in depreciation method.[29] The results of the study showed a moderate shift in the decision behavior of individuals, a phenomenon similar to what Change and Birnberg called the weak form of fixation. In addition, they found that groups exhibited a higher degree of fixation than did individuals. Amon the reasons given for this difference were the following: "One explanation is that the group process inhibited the collective or individual intellectual functioning of its members; yet another is that the groups incurred a higher cost in developing a new decision rule in response to the accounting change than did the individuals."[30] Another explanation was that the difference could be a reflection of the nature of the task, which consisted of the need both to reach a decision within the group on a decision rule and to make a decision on the task.[31]

Another accounting study provided evidence of functional fixation without being based on Ashton's and Ijiri, Jaedicke, and Knight's paradigms. A National Association of Accountants (NAA) research study on the effects of software accounting policies on bank lending decisions and stock prices showed clear evidence of fixation by loan officers making a decision on a loan to two fictional firms: the Campbell Corporation, which capitalized software expenditures; and the Edwards Corporation, which expensed all software costs.[32] Without mentioning data fixation per se, the results are indicative of the presence of the phenomenon. Witness the following:

Campbell was favored over Edwards by 62.2% of the respondents; Edwards was favored by 11.1%; 13.3% would treat the companies equally, but did not given any reason for the equal treatment; and 13.3% would treat the companies equally because a company's software policy would not influence the lending decision. Only 27.3% of the bankers would grant a $3 million, five year unsecured loan to Edwards; compare with 61.4% for Campbell. Of those respondents that gave an interest rate for both companies, 55% would charge Campbell a lower rate, 5% would charge Edwards a lower rate, and 40% would charge the same rate to both companies.[33]

A similar finding was made in another study. Belkaoui conducted an experiment in which bank loan officers evaluated a loan application that was accompanied by financial statements based on either accrual or modified cash accounting.[34] The loan officers in the experiment believed that the loan applicant presenting accrual accounting financial statements (1) was more likely to repay the loan, (2) was more likely to be granted the loan, (3) was given a different interest rate premium, and (4) had statements that were more reliable and freer of clerical errors.

Other Data-Fixation Research

Other accounting research studies have used the Ijiri-Jaedicke-Knight paradigm to explain their own results. This strategy has taken place both in the research of investor decisions and in capital market research.

In the research of investor decisions, a cross-sectional orientation was given to functional fixation as it was applied to alternative accounting methods rather than to changes in accounting methods over time. Jensen examined the impact of alternative depreciation and inventory costing methods on investor decisions.[35] To explain his findings that alternative accounting techniques affected decision making, he suggested that his subjects might be functionally fixated on net earnings. Livingstone examined the effects of alternative, interperiod tax-allocation methods on regulatory rate-of-return decisions affecting the electric utility industry.[36] In light of his findings that some rate-making books focus on "raw" rates of return and ignore the effects of alternative tax-allocation methods, he offered the explanation that some predictions might be functionally fixated on net operating revenue. Livingstone stated the following:

It is therefore hypothesized that the reason that original cost jurisdictions have been so much slower to adjust for alternative treatments of deferred taxes is that they are functionally fixated with respect to financial statement data. Since normalizing changes the amount but not the name of net operating revenue, it is intended that original-cost jurisdictions tend to view net operating revenue under normalizing as being the same as without it.[37]

He also suggested that users of accounting information could have formed a *learning set* after having experience with a significant number of different problems, all of which can be solved in the same manner. One solution went as follows: "If the hypothesis of a learning set with respect to alternative accounting methods is valid, multi-informational accounting statements would tend to stimulate learning and reduce functional fixation by providing users with information on accounting alternatives."[38] Mlynarczyk examined the effect of alternative tax-accounting methods on common-stock prices of electric utility companies and related functional fixation to his work.[39]

In capital market research, the functional-fixation hypothesis has been used to explain the lack of efficiency in the capital market. Beaver argued, however, that the market is not functionally fixated.[40] He stated the following:

In essence, the implication of the functional fixation hypothesis is that two firms (securities) could be alike in all "real" economic respects and yet sell for different prices, simply because of the way the accountant reported the results of operations. The implication is that the market ignores the fact that observed signals are generated from different information systems. Hence, it does not distinguish between numbers generated by different accounting methods either over time or across firms. Needless to say, this implies market inefficiency . . . The functional fixation hypothesis as described above is a rather extreme form of the market inefficiency argument, in that it implies that disequilibrium could exist indefinitely and presumably permanently.[41]

DATA FIXATION AND FUNCTIONAL FIXATION IN ACCOUNTING AND PSYCHOLOGY

As stated earlier, most accounting research has focused on data fixation, while psychological research has focused on functional fixation. The exceptions to his are a data-fixation study in psychology by Knight and a mixed data-fixation/functional-fixation study in accounting by Barnes and Webb.[42]

Knight conducted an experiment to investigate the impact of the successful solving of n water jug problems on the problem-solving techniques used in trial n+1. The results showed that a series of successes caused the subject to persist in his early behavior, making it difficult for him to see the alternative (correct) approach. Furthermore, the subject would give complex, correct solutions to even trivial problems in cases where the complex solutions had led to successful results in the previous n trials.

Barnes and Webb were interested in the investigation of both the data-fixation and the functional-fixation hypothesis in accounting. Actual managers were asked to make price decisions based on real-life case studies that differed in their method of inventory valuation (full-costing versus direct-costing). The data-fixation hypothesis was confirmed in that the subjects were fixated by the total costs figure, altering their project price in response to the changes in reported costs caused by the measurement change. However, the functional-fixation hypothesis was not confirmed because the subjects did not try to recover overhead costs, even though they were instructed that this was unnecessary, simply because they were not used to doing so. The lack of evidence for the functional-fixity hypothesis, a phenomenon widely observed in psychology, was attributed to the use of highly experienced and intelligent scientists. This is not surprising since intelligence has been found to mitigate fixity.[43]

DETERMINANTS OF FUNCTIONAL FIXATION IN ACCOUNTING
The Conditioning Hypothesis

The impact of accounting data on users and their behavior has always been a subject of interest for social scientists. On extreme concern, expressed by Schumpeter, goes as follows:

Capitalist practice turns the unit of money into a tool or rational cost-profit calculations, of which the towering monument is double-entry bookkeeping. . . . Primarily a product of the evolution of economic rationality, the cost-profit calculus in turn reacts upon that rationality; by crystallizing and defining numerically, it powerfully propels the logic of enterprise. . . .This type of logic or attitude or method then starts upon its conqueror's career subjugating- rationalizing- man's tool and philosophies, his medical practice, his picture of the cosmos, his outlook on life, everything in fact, including his concepts of beauty and justice and his spiritual ambitions.[44]

Accounting researchers have not reached the point of Schumpeter's consensus, but they also have stressed the notion that the socialization of accountants, with its emphasis on particular cost and income considerations, can lead to a form of conditioning and might explain some of the empirically observed decision processes. The argument is that users, individually or in aggregate, react because they have been conditioned to react to accounting data rather than because the data have any informational content. For example, Sterling contends that

if the response of receivers to accounting stimuli is to be taken as evidence that certain kinds of accounting practices are justified, then we must not overlook the possibility that those responses were conditioned. Accounting reports have been issued for a long time, and their issuance has been accompanied by a rather impressive ceremony performed by the managers and accountants who issue them. The receivers are likely to have gained the impression that they ought to react and have noted that others react, and thereby have become conditioned to react.[45]

It may also be argued that the recipients of accounting information react when they should not react or should not react the way they do. The conditioning hypothesis has also been advanced by Revsine as follows:

The process by which users may be conditioned to the data they could occur in at least two ways. First, as students in business training curricula, the prospective users are introduced to generally accepted accounting principles and the financial statements that result from the applications of these principles and their derivative procedures. Furthermore, they are taught manipulative operations and techniques such as ratio and funds flow analysis that utilize accounting data as a means for evaluating enterprise performance and prospects. In short, users are generally indoctrinated concerning the relevance and utility of traditionally disseminated information. Second, this formal conditioning is continually reinforced by each external report that users receive.[46]

One explanation of the data-fixation findings may be that the subjects of the experiments, mostly accounting students, have been conditioned to react to some form of accounting outputs (for instance, cost or income outputs), and have failed to adjust their decision processes in response to a "well-disclosed" accounting change. The conditioning phenomenon inhibits the subjects from adopting the correct behavior, which is to adjust to the accounting change, and has led them to act as they have been conditioned to act in their previous behaviors or socialization sessions. Thus, the conditioning phenomenon is a form of functional fixation, as the subjects no longer are able to discriminate.

Prospect Theory and the Framing Hypothesis

Kahneman and Tversky's prospect theory states the potential gains and losses are evaluated by an S-shaped value function, one that is convex (indicating a risk-averse orientation) for losses.[47] Four effects are observable in the process of choosing among bets:

1. *Certainty effect:* "People overweigh outcomes that are considered certain relative to outcomes which are merely probable."[48]

2. *Reflection effect:* "The selection of prospects around 0 reverses the preference order."[49]
3. *Aversion to probabilistic insurance:* Subjects do not like the idea of probabilistic insurance because it pays off with a probability of less-than-one but diminishes the premium.
4. *Isolation effect:* "In order to simplify the choice between alternatives, people often disregard components that distinguish them."[50]

The concept of framing options adds the key idea that the frame of the decision is simply the decision maker's concept of the decision problem or its structure. The *frame* is defined as follows: "The decision-maker's conception of the acts, outcomes and contingencies associated with a particular choice. The frame that a decision-maker adopts is controlled partly by the formulation of the problem and partly by the norms, habits and personal characteristics of the decision-maker."[51]

Framing occurs because the working of a question has the potential to alter a subject's response. Functional fixation may be viewed as a result of the particular choice of framing options made by the subjects in the experiments. The formulation of the decision tasks as well as the norms, habits, and personal characteristics of the subjects affect the framing of the decision and lead to the functional- or data- fixation results.

Inference Theory: Stimulus Encoding versus Retroactive Intuition

The *learning theory* holds that prior knowledge can either interfere with or facilitate effective decision making. The *interference theory* emerged from the two possible outcomes of the *transfer-of-training hypothesis*. According to the latter hypothesis, the transfer of training may have either facilitating or inhibitory effects. When a subject learns two tasks, task 1 and task 2, then is asked to perform task 1, the effects of the transfer of training are as follows: "Transfer may facilitate the learning of the second task, or conceivably have an inhibitory effect and interfere with the second learning and the mastery of the second task may help or hinder the subsequent performance of the first task."[52] What results, then, are two possible effects:

1. A negative transfer is labeled *retroactive inhibition or retroactive interference*.[53] In such a case the learning of task 2 affects the performance of the first task. The design used for the study of *retroactive interference* is as follows:[54]

   Experimental group: Learn Task 1   Learn Task 2   Test Task 1

   _____

   Control Group: Learn Task 1   Test Task 1

   Functional fixity has been viewed as "a classic case of negative transfer."[55]

2. A positive or facilitator effect is labeled *retroactive facilitation*. This positive transfer motivates the *stimulus-encoding hypothesis*, whereby a distinction is made between the nominal stimulus provided by the experiments and the functional stimulus perceived by the subject. No functional fixity would result from the stimulus-encoding process.

Haka, Friedman, and Jones used the above interference theory to test the hypothesis that exposure to cost and income measures causes fixated responses in a decision-making setting where market value is the appropriate response.[56] If subjects are presented with two stimulus-response pairs for market price (A-B) and one for cost or income (C-D), with separate stimulus and responses for each, and if C is confused with A, resulting in an A-B, C-B paradigm, then response B become the fixated response because of the retroactive interference. In other words:

The hypothesis posited that prevalence of cost and profit information interferes with (that is, causes fixation) or facilitates appropriate market-based decision models. In particular, if stimulus encoding is dominant, then subjects with more cost and profit exposure should be more likely to use the market price data than those with less exposure. If retroactive inhibition dominates, then the opposite effect should be discerned.[57]

The results of the study did not support the proposition that exposure to accounting concepts in accounting courses interferes with decision processes. In addition, only some moderate support was found for the theory that stimulus encoding causes some retroactive facilitation.

Primacy versus Recency and Ego Involvement

The findings on data fixation in accounting for the most part have been obtained by having students placed in a stressful situation make a given choice (for example, a price decision) before and after an accounting change. The students know the nature of the accounting change (such as from full costing to variable costing) from their courses and the learning process preceding the experiment. A relevant research question would be the impact of this learning order on the acceptance of accounting techniques and on the results observed in data-fixation research. The impact should be more obvious is the students are placed under stress. This is related to a general hypothesis in psychology which specifies that under stress an organism will respond with the behavior appropriate to the situation that was learned first.[58] Consequently, Belkaoui tested the specific hypothesis that if a student learns two alternative responses to an accounting problem or stimulus and is placed under stress unrelated to the behavior being observed, he or she will respond to the stimulus with the first-learned method.[59]

The results supported the hypothesis. Few implications of importance to the data-fixation hypothesis were made:

1. The appraisal of the usefulness of accounting technique cannot be ascertained when subjects are exposed to a stressful situation.

2. Given that stressful situations are likely to be present in both classroom and professional situation, there will be a predisposition to the use of the first learned accounting method.

3. Finally, the theoretical justifications pertaining to the choice of the appropriate accounting procedure by the firms can be reinforced by the learning order and the learning techniques to which the accountants have been exposed in their schools.[60]

The communication literature had addressed extensively the problem of the effects of order of presentation.[61] Known as the primacy-recency question, it is expressed by the following question: When both sides of a problem are presented successively, does the first-presented side (primacy) or the last-presented side (recency) have the advantage?

Different studies have supported the principle of primacy,[62] while other studies have created a controversy by reporting primacy effects under some conditions[63] and recency effects under others.[64] Consequently, Hovland, Jarvis, and Kelly recommended conducting research on the factors leading to the inconsistent effects of primacy and recency in the various experiments.[65] Examples of these factors include reinforcement, strength, involvement, and commitment. Ego involvement is also believed to be a variable that affects primacy and recency. Morteson noted:

Despite an absence of research, there is reason to believe that ego involvement may work against either primacy or recency, and often in a brutal way. Stated as a hypothesis, we may say that the more highly involved one is on a belief-discrepant topic, the less is the chance for either a primacy or recency effect.[66]

Belkaoui investigated the impact on the primacy and recency effects of ego involvement or commitment to one's stand on an accounting topic.[67] He reasoned that under conditions of ego involvement, the forces for reinforcement were likely to be particularly active and the impact of primacy or recency to be particularly passive. Subjects coming in contact with a stressful situation, in the form of resolving an accounting problem, would revert to the technique or the side of the message that was more clear or basic to them. The results of his experiments, which used accounting students, showed that the students under stress responded with the "accounting behavior" that was more clear or basic to them. In other words, in matters of ego involvement with an accounting technique just learned, subjects will give importance to what is perceived as relevant, significant, or meaningful. This could explain some of the data-fixation findings where the subjects have reverted to either the use of the first-learned method (primacy) or the second-learned method (recency), or to the method more clear or basic to their ego involvement.

PROBLEMS IN DATA-FIXATION RESEARCH

Several problems exist in the present state of data-fixation research.

1. Most studies have not distinguished between data fixation, with its focus on output, and functional fixation, with its focus on function. Research is needed on both concepts, as they provide insight into and represent different aspects of the behavior of decision makers.

2. Extrapolations made by accounting researchers could contain serious flaws if the simple fact of ignorance is confused with the psychological phenomenon of functional fixation, especially since most of the subjects used have been students rather than actual decision makers. This was Pearson's main criticism of Ashton's study; Pearson claimed that the inability of the subjects to adjust their decision process was entirely due to ignorance.[68] This fact was explicitly recognized by Barnes and Webb when they stated: "It is our view that functional fixity and ignorance are separate phenomenon and that in order to identify the former empirically, the absence of the latter needs to be insured."[69]

3. Fundamental evidence points to the fact that intelligence mitigates fixity. The point has been recognized both in the psychological [70] and the accounting experiments.[71] Again, Barnes and Webb have stated:

It would appear that those who were not fixated were less concerned with financial matters than their colleagues, as they were more concerned with providing an intellectual stimulus for their staff. Two groups appear therefore: those who can see around "trivial" financial matters and are concerned with "high matters" and those who are not. The implication again is that intelligence mitigates fixity.[72]

4. There are two methodologies in the functional-fixation research: *(a) The "one-object" approach*, where subjects are given an experimental task to perform and a novel or new way can be used in the solution. Fixity occurs when only a small number of solutions emerge from the group of subjects, for whom the usual function of an object is accentuated. *(b) The "two-objects" approach*, where subjects are given two objects and a control group is given the use of one of the objects. Functional fixation results from the tendency of the subjects to use that object in the critical problem whose function has not been accentuated. All the accounting studies have used the "one-object" approach, and therein lies a problem, which has been expressed by Flavell, Cooper, and Loisell:

While functional fixedness in the first case is a matter of solution vs. non-solution . . ., it is, in the second case a matter of choice of objects or means for the solution of a comparatively simple problem. It is to be expected that the last method is the one that gives the purest measure of functional fixedness. In the first method a difficult problem is used and the non-solution of this problem may very well be attributed to other factors than functional fixation.[73]

Thus, there is a need for evidence from accounting research that uses the "two-object" approach.

5. Most accounting research on data fixation has been concerned with whether fixity exists rather than why it exists. While the exception of the study by Haka, Friedman, and Jones, none of the accounting experiments has offered explanations about why fixity exists or has provided ways to remove it. In contrast, the psychological literature began to focus on its causes immediately after discovering the phenomenon. Removing fixation became the objective as experiments investigated factors such as time and the number of "other functions" shown for the fixated objects such as time and the number of "other functions" shown for the fixated objects that affect the degree of fixity.[74] Later studies focused on the various ways of providing hints and cues to overcome fixation.[75] Needless to say, accounting research should now deal with the question of why fixity exists and how it can be mitigated. Wilner and Birnberg have stated the following to that effect:

Despite the popularity among accounting researchers of the question of whether decision makers are fixated, the critical question would appear to be why at least a portion of decision makers exhibit fixation. Given that we know from various non-accounting studies that certain factors do inhibit creative problem analysis and solving, the role of accounting research should be to ascertain which of these inhibiting factors operate in the domain of accounting and to ascertain how we can reduce their detrimental effect.[76]

6. Wilner and Birnberg have pointed to the following problems in the design of existing studies on fixation:

1. The studies used an input-output methodology and the divergence between the inputs and the expected outputs were attributed to functional fixation while in fact there may be other reasons why a subject fails to alter his information processing after an accounting change.

2. While random assignment of subjects to tasks is used to lessen the effects of individual differences, it still remains that it cannot

overcome the systematic characteristics which prevent all subjects from understanding the task.

3. Most of the subjects used in these experiments are not sophisticated enough for the risks which suggests that they were not fixated but rather naïve or ignorant.

4. Unlike the psychological experiments which provided feedback to subjects, the accounting experiments not only did not provide any feedback, but used experimental tasks that were judgmental rather than optimal (right or wrong), which suggests that the subjects in the accounting experiments never knew if their behavior was appropriate.

5. Some knowledgeable subjects may have resisted changing their decision (model) following the accounting change for reasons other than fixation if a) he/she viewed the change as irrelevant, b) if he/she viewed changing his decision process as not worthwhile in that it leads to a different action than that already performed, c) if he/she viewed the benefits of "better decisions" as not outweighing the costs of learning how to process the change, d) if he/she thought it beneficial for him to act in a fixated manner because of his double role as an information sender as well as an information user, and e) if possibly he/she formed a set which he/she cannot overcome.[77]

ALTERNATIVE METHODOLOGY FOR DATA-FIXATION RESEARCH

Most of the empirical studies in data-fixation research have been based on laboratory or field experiments, with the exception of one single case based on a survey. In addition, with few exceptions, these experiments have used students as subjects, thereby raising problems of external validity. The tasks have not been realistic or motivating and have required judgmental rather than optimal behavior. What stands out upon review of the accountancy and psychological literature on the phenomenon is the urgent need for a better methodology, one that will allow direct observation of the process by which a decision is made. An appropriate methodology would be some form of protocol analysis, in which the subjects are asked to think aloud while solving the requirements of an experimental task. Such an approach would answer some very important questions:

1. Did the subject note the change?

2. Did the subject give any indication of appreciating its relevance?
3. Was the change understood?
4. Was the change ignored on grounds of its materiality, etc.?[78]

Better insights on the phenomenon of functional fixation may be possible through the use of protocol analysis, as the experiments use richer tasks, smaller pools of subjects, and better debriefing.

CONCLUSION

Functional fixation as observed in psychology, functional fixation, and data fixation as observed in accounting need to be explained. Future research should provide theoretical as well as empirical explanations of the reasons why subjects in accounting experiments persist in failing to adjust their decision process in response to accounting changes. In addition, richer and more realistic experimental tasks, sophisticated subjects, as well as protocol analysis ought to be used to provide better explanations of the phenomenon if it exists.

NOTES

1. N. R. F. Maier, "Reasoning in Humans: The Mechanisms of Equivalent Stimuli and Reasoning," *Journal of Experimental Psychology* (April 1945): 349-360.

2. K. Dunker, "On Problem Solving," *Psychological Monographs* 58, no. 5 (1945).

3. H. G. Birch and H. S. Rabinowitz, "The Negative Effect of Previous Experience on Productive Thinking," *Journal of Experimental Psychology* (February 1951): 121-125.

4. J. H. Flavell, A. Cooper, and R. H. Loisell, "Effect of the Number of Preutilization Functions on Functional Fixedness in Problem Solving," *Psychological Reports* (June 1958): 343-350.

5. R. E. Adamson, "Functional Fixedness as Related to Problem Solving: A Repetition of Three Experiments," *Journal of Experimental Psychology* (October 1952): 288-291.

6. Ibid., p. 288.

7. R. E. Adamson and D. W. Taylor, "Functional Fixedness as Related to Elapsed Time and to Set," *Journal of Experimental Psychology* (February 1954): 122-126.

8. S. Glucksberg and J. H. Danks, "Functional Fixedness: Stimulus Equivalence Mediated by Semantic-Acoustic Similarity," *Journal of Experimental Psychology* (July 1967): 400-405; J. Jensen, "On Functional Fixedness: Some Critical Remarks," *Scandinavian Journal of Psychology* (Winter 1960): 157-162.

9. Adamson and Taylor, "Functional Fixedness."

10. Duncker, "On Problem Solving."

11. P. Staugstad and K. Raaheim, "Problem Solving, Past Experience and Availability of Functions," *British Journal of Psychology* (May 1960): 97-104.

12. A. S. Luchins and E. H. Luchins, "New Experimental Attempts at Presenting Mechanization in Problem Solving," in P. C. Watson and P. N. Johnson Laird, eds., *Thinking and Reasoning: Selected Readings* (Hammondsworth, Eng.: Penguin, 1968), pp. 42-44.

13. Y. Ijiri, R. K. Jaedicke, and K. E. Knight, "The Effects of Accounting Alternatives on Management Decisions," in R. K. Jaedicke, Y. Ijiri, and O. Nielson, ed., *Research in Accounting Measurement* (Sarasota, Fla.: American Accounting Association, 1966), pp. 186-199.

14. Ibid., p. 194.

15. Ibid., p. 194.

16. K. E. Knight, "Effect of Effort on Behavioral Rigidy in Luchins' Water Jar Task," *Journal of Abnormal and Social Psychology* (1960): 192-194; Paul Barnes and John Webb, "Management Information Changes and Functional Fixation: Some Experimental Evidence from the Public Sector," *Accounting, Organizations, and Society* (February 1986): 1-18.

17. R. H. Ashton, "Cognitive Changes Induced by Accounting Changes: Experimental Evidence on the Functional Fixation Hypothesis," supplement to *Journal of Accounting Research* (1976): 1-7.

18. Ibid., p. 5.

19. Ibid., pp. 1-7.

20. Robert Libby, "Discussion of Cognitive Changes Induced by Accounting Changes: Experimental Evidence on the Functional Fixation Hypothesis," supplement to *Journal of Accounting Research* (1976): 18-24.

21. Ibid., p. 23.

22. David B. Pearson, "Discussion of Cognitive Changes Induced by Accounting Changes: Experimental Evidence on the Functional Fixation Hypothesis," supplement to *Journal of Accounting Research* (1976): 25-28.

23. R. J. Swieringa, T. R. Dyckman, and R. E. Hoskin, "Empirical Evidence about the Effects of an Accounting Change on Information Processing," in T. J. Burns, ed., *Behavioral Experiments in Accounting II* (Columbus: Ohio State University Press, 1979), pp. 225-259.

24. T. R. Dyckman, R. E. Hoskin, and R. J. Swieringa, "An Accounting Change and Information Processing Changes," *Accounting, Organizations, and Society* (February 1982): 1-11.

25. D. L. Chang and J. G. Birnberg, "Functional Fixity in Accounting Research: Perspective and New Data," *Journal of Accounting Research* (Autumn 1977): 300-312.

26. Ibid., p. 311.

27. R. A. Abdel-Khalik and T. F. Feller, "Earnings or Cash Flows: An Experiment on Functional Fixation and the Valuation of the Firm." *Studies in Accounting Research* 16 (Sarasota, Fla: American Accounting Association, 1979).

28. Ibid., p. 17.

29. Robert Bloom, Pieter T. Elgers, and Dennis Murray, "Functional Fixation in Product Pricing: A Comparison of Individuals and Groups," *Accounting, Organizations and Society* 9, no. 1 (1984): 1-11.

30. Ibid., p. 8.

31. Neil Wilner and Jacob Birnberg, "Methodological Problems in Functional Fixation Research: Criticism and Suggestions," *Accounting, Organizations and Society* (February 1986): 74.

32. Robert W. McGee, "Software Accounting, Bank Lending Decisions, and Stock Prices," *Management Accounting* (July 1984): 20-23.

33. Ibid., p. 20.

34. Ahmed Belkaoui, "Accrual Accounting, Modified Cash Basis of Accounting and the Loan Decision: An Experiment in Functional Fixation" (Unpublished manuscript, University of Illinois at Chicago, 1988).

35. Robert E. Jensen, "An Experimental Design for the Study of Effects of Accounting Variations in Decision Making," *Journal of Accounting Research* (Autumn 1966): 224-238.

36. J. L. Livingstone, "A Behavioral Study of Tax Allocation in Electric Utility Regulation," *Accounting Review* (July 1967): 544-552.

37. Ibid., pp. 520-551.

38. Ibid., p. 552.

39. F. A Mlynarczyk, Jr., "An Empirical Study of Accounting Methods and Stock Prices," supplement to *Journal of Accounting Research* (1969): 63-81.

40. W. H. Beaver, "The Behavior of Security Prices and Its Implications for Accounting Research Methods," supplement to *Accounting Review* (1972): 407-437.

41. Ibid., pp. 420-421.

42. K. E. Knight, "Effects of Effort on Behavioral Rigigity"; Barnes and Webb, "Management Information Changes and Functional Fixation."

43. Luchins and Luchins, "New Experimental Attempts."

44. J. A. Schumpeter, *Capitalism, Socialism and Democracy*, 3rd ed. (New York: Harper and Row, 1950), pp. 123-124.

45. Robert R. Sterling, "On Theory Construction and Verification," *Accounting Review* (July 1970): 433.

46. L. Revsine, *"Replacement Cost Accounting* (Englewood Cliffs, N.J.: Prentice-Hall, 1973), pp. 50-51.

47. D. Kahneman and A. Tversky, "Prospect Theory: An Analysis of Decision under Risk," *Econometrika* (March 1979): 263-291.

48. Ibid., p. 265.

49. Ibid., p. 268.

50. Ibid., p. 271.

51. R. S. Woodworth and H. Schosberg, *Experimental Psychology* (New York: Henry Holt and Co., 1954), p. 733.

52. Ibid.

53. G. E. Muller and F. Schumann, "Experimentelle Beitrage Zur Untersuchung des Gedachtnisses," *Zeitschrift fur Psychologie* (1894): 81-190, 257-339.

54. A. C. Catania, *Learning* (Englewood Cliffs, N. J.: Prentice-Hall, 1979).

55. J. Kagan and E. Havemann, *Psychology: An Introduction*, 3rd ed. (New York: Harcourt Brace Jovanovich, 1976), p. 149.

56. Susan Haka, Lauren Friedman, and Virginia Jones, "Functional Fixation and Interference Theory: A Theoretical and Empirical Investigation," *Accounting Review* (July 1986): 455-474.

57. Ibid., p. 460.

58. R. P. Barthol and Nari D. Ku, "Specific Regression under a Nonrelated Stress Situation," *American Psychologist* (February 1963): 482.

59. Ahmed Belkaoui, "Learning Order and the Acceptance of Accounting Techniques," *Accounting Review* (October 1975): 897-899.

60. Ibid., pp. 898-899.

61. C. Hovland, I. Jarvis, and H. Kelly, *Communication and Persuasion* (New Haven, Conn.: Yale University Press, 1953).

62. F. H. Lund, "The Psychology of Belief: IV. The Law of Primacy in Persuasion," *Journal of Abnormal and Social Psychology* (1925): 236-249; F. H. Kroner, "Experimental Studies of Changes in Attitudes: II. A Study of the Effect of Printed Arguments on Changes in Attitudes," *Social Psychology* (1936): 522-532.

63. R. Lana, "Controversy on the Topic and the Order of Presentation in Persuasive Communications," *Psychological Reports* (April 1963): 163-170.

64. C. A. Insko, "Primacy versus Recency in Persuasion as a Function of the Timing of Arguments and Measurement," *Journal of Abnormal and Social Psychology* (1964): 381-391.

65. Hovland, Jarvis, and Kelly, *Communication and Persuasion*.

66. David C. Morteson, *Communication: The Study of Human Interaction* (New York: McGraw-Hill, 1972).

67. Ahmed Belkaoui, "The Primacy-Recency Effect, Ego Involvement and the Acceptance of Accounting Techniques," *Accounting Review* (January 1977): 252-256.

68. Pearson, "Discussion of Cognitive Changes Induced by Accounting Changes."

69. Barnes and Webb, "Management Information Changes and Functional Fixation."

70. Luchins and Luchins, "New Experimental Attempts."

71. Barnes and Webb, "Management Information Changes and Functional Fixation."

72. Ibid., p. 12.

73. Flavell, Cooper, and Loisell, "Effect of the Number of Pre-utilization Functions."

74. Adamson and Taylor, "Functional Fixedness"; Flavell, Cooper, and Loisell, "Effect of the Number of Pre-utilization Functions."

75. N. A. Wilner and J. G. Birnberg, "A Comparison of the Accounting and Psychological Literature on Functional Fixation," (Unpublished working paper, 1984).

76. N. A. Wilner and J. G. Birnberg, "Methodological Problems in Functional Fixation Research: Criticisms and Suggestions," *Accounting, Organizations and Society* (February 1986): 75.

77. Ibid., pp. 75-78.

78. Ibid., pp. 78-79.

CHAPTER 7
THE PRACTICE OF SLACK: A REVIEW

Cyert and March advanced the concept of organizational slack as a hypothetical construct to explain overall organizational phenomena.[1] Lewin and Wolf, on the other hand, have made the following warning: "Slack is a seductive concept; it 'explains' too much and 'predicts' too little."[2] Indeed, slack research needs to be categorized along more precise dimensions that better explain its nature and its impact. Accordingly, this chapter reviews the research on slack by differentiating between *organizational slack and budgetary slack.*

VIEWS ON SLACK

Slack arises from the tendency of organizations and individuals to refrain from using all the resources available to them. It describes a tendency to not operate at peak efficiency. In general, tow types of slack have been identified in the literature, namely organizational slack and budgetary slack. Organizational slack basically refers to an unused capacity, in the sense that the demands put on the resources of the organization are less than the supply of these resources. Budgetary slack is found in the budgetary process and refers to the intentional distortion of information that results from an understatement of budgeted sales and an overstatement of budgeted costs.

The concepts of organizational slack and budgetary slack appear in other literature under different labels. Economists refer to an X-inefficiency in instances where resources are either not used to their full capacity or effectiveness or used in an extremely wasteful manner, as well as in instances where managers fail to make costless improvements. X-inefficiency is to be differentiated from allocative inefficiency, which refers to whether or not prices in a market are of the right kind, that is, whether they allocate input and output to those users who are willing to pay for them.[3] Categories of inefficiency of a nonallocative nature, or X-inefficiency, include inefficiency in (1) labor utilization, (2) capital utilization, (3) time sequence, (4) extent of employee cooperation, (5) information flow, (6) bargaining effectiveness, (7) credit availability utilization, and (8) heuristic procedures.[4]

Agency theory also refers to slack behavior. The problem addressed by the agency theory literature is how to design an incentive contract such that the total gains can be maximized, given (1) information asymmetry between principal and agent, (2) pursuit of self-interest by the agent, and (3) environmental uncertainty affecting the outcome of the agent's decisions.[5] Slack can occur when managers dwell in an "excess consumption of perquisites" or in a "tendency to shrink." Basically, slack is the possible "shrinking" behavior of an agent.[6]

The literature in organizational behavior refers to slack in terms of defensive, tactical responses and deceptive behavior. By viewing organizations as political environments, the deceptive aspects of individual power-acquisition behavior become evident.[7] A variety of unobtrusive tactics in the operation of power,[8] covert intents and means of those exhibiting power-acquisition behaviors,[9] and a "wolf in sheep's clothing" phenomenon, whereby individuals profess a mission or goal strategy while practicing an individual-maximization strategy,[10] characterize these deceptive behaviors, which are designed to present an illusionary or false impression. Schein has provided the following examples of deceptive behaviors in communication, decision making, and presentation of self:

Communication. With regards to written or oral communications, there may be an illusion that these communications include all the information or that these communications are true, which masks the reality either of them consisting of only partial information or of their actually distorting the information.

Decision-Making. A manager may present the illusion that he is actually compromising or giving in with regard to a decision, whereas in reality he is purposely planning to lose this particular battle with the long-range objective of winning the war. Or a manager or a subunit may initiate a particular action and then work on plans and activities for implementing a program. This intensive planning and studying, however, may in reality be nothing more than a delaying tactic during which time the actual program will die or be forgotten. Underlying this illusion that one is selecting subordinates, members of boards of directors, or successors on the basis of their competency may be the reality that these individuals are selected for loyalty, compliancy, or conformity to the superior's image.

Presentation of Self. Many managers exude an apparent confidence, when in reality they are quite uncertain. Still other managers are skilled in organizing participatory group decision-making sessions, which in reality have been set up to produce a controlled outcome.[11]

Schein then hypothesized that the degree to which these behavior are deceptive seems to be a function of both the nature of the organization and of the kinds of power exhibited (work-related or personal).[12] She relied on Cyert and March's dichotomization of organizations as either low-or high-slack systems.[13] Low-slack systems are characterized by a highly competitive environment that requires rapid and nonroutine decision making on the part of its members and a high level of productive energy and work outcomes to secure an effective performance. High-slack systems are characterized by a reasonably stable environment that requires routine decision making to secure an effective performance. Given these dichotomizations, Schein suggested that:

1. The predominant form of power acquisition behavior is personal in a high-slack organization and work-related in a low-slack organization.
2. The underlying basis of deception is an inherent covert nature of personal power acquisition behaviors in a high-slack organization and an organization illusion as to how work gets done in a low-slack organization.
3. The benefits of deception to members are the provisions of excitement and personal rewards in a high-slack organization and the facilitation of work accomplishment and organizational rewards in a low-slack organization.
4. The benefits of deception to organization are to foster illusion of a fast paced, competitive environment in a high-slack organization and to maintain an illusion of workability of the formal structure in a low-slack organization.[14]

ORGANIZATIONAL SLACK
Nature of Organizational Slack

There is no lack of definitions for organizational slack as can be seen from the definitions provided by Cyert and March,[15] Child,[16] Cohen, March, and Olsen,[17] Dimmick and Murray,[19] Litschert and Bonham,[20] and March,[21] and as shown in Exhibit 7.1.

Exhibit 7.1

Definitions of Organizational Slack

Cyert & March [1963]

"[The] disparity between the resources available to the organization and the payments required to maintain the coalition" [p. 36].

E.g.: Excess dividends to stockholders

    Prices lower than necessary to keep buyers

    Wages greater than needed to keep labor

    Perquisites to executives

    Subunit growth beyond relative rate of contribution

"Supply of uncommitted resources" [p. 54].

"Resources funneled into the satisfaction of individual and sub-group [vs. organizational] objectives" [p. 98].

Child [1972]

"The margin or surplus [performance exceeding "satisficing" level] which permits an organization's dominant coalition to adopt structural arrangements which accord with their own preferences [vs. "goodness of fit" dictates of contingency theory], even at some extra administrative cost" [p. 11].

Cohen, March, & Olsen [1972]

"The difference between the resources of the organization and the combination of demands made on it" [p. 12].

March & Olsen [1976]

"The difference between existing resources and activated demands" [p. 87].

Dimmick & Murray [1978]

"Those resources which an organization has acquired which are not committed to a necessary expenditure. In essence, these are resources which can be used in a discretionary manner" [p. 616].

Operation = Avg. profit over 5 yrs., controlled for size ($ sales)

Litschert & Bonham [1978]

Using Cyert and March's [1963] definition, they gave the following suggested operation: Slack = the variation, from the average among comparable organizations on: ROE, ROTA, Net Sales, and Gross Profit as a percentage of Sales.

March [1979]

"Since organizations do not always optimize, they accumulate spare resources and unexploited opportunities which then become a buffer against bad times. Although the buffer is not necessarily intended, slack produces performance smoothing, reducing performance during good times and improving it during bad times" [quoted in *Stanford GSB*, p. 17].

Source: L. J. Bourgeois, "On the Measurement of Organizational Slack," *Academy of Management Review* 6, no. 1 (1981): 30. Reprinted with permission.

What appears from these definitions is that organizational slack is a buffer created by management in its use of available resources to deal with internal as well as external events that may arise and threaten an establish coalition. Slack, therefore, will be used by management as an agent of change in response to changes in both the internal and external environments.

Cyert and March's model explains slack in terms of cognitive and structural factors.[22] It provides the rationale for the unintended creation of slack. Individuals are assumed to "satisfice," in the sense that they set aspiration levels for performance rather than a maximization goal. These aspirations adjust upward or downward, depending on actual performance, and in a slower fashion than actual changes in performance. It is this lag in adjustment that allows excess resources from superior performance to accumulate in the form of organizational slack. This slack is then used as a stabilizing force to absorb excess resources in good times without requiring a revision of aspirations and intentions regarding the use of these excess resources. "By absorbing excess resources it retards upward adjustment of aspirations during relatively good times . . . by providing a pool of emergency resources, it permits aspirations to be maintained during relatively bad times."[23]

Williamson has proposed a model of slack based on managerial incentives.[24] This model provides the rationale for managers' motivation and desire for slack resources. Under conditions where managers are able to pursue their own objectives, the model predicts that the excess resources available after target levels of profit have been reached are not allocated according to profit-maximization rules. Organizational slack becomes the means by which a manager achieves his or her personal goals, as characterized by four motives: income, job security, status, and discretionary control over resources. Williamson makes the assumption that the manager is motivated to maximize his or her personal goals subject to satisfying organizational objectives and that the manager achieves this by maximizing slack resources under his or her control. Williamson has suggested that there are four levels of profits: (1) a maximizing profit equal to the profit the firm would achieve when marginal revenue equals marginal cost, (2) actual profit equal to the true profit achieved by the firm, (3) reported profit equal to the accounting profit reported in the annual report, and (4) minimum profit equal to the profit needed to maintain the organizational coalition. If the market is noncompetitive, various forms of slack emerge: (1) *slack absorbed as staff* equal to the difference between maximum profit and actual profit, (2) *slack in the form of cost* equal to the difference between reported and minimum profits, and (3) *discretionary spending for investment* equal to the difference between reported and minimum profits.

Income smoothing can be used to substantiate the efforts of management to neutralize environmental uncertainty and to create organizational slack by means of an accounting manipulation of the level of earnings. Kamin and Ronen have related organizational slack to income smoothing by reasoning that the decisions that affect the allocation of costs- such as budget negotiations, which often result in slack accumulation- are aimed at smoothing earnings.[25] They hypothesized that management-controlled firms were more likely to be engaged in smoothing as a manifestation of managerial discretion and slack. "Accounting" and "real" smoothing were tested by observing the behavior of discretionary expenses vis-à-vis the behavior of income numbers. Their results showed that (1) a majority of the firms behaved as if they were income smoothers, and (2) a particularly strong majority was found among management-controlled firms with high barriers to entry. This line of reasoning was pursued by Belkaoui and Picur.[26] Their study tested the effects of the dual economy on income-smoothing behavior. It was hypothesized that a higher degree of smoothing of income numbers would be exhibited by firms in the periphery sector than by firms in the core sector in reaction to different opportunity structures and experiences. Their results indicated that a majority of the firms may have been resorting to income smoothing. A higher number was found among firms in the periphery sector.

Lewin and Wolf proposed the following statements as a theoretical framework for understanding the concept of slack:

(1) Organizational slack depends on the availability of excess resources.

(2) Excess resources occur when an organization generates or has the potential to generate resources in excess of what is necessary to maintain the organizational coalition.

(3) Slack occurs unintentionally as a result of the imperfection of the resource allocation decision making process.

(4) Slack is created intentionally because managers are motivated to maximize slack resources under their control to insure achievement of personal goals subject to the achievement of organizational goals.

(5) The disposition of slack resources is a function of a manager's expense preference function.

(6) The distribution of slack resources is an outcome of the bargaining process setting organization and reflects the discretionary power of organization members in allocating resources.

(7) Slack can be present in a distributed or concentrated form.

(8) The aspiration of organizational participants for slack adjusts upward as resources become available. The downward adjustment of aspirations for slack resources, when resources become scarce, is resisted by organizational participants.

(9) Slack can stabilize short-term fluctuations in the firm's performance.

(10) Beyond the short-term, the reallocation of slack requires a change in organizational goals.

(11) Slack is directly related to organizational size, maturity and stability of the external environment.[27]

Functions of Organizational Slack

Because the definition of slack is often intertwined with a description of the functions that slack serves, Bourgeois discussed these functions as a means of making palpable the ways of measuring slack.[28] From a review of the administrative theory literature, he identified organizational slack as an independent variable that either "causes" or serves four primary functions: "(1) as an inducement for organizational actors to remain in the system, (2) as a resource for conflict resolution, (3) as a buffering mechanism in the work flow process, or (4) as a facilitator of certain types of strategic or creative behavior within the organization."[29] Exhibit 7.2 summarizes basic information on the first three of these functions.

Exhibit 7.2
Functions of Slack for Internal Maintenance

	Inducement (to maintain the coalition)	Conflict Resolution	Work flow Buffer
Authors and Concepts	I/C ratio [Barnard, 1937] I/C >1 [March & Simon, 1958] I > 1 = C [Cyert & March, 1963]	Goal incongruence [Pondy, 1967] Local rationality, goal conflict, local optimization [Cyert & March, 1963]	Technical core buffer (inven- tories, adver- tising) [Thompson, 1967] Systems model [Pondy, 1967] Reduced information- processing require- ments [Galbraith, 1973]
Operation	I = Excess dividends Low prices High wages Income and prestige Executive "perks"	Pursuit of pet projects Lowered ROI hurdle Increased/decreased financial authority	Δ in inventory Δ in administrative intensity * * * Reduced performance levels Longer delivery times Hire more labor Buy more equipment
Unit of Analysis	Individual (Σ for organization)	Subunit	Organization
Data Source	Questionnaire	Archival	Archival
Measure	$: static (one point in time)	$ or : relative (compared to previous period)	$: relative Time Labor intensity Static Excess capacity
Problems	Perceptual data Threatening Individual (vs. organi- zational) phenomenon	Sensitive data Subunit slack ≠ organi- zational slack	Slack consumption vs. slack creation

$ = Quantified in terms of monetary value

Δ = Change

Source: L. J. Bourgeois, "On the Measurement of Organizational Slack," *Academy of Management Review* 6, no. 1 (1981): 32. Reprinted with permission.

The concept of slack as an inducement to maintain the coalition was first introduced by Barnard in his treatment of the inducement/ contribution ratio (I/C) as a way of attracting organizational participants and sustaining their membership.[30] March and Simon later described slack resources as the source of inducements through which the inducement/ contribution ratio might exceed a value of one, which is equivalent to paying an employee more than would be required to retain his or her services.[31] The concept of slack was then explicitly introduced by Cyert and March as consisting of payments to members of the coalition in excess of what is required to maintain the organization.[32]

Slack as a resource for conflict resolution was introduced in Pondy's goal model.[33] In this model subunit goal conflicts are resolved partly by sequential attention to goals and partly by adopting a decentralized organizational structure. A decentralized structure is made possible by the presence of organizational slack.

A notion of slack as a technical buffer from the variances and discontinuities caused by environmental uncertainty was proposed by Thompson.[34] It was also acknowledged in Pondy's system model, which described conflict as a result of the lack of buffers between interdependent parts of an organization.[35] Galbraith saw buffering as an information processing problem: "Slack resources are an additional cost to the organization or the customer. . . . The creation of slack resources, through reduced performance levels, reduces the amount of information that must be processed during task execution and prevents the overloading of hierarchical channels."[36]

According to Bourgeois slack facilitates three types of strategic or creative behavior within the organization: (1) providing resources for innovative behavior, (2) providing opportunities of a satisficing behavior, and (3) affecting political behavior.[37] Exhibit 7.3 summarizes the fundamental characteristic of these types of behavior and their strategic implications for the organization.

Exhibit 7.3

Slack as a Facilitator of Strategic Behavior

	Innovation	Satisficing	Politics
Authors and Concepts	Experimentation with new strategies [Hambrick & Snow, 1977] Funds for innovation [Cyert & March, 1963]	Bounded search [Simon, 1957; March & Simon, 1958]	Bargaining activity [Cyert & March, 1963] Self-aggrandizement; conflict and coalition [Astley, 1978]
Opera-tions	New products New markets New processes R&D and market research	Search time Search team Number of alterna-tives generated or considered	New resource infu-sion and subsequent distribution Policy conflicts between managers, coalition formation
Unit of Analysis	Organization	Organization or top management team	Organization or top management team
Data Source	Archival Interview	Interview	Archival Interview Organization
Measure	Products Clients, longitu- region dinal $: static	Time $ longitudinal Process	$ longitu- Behavior dinal

$ = quantified in terms of monetary value.

Source: L. J. Bourgeois, "On the Measurement of Organizational Slack," *Academy of Management Review* 6, no. 1 (1981): 35. Reprinted with permission.

First, as a facilitator of innovative behavior, slack tends to create conditions that allow the organization to experiment with new strategies[38] and introduce innovation.[39] Second, as a facilitator of suboptimal behavior, slack defines the threshold of acceptability of a choice, or "bounded search,"[40] by people whose bounded rationality leads them to satisfice.[41] Third, the notion that slack affects political activity was advanced by Cyert and March, who argued that slack reduces both political activity and the need for bargaining and coalition-forming activity.[42] Furthermore, Astley has argued that slack created by success results in self-aggrandizing behavior by managers, who engage in political behavior to capture more than their fair share of the surplus.[43]

Measurement of Organizational Slack

One problem in investigating empirically the presence of organizational slack relates to the difficulty of securing an adequate measurement of the phenomenon. As exhibits 7.2 and 7.3 show, various methods have been suggested. In addition to these methods, eight variables that appear in public data, whether they are created by managerial actions or made available by the environment, may explain a change in slack.[44] The mode, suggested by Bourgeois, is as follows:

Slack = f(RE, DP, GαA, WC/S, D/E, CR, I/P, P/E)

where

RE = retained earnings

DP = Dividend payout

GαA = General and administrative expense

WC/S = Working capital as a percentage of sales

D/E = Debt as a percentage of equity

CR = Credit rating

I/P = Short-term loan interest compared to prime rate

P/E = Price/earnings ratio

RE, GαA, WC/S, and CR are assumed to have a positive effect on changes in slack, whereas DP, D/E, P/E, and I/P are assumed to have a negative effect on changes in slack.

Some of these measures have also been suggested by other researchers. For example, Rosner used profit and excess capacity as slack measures,[45] and Lewin and Wolf used selling, general, and administrative expenses as surrogates for slack.[46] Bourgeois and Singh refined these measures by suggesting that slack could be differentiated on an "ease-of-recovery" dimension.[47] Basically, they considered excess liquidity to be *available slack*, not yet earmarked for particular uses. Overhead costs were termed *recoverable slack*, in the sense that they are absorbed by various organizational functions but can be recovered when needed elsewhere. In addition, the ability of a firm to generate resources from the environment, such as the ability to raise additional debt or equity capital, was considered *potential slack*. All of these measures were divided by sales to control for company size.

Building on Bourgeois and Singh's suggestions, Lant opted for the four following measures:

1. Administrative Slack = (General and Administrative Expenses)/ Cost of Goods Sold
2. Available Liquidity = (Cash + Marketable Securities – Current Liabilities)/Sales
3. Recoverable Liquidity = (Accounts Receivable + Inventory)/Sales
4. Retained Earnings = (Net Profit – Dividends)/ Sales[48]

Lant used these measures to show empirically that (a) available liquidity and general and administrative expenses have significantly higher variance than profit across firms and across time, and (b) the mean change in slack is significantly greater than the mean change in profit. She concluded as follows:

Their results are logically consistent with the theory that slack absorbs variance in actual profit. They also suggest that the measures used are reasonable measure for slack. Thus, it supports prior work which has used these measures, and implies that further large sample models using slack as a variable is feasible since financial information is readily available for a large number of firms. Before these results can be generalized, however, the tests conducted here should be replicated using different samples of firms from a variety of industries.[49]

BUDGETARY SLACK
Nature of Budgetary Slack

The literature on organizational slack shows that managers have the motives necessary to desire to operate in a slack environment. The literature on budgetary slack considers the budget as the embodiment of that environment and, therefore, assumes that managers will use the budgeting process to bargain for slack budgets. As stated by Schiff and Lewin, "managers will create slack in budgets through a process of *understating revenues and overstating costs*."[50] The general definition of budgetary slack, then, is the understatement of revenues and the overstatement of costs in the budgeting process. A detailed description of the creation of budgetary slack by managers was reported by Schiff and Lewin in their study of the budget process of three divisions of multidivision companies.[51] They found evidence of budgetary slack through underestimation of gross revenue, inclusion of discretionary increases in personnel requirements, establishment of marketing and sales budgets with internal limits on funds to be spent, use of manufacturing costs based on standard costs that do not reflect process improvements operationally available at the plant, and inclusion of discretionary "special projects."

Evidence of budgetary slack has also been reported by others. Lowe and Shaw found a downward bias, introduced through sales forecasts by line managers, which assumed good performance where rewards were related to forecasts.[52] Dalton reported various examples of department managers allocating resources to what they considered justifiable purposes even though such purposes were not authorized in their bugets.[53] Shillinglaw noted the extreme vulnerability of budgets used to measure divisional performance given the great control exercised by divisional management in budget preparation and the reporting of results.[54]

Slack creation is a generalized organizational phenomenon. Many different organizational factors have been used to explain slack creation, in particular organizational structure, goal congruence, control system, and managerial behavior. Slack creation is assumed to occur in cases where a Tayloristic organizational structure exists,[55] although it is also assumed to occur in a participative organizational structure.[56] It may be due to conflicts that arise between the individual and organizational goals, leading managers intentionally to create slack. It may also be due to the attitudes of management toward the budget and to workers' views of the budgets as a device used by management to manipulate them.[57] Finally, the creation of slack may occur whether or not the organization is based on a centralized or decentralized structure.[58] With regard to this last issue, Schiff and Lewin have reported that the divisional controller appears to have undertaken the tasks of creating and managing divisional slack and is most influential in the internal allocation of slack.

Budgeting and the Propensity to Create Budgetary Slack

The budgeting system has been assumed to affect a manager's propensity to create budgetary slack, in the sense that this propensity can be increased or decreased by the way in which the budgeting system is designed or complemented. Onsi was the first to investigate empirically the connections between the type of budgeting system and the propensity to create budgetary slack.[59] From a review of the literature, he stated the following four assumptions:

(1) Managers influence the budget process through bargaining for slack by understating revenues and overstating costs. . . .

(2) Managers build up slack in "good years" and reconvert slack into profit in "bad years." . . .

(3) Top management is at a "disadvantage" in determining the magnitude of slack. . . .

(4) The divisional controller is decentralized organizations participates in the task of creating the managing divisional slack.[60]

Personal interviews of 32 managers of five large, national and international companies and statistical analysis of a questionnaire were used to identify the important behavioral variables that influence slack buildup and utilization. The questionnaire's variables were grouped into the following eight dimensions:

1. *Slack attitude* described by the variables indicating a manager's attitude to slack.

2. *Slack manipulation* described by the variables indicating how a manager builds-up and uses slack.
3. *Slack institutionalization* described by the variables that make a manager less inclined to reduced his slack.
4. *Slack detection* described by the variables indicating the superior's ability to detect slack based on the amount of information he receives.
5. *Attitude towards the top management control system* described by the variables indicating an authoritarian philosophy towards budgeting being attributed to top management by divisional managers.
6. *Attitudes towards the divisional control system* described by variables on attitudes toward subordinates, sources of pressure, budget autonomy, budget participation, and supervisory uses of budgets.
7. *Attitudes towards the budget described* by variables on attitude towards the level of standards, attitude towards the relevancy of budget attainment to valuation of performance, and the manager's attitude (positive or negative) towards the budgetary system in general, as a managerial tool.
8. *Budget relevancy* described by variables indicating a manager's attitudes towards the relevancy of standards for his department's operation.[61]

Factor analysis reduced these dimensions to seven factors and showed a relationship between budgetary slack and what Onsi called "an authoritarian top management budgetary control system." Thus, he stated:

Budgetary slack is created as a result of pressure and the use of budgeted profit attainment as a basic criterion in evaluating performance. Positive participation could encourage less need for building-up slack. However, the middle managers' perception of pressure was an overriding concern. The positive correlation between managers' attitudes and attainable levels of standards is a reflection of this pressure.[62]

Cammann explored the moderating effects of subordinates' participation in decision making and the difficulty of subordinates' jobs on their responses to different uses of control systems by their superiors.[63] His results showed that the use of control systems for contingent reward allocation produced defensive responses by subordinates under all conditions, which included the creation of budgetary slack. Basically, when superiors used budgeting information as a basis for allocating organizational rewards, their subordinates' responses were defensive. Allowing participation in the budget processes reduced this defensiveness.

Finally, Merchant conducted a field study designed to investigate how managers' propensities to create a budgetary slack are affected by the budgeting system and the technical context.[64] He hypothesized that the propensity to create budgetary slack is positively related to the importance placed on meeting budget targets and negatively related to the extent of participation allowed in budgeting processes, the degree of predictability in the production process, and the superiors' abilities to create slack. Unlike earlier studies that had drawn across functional areas, 170 manufacturing managers responded to a questionnaire measuring the propensity to create slack, the importance of meeting the budget, budget participation, the nature of technology in terms of work-flow integration and product standardization, and the ability of superiors to detect slack. The results suggested that managers' propensities to create slack (1) do vary with the setting and with how the budgeting system is implemented; (2) are lower where managers actively participate in budgeting, particularly when technologies are relatively predictable; and (3) are higher when a tight budget requires frequent tactical responses to avoid overruns.

Budgetary Slack Information Distortion and Truth-Inducing Incentive Schemes

Budgetary slack involves a deliberate distortion of input information. Distortion of input information in a budget setting arises, in particular, from the need of managers to accommodate their expectations about the kinds of payoffs associated with different possible outcomes. Several experiments have provided evidence of such distortion of input information. Cyert, March, and Starbuck showed in a laboratory experiment that subjects adjusted the information they transmitted in a complex decision-making system to control their payoffs.[65] Similarly, Lowe and Shaw have shown that in cases where rewards were linked to forecasts, sales managers tended to distort the input information and to induce biases in their sales forecast.[66] Dalton also provided some rich situational descriptions of information distortion in which lower-level managers distorted the budget information and allocated resources to what were perceived to be justifiable objectives.[67] Finally, given the existence of a payoff structure that can induce a forecaster to bias intentionally his or her forecast, Barefield provided a model of forecast behavior that showed a "rough" formulation of a possible link between a forecaster's biasing and the quality of the forecaster as a source of data for an accounting system.[68]

Taken together, these studies suggest that budgetary slack, through systematic distortion of input information, can be used to accommodate the subjects' expectations about the payoffs associated with various possible outcomes. They fail, however, to provide a convincing rationalization of the link between distortion of input information and the subjects' accommodation of their expectations. Agency theory and issues related to risk aversion may provide such a link. Hence, given the existence of divergent incentives and information asymmetry between the controller (or employer) and the controllee (or employee) and the high cost of observing employee skill or effort, a budget-based employment contact (that is, where employee compensation is contingent on meeting the performance standard) can be Pareto-superior to fixed pay or linear sharing rules (where the employer and employee split the output).[69] However, the budget-based schemes impose a risk on the employee, as job performance can be affected by a host of uncontrollable factors. Consequently, risk-averse individuals may resort to slack budgeting through systematic distortion of input information. In practice, moreover, any enhanced (increased) risk aversion would lead the employee to resort to budgetary slack. One might hypothesize that, without proper incentives for truthful communication, the slack budgeting behavior could be reduced. One suggested avenue is the use of truth-inducing, budget-based schemes.[70] These schemes, assuming risk neutrality, motivate a worker to reveal truthfully private information about future performance and to maximize performance regardless of the budget.

Accordingly, Young conducted an experiment to test the effects of risk aversion and asymmetric information on slack budgeting.[71] Five hypotheses related to budgetary slack were developed and tested using a laboratory experiment. The hypotheses were as follows:

Hypothesis 1: A subordinate who participates in the budgeting process will build slack into the budget. . . .

Hypothesis 2: A risk-averse subordinate will build in more budget slack than a non-risk-averse subordinate. . . .

Hypothesis 3: Social pressure not to misrepresent productive capability will be greater for a subordinate whose information is known by management than for a subordinate having private information. . . .

Hypothesis 4: As social pressure increases for the subordinate, there is a lower degree of budgetary slack. . . .

Hypothesis 5: A subordinate who ha private information builds more slack into the budget than a subordinate whose information is known by management.[72]

The results of the experiment confirmed the hypotheses that a subordinate who participates builds in budgetary slack and that slack is, in part, attributable to a subordinate's risk preferences. Given state uncertainty and a worker-manager information asymmetry about performance capability, the subjects in the experiment created slack even in the presence of a truth-inducing scheme. In addition, risk-averse workers created more slack than non-risk-averse workers did. Similarly, Chow, Cooper, and Waller provided evidence that, given a worker-manager information asymmetry about performance capability, slack is lower under a truth-inducing scheme than under a budget-based scheme with an incentive to create slack.[73]

Both Young's and Chow, Cooper, and Waller's studies were found to have limitations.[74] With regard to Young's study, Waller found three limitations:

First, unlike the schemes examined in the analytical research, the one used in his study penalized outperforming the budget, which limits its general usefulness. Second, there was no manipulation of incentives, so variation in slack due to incentives was not examined. Third, risk preferences were measured using the conventional lottery technique of which the validity and reliability are suspect.[75]

With regard to Chow, Cooper, and Waller's study, Waller found to be limitations the assumption of state certainty and the failure to take risk preference into account. Accordingly, Waller conducted an experiment under which subjects participatively set budgets under either a scheme with an incentive for creating slack or a truth-incentive scheme like those examined in the analytical research. In addition, risk neutrality was induced for one-half of the subjects and constant, absolute risk aversion for the rest, using a technique discussed by Berg, Daley, Dickhaut, and O'Brien that allows the experimenter to induce (derived) utility functions with any shape.[76] The results of the experiment show that when a conventional truth-inducing scheme is introduced, slack decreases for risk-neutral subjects but not for risk-averse subjects. Added to the evidence provided by the other studies, this study indicates that risk preference is an important determinant of slack, especially in the presence of a truth-inducing scheme.

Budgetary Slack and Self-Esteem

The enhancement of risk aversion and the resulting distortion of input information can be more pronounced when self-esteem is threatened. It was found that persons who have low opinions of themselves are more likely to cheat than persons with higher self-esteem.[77] A situation of dissonance was created in an experimental group by giving out positive feedback about a personality test to some participants and negative feedback to others. All the participants were then asked to take part in a competitive game of cards. The participants who received a blow to their self-esteem cheated more often than those who had received positive feedback about themselves. Could it also be concluded that budgetary slack through information distortion may be a form of dishonest behavior, arising from the enhancement of risk aversion caused by a negative feedback on self-esteem? A person's expectations can be an important determinant of his or her behavior. A negative impact on self-esteem can lead to an individual to develop an expectation of poor performance. At the same time, the individual who is given negative feedback about his or her self-esteem would be more risk averse than others and would be ready to resort to any behavior to cover the situation. Consequently, the person may attempt to distort the input information in order to have an attainable budget. Belkaoui accordingly tested the hypothesis that individuals given negative feedback about their self-esteem would introduce more bias into estimates than individuals given positive or neutral feedback about their self-esteem.[78] One week after taking a self-esteem test, subjects were provided with false feedback (either positive or negative) and neutral feedback about their self-esteem score. They were then asked to make two budgeting decisions, first one cost estimate and then one sales estimate for a fictional budgeting decision. The results showed that, in general, the individuals who were provided with information that temporarily caused them to lower their self-esteem were more apt to distort input information than those who were made to raise their self-esteem. It was concluded that, whereas slack budgeting may be consistent with generally low self-esteem feedback, it is inconsistent with generally high or neutral self-esteem feedback.

Toward a Theoretical Framework for Budgeting

A theoretical framework aimed at structuring knowledge about biasing behavior was proposed by Lukka.[79] It contains an explanatory model for budgetary biasing and a model for budgetary biasing at the organizational level.

The explanatory model of budgetary biasing at the individual level is presented in Exhibit 7.4. It draws from the management accounting and organizational behavior literature and related behavioral research to suggest a set of intentions and determinants of budgetary biasing. Budgetary biasing is at the center of many interrelated and sometimes contradictory factors with the actor's intentions as the synthetic core of his or her behavior.

Exhibit 7.4
Intentions and Determinants of Budgetary Biasing

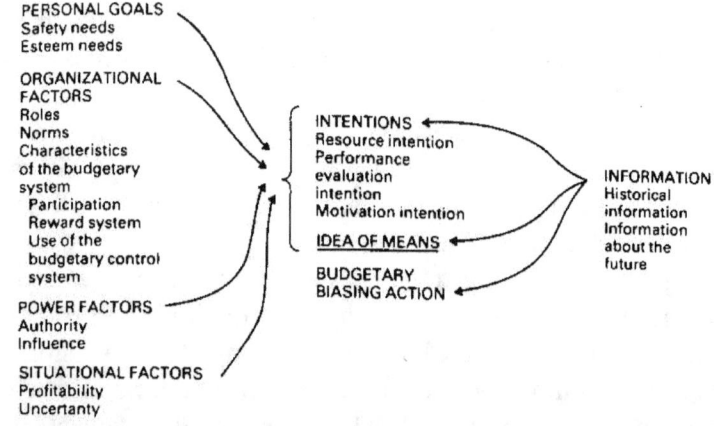

Source: Kari Lukka, "Budgetary Biasing in Organizations: Theoretical Framework and Empirical Evidence," *Accounting, Organizations and Society* (February 1988): 291. Reprinted with permission.

Exhibit 7.5
Budgetary Process from the Biasing Viewpoint

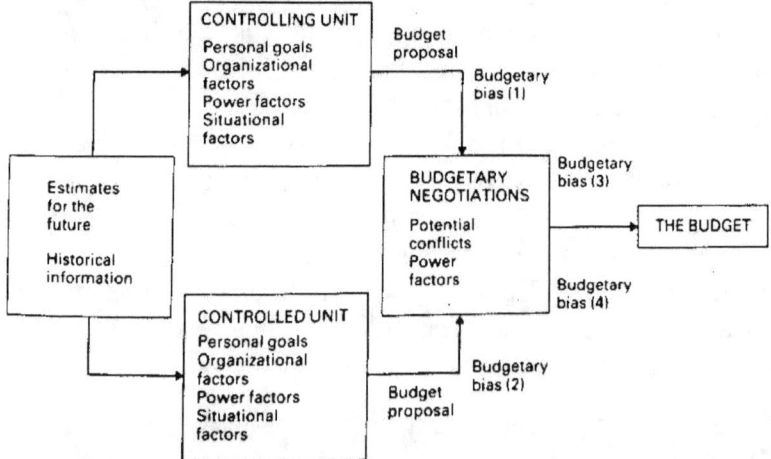

Source: Kari Lukka, "Budgetary Biasing in Organizations: Theoretical Framework and Empirical Evidence," *Accounting, Organizations and Society* (February 1988): 292. Reprinted with permission.

The model for budgetary biasing at the organizational level is presented in Exhibit 7.5. It shows that the "bias contained in the final budget is not the result of one actor's intentional behavior, but rather the result of the dialects of the negotiations.[80] While budgetary biases 1 and 2 are the original biases created in the budget by the controlling unit and the controlled unit, biases 3 and 4 are the final biases to end up in the budget after the budgetary negotiations, which are characterized by potential conflict and power factors. The results of semi-structured interviews at different levels of management of a large decentralized company verified the theoretical framework. The usefulness of this theoretical framework rests on further reinfinements and empirical testing.

Positive versus Negative Slack

Although the previous sections have focused on budgetary, or positive, slack, budgetary bias is in fact composed of both budgetary slack and an upward bias, or a negative slack. While budgetary slack refers to bias in which the budget is designed intentionally so as to make it easier to achieve the forecast, upward bias refers to overstatement of expected performance in the budget. Otley has described the difference as follows: "Managers are therefore likely to be conservative in making forecasts when future benefits are sought (positive slack) but optimistic when their need for obtaining current approval dominates (negative slack)."[81]

Evidence for negative slack was first provided by Read, who showed that managers distort information to prove to their superiors that all is well.[82] He cited several empirical studies of budgetary control that indicated that managers put a lot of effort and ingenuity into assuring that messages conveyed by budgetary information serve their own interests.[83] Following earlier research by Barefield, Otley argued that forecasts may be the mode, rather than the means, of people's intuitive probability distributions.[84] Given that the distribution of cost and revenue is negatively skewed, there will be a tendency for budget forecasts to become unintentionally biased in the form of negative slack. Data collected from two organizations verified the presence of negative slack.

Reducing Budgetary Slack: A Bonus-Based Technique

In general, firms use budgeting and bonus techniques to overcome slack budgeting. One such approach consists of paying higher rewards when budget are set high and achieved, and lower rewards when budgets are either set high but no met or set low and achieved. Mann presented a bonus system that gave incentives for managers to set budget estimates as close to achievable levels as possible.[85] The following two formulas were proposed:

Formula 1 applies for bonus if actual performance is equal to or greater than budget.

(Multiplier no. 2 X budget goal) + (multiplier no. 1 X [actual level achieved – budget goal])

Formula 2 applies for bonus if actual performance is less than budget.

(Multiplier no. 2 X budget goal) + (multiplier no. 3 X [actual level achieved – budget goal])

The three multipliers set by management served as factors in calculating different components of bonuses. They were defined as follows:

Multiplier no. 1 (which must be less than multiplier no. 2, and which in turn must be less than multiplier no. 3) is used when actual performance is greater than budget. It provides a smaller bonus per unit for the part of actual performance that exceeds the budgeted amount. . . .

Multiplier no. 2 is the rate per unit used to determine the basic bonus component. It is based on the budgeted level of activity which equals multiplier no. 2 times the budgeted level.

Multiplier no. 3 is the rate used to reduce the bonus when the achieved level is less than the budget (multiplier no. 3 times work of units by which actual performance fell short of budget).[86]

Exhibit 7.6 shows an illustration of the application of the method and the effect of variations in multipliers or bonuses. As the exhibits shows, the manager will be rewarded for accurate estimation of the level of rates. In addition, the multipliers can be set with greater flexibility for controlling the manager's estimates.

Exhibit 7.6

Reducing Slack through a Bonus System

(1) Budget Sales	(2) Actual Sales	(3) State of Nature	(4) Bonus I Multiple No. 1 = $.05 Multiple No. 2 = $.10 Multiple No. 3 = $.15	(5) Bonus II Multiple no. 1 = .01 Multiple no. 2 = .10 Multiple No. 3 = .30
200,000	180,000	Over estimation	$17,000	$14,000
200,000	200,000	Actual = Budget	20,000	20,000
200,000	220,000	Under estimation	21,000	22,000

CONCLUSION

Organizational slack and budgetary slack are two hypothetical constructs to explain organizational phenomena that are prevalent in all forms of organizations. Evidence linking both constructs to organizational, individual, and contextual factors is growing and in the future may contribute to an emerging theoretical framework for an understanding of slack. Further investigation into the potential determinants of organizational and budgetary slack remains to be done. This effort is an important one, as the behavior of slack is highly relevant to the achievement of internal economic efficiency in organizations.

NOTES

1. Richard M. Cyert and James G. March, eds., *A Behavioral Theory of the Firm* (Englewood Cliffs, N.J.: Prentice-Hall, 1963).

2. Arie Y. Lwein and Carl Wolf, "The Theory of Organizational Slack: A Critical Review," *Proceedings: Twentieth International Meetings of TIMS* (1976): 648-654.

3. Harvey Leibenstein, "Allocative Efficiency vs. 'X-Efficiency,'" *American Economic Review* (June 1966): 392-415.

4. Harvey Leibenstein, "X-Efficiency: From Concept to Theory," *Challenge* (September-October 1979): 13-22.

5. Nandan Choudhury, "Incentives for the Divisional Manager," *Accounting and Business Research* (Winter 1985): 11-21.

6. S. Baiman, "Agency Research in Managerial Accounting: A Survey," *Journal of Accounting Literature* (Spring 1982): 154-213.

7. D. Packard, *The Pyramid Climber* (New York: McGraw-Hill, 1962); E. A. Buttler, "Corporate Politics- Monster or Friend?" *Generation 3* (1971): 54-58, 74; A. N. Schoomaker, *Executive Career Strategies* (New York: American Management Association, 1971).

8. J. Pfeffer, "Power and Resource Allocation in Organizations," in B. M. Shaw and G. R. Salancik, eds., *New Directions in Organizational Behavior* (Chicago: St. Clair Press, 1977).

9. V. E. Schein, "Individual Power and Political Behaviors in Organizations: An Inadequately Explored Reality," *Academy of Management Review* (January 1977): 64-72.

10. B. Bozeman and W. Malpive, "Goals and Bureaucratic Decision-Making: An Experiment," *Human Relations* (June 1977): 417-429.

11. V. E. Schein, "Examining an Illusion: The Role of Deceptive Behaviors in Organizations," *Human Relations* (October 1979): 288-289.

12. Ibid., p. 290.

13. Cyert and March, *A Behavioral Theory of the Firm.*

14. Schein, "Examining an Illusion," p. 293.

15. Cyert and March, *A Behavioral Theory of the Firm.*

16. John Child, "Organizational Structure, Environment, and Performance: The Role of Strategic Choice," *Sociology* 6, no. 1 (1972): 2-22.

17. M. D. Cohen, J. G. March and J. P. Olsen, "A Garbage Can Model of Organizational Choice," *Administrative Science Quarterly* 17, no. 1 (1972): 1-25.

18. J. G. March and J. P. Olsen, *Ambiguity and Choice* (Bergen: Universitetsforlagt, 1976).

19. D. E. Dimmick and V. V. Murray, "Correlates of Substantive Policy Decisions in Organizations: The Case of Human Resource Management," *Academy of Management Journal* 21, no. 4 (1978): 611-623.

20. R. J. Litschert and T. W. Bonham, "A Conceptual Model of Strategy Formation," *Academy of Management Review* 3 no. 2 (1978) 211-219.

21. James G. March, interview by Stanford Business School Alumni Association, *Stanford GSB* 47, no. 3 (1978-79): 16-19.

22. Cyert and March, *A Behavioral Theory of the Firm.*

23. Ibid., p. 38.

24. Oliver E. Williamson, "A Model of Rational Managerial Behavior," in Richard M. Cyert and James G. March, eds., *A Behavioral Theory of the Firm* (Englewood Cliffs, N. J.: Prentice-Hall, 1963); idem, *The Economics of Discretionary Behavior:*

Managerial Objectives in a Theory of the Firm (Englewood Cliffs, N.J.: Prentice-Hall, 1964).

25. J. Y. Kamin and J. Ronen, "The Smoothing of Income Numbers: Some Empirical Evidence on Systematic Differences among Management-Controlled and Owner-Controlled Firms," *Accounting, Organizations, and Society* (October 1978): 141-157.

26. Ahmed Belkaoui and R. D. Picur, "The Smoothing of Income Numbers: Some Empirical Evidence on Systematic Differences between Core and Periphery Industrial Sectors," *Journal of Business Finance and Accounting* (Winter 1984): 527-545.

27. Lewin and Wolf, "The Theory of Organizational Slack," p. 653.

28. L. J. Bourgeois, "On the Measurement of Organizational Slack," *Academy of Management Review* 6, no. 1 (1981): 29-39.

29. Ibid., p. 31.

30. C. I. Barnard, *Functions of Executive* (Cambridge, Mass.: Harvard University Press, 1938).

31. James G. March and H. A. Simon, *Organizations* (New York: John Wiley and Sons, 1958).

32. Cyert and March, *A Behavioral Theory of the Firm*, p. 36.

33. L. R. Pondy, "Organizational Conflict: Concepts and Models," *Administrative Science Quarterly* 12, no. 2 (1967): 296-320.

34. J. D. Thompson, *Organizations in Action* (New York: McGraw-Hill, 1967).

35. Pondy, "Organizational Conflict."

36. Jay Galbraith, *Designing Complex Organizations* (Reading, Mass.: Addison-Wesley, 1973), p. 15.

37. Bourgeois, "On the Measurement of Organizational Slack," p. 34.

38. D. C. Hambrick and C. C. Snow, "A Contextual Model of Strategic Decision Making in Organizations," in R. L. Taylor, J. J. O'Connell, R. A. Zawaki and D. D. Warrick, eds., *Academy of Management Proceedings* (1977): 109-112.

39. Cyert and March, *A Behavioral Theory of the Firm.*

40. March and Simon, *Organizations*.

41. H. A. Simon, *Administrative Behavior* (New York: Free Press, 1957).

42. Cyert and March, *A Behavioral Theory of the Firm*.

43. W. G. Astley, "Sources of Power in Organizational Life" (Ph.D. diss., University of Washington, 1978).

44. Bourgeois, "On the Measurement Organization Slack," p. 38.

45. Martin M. Rosner, "Economic Determinant of Organizational Innovation," *Administrative Science Quarterly* 12 (1968): 614-625.

46. Arie Y. Lewin and Carl Wolf, "Organizational Slack: A Test of the General Theory," *Journal of Management Studies* (Forthcoming).

47. L. J. Bourgeois and Jitendra V. Singh, "Organization Slack and Political Behavior within Top Management Teams," (Working paper, Graduate School of Business, Stanford University, 1983).

48. Theresa K. Lant, "Modeling Organizational Slack: An Empirical Investigation," Stanford University Research Paper, No. 856 (July 1986).

49. Ibid., p. 14.

50. Michael Schiff and Arie Y. Lewin, "The Impact of People Budgets," *Accounting Review* (April 1970): 259-268.

51. Michael Schiff and Arie Y. Lewin, "Where Traditional Budgeting Fails," *Financial Executive* (May 1968): 51-62.

52. A. E. Lowe and R. W. Shaw, "An Analysis of Managerial Biasing: Evidence from a Company's Budgeting Process," *Journal of Management Studies* (October 1968): 304-315.

53. M. Dalton, *Men Who Manage* (New York: John Wiley and Sons, 1961), pp. 36-38.

54. G. Shillinglaw, "Divisional Performance Review: An Extension of Budgetary Control," in C. P. Bonini, R. K. Jaedicke, and H. M. Wagner, eds., *Management Controls: New Directors in Basic Research* (New York: McGraw-Hill, 1964), pp. 149-163.

55. C. Argyris, *The Impact of Budgets on People* (New York: Controllership Foundation, 1952), p. 25.

56. E. H. Caplan, *Management Accounting and Behavioral Sciences* (Reading, Mass.: Addison-Wesley, 1971).

57. Argyris, *The Impact of Budgets on People.*

58. Schiff and Lewin, "Where Traditional Budgeting Fails," pp. 51-62.

59. Mohamed Onsi, "Factor Analysis of Behavioral Variables Affecting Budgetary Slack," *Accounting Review* (July 1973): 535-548.

60. Ibid., p. 536.

61. Ibid., p. 539.

62. Ibid., p. 546.

63. Cortlandt Cammann, "Effects of the Use of Control Systems," *Accounting, Organizations and Society* (January 1976): 301-313.

64. Kenneth A. Merchant, "Budgeting and the Propensity to Create Budgetary Slack," *Accounting, Organizations and Society* (May 1985): 201-210.

65. Richard M. Cyert, J. G. March, and W. H. Starbuck, "Two Experiments on Bias and Conflict in Organizational Estimation," *Management Science* (April 1961): 254-264.

66. Lowe and Shaw, "An Analysis of Managerial Biasing,"

67. Dalton, *Men Who Manage.*

68. R. M. Barefield, "A Model of Forecast Biasing Behavior," *Accounting Review* (July 1970): 490-501.

69. J. S. Demski and G. A. Feltham, "Economic Incentives in Budgetary Control Systems," *Accounting Review* (April 1978): 336-359.

70. Y. Ijirir, J. Kinard, and F. Putney, "An Integrated Evaluation System for Budget Forecasting and Operating Performance with a Classified Budgeting Bibliography," *Journal of Accounting Research* (Spring 1978): 103-121; P. Jennergren, "On the Design of Incentives in Business Firms- A Survey of Some Research," *Management Science* (February 1980): 180-201; M. Weitzman, "The New Soviet Incentive Model," *Bell Journal of Economics* (Spring 1976): 251-257.

71. Mark S. Young, "Participative Budgeting: The Effects of Risk Aversion and Asymmetric Information on Budgetary Slack," *Journal of Accounting Research* (Autumn 1985): 829-842.

72. Ibid., pp. 831-832.

73. C. Chow, J. Cooper, and W. Waller, "Participative Budgeting: Effects of a Truth-Inducing Pay Scheme and Information Asymmetry on Slack and Performance" (Working paper, 1986).

74. William S. Waller, "Slack in Participative Budgeting: The Joint Effect of a Truth-Inducing Pay Scheme and Risk Preferences," *Accounting, Organizations and Society* (December 1987): 87-98.

75. Ibid., p. 88.

76. J. Berg, L. Daley, J. Dickhaut, and J. O'Brien, "Controlling Preferences for Lotteries on Units of Experimental Exchange," *Quarterly Journal of Economics* (May 1986): 281-306.

77. E. Aronson and D. R. Mettee, "Dishonest Behavior as a Function of Differential Levels of Induced Self-Esteem," *Journal of Personality and Social Psychology* (January 1968): 121-127.

78. Ahmed Belkaoui, "Slack Budgeting, Information Distortion and Self-Esteem," *Contemporary Accounting Research* (Fall 1985): 111-123.

79. Kari Lukka, "Budgetary Biasing in Organizations: Theoretical Framework and Empirical Evidence," *Accounting, Organizations and Society* (February 1988): 281-301.

80. Ibid., p. 292.

81. David T. Otley, "The Accuracy of Budgetary Estimates: Some Statistical Evidence," *Journal of Business Finance and Accounting* (Fall 1985): 416.

82. W. H. Read, "Upward Communication in Industrial Hierarchies," *Human Relations* (1962): 3-16.

83. G. H. Hofstede, *The Game of Budget Control* (London: Tavistock, 1968); A. G. Hopwood, "An Empirical Study of the Role of Accounting Data in Performance Evaluation," supplement to *Journal of Accounting Research* (1972): 156-182; David T. Otley, "Budget Use and Managerial Performance," *Journal of Accounting Research* (Spring 1978): 122-149.

84. R. M. Barefield, "Comments on a Measure of Forecasting Performance," *Journal of Accounting Research* (Autumn 1969): 324-327; Otley, "The Accuracy of Budgetary Estimates."

85. G. S. Man, "Reducing Budget Slack," *Journal of Accounting* (August 1988): 118-122.

86. Ibid., p. 119.

APPENDIX TO CHAPTER 7
PLANNING, BUDGETING, AND
INFORMATION DISTORTION

INTRODUCTION

In both the process of planning and budgeting, managers may be tempted to distort the information in a process better known as slack behavior. Richard M. Cyert and James G. March advanced the concept of organizational slack as a hypothetical construct to explain overall organizational phenomena.[1] Arie Y. Lewin and Carl Wolf, on the other hand, have made the following warning: "Slack is a seductive concept; it 'explains' too much and 'predicts' too little."[2] Indeed, slack research needs to be categorized along more precise dimensions that better explain its nature and its impact. Accordingly, this chapter reviews the research on slack by differentiating between *organizational slack* and *budgetary slack*.

VIEWS OF SLACK

Slack arises from the tendency of organizations and individuals to refrain from using all the resources available to them. It describes a tendency to not operate at peak efficiency. In general, two types of slack have been identified in the literature, namely organizational slack and budgetary slack. Organizational slack basically refers to an unused capacity, in the sense that the demands put on the resources of the organization are less than the supply of these resources. Budgetary slack is found in the budgetary process and refers to the intentional distortion of information that results from an understatement of budgeted sales and an overstatement of budget costs.

The concepts of organizational slack and budgetary slack appear in other literature under different labels. Economists refer to an X-inefficiency in instances where resources are either not used to their full capacity or effectiveness or are used in an extremely wasteful manner, as well as in instances where managers fail to make costless improvements. X-inefficiency is to be differentiated from allocative inefficiency, which refers to whether or not prices in a market are of the right land, that is, whether they allocate input and output to those users who are willing to pay for them.[3] Categories of inefficiency of a nonallocative nature, or X-inefficiency, include inefficiency in (1) labor utilization, (2) capital utilization, (3) time sequence, (4) extent of employee cooperation, (5) information flow, (6) bargaining effectiveness, (7) credit availability utilization, and (8) heuristic procedures.[4]

Agency theory also refers to slack behavior. The problem addressed by the agency theory literature is how to design an incentive contract such that the total gains can be maximized, given (1) information asymmetry between principal and agent, (2) pursuit of self-interest by the agent, and (3) environmental uncertainty affecting the outcome of the agent's decisions.[5] Slack can occur when managers dwell in an "excess consumption of perquisites" or in a "tendency to shrink." Basically, slack is the possible "shrinking" behavior of an agent.[6]

The literature in organizational behavior refers to slack in terms of defensive tactical responses and deceptive behavior. By viewing organizations as political environments, the deceptive aspects of individual power-acquisition behavior become evident.[7] A variety of unobstrusive tactics in the operation of power,[8] covert intents and means of those exhibiting power-acquisition behaviors,[9] and a "wolf in sheep's clothing" phenomenon, whereby individuals profess a mission or goal strategy while practicing an individual-maximization strategy,[10] characterize these deceptive behaviors, which are designed to present an illusionary or false impression. V. E. Schein has provided the following examples of deceptive behaviors in communication, decision making, and presentation of self.

Communication With regard to written or oral communications, there may be an illusion that these communications include all the information or that these communications are true, which masks the reality of either of them consisting of only partial information or of their actually distorting the information.

Decision making. A manager may present the illusion that he is actually compromising or giving in with regard to a decision, whereas in reality he is purposely planning to lose this particular battle with the long-range objective of winning the war. Or a manager or a subunit may initiate a particular action and then work on plans and activities for implementing a program. This intensive planning and studying, however, may in reality be nothing more than a delaying tactic, during which delay the actual program will die or be forgotten. Underlying this illusion that one is selecting subordinates, members of boards of directors, or successors on the basis of their competency may be the reality that these individuals are selected for loyalty, compliancy, or conformity to the superior's image.

Presentation of self. Many managers exude an apparent confidence, when in reality they are quite uncertain. Still other managers are skilled in organizing participatory group decision-making sessions, which in reality have been set up to produce a controlled outcome.[11]

Schein then hypothesized that the degree to which these behaviors are deceptive seems to be a function of both the nature of the organization and the lands of power exhibited (work-related or personal).[12] She relied on Cyert and March's dichotomization of organizations as either low- or high-slack systems.[13] Low-slack systems are characterized by a highly competitive environment that requires rapid and nonroutine decision making on the part of its members and a high level of productive energy and work outcomes to secure an effective performance. High-slack systems are characterized by a reasonably stable environment that requires routine decision making to secure an effective performance. Given these dichotomizations, Schein suggested that:

1. The predominant form of power acquisition behavior is personal in a high-slack organization and work-related in a low-slack organization.
2. The underlying basis of deception is an inherent covert nature of personal power acquisition behaviors in a high-slack organization and an organization['s] illusion as to how work gets done in a low-slack organization.
3. The benefits of deception to members are the provisions of excitement and personal rewards in a a high-slack organization and the facilitation of work accomplishment and organizational rewards in a low-slack organization.
4. The benefits of deception to organization are to foster [the] illusion of a fast-paced, competitive environment in a high-slack organization

and to maintain an illusion of workability of the formal structure in a low-slack organization.[14]

ORGANIZATIONAL SLACK
Nature of Organizational Slack

There is no lack of definitions for organizational slack, as can be seen from the definitions provided by Cyert and March,[15] Child,[16] M. D. Cohen, March, and J. P. Olsen,[17] March and Olsen,[18] D. E. Dimmick and V. V. Murray,[19] R. J. Litschert and T. W. Bonham,[20] and March.[21]

What appears from these definitions is that organizational slack is a buffer created by management in its use of available resources to deal with internal as well as external events that may arise and threaten an established coalition. Slack, therefore, is used by management as an agent of change in response to changes in both the internal and external environments.

Cyert and March's model explains slack in terms of cognitive and structural factors.[22] It provides the rationale for the unintended creation of slack. Individuals are assumed to "satisfice," in the sense that they set aspiration levels for performance rather than a maximization goal. These aspirations adjust upward or downward, depending on actual performance, and in a slower fashion than actual changes in performance. It is this lag in adjustment that allows excess resources from superior performance to accumulate in the form of organizational slack. This slack is then used as a stabilizing force to absorb excess resources in good times without requiring a revision of aspirations and intentions regarding the use of these excess resources. "By absorbing excess resources it retards upward adjustment of aspirations during relatively good times . . . by providing a poll of emergency resources, it permits aspirations to be maintained during relatively bad times."[23]

Oliver E. Williamson has proposed a model of slack based based on managerial incentives.[24] This model provides the rationale for managers' motivation and desire for slack resources. Under conditions where managers are able to pursue their own objectives, the model predicts that the excess resources available after target levels of profit have been reached are not allocated according to profit-maximization rules. Organizational slack becomes the means by which a manager achieves his or her personal goals, as characterized by four motives: income, job security, status, and discretionary control over resources. Williamson makes the assumption that the manager is motivated to maximize his or her personal goals subject to satisfying organizational objectives and that the manager achieves this by maximizing slack resources under his or her control. Williamson has suggested that there are four levels of profits: (1) a maximizing profit equal to the profit the firm would achieve when marginal revenue equals marginal cost, (2) actual profit equal to the true profit achieved by the firm, (3) reported profit equal to the accounting profit reported in the annual report, and (4) minimum profit equal to the profit needed to maintain the organizational coalition. If the market is noncompetitive, various forms of slack emerge: (1) *slack absorbed as staff* equal to the difference between maximum profit and actual profit, (2) *slack in the form of cost* equal to the difference between reported and minimum profits, and (3) *discretionary spending for investment* equal to the difference between reported and minimum profits.

Income smoothing can be used to substantiate the efforts of management to neutralize environmental uncertainty and to create organizational slack by means of an accounting manipulation of the level of earnings. J. Y. Kamin and J. Ronen have related organizational slack to income smoothing by reasoning that the decisions that affect the allocation costs- such as budget negotiations, which often result in slack accumulation- are aimed at smoothing earnings.[25] They hypothesized that management-controlled firms were more likely to be engaged in smoothing as a manifestation of managerial discretion and slack. "Accounting" and "real" smoothing were tested by observing the behavior of discretionary expenses vis-à-vis the behavior of income numbers. Their results showed that (1) a majority of the firms behaved as if they were income smoothers and (2) a particularly strong majority was found among management-controlled firms with high barriers to entry. This line of reasoning was pursued by Ahmed Belkaoui and

R. D. Picur.[26] Their study tested the effects of the dual economy on income-smoothing behavior. It was hypothesized that a higher degree of smoothing of income numbers would be exhibited by firms in the periphery sector than by firms in the core sector in reaction to different opportunity structures and experiences. Their results indicated that a majority of the firms may have been resorting to income smoothing. A higher number were found among firms in the periphery sector.

Lewin and Wolf proposed the following statements as a theoretical framework for understanding the concept of slack:

1. Organizational slack depends on the availability of excess resources.
2. Excess resources occur when an organization generates or has the potential to generate resources in excess of what is necessary to maintain the organizational coalition.
3. Slack occurs unintentionally as result of the imperfection of the resource allocation decision-making process.
4. Slack is created intentionally because managers are motivated to maximize slack resources under their control to ensure achievement of personal goals subject to the achievement of organizational goals.
5. The disposition of slack resources is a function of a manager's expense preference function.
6. The distribution of slack resources is an outcome of the bargaining process setting organization and reflects the discretionary power of organization members in allocating resources.
7. Slack can be present in a distributed or concentrated form.
8. The aspiration of organizational participants for slack adjusts upward as resources become available. The downward adjustment of aspirations for slack resources, when resources become scarce, is resisted by organizational participants.
9. Slack can stabilize short-term fluctuations in the firm's performance.
10. Beyond the short term, the reallocation of slack requires a change in organizational goals.
11. Slack is directly related to organizational size, maturity, and stability of the external environment.[27]

Functions of Organizational Slack

Because the definition of slack is often intertwined with a description of the functions that slack serves, L. J. Bourgeois discussed these functions as a means of making palpable the ways of measuring slack.[28] From a review of the administrative theory literature, he identified organizational slack as an independent variable that either "causes" or serves four primary functions: "(1) as an inducement for organizational actors to remain in the system, (2) as a resource for conflict resolution, (3) as a buffering mechanism in the work flow process, or (4) as a facilitator of types or creative behavior within the organization."[29]

The concept of slack as an inducement to maintain the coalition was first introduced by C. I Barnard in his treatment of the inducement/contribution ratio (I/C) as a way of attracting organizational participants and sustaining their membership.[30] March and H. A. Simon later described slack resources as the source of inducements through which the inducement/contribution ratio might exceed a value of one, which is equivalent to paying an employee more than would be required to retain his or her services.[31] This concept of slack was then explicitly introduced by Cyert and March as consisting of payments to members of the coalition in excess of what is required to maintain the organization.[32]

Slack as a resource for conflict resolution was introduced in L. R. Pondy's goal model.[33] In this model subunit goal conflicts are resolved partly be sequential attention to goals and partly by adopting a decentralized organizational structure. A decentralized structure is made possible by the presence of organizational slack.

A notion of slack as a technical buffer from the variances and discontinuities caused by environmental uncertainty was proposed by J. D. Thompson.[34] It was also acknowledged in Pondy's system model, which described conflict as a result of the lack of buffers between interdependent parts of an organization.[35] Jay Galbraith saw buffering as an information-processing problem: "Slack resources are an additional cost to the organization or the customer. . . . The creation of slack resources, through reduced performance levels, reduces the amount of information that must be processed during task execution and prevents the over loading of hierarchical channels."[36]

According to Bourgeois, slack facilitates three types of strategic or creative behavior within the organization: (1) providing resources for innovative behavior, (2) providing opportunities for a satisficing behavior, and (3) affecting political behavior.[37]

First, as a facilitator of innovative behavior, slack tends to create conditions that allow the organization to experiment with new strategies[38] and introduce innovation.[39] Second, as a facilitator of suboptimal behavior, slack defines the threshold of acceptability of a choice, or "bounded search,"[40] by people whose bounded rationality leads them to satisfice.[41] Third, the notion that slack affects political activity was advanced by Cyert and March, who argued that slack reduces both political activity and the need for bargaining and coalition-forming activity.[42] Furthermore, W. G. Astley has argued that slack created by success results in self-aggrandizing behavior by managers who engage in political behavior to capture more than their fair share of the surplus.[43]

W. Richard Scott argued that lowered standards create slack-unused resources- that can be used to create ease in the system.[44] Notice the following comment: "Of course, some slack in the handling of resources is not only inevitable but essential to smooth operations. All operations require a margin of error to allow for mistakes, waste, spoilage, and similar unavoidable accompaniments of work."[45] But the inevitability of slack is not without consequences:

The question is not whether there is to be slack but how much slack is permitted. Excessive slack resource increase costs for the organization that are likely to be passed on to the consumer. Since creating slack resources is a relatively easy and painless solution available to organizations, whether or not it is employed is likely to be determined by the amount of competition confronting the organization in its task environment.[46]

Measurement of Organizational Slack

One problem in investing empirically the presence of organizational slack relates to the difficulty of securing an adequate measurement of the phenomenon. Various methods have been suggested. In addition to these methods, eight variables that appear in public data, whether they are created by managerial actions or

made available by environment, may explain a change in slack.[47]
The model, suggested by Bourgeois, is as follows:

Slack = f(RE, DP, G&A WC/S, D/E, CR, I/P, P/E)

where:

RE = Retained earnings

DP = Dividend payout

G&A = General and administrative expense

WC/S = Working capital as a percentage of sales

D/E = Debt as a percentage of equity

CR = Credit Rating

I/P = Short-term loan interest compared to prime rate

P/E = Price/earnings ratio.

Here RE, G&A, WC/S, and CR are assumed to have a positive effect on changes in slack, whereas DP, D/E, P/E, and I/P are assumed to have a negative effect on changes in slack.

Some of these measures have also been suggested by other researchers. For example, Martin M. Rosner used profit and excess capacity as slack measures,[48] and Lewin and Wolf used selling, general, and administrative expenses as surrogates for slack.[49] Bourgeois and Jitendra V. Singh refined these measures by suggesting that slack could be differentiated on an "ease-or-recovery" dimension.[50] Basically, they considered excess liquidity to be *available slack*, not yet earmarked for particular uses. Overhead costs were termed *recoverable slack*, in the sense that they are absorbed by various organizational functions but can be recovered when needed elsewhere. In addition, the ability of a firm to generate resources from the environment, such as the ability to raise additional debt or equity capital, was considered *potential slack*. All of these measures were divided by sales to control for company size.

Building on Bourgeois and Singh's suggestions, Theresa K. Lant opted for the four following measures:

1. Administrative slack = (General and administrative expenses)/cost of goods sold
2. Available liquidity = (Cash + marketable securities – current liabilities)/sales
3. Retained earnings = (Net profit – dividends)/sales[51]

Lant used these measures to show empirically that (1) available liquidity and general and administrative expenses have significantly higher variance than profit across firms and across time and (2) the mean change in slack is significantly greater than the mean change in profit. She concluded as follows:

These results are logically consistent with the theory that slack absorbs variance in actual profit. They also suggest that the measures used are reasonable measures for slack. Thus, it supports prior work which has used these measures, and implies that further large sample models using slack as a variables feasible since financial information is readily available for a large number of firms. Before these results can be generalized, however, the tests conducted here should be replicated using different samples of firms from a variety of industries.[52]

BUDGETARY SLACK
Nature of Budgetary Slack

The literature on organizational slack shows that managers have the motives necessary to desire to operate in a slack environment. The literature on budgetary slack considers the budget as the embodiment of that environment and, therefore, assumes that managers will use the budgeting process to bargain for slack budgets. As stated by Schiff and Lewin, "Managers will create slack in budgets through a process of *understating revenues and over-stating costs*."[53] The general definition of budgetary slack, then, is the understatement of revenues and the overstatement of costs in the budgeting process. A detailed description of the creation of budgetary slack by managers was reported by Schiff and Lewin in their study of the budget process of three divisions of multidivision companies.[54] They found evidence of budgetary slack through underestimation of gross revenue, inclusion of discretionary increases in personnel requirements, establishment of marketing and sales budgets with internal limits on funds to be spent, use of manufacturing costs based on standard costs that do not reflect process improvements operationally available at the plant, and inclusion of discretionary "special projects."

Evidence of budgetary slack has also bee reported by others. A. E. Lowe and R. W. Shaw found a downward bias, introduced through sales forecasts by line managers, which assumed good performance where rewards were related to forecasts.[55] M. Dalton reported various examples of department managers allocating resources to what they considered justifiable purposes even though such purchases were not authorized in their budgets.[56] G. Shillinglaw noted the extreme vulnerability of budgets used to measure divisional performance given the great control exercised by divisional management in budget preparation and the reporting of results.[57]

Slack creation is a generalized organizational phenomenon. Many different organizational factors have been used to explain slack creation, in particular, organizational structure, goal congruence, control system, and managerial behavior. Slack creation is assumed to occur in cases where a Tayloristic organizational structure exists,[58] although it is also assumed to occur in a participative organizational structure.[59] It may be due to conflicts that arise between the individual and organizational goals, leading managers intentionally to create slack. It may also be due to the attitudes of management toward the budget and to workers' views of the budgets as a device used by management to manipulate them.[60] Finally, the creation of slack may occur whether or not the organization is based on a centralized or decentralized structure.[61] With regard to this last issue, Schiff and Lewin have reported that the divisional controller appears to have undertaken the tasks of creating and managing divisional slack and is most influential in the internal allocation of slack.

Budgeting and the Propensity to Create Budgetary Slack

The budgeting system has been assumed to affect a manager's propensity to create budgetary slack, in the sense that this propensity can be increased or decreased by the way in which the budgeting system is designed or complemented. Mohamed Onsi was the first to investigate empirically the connections between the type of budgeting system and the propensity to create budgetary slack.[62] From a review of the literature, he stated the following four assumptions:

1. Managers influence the budget process through bargaining for slack by understating revenues and overstating costs. . . .
2. Managers build up slack in "good years" and reconvert slack into profit in "bad years."
3. Top management is at a "disadvantage" in determining the magnitude of slack. . . .
4. The divisional controller in decentralized organizations participates in the task of creating and managing divisional slack.[63]

Personal interviews of thirty-two managers of five large national and international companies and statistical analysis of a questionnaire were used to identify the important behavioral variables that influence slack buildup and utilization. The questionnaire's variables were grouped into the following eight dimensions:

1. *Slack attitude* described by the variables indicating a manager's attitude to slack.
2. *Slack manipulation* described by the variables indicating how a manager builds up and uses slack.
3. *Slack institutionalization* described by the variables that make a manager less inclined to reduce his slack.
4. *Slack detection* described by the variables indicating the superior's ability to detect slack based on the amount of information he receives.
5. *Attitude toward the top management control system* described by the variables indicating an authoritarian philosophy toward budgeting being attributed to top management by divisional managers.
6. *Attitudes toward the divisional control system* described by variables on attitudes toward subordinates, sources of pressure, budget autonomy, budget participation, and supervisory uses of budgets.
7. *Attitudes toward the budget* described by variables on attitude toward the level of standards, attitude toward the relevancy of budget attainment to valuation of performance, and the manager's attitude (positive or negative) toward the budgetary system in general, as a managerial tool.
8. *Budget relevancy* described by variables indicating a manager's attitudes toward the relevancy of standards for his department's operation.[64]

Factor analysis reduced these dimensions to seven factors and showed a relationship between budgetary slack and what Onsi called "an authoritarian top management budgetary control system."

Thus, he stated: "Budgetary slack is created as a result of pressure and the use of budgeted profit attainment as a basic criterion in evaluating performance. Positive participation could encourage less need for building-up slack. However, the middle managers' perception of pressure was an overriding concern. The positive correlation between managers' attitudes and attainable level of standards is a reflection of this pressure."[65]

Cortlandt Cammann explored the moderating effects of subordinates' participation in decision making and the difficulty of subordinates' jobs based on their responses to different uses of control systems by their superiors.[66] His results showed that the use of control systems for contingent reward allocation produced defensive responses by subordinates under all conditions, which included the creation of budgetary slack. Basically, when superiors used budgeting information as a basis for allocating organizational rewards, their subordinates' responses were defensive. Allowing participation in the budget processes reduced this defensiveness.

Finally, Kenneth A. Merchant conducted a field study designed to investigate how managers' propensities to create budgetary slack are affected by the budgeting system and the technical context.[67] He hypothesized that the propensity to create budgetary slack is positively related to the importance placed on meeting budget targets and negatively related to the extent of participation allowed in budgeting processes, the degree of predictability in the production process, and the superiors' abilities to create slack. Unlike earlier studies that had drawn across functional areas, 170 manufacturing managers responded to a questionnaire measuring the propensity to create slack, the importance of meeting the budget, budget participation, the nature of technology in terms of work-flow integration and product standardization, and the ability of superiors to detect slack. The results suggested that managers' propensities to create slack (1) do vary with the setting and with how the budgeting system is implemented; (2) are lower where managers actively participate in budgeting, particularly when technologies are relatively predictable;

and (3) are higher when a tight budget requires frequent tactical responses to avoid overruns.

The three studies by Onsi, Cammann, and Merchant provide evidence that participation may lead to positive communication between managers so that subordinates feel less pressure to create slack. This result is, in fact, contingent on the amount of information asymmetry existing between the principals (superiors) and the agents (the subordinates). Although participation in budgeting leads subordinates to communicate or reveal some of their private information, leading to budgetary slack. Accordingly, Alan s. Dunk proposed a link between participation and budgetary slack through two variables: superiors' budget emphasis in their evaluation of subordinate performance and the degree of information asymmetry between superior and subordinates:[68] "When participation, budget emphasis, and information asymmetry are high (low), slack will be high (low)[69] participation, budget emphasis, and information asymmetry. The results are stated as follows: The results of this study show that the relation between participation and slack is contingent upon budget emphasis and information asymmetry, but in a direction contrary to expectations.

The results provide evidence for the utility of participative budgeting, and little support for the view that high participation may result in increased slack when the other two predictors are high. Although participation may induce subordinates to incorporate slack in budgets, the results suggest that participation alone may not be sufficient. The findings suggest that slack reduction results from participation, except when budget emphasis is low.[70]

Budgetary Slack, Information Distortion, and Truth-Inducing Incentives Schemes

Budgetary slack involves a deliberate distortion of input information. Distortion of input information in a budget setting arises, in particular, from the need of managers to accommodate their expectations about the kinds of payoffs associated with different possible outcomes. Several experiments have provided evidence of such distortion of input information. Cyert, March, and W. H. Starbuck showed in laboratory experiments that subjects adjusted the information they transmitted in a complex decision-making system to control their payoffs.[71] Similarly, Lowe and Shaw have shown that in cases where rewards were linked to forecasts, sales managers tended to distort the input information and to induce biases in their sales forecast.[72] Dalton also provided some rich situational descriptions of information and allocated resources to what were perceived to be justifiable objectives.[73] Finally, given the existence of a payoff structure that can induce a forecaster to bias intentionally his or her forecast, R. M. Barefield provided a model of forecast behavior that showed a "rough" formulation of a possible link between a forecasters' biasing and the quality of the forecaster as a source of data for an accounting system.[74]

Taken together, these studies suggest that budgetary slack, through systematic distortion of input information, can be used to accommodate the subjects' expectations about the payoffs associated with various possible outcomes. They fail, however, to provide a convincing rationalization of the link between distortion of input information and the subjects' accommodation of their expectations. Agency theory and issues related to risk aversion may provide such a link. Hence, given the existence of divergent incentives and information asymmetry between the controller (or employer) and the controllee (or employee) and the high cost of observing employee skill or effort, a budget-based employment contract (that is, where employee compensation is contingent on meeting the performance standard) can be Pareto-superior to fixed-pay or linear-sharing rules (where the employer and employee split the output).[75] However, the budget-based schemes impose a risk on the employee, as job performance can be affected by a host of uncontrollable factors. Consequently, risk-averse individuals may resort to slack budgeting through systematic distortion of input information. In practice, moreover, any enhanced (increased) risk aversion would lead the employee to resort to budgetary slack. One might hypothesize that, without proper incentives for truthful communication, the slack budgeting behavior could be reduced. One suggested avenue is the use of truth-inducing, budget-based schemes.[76] These schemes, assuming risk neutrality, motivate a worker to reveal private information truthfully about future performance and to maximize performance regardless of the budget.

Accordingly, Mark S. Young conducted an experiment to test the effects of risk aversion and asymmetrical information on slack budgeting.[77] Five hypotheses related to budgetary slack were developed and tested using a laboratory experiment. The hypotheses were as follows:

Hypothesis 1: A subordinate who participates in the budgeting process will build slack into the budget. . . .

Hypothesis 2: A risk-averse subordinate will build in more budget slack than a non-risk-averse subordinate. . . .

Hypothesis 3: Social pressure not to misrepresent productive capability will be greater for a subordinate whose information is known by management than for a subordinate having private information. . . .

Hypothesis 4: As social pressure increases for the subordinate, there is a lower degree of budgetary slack. . . .

Hypothesis 5: A subordinate who has private information builds more slack into the budget than a subordinate whose information is known by management.[78]

The results of the experiment confirmed the hypothesis that a subordinate who participates builds in budgetary slack and that slack is, in part, attributable to a subordinate's risk preferences. Given state uncertainty and a worker-manager information asymmetry about performance capability, the subjects in the experiment created slack even in the presence of a truth-inducing scheme. In addition, risk-averse workers created more slack than non-risk-averse workers did. Similarly, C. Chow, Cooper, and Waller's studies were found to have limitations.[80] With regard to Young's study, William S. Waller found three limitations: "First, unlike the schemes examined in the analytical research, the one used in his study penalized outperforming the budget, which limits its general usefulness. Second, there was no manipulation of incentives, so variation in slack due to incentives was not examined. Third, risk performances were measured using the conventional lottery technique of which the validity and reliability are suspect."[81] With regard to Chow, Cooper, and Waller's study. Waller found the limitations to be the assumption of state certainty and the failure to take risk preference into account. Accordingly, Waller conducted an experiment under which subjects participatively set budgets under either a scheme with an incentive for creating slack or a truth-incentive scheme like those examined in the analytic research. In addition, risk neutrality was induced for one half of the subjects and constant, absolute risk aversion for the rest, using a technique discussed by J. Berg, L. Daley, J. Dickhaut, and J. O'Brien that allows the experimenter to induce (derived) utility functions with any shape.[82] The results of the experiment show that when a conventional truth-inducing scheme is introduced, slack decreases for risk-neutral subjects but not for risk-averse subjects. Added to the evidence provided by the other studies, this study indicates that risk preference is an important determinant of slack, especially in the presence of a truth-inducing scheme.

Basically, there is preliminary evidence that risk-averse workers create more budgetary slack than risk-neutral ones. In addition, "truth inducing incentive schemes" reduce budgetary slack for risk-neutral subjects but not for risk-averse subjects. It seems that resource allocations within organizations are mediated by perceptions of risk, where risk is a stable personal trait. Accordingly, D. C. Kim tested whether risk preferences are domain-specific; that is, latent risk preferences translate into differing manifest risk preferences according to the context.[83] He relied on an experiment simulating the public accountants' budgeting of billable bonus to test the hypothesis that subject preference for tight or safe budget behavior depends on the performance of co-workers and domain-specific risk preferences. The results supported the view that subordinates' risk preferences are influenced by a situation-dependent variable. As stated by Kim: "The reversal of risk preferences around a neutral reference point is statistically significant for both dispositionally risk-averse and dispositionally risk-seeking subjects. The dispositional variable also contributes to the explanation of variation in subjects' manifest risk preferences. Thus the propensity to induce budgetary slack seems to be a joint function of situations and dispositions."[84]

Budgetary Slack and Self-Esteem

The enhancement of risk aversion and the resulting distortion of input information can be more pronounced when self-esteem is threatened. It was found that persons who have low opinions of themselves are more likely to cheat than persons with higher self-esteem.[85] A situation of dissonance was created in an experimental group by giving out positive feedback about a personality test to some participants and negative feedback to others. All the participants who received a blow to their self-esteem cheated more often than those who had received positive feedback about themselves. Could it also be concluded that budgetary slack through information distortion may be a form of dishonest behavior, arising from the enhancement of risk aversion caused by a negative feedback on self-esteem? A person's expectations can be an important determinant of his or her behavior. A negative impact on self-esteem can lead an individual to develop an expectation of poor performance. At the same time, the individual who is given negative feedback about his or her self-esteem would be more risk averse than others and would be ready to resort to any behavior to cover the situation. Consequently, the person may attempt to distort the input information in order to have an attainable budget. Belkaoui accordingly tested the hypothesis that individuals given negative feedback about their self-esteem would introduce more bias into estimates than individuals given positive or neutral feedback about their self-esteem.[86] One week after taking a self-esteem test, subjects were provided with false feedback (either positive or negative) and neutral feedback about their self-esteem score. They were then asked to make two budgeting decisions, first one cost estimate and then one sales estimate for a fictional budgeting decision. The results showed that, in general, the individuals who were provided with information that temporarily caused them to lower their self-esteem were more apt to distort input information than those who were made to raise their self-esteem. It was concluded that whereas slack budgeting may be consistent with generally low self-esteem feedback, it is inconsistent with generally high or neutral self-esteem feedback.

Toward a Theoretical Framework for Budgeting

A theoretical framework aimed at structuring knowledge about biasing behavior was proposed by Kari Lukka.[87] It contains an explanatory model for budgetary biasing and a model for budgeting biasing at the organizational level.

The explanatory model of budgetary biasing at the individual level draws from the management accounting and organizational behavior literature and related behavioral research to suggest a set of intentions and determinants of budgetary biasing. Budgetary biasing is at the center of many interrelated and sometimes contradictory factors with the actor's intentions as the synthetic core of his or her behavior.

The model for budgetary biasing at the organizational level shows that the "bias contained in the final budget is not the result of the dialectics of the negotiations."[88] Whereas budgetary biases 1 and 2 are the original biases created in the budget by the controlling unit and the controlled unit, biases 3 and 4 are the final biases to end up in the budget after the budgetary negotiations, which are characterized by potential conflicts and power factors. The results of semistructured interviews at different levels of management of a large decentralized company verified the theoretical framework. The usefulness of this theoretical framework rests on further refinements and empirical testing.

Positive Versus Negative Slack

Although the previous sections have focused on budgetary, or positive, slack, budgetary bias is, in fact, composed of both budgetary slack and an upward bias, or a negative slack. Whereas budgetary slack refers to bias in which the budget is designed intentionally so as to make it easier to achieve the forecast, upward bias refers to overstatement of expected performance in the budget. David T. Otley has described the difference as follows: "Managers are therefore likely to be conservative in making forecasts when future benefits are sought (positive slack) but optimistic when their need for obtaining current approval dominates (negative slack)."[89]

Evidence for negative slack was first provided by W. H. Read, who shoed the mangers distort information to prove to their superiors that all is well.[90] He cited several empirical studies of budgetary control that indicated that mangers put a lot of effort and ingenuity into assuring that messages conveyed by budgetary information serve their own interests.[91] Following earlier research by Barefield, Otley argued that forecasts may be the mode, rather than the means, of peoples' intuitive probability distributions.[92] Given that the distribution of cost and revenue is negatively skewed, there will be a tendency for budget forecasts to become unintentionally biased in the form of negative slack. Data collected from two organizations verified the presence of negative slack.

Reducing Budgetary Slack: A Bonus-Based Technique

In general, firms use budgeting and bonus techniques to overcome slack budgeting. One such approach consists of paying higher rewards when budgets are set high and achieved, and lower rewards when budgets are either set high but not met or set low and achieved. G. S. Mann presented a bonus system that gave incentives for managers to set budget estimates as close to achievable levels as possible.[93] The following two formulas were proposed:

Formula 1 applies for bonus if actual performance is equal to or greater than budget.

(multiplier no. 2 X budget goal) + [multiplier no. 1 X (actual level achieved budget goal)]

Formula 2 applies for bonus if actual performance is less than budget.

(multiplier no. 2 X budget goal) + [multiplier no. 3 X (actual level achieved – budget goal)]

The three multipliers set by management served as factors in calculating different components of bonuses. They were defined as follows:

Multiplier no. 1 (which must be less than multiplier no. 2, and which in turn must be less than multiplier no. 3) is used when actual performance is greater than budget. It provides a smaller bonus per unit for the part of actual performance that exceeds the budgeted amount. . . .

Multiplier no. 2 is the rate per unit used to determine the basic bonus component. It is based on the budgeted level of activity which equals multiplier no. 2 times the budgeted level.

Multiplier no. 3 is the rate used to reduce the bonus when the achieved level is less than the budget (multiplier no. 3 times work of units by which actual performance fell short of budget).[94]

Exhibit Appendix 7.1.1 shows an illustration of the application of the method and the effect of variations in multipliers or bonuses. As the exhibit shows, the manager will be rewarded for accurate estimation of the level of rates. In addition, the multipliers can be set with greater flexibility for controlling the manager's estimates.

CONCLUSIONS

Organizational slack and budgetary slack are two hypothetical constructs to explain organizational phenomena that are prevalent in all forms of organizations. Evidence linking both constructs to organizational, individual, and contextual factors is growing and in the future may contribute to an emerging theoretical framework for an understanding of slack. Further investigation into the potential determinants of organizational and budgetary slack remains to be done. This effort is an important one because the behavior of slack is highly relevant to the achievement of internal economic efficiency in organizations. Witness the following comment: "The effective organization has more rewards at its disposal, or more organizational slack to play with, and thus can allow all members to exercise more discretion, obtain more rewards, and feel that their influence is higher."[95]

Exhibit Appendix 7.1
Reducing Slack through a Bonus System

(1)	(2)	(3)	(4) Bonus I	(5) Bonus II
Budget Sales	Actual Sales	State of Nature	Multiple No. 1 = $.05 Multiple No. 2 = $.10 Multiple No.3 = $.15	Multiple no. 1 = .01 Multiple no. 2 = .10 Multiple no. 3 = .30
200,000	180,000	Over estimation	$17,000	$14,000
200,000	200,000	Actual = Budget	20,000	20,000
200,000	220,000	Under estimation	21,000	22,000

NOTES

1. Richard M. Cyert and James G. March, eds., *A Behavioral Theory of the Firm* (Englewood Cliffs, NJ: Prentice-Hall, 1963).

2. Arie Y. Lewin and Carl Wolf, "The Theory of Organizational Slack: A Critical Review," *Proceedings: Twentieth International Meeting of TIMS* (1976): 648-54.

3. Harvey Leibenstein, "Allocative Efficiency vs. 'X-Efficiency," *American Economic Review* (June 1966): 392-415.

4. Harvey Leibenstein, "X-Efficiency: From Concept to Theory," *Challenge* (September-October 1979): 13-22.

5. Nandan Choudhury, "Incentives for the Divisional Manager," *Accounting and Business Research* (Winter 1985): 11-21.

6. S. Baiman, "Agency Research in Managerial Accounting: A Survey," *Journal of Accounting Literature* (Spring 1982): 154-213.

7. D. Packard, *The Pyramid Climber* (New York: McGraw-Hill, 1962); E. A. Buttler, "Corporate Politics: Monster of Friend?" *Generation* 3 (1971): 54-58, 74; A.N. Schoomaker, *Executive Career Strategies* (New York: American Management Association, 1971).

8. J. Pfeffer, "Power and Resources Allocation in Organizations," in *New Directions in Organizational Behavior*, ed. B. M. Shaw and G. R. Salancik (Chicago: St. Clair Press, 1977).

9. V. E. Schein, "Individual Power and Political Behaviors in Organizations: An Inadequately Explored Reality," *Academy of Management Review* (January 1977): 64-72.

10. B. Bozeman and W. Malpive, "Goals and Bureaucratic Decision-Making: An Experiment," *Human Relations* (June 1977): 417-29.

11. V. E. Schein, "Examining an Illusion: The Role of Deceptive Behaviors in Organizations," *Human Relations* (October 1979): 288-89.

12. Ibid., 290.

13. Cyert and March, *A Behavioral Theory of the Firm*.

14. Schein, "Examining an Illusion," 293.

15. Cyert and March, *A Behavioral Theory of the Firm.*

16. John Child, "Organizational Structure, Environment, and Performance: The Role of Strategic Choice," *Sociology* 6, no. 1 (1972): 2-22.

17. M. D. Cohen, J. G. March, and J. P. Olsen, "A Garbage Can Model of Organizational Choice," *Administrative Science Quarterly* 17, no. 1 (1972): 1-25.

18. J. G. March and J. P. Olsen, *Ambiguity and Choice* (Bergen, Ger.: Universitetsforlagt, 1976).

19. D. E. Dimmick and V. V. Murray, "Correlates of Substantive Policy Decisions in Organizations; The Case of Human Resource Management," *Academy of Management Journal* 21, no. 4 (1978): 611-23.

20. R. J. Litschert and T. W. Bonham, "A Conceptual Model of Strategy Formation," *Academy of Management Review* 3, no. 2 (1978): 211-19.

21. James G. March, interview by Stanford Business School Alumni Association, *Stanford GSB* 47, no. 3 (1978-79): 16-19.

22. Cyert and March, *A Behavioral Theory of the Firm.*

23. Ibid.

24. Oliver E. Williamson, "A Model of Rational Managerial Behavior," in *A Behavioral Theory of the Firm* ed. Richard M. Cyert and James G. March (Englewood Cliffs, NJ: Prentice-Hall, 1963); idem, *The Economics of Discretionary Behavior: Managerial Objectives in a Theory of the Firm* (Englewood Cliffs, NJ: Prentice-Hall, 1964).

25. J. Y. Kamin and J. Ronen, "The Smoothing of Income Numbers: Some Empirical Evidence on Systematic Differences among Management-Controlled and Owner-Controlled Firms," *Accounting, Organizations and Society* (October 1978): 141-57.

26. Ahmed Belkaoui and R. D. picur, "The Smoothing of Income Numbers: Some Empirical Evidence on Systematic Differences between Core and Periphery Industrial Sector," *Journal of Business Finance and Accounting* (Winter 1984): 527-45.

27. Lewin and Wolf, "Theory of Organizational Slack," 653.

28. L. J. Bourgeois, " On the Measurement of Organizational Slack," *Academy of Management Review* 6, no. 1 (1982): 29-39.

29. Ibid., 31.

30. C. I. Barnard, *Functions of the Executive* (Cambridge, MA: Harvard University Press, 1938).

31. James G. March and H. A. Simon, *Organizations* (New York: Wiley, 1958).

32. Cyert and March, *A Behavioral Theory of the Firm*, 36.

33. L. R .Pondy, "Organizational Conflict: Concepts and Models," *Administrative Science Quarterly* 12, no. 2 (1967): 296-320.

34. J. D. Thompson, *Organizations in Action* (New York: McGraw-Hill, 1967).

35. Pondy, "Organizational Conflict."

36. Jay Galbraith, *Designing Complex Organizations* (Reading, MA: Addison-Wesley, 1973), 15.

37. Bourgeois, "On the Measurement of Organizational Slack," 34.

38. D. C. Hambrick and C. C. Snow, "A Contextual Model of Strategic Decision Making in Organizations," in *Academy of Management Proceedings*, ed. R. L. Taylor, J. J. O'Connell, R. A. Zawala, and D. D. Warrick (1977): 109-12.

39. Cyert and March, *A Behavioral Theory of the Firm*.

40. March and Simon, *Organizations*.

41. H. A. Simon, *Administrative Behavior* (New York: Free Press, 1957).

42. Cyert and March, *A Behavioral Theory of the Firm*.

43. W. G. Astley, "Sources of Power in Organizational Life," in Ph.D. diss., University of Washington, 1978.

44. W. Richard Scott, *Organizations: Rational, Natural and Open Systems* (Englewood Cliffs, NJ: Prentice-Hall, 1981), 216.

45. Ibid.

46. Ibid.

47. Bourgeois, "On the Measurement of Organizational Slack," 38.

48. Martin M. Rosner, "Economic Determinant of Organizational Innovation," *Administrative Science Quarterly* 12 (1968): 614-25.

49. Arie Y. Lewin and Carl Wolf, "Organizational Slack: A Test of the General Theory," *Journal of Management Studies* (forthcoming).

50. L. J. Bourgeois and Jitendra V. Singh, "Organizational Slack and Political Behavior within Top Management Teams," working paper, Graduate School of Business, Stanford University, 1983.

51. Theresa K. Lant, "Modeling Organizational Slack: An Empirical Investigation," Stanford University Research Paper, no. 856, July 1986.

52. Ibid., 14.

53. Michael Schiff and Arie Y. Lewin, "The Impact of People on Budgets," *Accounting Review* (April 1970): 259-68.

54. Michael Schiff and Arie Y. Lewin, "Where Traditional Budgeting Fails," *Financial Executive* (May 1968): 51-62.

55. A. E. Lowe and R. W. Shaw, "An Analysis of Managerial Biasing: Evidence from a Company's Budgeting Process," *Journal of Management Studies* (October 1968): 304-15.

56. M. Dalton, *Men who Manage* (New York: Wiley, 1961), 36-38.

57. G. Shillinglaw, "Divisional Performance Review: An Extension of Budgetary Control," in *Management Controls: New Directors in Basic Research*, ed. C. P. Bonini, R. K. Jaedicke, and H. M. Wagner (New York: McGraw-Hill, 1964), 149-63.

58. C. Argyris, *The Impact of Budgets on People* (New York: Controllership Foundation, 1952), 25.

59. E. H. Caplan, *Management Accounting and Behavioral Sciences* (Reading, MA: Addison-Wesley, 1971).

60. Argyris, *The Impact of Budgets on People*.

61. Schiff and Lewin, "Where Traditional Budgeting Fails," 51-62.

62. Mohamed Onsi, "Factor Analysis of Behavioral Variables Affecting Budgetary Slack," *The Accounting Review* (July 1973): 535-48.

63. Ibid., 536.

64. Ibid., 539.

65. Ibid., 546.

66. Cortlandt Cammann, "Effects of the Use of Control Systems," *Accounting, Organizations and Society* (January 1976): 301-13.

67. Kenneth A. Merchant, "Budgeting and the Propensity to Create Budgetary Slack," *Accounting, Organizations and Society* (May 1985): 201-10.

68. Alan S. Dunk, "The Effect of Budget Emphasis and Information Asymmetry on the Relation between Budgetary Participation and Slack," *The Accounting Review* (April 1993): 400-410.

69. Ibid., 400.

70. Ibid., 408-9.

71. Richard M. Cyert, J. G. March, and W. H. Starbuck, "Two Experiments on Bias and Conflict in Organizational Estimation," *Management Science* (April 1961): 254-64.

72. Lowe and Shaw, "Analysis of Managerial Biasing."

73. Dalton, *Men who Manage*.

74. R. M. Barefield, "A Model of Forecast Biasing Behavior," *The Accounting Review* (July 1970): 490-501.

75. J. S. Demski and G. A. Feltham, "Economic Incentives in Budgetary Control Systems," *The Accounting Review* (April 1978): 336-59.

76. Y. Ijiri, J. Kinard, and F. Putney, "An Integrated Evaluation System for Budget Forecasting and Operating Performance with a Classified Budgeting Bibliography," *Journal of Accounting Research* (Spring 1968): 1-28; M. Loeb and W. Magat, "Soviet Success Indicators and the Evaluation of Divisional Performance," *Journal of Accounting Research* (Spring 1978): 103-21; P. Jennergren, "On the Design of Incentives in Business Firms- A Survey of Some Research," *Management Science* (February 1980): 180-20; M. Weitzman, "The New Soviet Incentive Model," *Bell Journal of Economics* (Spring 1976): 251-57.

77. Mark S. Young, "Participative Budgeting: The Effects of Risk Aversion and Asymmetric Information on Budgetary Slack," *Journal of Accounting Research* (Autumn 1985): 829-42.

78. Ibid., 831-32.

79. C. Chow, J. Cooper, and W. Waller, "Participative Budgeting: Effects of a Truth-Inducing Pay Scheme and Information Asymmetry on Slack and Performance," working paper. University of Arizona, Tucson, 1986.

80. William S. Waller, "Slack in Participative Budgeting: The Joint Effect of a Truth-Inducing Pay Scheme and Risk Preferences," *Accounting Organizations and Society* (December 1987): 87-98.

81. Ibid., 88.

82. J. Berg, L. Daley, J. Dickhaut, and J. O'Brien, "Controlling Preferences for Lotteries on Units of Experimental Exchange," *Quarterly Journal of Economics* (may 1986): 281-306.

83. D. C. Kim, "Risk Preferences in Participative Budgeting," *The Accounting Review* (April 1992): 303-18.

84. Ibid., 304.

85. E. Aronson and D. R. Mettee, "Dishonest Behavior as a Function of Differential Levels of Induced Self-Esteem," *Journal of Personality and Social Psychology* (January 1968): 121-27.

86. Ahmed Belkaoui, "Slack Budgeting, Information Distortion and Self-Esteem," *Contemporary Accounting Research* (Fall 1985): 111-23.

87. Kari Lukka, "Budgetary Biasing in Organizations: Theoretical Framework and Empirical Evidence," *Accounting Organizations and Society* (February 1988): 281-301.

88. Ibid., 292.

89. David T. Otley, "The Accuracy of Budgetary Estimates: Some Statistical Evidence," *Journal of Business Finance and Accounting* (Fall 1985): 416.

90. W. H. Read, "Upward Communication in Industrial Hierarchies," *Human Relations* (1962): 3-16.

91. G. J. Hofstede, *The Game of Budget Control* (London: Tavistock, 1968); A. G. Hopwood, "An Empirical Study of the Role of Accounting Data in Performance Evaluation," supplement to

Journal of Accounting Research (1972): 156-82; David T. Otley, "Budget Use and Managerial Performance," *Journal of Accounting Research* (Spring 1978): 122-49.

92. R. M Barefield, "Comments on a Measure of Forecasting Performance," *Journal of Accounting Research* (Autumn 1969): 324-27; Otley, "Accuracy of Budgetary Estimates."

93. G. S. Mann, "Reducing Budget Slack," *Journal of Accountancy* (August 1988): 118-22.

94. Ibid., 119.

95. Charles Perrow, *Complex Organizations: A Critical Essay* (Glenview, IL: Scott, Foresman, 1972), 140.

CHAPTER 8
COGNITIVE RELATIVISM

INTRODUCTION

What happens when people make decisions about a phenomenon, amid the pressures, constraints, dangers, and opportunities of today's environment?[1] This chapter presents a model which focuses on the cognitive processes employed by a decision maker attempting to use his/her judgment to make a decision about a phenomenon. Basically, both judgment and decision are the products of a set of social cognitive operations that include the observation of information on the phenomenon and the formation of a schema to represent the phenomenon that is stored in memory and later retrieved when needed to allow the formation of a judgment and a decision. Before presenting the model an elaboration on the notion and use of schemata in cognitive psychology is necessary.

SCHEMATA IN COGNITIVE PSYCHOLOGY
The Notion of Schema-Guided Processes

The schema theory as developed by F. C. Bartlett[2] served as the stimulus for all schema theories. As defined by Bartlett, a schema is "an active organization of past reactions, or past experiences, which must always be supposed to be operating in any well-adapted organic response."[3] They are complex unconscious knowledge, as "masses of organized past experiences."[4] They are generic cognitive representations, in the sense that they constitute a process that can deal with an indefinitely large number of new instances.

Modern views of schemata refer generally to cognitive structures that represent organized knowledge about a given concept or a given stimulus and that serve as mechanisms for the interaction of old knowledge and new knowledge in perception, language, thought, and memory.

Schemata are generally regarded as fundamental elements upon which all information processing depends. They constitute a theory about knowledge: how knowledge is represented, and how that representation facilitates the use of knowledge in numerous ways. As stated by D. E. Rumelhart, "schemata are employed in the process of interpreting sensory data, in retrieving information from memory, in organizing actions, in the determining of goals and sub-goals, in the allocation of resources and generally in guiding the flow of processing in the system."[5] In fact, useful analyses of schemata suggested by Rumelhart include plays, theories, procedures, and parsers.[6] Properties of schemas include the following:

1. A schema represents a prototypical abstraction of the complex concept it represents.
2. A schema is induced from past experiences with numerous exemplars of the complex concept it represents.
3. A schema can guide the organization of incoming information into clusters of knowledge that are "instantiations" of the schema itself.
4. When one of the constituent concepts of a schema is missing in the input, its features can be inferred from "default values" in the schema.[7]

Schemata versus Categories

Jean Randler made an unusual distinction between two types of representations- categories and schemata. Categories are denoted by verbal or nonverbal symbols (i.e., "names") and are represented by a set of features that serve as the basis for inferring membership in it. Schemata, on the other hand, are cognitive representations whose features, like those of categories, are organized according to specific a priori spatial, temporal, or logical criteria.[8] Categories and schemata function differently. As Robert S. Wyer and S. E. Gordon note:

Information about a set of attributes processed by the members of a particular category may not spontaneously activate this category unless either (a) the attributes are very strongly and uniquely associated with it, (b) one has a specific objective that leads the object being described to be classified, or (c) a category and its characteristic features are already activated at the time the information is received. . . . In contrast, information that describes the characteristic features of a schema may become more inclined to activate the schema spontaneously.[9]

Schema Growth and Change

In considering schema growth and change the evidence favors a perseverance effect whereby generic schemata are resistant to change even in the face of contrary evidence.[10] In fact, people may even interpret expectations as proving given schema,[11] unless they are asked to counter-argue it, to explain why their favorite theory might be wrong.[12]

Schemata are developed from experience with instances of the category in question and become more complex, more abstract, and more organized with experience. With increasing experience a schema becomes more mature and more complex. Hence, the schemata of experts contain more informational elements than those of novices, are more organized, contain more links, and may have a more complex hierarchy.[13-15]

Sources of Activation for Schemas

D.G. Bobrow and D. A. Norman distinguish between two basic sources of activation for schemata: conceptually driven and data-driven processing.[16] In conceptually driven processing, and activated schema in turn activates a subschemata with the expectation that this will account for some portion of the input data. In data-driven processing, the activated subschema causes the activation of the various schemas of which it is a component. Data-driven processing goes from part to the whole. In another source of activation, known as schema-directed processing, the activation is assumed to go in both directions. It proceeds as follows:

Some events occur at the sensory system. The occurrence of this event "automatically activates certain low level" schemata (much schemata might be called "*feature detectors*"). The low level schemata, in turn, activates (in a data driven fashion) certain of the "higher level" schemata (the most probable ones) of which they are constituents. These "higher level" schemata then initiate conceptually driven processing by activating the subschemata not already activated in an attempt to evaluate their goodness of fit.[17]

Encoding of Information in a Schema

For W. F. Brewer and G. V. Nakamura, the interaction of old knowledge with new knowledge involves two processes: one refers to the modification of the generic knowledge in the relevant schema, while the other refers to the construction of a specified instantiated memory representation, where the instantiated schema is the cognitive structure that results from the interaction of the old information and the new information from the episodic unit.[18]

The encoding of information is in fact subject to at least two interpretations. First, the interpretations proposed by R. S. Woodswork and H. Schlosberg[19] postulates that once a schema is activated by incoming episodic information, features that are inconsistent with the implications of this schema are appended to the representation of information as "corrections." A second conceptualization proposed by A. C. Graesser, S. E. Gordon, and J. D. Sawyer,[20] known as the "script-pointer-plus-tag" formulation, postulates that when people receive information that is interpretable in terms of a prototypic event schema (script), they do not retain the information itself but a "pointer" to the general script, along with an indication of the values of the information that instantiate the script variables. If features of the information do not match attributes of the generic script, and thus cannot be reconstructed, they are appended to the representations as "tags." Basically, new information is represented by a series of "pointers" to prototypic event schemata that can be used to understand or describe the event, accompanied when necessary by "tags" denoting objects or events that cannot be derived from the event schemata alone.

Social Schema Research

Social schema research investigates self-schemata, person schemata, script or event schemata, and person-in-situation schemata.[21]

The self-schema contains cognitive generalizations about the self that are derived from past experiences. People are generally self-schematic on dimensions that are of importance to them, on which they perceive themselves as extreme, and on which they perceive the opposite to be untrue.[22] They are schematic on those dimensions perceived to be of lesser importance to them.

Research on perception shows that people who are schematic on a particular dimension recognize and filter rapidly incoming information about the dimension, notice the dimension in other people, and think harder about kinds of schema-relevant information.[23]

Research on memory shows that self-schematic people remember schema-relevant information, are difficult to change, have more accessible knowledge about others because of the sheer familiarity of self-knowledge, and are more affect-laden in knowledge about others, especially unfamiliar individuals.[24,25]

Research on inference shows that people make rapid predictions about their own behavior that are consistent with their self-schemata.[26] Under certain circumstances these predictions take longer than for aschematics,[27] especially if the judgment is novel.

The person-schema contains cognitive generalizations about trait and behavior information common to certain groups or types of people.

Research on perception shows that categories for people, like categories for objects, are organized hierachically.[28] Research on memory shows that schemata for people's traits and goals typically help the perceiver to remember schema-consistent information in more detail than would be possible without the schemata. Research on inference shows that person schemata affect subsequent inferences.

The evidence on person schemata is summarized as follows: Person schemata include protypical representations of traits such as extroversion and introversion, as well as notions of what behavior is consistent with a given goal. Person schemata of all sorts shape the processes of perception, memory, and inference to conform to our general assumptions about other people. The effects of schemata on perception, memory and inference are not necessarily well suited to accuracy in identifying individual instances. Schemata are used by the mind to manage such processes economically, if not accurately.[29]

The script or event schema contains cognitive generalizations that describe the appropriate sequence of events in a given situation.[30] Research on script or event schemata is summarized as follows:

Script or event schema describe sequences of activity from everyday life. They contain props, roles and sequence rules. Scripts also may be subdivided into segments (scenes). Like other schemata, scripts guide the perception of ambiguous information and often shape memory toward schema consistent information. Inferences can be seen as filling in gaps where information was missing, and gap filling appears to be exaggerated by repeated encounters with the script. Most of the functions of scripts echo those of other schemata, in their focus on relevant- and usually on consistent- information in perception, memory and inference.[31]

The person-in-situation or role schema contains cognitive generalizations about people in situations or scripts for behavior in situations. Role schemata not only help perception, memory, and inference but may be a way to account for stereotyping.

Research on perception shows that categorization instantiates the stereotypic content of the schema whether or not the person fits the category and in the process minimizes the amount of variability and complexity that may exist in the category.[32,33] In addition to minimizing variability and complexity, a schema slants perception of the content of what a person does.

Research on memory shows that the role schema shapes memory in a schemata-consistent fashion. In addition, the categorical information seems to override the details of the specific instance.[34] Schema-discrepant information is, however, likely to receive added attention at input, if task conditions allow. Attentional processes can facilitate remembering inconsistent information.[35]

A COGNITIVE VIEW OF THE JUDGMENT/DECISION PROCESS

In what follows a model of the judgment/decision process is proposed as an exercise in social perception and cognition, requiring both formal and implicit judgment.[36] The primary input to this process is a problem or phenomenon that needs to be solved and requires a judgment preceding either a preference or a decision. The model consists of the following steps:

1. Observation of the accounting phenomenon by the decision maker
2. Schema formation or building of the phenomenon
3. Schema organization or storage

4. Attention and recognition process triggered by a stimulus
5. Retrieval of stored information needed for the judgment decision
6. Reconsideration and integration of retrieved information with new information
7. Judgment process
8. Decision/action response

Observation of the Phenomenon by the Decision Maker

The decision maker is assumed to have the opportunity to observe the phenomenon. To understand the phenomenon, the decision maker may be given some information which is deemed diagnostic. If this information if not provided, the decision maker may seek the information and test available information judged most relevant to the phenomenon. Following H. H. Kelly's approach to causal attribution,[37] the search behavior may concentrate on these types of available information:

1. *Consensus information:* how this phenomenon and other phenomena were rated or performed on given dimensions
2. *Distinctiveness information*: how this phenomenon was rated or performed on various other dimensions
3. *Consistency information*: how this phenomenon was rated or performed on important dimensions in the past

Evidence shows that subjects tend to focus more on distinctiveness or consistency information than on consensus information.[38]

The search behavior is not misguided. It is fair to assume that the decision maker has some expectations about the phenomenon which may determine the type of information sought. These expectations are termed *preconceived notions* in A. S. De Nisi et al.'s model.[39] They result from the decision maker's previous experiences with the phenomenon. These expectations or preconceived notions may bias the decision maker toward choosing some information rather than other information. Providing background information prior to observation contributes to this phenomenon.[40,41] R. S. Wyer and T. K. Srull maintain that prior information predisposes the subject to select one of a number of frames of references.[42] Bias is a result of the tendency to seek evidence confirming preconceived notions rather than neutral or disconfirming evidence.[43,44]

Schema Formation or Building

Once the phenomenon has been observed, the relevant information is encoded in the sense that it is categorized on the basis of experience and organized in memory along schemata or knowledge structures. As put by R. E. Nisbett and L. Ross:

Few, if any, stimuli are approached for the first time by the adult. Instead, they are processed through pre-existing systems of schematized and abstracted knowledge-beliefs, theories, propositions and schemas. These knowledge structures label and categorize objects and events quickly and, for the most part, accurately. They also define a set of expectations about objects and events and suggest appropriate responses to them.[45]

A schema can be simply an update of templates that existed prior to the occurrence of a known phenomenon or a new template generated by the occurrence of a new phenomenon. In the first case, little ambiguity is assumed to exist and therefore the encoding follows an automatic process.[46] In the second case, no immediate available schema exists, and a controlled categorization process is triggered to determine which schema is consistent with the dimensions of the phenomenon. Both processes are suggested in the case of the encoding of information or performance appraisal:

Thus, both the automatic and controlled processes have the same end result: the assignment of a person to a category based on prototype-matching process. The difference is whether the stimulus person's behavior is sufficiently consistent with other cues to allow the categorization to proceed automatically or whether a controlled process must be used to determine which category is consistent with the individual's behavior. The actual category assignment is a function of contextual factors influencing the salience of particular categories and stimulus characteristics, as well as individual differences among perceivers that render some categories and their prototypes more available than others and some stimulus features more salient than others.[47]

Basically, a phenomenon may be categorized in a given schema, by virtue of its possession of obvious or salient attributes known to the perceiver. When no salient category prototype or schema provides a natural framework, the automatic process is superseded by a controlled process or a consciously monitored process.[48]

The controlled process can be triggered by either a new phenomenon or new features of a known phenomenon that are inconsistent with a previous categorization. In the latter case a recategorization is invoked until the inconsistency is resolved and a new schema is used to describe the phenomenon, causing a reconstruction of memories about the phenomenon such that memories consistent with the new categorization are more available.

Schema Organization and Storage

After information about a given phenomenon is encoded to form a representation or schema, it is stored and maintained in long-term memory. E. Tulving distinguishes between episodic and semantic memory.[49] Basically, a person's episodic memories are personal while semantic memory is knowledge of words and symbols, their meanings and referent knowledge of the relations among words, and the rules or algorithms for manipulating words, symbols, and the relations among them. R. C. Atkinson and R. M. Schiffrin maintain that the basic structural features of episodic memory are three memory stores: the sensory register, the short-term store, and the long-term store.[50] Information enters the memory system through the various senses and goes first to the sensory register whose function is to preserve incoming information long enough for it to be selectively transmitted into the memory system. It is kept there less than a second and is lost either through decay or erasure by overwriting.

The information then goes to the short-term store, "working in memory" where conscious mental processes are performed. It is where consciousness exercises its function. Information can be kept indefinitely here provided that it is given constant attention; if not, it is lost through decay in twenty to thirty seconds.

The information next goes to the long-term store through a conscious or unconscious process where it can be held indefinitely and often permanently (although it can be lost due to decay or interference or various sorts). The long-term store is assumed to have unlimited capacity. In this multistore model information about the phenomenon moves through different and separate memory systems, ending with a long-term store where semantic information is maintained along meaning-based codes or schemata. It is important to realize at this stage that if the person intends to remember the phenomenon for all time, he/she must perform a different analysis on the input than when his/her intentions are temporary.[51] A person's intention determines whether the storage of the information on the phenomenon is permanent or temporary. A different coding is used: a memory code for permanent storage and a perceptual role for temporary storage.

Different codes have different permanence. Codes of the sensory aspects of an input, such as appearance, are short lived. hence, a person who looked at a word to decide whether it was printed in red or green would not remember the word's name very long because his coding would have emphasized color, not meaning. In contrast, a person who looked at a word to decide whether it was a synonym for some other word would form a semantic code, and he/she would remember the name of the examined word for quite a while.[52]

Stimulus and Attention and Recognition Processes

Upon observation of a triggering event or stimulus, the schema in the phenomenon is activated. The activation, as a process of detection, search, and attention, can be either a controlled or an automatic processing.[53]

Basically, automatic detection, triggered by the recognition of a stimulus, operates independently of the person's control. Automatic processing is the apprehension of stimuli by the use of previously learned routines that are in the long-term storage.

Automatic processing as learned in long-term store, is triggered by appropriate inputs, and then operates independently of the subject's control. An automatic sequence can contain components that control information flow, attract attention, or govern overt responses. Automatic sequences do not require attention, though they may attract it I training is appropriate, and they do not use up short-term capacity. They are learned following the earlier use of controlled processing that links the same nodes in sequence. In search, detection, and attention tasks, automatic detection develops when stimuli are consistently mapped to responses; then the targets develop the ability to attract attention and initiate responses automatically, immediately, and regardless of other input or memory load.[54]

In these automatic processes, no conscious effort is involved in the search as well as in demanding attention due to the learned sequence of the elements composing the schemata. On the other hand, controlled processes involve a temporary activation of novel sequences of processing steps that require attention, use short-term memory, and involve a conscious effort.

It is important to realize that in both processes, the use of schemata for encoding or retrieving information depends on accessibility in memory, where the accessibility of schemata is the probability that they can be activated, either for use in storage of incoming information or for retrieval of previously stored informaiton.[55,56]

Accessibility of a schema depends upon such factors as the strength of the stored information, the extent of the overlap or match between input and schema, and the recency and frequency of previous activations. Each time a schema is activated for use, it becomes more accessible for successive activations. The instrumental effort of an activation on the accessibility of a schema is presumably a decreasing function of its prior strength. That is, a weak schema benefits more from an activation than a strong one.[57]

Empirical evidence on the increased accessibility of information with the frequency of activation is available.[58,59]

Retrieval of Stored Information Needed for Judgment/Decision

Either the automatic or controlled search processes activate the appropriate schema for the phenomenon and allow the retrieved of information on the phenomenon. It is, however, the schema, a representation of the phenomenon, that is recalled rather than the actual phenomeon.[60,61] The effect becomes stronger as the time between observation and recall increases.[62]

The potential for different types of biases exists at this stage. For example, people may be more likely to recall information consistent with a schema confirming an expectation,[63] or may recall schema-consistent information which they never saw.[64] A good deal of evidence also suggests that schema-inconsistent information is more likely to be recalled[65] because of its novelty, saliency, and difficulty of incorporation into a schema.[66]

What is more likely to be recalled when faced with a phenomenon, what types of biases affect the recall of schemata of phenomena, and what can be done to reduce or eliminate the distortions in recall are some of the important questions in need of investigation. This model will assume that familiarity with the phenomenon through constant record keeping and other forms of monitoring may result in less biased recall. The solution, in fact, is more complex and depends on the type of relationship between memory and judgment. Reid Hastie and Bernadette Park investigated these relationships and distinguished between two types of judgment tasks, memory-based and on-line. They also identified five information-processing models that relate memory for evidence to judgment based on the evidence: (1) independent processing, (2) availability, (3) biased retrieval, (4) biased encoding, and (5) incongruity-biased encoding.[67]

With regard to the five information-processing models, the distinction is threefold: (1) cases where there is no relation between judgment and memory processes which include the independent processing model; (2) cases where memory availability cause judgment which include the availability-based information-processing model and the automatic search process described earlier; and (3) cases where judgment causes memory which include the biased retrieval, the biased encoding, and incongruity-biased encoding models. The biased retrieval model is selective in the sense that traces which "fit" the judgment are more likely to be found at the memory decision stage. Such biases have been termed *selective recall, confirmatory memory,* and *access-biased memory.*[68,69]

The biased encoding model assumes that biasing takes place at the time of the encoding of evidence information and memory search will locate a biased sample of information reflecting the initial encoding bias.

The incongruity-based encoding model assumes after the initial encoding, incoming information that is incongruent or contradictory is given special processing to enhance its memorability by being placed in "special tags" that strongly attach to memory. In memory search, the subject is more likely to find the incongruent information.[70,71]

This model assumes that where the phenomenon calls for an online task, the availability or automatic search model will characterize the retrieval of stored information needed for judgment decision. Selection of a processing model will depend on the individual objectives of the subject and the perceived consequences of his/her judgments on his/her economic and psychological welfare.

Reconsideration and Integration of Retrieved Information with Other Available Information

At this stage the process involves the integration of the information retrieved from memory and other available information into a single evaluation of the phenomenon.

Where familiarity with the phenomenon is present and previously learned routines are retrieved active integration will not take place. An earlier integration is recalled from past stored output on the phenomenon. "What was once accomplished by slow, conscious, deductive reasoning is now arrived at by fast, unconscious perceptual processing."[72]

Where the phenomenon presents challenging and novel dimensions and where controlled processes were involved in attention and recognition, a cognitive integration of all the information is required to reach a single evaluation of the phenomenon. G. Mandler describes the process of "response learning" as follows:

First, the organism makes a series of discrete responses, often interrupted by incorrect ones. However, once errors are dropped out and the sequence of behavior becomes relatively stable- as in running a maze, speaking a word, reproducing a visual pattern- the various components of the total behavior required in the situation are "integrated." Integration refers to the face that previously discrete parts of a sequence come to behave functionally as a unit; the whole sequence is elicited as a unit and behaves as a single component response has in the past; any part of it elicits the whole sequence.[73]

Brunswick's lens model and Anderson's weighted average model provide support to the types of integration of information that take place.[74] The integration process is, however, also subject to various biases:

1. People may attach and give great weight to some type of information. For example, evidence in the employee appraisal literature shows that negative information has greater weight.[75,76]
2. There is evidence of an underutilization or underweighting of base rate or consensus information.[77]
3. There is ample evidence of the effect of various heuristics involved in decisions on and about accounting phenomena. They include (1) representativeness, (2) availability, (3) confirmation bias, (4) anchoring and adjustment, (5) conjunction fallacy, (6) hindsight bias, (7) illusory correlation and contingency judgments, (8) selective perception, (9) frequency, (10) concrete information, (11) data presentation, (12) inconsistency, (13) conservation, (14) nonlinear extrapolation, (15) law of small numbers, (16) habit/ "rules of thumb," (17) "best-guess" strategy, (18) complexity in the decision environment, (19) social pressures in the decision environment, (20) consistency of information sources, (21) question format, (22) scale effects, (23) wishful thinking, (24) outcome-irrelevant learning structures, (25) misperceptions of chance fluctuations (Gambler's fallacy), (26) success/failure attributions, and (27) logical fallacies in recall.[78]

The Judgment Process

The judgment process is the result of the integration process of information and the forming of a single evaluation of the phenomenon if the attention, recognition, and integration processes are the result of controlled processes. The judgment made in this case requires a conscious access to all the mental processes implied in the model. If, however, the attention, retrieval recognition, and integration processes were the result of automatic processes, the judgment is not and will not be conscious. It does not require the conscious use of all the mental processes implied in this model.[79,80] It is a routine judgment.

Routine judgment involves the rapid matching of immediate perceptions to a template which provides, and executes, a specific response, "if total debts do not equal total credits, re-add the total balance."

In the above example, there is no awareness of how the brain actually decides that the debits do not equal the credits. Even if awareness were possible, it is not normally necessary- a great many of our routine activities, such as keeping our eyes open or holding our pencils, are done without any particular conscious awareness, at least until something causes us to become aware.[81]

Decision/Action (Response)

The final step of the model is the decision or selection of a response to the phenomenon. It is a conscious response preference resulting from the judgment process. It is an output of the judgment process and is clearly influenced by all the mental processes and biases described earlier. As a result, a new schema on the phenomenon will develop that will be part of the knowledge structure or the phenomenon stored in long-term memory.

The move from judgment to decision is a bridging process. It assumes that no obstacles stand in the way.

The decision/action has been investigated in various environments and using various phenomena. It has been found to differ from various normative decision models, including Bayerian-decision theory and expected value models.[82,83]

The bridging process, however, will be influenced by the cognitive steps described to his model as well as by other factors including the possible consequences of the decision on the phenomenon. Gibbins, for instances, cites the following factors:

Personal attitudes may play a direct role, much as determining priorities within the search process. For example, some public accountants may use financial return as their first selection criterion; others may use moral propriety as their first. Personal attitudes can also play an indirect role, limiting past actions and thus limiting the experiences on which judgment guides are built. The applications of such attitudes to the judgment process need to be conscious- particularly for deeply ingrained beliefs.[84]

CONCLUSIONS

The essence of cognitive relativism is the presence of a cognitive process that is assumed to guide the judgment/decision process. The model in this chapter shows that judgments and decisions made about a phenomena are the products of a set of social cognitive operations that include the observation of information on the phenomena and the formation of schemata that are stored in memory and later retrieved to allow the formation of judgments and/or decisions when needed.

NOTES

1. W. L. Felix, Jr., and W. R. Kinney, Jr., "Research in the Auditor's Opinion Formulation Process: State of the Art," *Accounting Review* (Apr. 1988); 245-71.

2. F. C. Bartlett, *Remembering* (London: Cambridge University Press, 1932).

3. Ibid., 201.

4. Ibid., 197-98.

5. D. E. Rumelhart, "Schemata and the Cognitive System," in R. S. Wyer, Jr., and T. K. Srull, eds., *Handbook of Social Cognition* (Hillsdale, N.J.: Erlbaum, 1984), 1: 162.

6. Ibid.

7. Perry W. Thoradyke and B. Hayes-Roth, "The Use of Schemata in the Acquisition and Transfer of Knowledge," *Cognitive Psychology* 11 (1979): 83.

8. Jean Mandler, "Categorical and Schematic Organization in Memory," in R. C. Ruff, *Memory, Organization and Structure* (New York: Academic Press, 1979).

9. Robert S. Wyer, Jr., and S. E. Gordon, "The Cognitive Representation of Social Information," in R. S. Wyer, Jr., and T. K. Srull, eds,. *Handbook of Social Cognition* (Hillsdale, N. J.: Erlbaum, 1984), 2:82.

10. L. Ross, M. R. Lepper, and M. Hubbard, "Perseverance in Self-Perception and Social Perception: Biased Attribution Processes in the Debriefing Paradigm," *Journal of Personality and Social Psychology* 32 (1975): 880-92.

11. C. A. Anderson, "Inoculation and Counter-Explanation: Debasing Techniques in the Perseverance of Social Theories," *Social Cognition* 1 (1982): 126-35.

12. W. G. Chase and H. A. Simon, "The Mind's Eye in Chess," in W. G. Chase, ed., *Visual Information Processing* (New York: Academic Press, 1982).

13. M. T. H. Chi and R. Koeske, "Network Representations of a Child's Dinosaur Knowledge," *Developmental Psychology* 19 (1983): 29-35.

14. J. H. Larkin, et al., "Models of Competence in Solving Physics Problems," *Science* 200 (1980): 1335-42.

15. K. B. McKeithen, et al., "Knowledge Organization and Skill Differences in Computer Programmers, *Cognitive Psychology* 13 (1981): 307-25.

16. D. G. Brobow and D. A. Norma, "Some Principles of Memory Schemata," in D. G. Bobrow and and A. M. Collins, ed., *Representations and Understanding: Studies in Cognitive Science* (New York: Academic Press, 1975): 25-32.

17. D. E. Rumelhart, "Schemata and the Cognitive System," in R. S. Wyer, Jr., and T. K. Srull, *Handbook of Social Cognition* (Hillsdale, N.J.: Erlbaum, 1984), 1:170.

18. W. F. Brewer and G. V. Nalsamura, "The Nature and Functions of Schemas," in R. S. Wyer, Jr. and T. K. Srull, *Handbook of Social Cognition*, (Hillsdale, N. J.: Erlbaum, 1984), 1:141.

19. R. S. Woodswork and H. Schlosberg, *Experimental Psychology* (New York: Holt, 1954).

20. A. C. Graesser, S. E. Gordon, and J. D. Sawyer, "Memory for Typical and Atypical Actions in Script Activities: Test of a Script Pointer + Tag Hypothesis," *Journal of Verbal Learning and Behavior* 18 (1979): 503-15.

21. S. E. Taylor, and J. Crocker, "Schematic Bases of Social Information Processing," in E. T. Higgins, C. P. Herman, and M. P. Zanna, eds., *Social Cognition: The Ontario Symposium*, vol. 1 (Hillsdale, N.J.: Erlbau, 1981).

22. H. Markus, "Self-Schemata and Processing Information about the Self," *Journal of Personality and Social Psychology* 38 (1980): 231-48.

23. H. Markus, and K. P. Sentis, "The Self in Social Information Processing," in J. Suls, ed., *Psychological Perspectives on the Self*, vol. 1 (Hillsdale, N.J.: Erlbaum, 1982).

24. J. A. Bargh, "Attention and Automaticity in the Processing of Self-Relevant Information," *Journal of Personality and Social Psychology* 43 (1982): 425-36.

25. T. J. Ferguson, B. G. Rule, and D. Carlson, "Memory for Personally Relevant Information," *Journal of Personality and Social Psychology* 44 (1983): 251-61.

26. H. Rankus, "Self-Schema DNA Processing Information about the Self," *Journal of Personality and Social Psychology* 35 (1977): 63-78.

27. N. A. Kuiper, "Convergent Evidence for the Self as a Prototype," *Personality and Social Psychology Bulletin* 7 (1981): 483-43.

28. N. Canton and W. Mischel, "Prototypes in Person Perception," in L. Berkowitz, ed., *Advances in Experimental Psychology*, vol. 12 (New York: Academic Press, 1979).

29. S. T. Fiske and S. E. Taylor, *Social Cognition* (New York: Random House, 1984), 154.

30. R. P. Abelson, "The Psychological Status of the Script Concept," *American Psychologist* 36 (1981): 715-25.

31. Fiske and Taylor, *Social Cognition*, 169.

32. R. S. Malpass, H. Lavingnern, and D. E. Weldon, "Verbal and Visual Training in Face Recognition," *Perception and Psychophysics* 14 (1973): 285-92.

33. P. W. Linville and E. E. Jones, "Polonized Appraisals of Outgroup Members," *Journal of Personality and Social Psychology* 36 (1978): 193-211.

34. S. E. Taylor, et al., "Categorical Bases of Person Memory and Stereotyping," *Journal of Personality and Social Psychology* 36 (1978): 778-93.

35. R. Hastie, "Memory for Behavioral Information That Confirms or Contradicts a Personality Impression," in R. Hastie, et al., eds., *Person Memory: The Cognitive Basis of Social Perception* (Hillsdale, N.J.: Erlbaum, 1981).

36. Similar models have been proposed for the performance appraisal process. See, e.g., A. S. De Nisi, T. P. Cafferty, and B. M. Meglino, "A Cognitive View of the Performance Appraisal Process: A Model and Research Proposition," *Organizational Behavior and Human Performance* 33 (1984): 360-96; J. M. Feldman, "Beyond Attribution Theory: Cognitive Processes in Performance Appraisal," *Journal of Applied Psychology* 66/2 (1981): 127-48.

37. H. H. Kelly, "Attributions in Social Interactions," in E. E. Jones et al., eds., *Attributions: Perceiving the Causes of Behavior* (Norristown, N.J.: General Learning Process, 1972).

38. B. Major, "Information Acquisition and Attribution Processes," *Journal of Personality and Social Psychology* 39 (1980): 1010-23.

39. De Nisi, Cafferty, and Meglino, "Performance Appraisal Decision," 367-68.

40. Hl Tajfel, "Social Perception," in G. Lidzey and E. Aronson, eds., *Handbook of Social Psychology*, vol. 1 (Reading, Mass.: Addison-Wesley, 1969).

41. P. Slovic, B. Fischoff, and S. Lichtenstein, "Behavioral Decision Theory," *Annual Review of Psychology* 28 (1977): 119-39.

42. R. S. Wyer and T. K. Srull, "Category Accessibility: Some Theoretical and Empirical Issues Concerning the Processing of Social Stimulus Information," in E. Higgins, C. Herman, and M. Zanna, eds., *Social Cognition: The Ontario Symposium,* vol. 1 (Hillsdale, N.J.: Erlbaum, 1981).

43. M. Snyder and N. Cantor, "Treating Hypotheses about Other People," in M. Higgins, E. C. Herman, and M. Zarma, eds., *Social Cognition: The Ontario Symposium* (Hillsdale, N.J.: Erlbaum, 1981), 1:33.

44. E. B. Ebbesen, "Cognitive Processes in Inferences about a Person's Personality," in M. Higgins, E. C. Herman, and M. Zarma,

eds., *Social Cognition: The Ontario Symposium* (Hillsdale, N.J.: Erlbaum, 1981), 1:55.

45. R. E. Nisbett and L. Ross, *Human Inference: Strategies and Shortcomings of Social Judgment* (Englewood Cliffs, N.J.: Trent and Hall, 1980), 7.

46. Wyer and Srull, "Category Accessibility."

47. Feldman, "Beyond Attribution Theory," 129.

48. M. Snyder and S. W. Uranowity, "Reconstructing the Past: Some Cognitive Consequences of Person Perception," *Journal of Personality and Social Psychology* 37 (1979): 1660-72.

49. E. Tulving, "Episodic and Semantic Memory," in E. Tulving and W. Donaldson, eds., *Organizations of Memory* (New York: Academic Press, 1972).

50. R. C. Atkinson and R. M. Shiffrin, "Human Memory: A Proposed System and Its Control Processes," in K. W. Spence and J. T. Spence, eds., *Advances in the Psychology of Learning and Motivation Research and Theory*, vol. 2 (New York: Academic Press, 1968).

51. R. I .Craig, and R. S. Lockart, "Levels of Processing: A Framework for Memory Research," *Journal of Verbal Learning and Verbal Behavior* 11 (1972): 671-84.

52. R. Lachman, J. L Lachman, and Earl C. Butterfield, *Cognitive Psychology: An Introduction* (Hillsdale, N.J.: Erlbaum, 1979), 274.

53. Walter Schneider and Richard M. Shiffrin, "Controlled and Automatic Human Information Processing: I. Detection, Search, and Attention," *Psychological Review* (Jan, 1977): 1-53.

54. Ibid., 51.

55. E. Tulving and Z. Pearlstone, "Availability versus Accessibility of Information in Memory for Words," *Journal of Verbal Learning and Verbal Behavior* 5 (1966): 381-91.

56. B. Hayes-Roth, "Evolution of Cognitive Structures and Processes," *Psychological Review* 84 (1977): 260-78.

57. P. W. Thorndyke and B. Hayes-Roth, "The Use of Schemata in the Acquisition and Transfer of Knowledge," *Cognitive Psychology* 11 (1979): 86-87.

58. J. Perlmutter, P. Source, and J. L. Myers, "Retrieval Process in Recall," *Cognitive Psychology* 8 (1976): 32-63.

59. B. Hayes-Roth and F. Hayes-Roth, "Plasticity in Memorial Networks," *Journal of Verbal Learning and Verbal Behavior* (1979).

60. Ibid.

61. A. G. Greenwald, "Cognitive Learning, Cognitive Response to Pervasion (?), and Attitude Change," in A. Greenwald, T. Brock, and T. Ostron, eds., *Psychological Foundations of Attitudes* (New York: Academic press, 1960).

62. R. Schanke and R. Abelson, *Scripts, Plans, Goals, and Understanding* (Hillsdale, N.J.: Erlbaum, 1977).

63. T. K. Srull and R. S. Wyer, "Category Accessibility and Social Perception: Some Implications for the Study of Person, Memory and Interpersonal Judgments," *Journal of Personality and Social Psychology* 38 (1980): 841-56.

64. K. P. Sentis and E. Burnstein, "Remembering Schema Consistent Information; Effects on Balance Schema on Recognition Memory," *Journal of Personality and Social Psychology* 37 (1979): 2200-11.

65. C. E. Cohen, "Pearson Categories and Social Perception: Testing Some Boundaries of the Processing Effects of Prior Knowledge," *Journal of Personality and Social Psychology* 40 (1981): 441-52.

66. S. E. Taylor, et al., "The Generalizability of Salience Effects," *Journal of Personality and Social Psychology* 37 (1979): 357-68.

67. R. I. Craig and E. Tulving, "Depth of Processing and the Retention of Words in Episodic Memory," *Journal of Verbal Learning and Verbal Behavior* 11 (1972): 671-84.

68. R. Hastie and Bernadette Park, "The Relationship Between Memory and Judgment Depends on Whether the Judgment Task Is Memory-Based or On-Line," *Psychological Review* 93/3 (1986): 258-68.

69. E. J. Learner, A. Blank, and B. Chanowitz, "The Mindlessness of Ostensibly Thoughtful Action; The Role of Placebo

Information in Interpersonal Interaction," *Journal of Personality and Social Psychology* 36 (1978): 635-42.

70. E. E. Learner, "False Models and Post-Data Model Construction," *Journal of the American Statistical Association* 69 (1974): 122-31.

71. E. E. Learner, "Explaining Your Results as Accent-Biased Memory," *Journal of the American Statistical Association* 70 (1975): 88-93.

72. M. Snyder and W. Uranowitz, "Reconstructing the Past: Some Cognitive Consequences of Person Perception," *Journal of Personality and Social Psychology* 36 (1978): 941-45.

73. A. C. Graeser and G. V. Nalsamura, "The Impact of Schema on Comprehension and Memory," *Psychology of Learning and Memory* 16 (1982): 60-102.

74. Graesser, Gordon, and Sawyer, "Memory for Typical and Atypical Actions in Scripted Activities," 319-32.

75. Chase and Simon, "Perception in Chess," 55-81.

76. G. Mandler, "From Association to Structure," *Psychological Review* 69 (1962): 415-27.

77. Ahmed Belkaoui, *Human Information Processing in Accounting* (Westport, Conn: Quorum Books, 1989).

78. D. L. Hamilton and L. J. Huffman, "Generality of Impression Formation for Evaluative and Non-evaluative Judgments," *Journal of Personality and Social Psychology* 20 (1971): 200-207.

79. R. S. Wyer and H. L. Hinlel, "Information Factor Underlying Inferences about Hypothetical People," *Journal of Personality and Social Psychology* 34 (1976): 481-95.

80. Belkaoui, *Human Information Processing in Accounting*.

81. Ibid.

82. J. Jaynes, *The Origin of Consciousness in the Breakdown of the Bicameral Mind* (Toronto: University of Toronto Press, 1978).

83. R. E. Nisbett and T. D. Wilson, "Telling More Than We Can Know: Verbal Reports on Mental Processes," *Psychological Review* (May 1977): 231-59.

84. Gibbins, "Propositions about the Psychology of Professional Judgments in Public Accounting," 113.

85. Belkaoui, *Human Information Processing in Accounting.*

86. R. M. Hogarth, *Judgment and Choice: The Psychology of Decision* (Chichester: Wiley, 1980).

87. Gibbins, "Propositions about the Psychology of Professional Judgment in Public Accounting," 114.

CHAPTER 9
CULTURAL RELATIVISM

People from different cultures react differently to a phenomena. Basically, the model in this chapter postulates that culture, through its components, elements, and dimensions, dictates the organizational structures adopted, the micro-organizational behavior, and the cognitive functioning of individuals faced with a phenomenon.

Before presentation of the model, the chapter presents selected issues in the history of the theories of culture, the diverse concepts of culture, and the conduct of cross-culture research for a better appreciation of the cultural relativism paradigm.

HISTORY OF THE THEORIES OF CULTURE

By the middle of the eighteenth century, efforts were being made to develop scientific theories of cultural differences. Cultural differences were then attributed to the different degrees of intellectual and moral progress achieved by different peoples. Scholars such as Adam Smith,[1] Adam Ferguson,[2] Jean Turgot,[3] and Denis Diderot[4] held this view of the role of progress in defining cultural differences. The nineteenth century saw the emergence of the concept of *cultural evolution*, which posited that cultures move through various stages of development. Scholars such as Auguste Comte,[5] George Wilheml Friedrich Hegel,[6] and Lewis Henry Morgan[7] held this view of progression of cultures from one state to another. Morgan's stages were savagery, barbarism, and civilization.[8] In the case of Comte they included theological, metaphysical, and positivistic modes of thought.[9] In all these schemes culture was viewed as evolving in conjunction with the evolution of human biological types and races, an idea started with social philosophers such as Thomas Malthus[10] and Herbert Spencer[11] and espoused by Charles Darwin.[12] The resulting movement, called Social Darwinism, postulates that cultural and biological progress results from the free play of competitive forces in the struggle of individual against individual, nation against nation, and race against race. Karl Marx also espoused the nineteenth-century evolution-and-progress paradigm of culture.[13] In his case the stages were primitive capitalism, slave society, feudalism, capitalism, and communism. The idea was also expressed by Friedrich Engels.[14]

The early twentieth saw the emergence of various challenges to the evolutionism theory of culture. One challenge, introduced by Franz Boas,[15] is known as historical particularism. Boas viewed each culture as having a long and unique history that offers the best way to understand it. In addition, cultural relativism holds that there are no higher or lower forms of culture and that the stages proposed by the evolutionists merely reflect their ethnocentrism. Another challenge to evolutionism, known as diffusionism, holds that cultural differences and similarities are merely the result of people imitating and borrowing from other cultures. However, diffusionism fails to recognize that similarities between societies may be caused by the effects of similar environments.[16] British challenges to evolutionism were functionalism and structural functionism. Functionalism advocates the descriptions of recurrent functions of customs and institutions rather than the origin of cultural differences and similarities.[17,18] All attempts to study the origin of cultural differences were viewed as speculative history. This new opposition, coupled with Frued's interpretation of cultures in psychological terms, shifted the emphasis to culture and personality theories, where cultural beliefs and practices were related to individual personality.[19,20]

More recently, dissatisfaction with anti-evolutionism has led to a return to some of the evolutionary theories of culture, a phenomenon spurred by Leslie White's linking of energy to the evolution of culture.[21] His basic law governing the evolution of culture is as follows: "Other factors remaining constant, culture evolves as the amount of energy harnessed per year is increased, or as the efficiency of the means of putting energy to work is increased."[22] This new evolutionism movement gave rise to the cultural ecology approach, advocated by Julian Steward, who identified the causes of cultural differences and similarities as the interaction of natural conditions with cultural factors.

With the popularity of dialectical materialism, which stresses the internal contradictions of sociocultural systems, and "dialectical" revolutions toward communism,[23] the new evolutionism led to the emergence of cultural materialism, which attributed cultural differences to the material constraints or conditions affected the conduct of life in each society.

The French contribution to the debate, advanced by Claude Levi-Strauss, is known as structuralism.[24] It stresses the similarities among cultures as a product of the structure of the human brain and of the unconscious thought processes, a structure characterized by binary contrasts.

Finally, despite the overwhelming evidence that culture is encoded in the brain rather than the genes, the units of biological heredity, there are still some racial determinism theories being offered to explain cultural differences. With the realization that most intelligence tests are culture-bound, and with increasing evidence of environmental influences, these theories do not constitute a dominant paradigm.

CONCEPTS OF CULTURE

The concept of culture has been subjected to various interpretations. In fact, some anthropologists have stated that culture in the abstract can be explained only by reference to specific cultures.[25] Anthropologists approach culture in at least three different ways: (1) the cultural universals approach, (2) the value systems approach, and (3) the systems approach.[26]

The cultural universals approach focuses on identifying certain universals common to all cultures, which does allow an examination of cultures in terms of how they contribute to these variables. An example of such a list is provided by G. P. Murdock.[27]

The value systems approach focuses on classifying cultures according to value systems. Instruments used to assess values among cultures include the Allport, Varnon, and Lindzey instrument,[28] Morris's "way of life" instrument,[29] Kluckhohn and Stradbeck's value theory,[30] Sarnoff's human value index,[31] and Rokeach's value survey.[32]

The systems approach focuses on the systems that make up a given culture. P. R. Harris and R. T. Moran identified eight subsystems in a culture: kinship, education, economy, politics, religion, association, health, and recreation.[33]

Some anthropologists view culture as information doubly coded- once chemically in the brain as memory, and once externally as a language, behavior, material, or document, and as a cultural pool from which each individual, each dyad, each group draws its particular culture.[34]

In short, culture remains the basis of anthropological research. Anthropologists differ as to what the concept of culture means, although they generally agree that it is learned rather than logically transmitted, that is shared by the members of a group, and that it is the foundation of the human way of life.[35] There is also a consensus on the issue of cultural utility in the sense that cultural practices have "functions" or reflect a society's "adaptations" to its environment.

[C]ulture is man's primary mode of achieving reproductive success. Hence particular sociocultural systems are arrangements of patterned behavior, thought, and feeling that contribute to the survival and reproduction of particular social groups. Traits contributing to the maintenance of a system may be said to have a *positive function* with respect to that system. Viable systems may be regarded as consisting largely of positive-functioned traits, since the contrary assumption would lead us to expect the system's extinction.[36]

[C]ustoms which diminish the survival chances of a society are not likely to persist . . . Those customs of a society that enhance survival chances are *adaptive* and are likely to persist. Hence we assume that, if a society has survived to be described in the annals of anthropology, much if not most of its cultural repertoires is adaptive, or was at one time.[37]

That cultural customs can be explained in practical materialist terms is well explained by anthropologist Marving Harris in his popular *Cows, Pigs, Wars and Witches: The Riddle of Culture.*[38]

Various concepts of culture exist in anthropology suggesting different themes for accounting research.[39]

1. Following Malinovski's functionalism,[40] culture may be viewed as an instrument serving biological and psychological needs.

2. Following Radcliffe-Brown's structural functionalism,[41] culture may be viewed as an adaptive regulatory mechanism that unites individuals with social structures.
3. Following Goodenough's ethnoscience,[42] culture may be viewed as a system of shared cognitions. The human mind thus generates culture by means of a finite number of rules.
4. Following Geert'z symbolic anthropology,[43] culture may be viewed as a system of shared symbols and meaning.
5. Following Levi-Strauss's structuralism,[44] culture may be viewed as a projection of the mind's universal unconscious infrastructure.

CROSS-CULTURAL RESEARCH
Approaches for Studying Cultures
There are at least six possible approaches to cross-cultural research:[45]
1. Parochial research is the study of one country conducted by local researchers. These are single-culture studies or domestic studies that assume the phenomenon researched to be universal.
2. Ethnocentric research attempts to replicate the findings in one culture in a second culture. These are second-culture studies searching for similarities between cultures.
3. Polycentric research is the study of one phenomenon in several cultures. These are studies in many cultures searching for differences and denying the universality of the phenomenon.
4. Comparative research focuses on identifying the similarities and dissimilarities in cultures around the world. These are studies contrasting many cultures.
5. The geocentric approach focuses on phenomena that apply in more than one culture. They are international management studies searching for similarities.
6. The synergistic approach focuses on creating universality while maintaining a certain level of cultural specificity.

Each of these types of research will address a different set of questions and will be based on different set assumptions.

The Search for Universals in Cross-Cultural Research

The establishment of universally valid laws is a worthwhile if not essential goal. Walter J. Lonner identified four consistent bases from which to make comparisons across cultures within a universalistic framework: biological, social, ecological, and psychological.[46] Basically a finite number of culture types are formed because three bases- biological, ecological, and social- converge in various patterns. Then the various types are compared along the psychological base. That comparison identifies an obvious array of universals in human behavior which far outweigh substantive differences.

For that matter culture (in the plural) may be viewed as an opaque veneer covering an essential universality or "psychic and romantic unity" just as the methodological characteristics of the earth's variable mantle stretch over a molten mass of common core substance. Understanding and explaining why the veneer of culture is metaphorically "thick" in some places and "thin" in others is therefore of major interest to cross-cultural researchers in psychology.[47]

Fons J. R. Van de Vijver and Ype H. Poortinga identify the following categories of universals along a dimension of "experimental rigor" or "strictness": (1) conceptual universals, (2) functionally equivalent (weak) universals, (3) metrically equivalent (strong) universals, and (4) scalar equivalent (strict) universals.[48] They are defined as follows:

In sum, conceptual universals refer to molar, theoretical concepts without any reference to measurement scales; functionally equivalent universals are concepts for which empirical referents have been specified and that are measured in qualitatively the same ways in each culture; metrically equivalent universals are concepts that have the same metric but not the same scale origin across cultures, and strictly equivalent universals have the same scale with the same origin in each culture.[49]

Those electing not to search for universals opt generally for the "traditional" cultural anthropology approach known under such names such as cultural relativism, contextualism, ideography, or configurationism. They are "relativists" in that they maintain that culture must be understood on no one else's terms but their own. To the relativists, some obvious generalizations and anthropological insights such as "the family is universal" are termed "fake universals" or "vague tautologies and forceless banalities."[50]

A comparison of both approaches would characterize the comparative approach as essentially nomothetic, focusing on universals, generalization, and similarities cross-culturally, and the relativist approach as essentially content-oriented, with ideographic interests, focusing on the detailed delineation of each culture and the importance of a holistic picture for valid interpretation.[51]

Both approaches have limitations. "Relativism in its extreme form foreclosed the possibility of cross-cultural generalization, whereas comparativism courted the danger of ethnocentrism in viewing cultures."[52]

The use of cross-cultural research may benefit from the use of both the comparative and the relativist approach. The relativist approach is necessary in order to understand the meaning of phenomenon in that it relates it to the myriad variables surrounding it. The comparative approach can follow if matters of contextual understanding are carefully considered. This strategy may be feasible using the following three-step procedure suggested by John W. Berry:

1. Aspects of behavior may be compared only where functional equivalence can be demonstrated. 2. (a) Existing descriptive categories and concepts then be applied to these behavior systems in a tentative way (imposed etic); (b) these must then be modified to the extent that they become an adequate description from within that system (emic); (c) shared categories can then be used to build up new categories valid for both systems (derived etic) and can be expanded (if desired) until they constitute a universal. 3. Instruments and techniques can then de devised, based upon the derived etic or universal, and satisfying the requirement of conceptual equivalances.[53]

Etic Versus Emic Approaches in Cross-Cultural Research

A research strategy is best characterized by the way it treats the relationship between what people say, think , and do as subjects and what they say, think, and do as objects of scientific inquiry. The researcher may view the thoughts and behavior of participants from either the perspective of the participants themselves, or the perspective of the observers. The terms *emic* and *etic* as introduced by K. L. Pike in *Language in Relation to a Unified Theory of the Structure of Human Behavior*[54] allow such a distinction. He suggests that the linguistic distinction between phonemics and phonetics can be used to delineate two different approaches to the study of cultural phenomena. Phonemics studies the sound in one particular language whole phonetics focuses on generalizing from phonemic studies in separate languages to a universal scheme relevant to all languages. Accordingly, the "emic" (from phonemics) differs from the "etic" (from phonetics) approach in cross-cultural research.

Berry typifies the emic-etic distinction as follows:[55]

Emic Approach	Etic Approach
studies behavior from within the system	studies behavior from outside the system
examines one culture	examines many cultures, comparing them
structure discovered by the analyst	structure created by the analyst
criteria are relative to internal characteristics	criteria are considered absolute or universal

The etic approach takes the perception of the observer as the important ingredient for the generation of scientifically productive theories about the causes of sociocultural differences and similarities. Basically it studies behavior from outside the system and examines phenomena from many cultures in order to extract the common elements across cultures.[56] It has been eloquently characterized as follows:

Rather than employ concepts that are necessarily real, meaningful, and appropriate from the native point of view, the observer is free to use alien categories and rules derived from the data language of science. Frequently, etic operations involve the measurement and juxtaposition of activities and events that native informants may find inappropriate or meaningless.[57]

What it amounts to is that the person adopting the etic approach, as an outside researcher, has his/her own categories by which the world is organized. Extreme advocates of the etic approach elevate the researcher as the best judge of the adequacy of the description or the analysis and dismiss the subject's opinion as potentially interesting but irrelevant.[58] Cross-Cultural research has also warned against the use of a "pseudo-etic approach," or as Berry calls it, "an imposed etic approach,"[59] which assumes that an emic dimension is etic when in fact there is no evidence to support such an assertion. Harry C. Triandis and Marvin Gerardo[60] give the example of administering an intelligence test in another culture without using the construct-validating procedures outlined by S. H. Irvine and W. K. Carroll[61] as an example of pseudo-etic given that cultures differ in their concepts of intelligence. Basically, a pseudo-etic approach would translate and use instruments composed of items reflecting Western conditions in other cultures with little regard for the reliability, validity, or relevance of the new instrument in the new culture.

The emic approach takes the perception of the participants as the most important ingredient for the generation of scientifically productive theories about a sociocultural system. Basically, it studies behavior from within the cultural system centering on the native, that is, the insider's or the "informant's" view of reality, and is therefore based on data from only one culture. Extreme advocates of the emic approach elevate the subject as the best judge of the adequacy of the research and analysis, and consider the subject's acceptance of the results of the research as a necessary and sufficient validation.[62,63] For example, *philotimo* is an emic concept that applies only in Greece. It refers to the extent to which the individual conforms to the expectation of his/her in-group.[64,65] Emic research techniques generally subsumed under the term *ethnoscience* include ethnosemantics (also known as ethnographic semantics or ethnographic ethnoscience), formal analysis, and componential analysis.[66] J. P. Spradley has operationalized many of these techniques of ethnoscience in a series of books.[67-69]

The emic-etic distinction helps in differentiating the particular from the universal. In the controversy centering on the choices of etic versus emic approaches, a consensus seems to be emerging toward the use of combined etic and emic measures in cross-cultural research. For example, P. J. Pelto indicates that there is an "embedded emicism" in most anthropological field work with a focus on native viewpoints, meanings and interpretations.[70] It follows, however, that as a researcher starts moving inductively up the levels of analysis searching for universal categories, an etic approach emerges. The emic categories are added to the etic categories to allow for a testing of propositions about human behavior.[71] Another example of the combination of etic and emic measures is suggested by Triandis[72] as a two-step approach. The first step elicits the concepts under study in both cultures, while the second step includes those attributes common to (etic) as well as frequently used in one culture but not in any other (emic).

Cross-cultural research in accounting will also be best served if it includes more emic (subjectivist/idiographic/qualitative/insider) perspectives to be later generally translated into etic (objectivist/quantitative/nomothetic/outsider) terms.

Design of Cross-Cultural Studies

In general, analysis of variance models is used to represent the design of many cross-cultural studies. A set of stimuli is administered to subjects from different cultural groups and can be represented by the following analysis of variance model:[73]

$$X_{sp(c)} = R + S_s + P_p PC_{pc} + C_c + SC_{sc} + SP_{sp}, SPC_{spc}, E_{spc}$$

where
R is the overall mean
$S_s (s = 1, \ldots, n_s)$ is the main effect for stimuli
P_p, PC_{pc} $(p = 1, \ldots, n_p)$ is the confounded effect for the main effect persons and the person by culture interaction
$C_c (c = 1, \ldots, n_c)$ is the main effect for culture
SC_{sc} is the interaction between stimulus and culture
$SP_{sp}, SPC_{spc}, E_{spc}$ is the confounding of the stimulus by person interaction, the stimulus by person by culture interaction, and the error term (E)

When the design of cross-cultural studies is represented by analysis of variance models, the stimulus by culture interaction is interpreted as bias.[74] Basically the effects of culture are perceived as an index of a valid cultural difference when the stimulus of culture interaction is small or insignificant.

Another approach may be used to determine whether the measurement refers to more universal or more specific aspects of behavior.

The concept of generalizability introduced by L. J. Cronbach et al.[75,76] is suggested by Van de Vijver and Poortinga.[77] Basically the generalizability theory dictates that estimation of the variance components be made first in order to compute coefficients of generalizability. Two coefficients of generalizability are deemed most important: (1) the coefficient estimating the stimulus by culture interaction $\hat{p}2(R_{sc})$; and (2) the coefficient estimating the combined contribution of the main effect of culture and the stimulus by culture interaction ($\hat{p}2(R_{c+sc})$). They are estimated as follows:

$$\hat{p}2(\mu S^C) = \frac{\sigma^2(SC)}{\sigma^2(SC) + \sigma^2(SP, SPC, E)/n^1p}$$

$$\hat{p}2(\mu^{C+SC}) = \frac{\sigma^2(C) + \sigma^2(SC)}{\sigma^2(C) + \sigma^2(SC) + \dfrac{\sigma^2(P, PC)}{n^1p} + \sigma^2(SP, SPC, E)/n^1p}$$

where n^1p =np for full sample estimates and $n^1p=1$. The suggested methodology is as follows:

1. Undertake a standard investigation of the significance of the F ratio to estimate the variance components.
2. If $\hat{p}2(R_{sc})$ differs substantially from zero, a meaningful quantitative comparison of scores is possible across cultures. The concept is either a conceptual universal or a functionally equivalent universal.
3. If $\hat{p}2(R_{sc})$ is equal to zero, then investigate $\hat{p}2(R_{c+sc})$. If it differs substantially from zero, then consistent cross-cultural differences exist and the concept is deemed to be a strong universal characterized by the same metric but a different origin across cultures.
4. If $\hat{p}2(R_{c+sc})$ is equal to zero or small, there is evidence for a strict universal, whereby the scales have the same metric with the same origin across all cultures.[78]

In conclusion, "when consistent cross-cultural differences are observed and the researcher is willing attribute these to real cross-cultural differences, circumstantial evidence is needed to validate this choice and to rule out alternative hypotheses."[79]

CULTURAL RELATIVISM
The Cultural Relativism Model

Edward T. Hall has stated that "culture is man's medium; there is not one aspect of human life that is not touched and altered by culture. This means personalities, how people express themselves (including show of emotions), the way they think, how they move, how problems are solved, how their cities are planned and laid out, how transportation systems function and are organized, as well as how economic and government systems are put together and function."[80] Culture in essence determines the judgment/decision process. The model, as illustrated in Exhibit 9.1, postulates that culture through its components, elements, and dimensions, dictates the organizational structures adopted, the micro-organizational behavior, and the cognitive functioning of individuals, in such a way as to ultimately affect their judgment/decision process when they are faced with a phenomenon.

Operationalization of Culture

This model avoids the two main problems that had beset earlier operationalization and use of culture: the equating of culture with nations and the ad hoc use of culture as a residual factor in explaining the variations that had not been explained by other factors.[81] Culture is viewed as collective mental programming.[82] That is, an ideological system forming the backdrop for human activity and providing people with a theory of reality.[83] This backdrop is composed of distinct elements and includes definite dimensions.

Those cultural elements generally assumed to affect the conduct of international business are language, religion, values and attitudes, law, education, politics, technology and material culture, and social organization each is assumed in this cultural relativism model to have the potential of dictating the organizational structure adopted, the cognitive functioning of individuals, and micro-organizational behavior, that may shape the judgment/decision process in accounting.

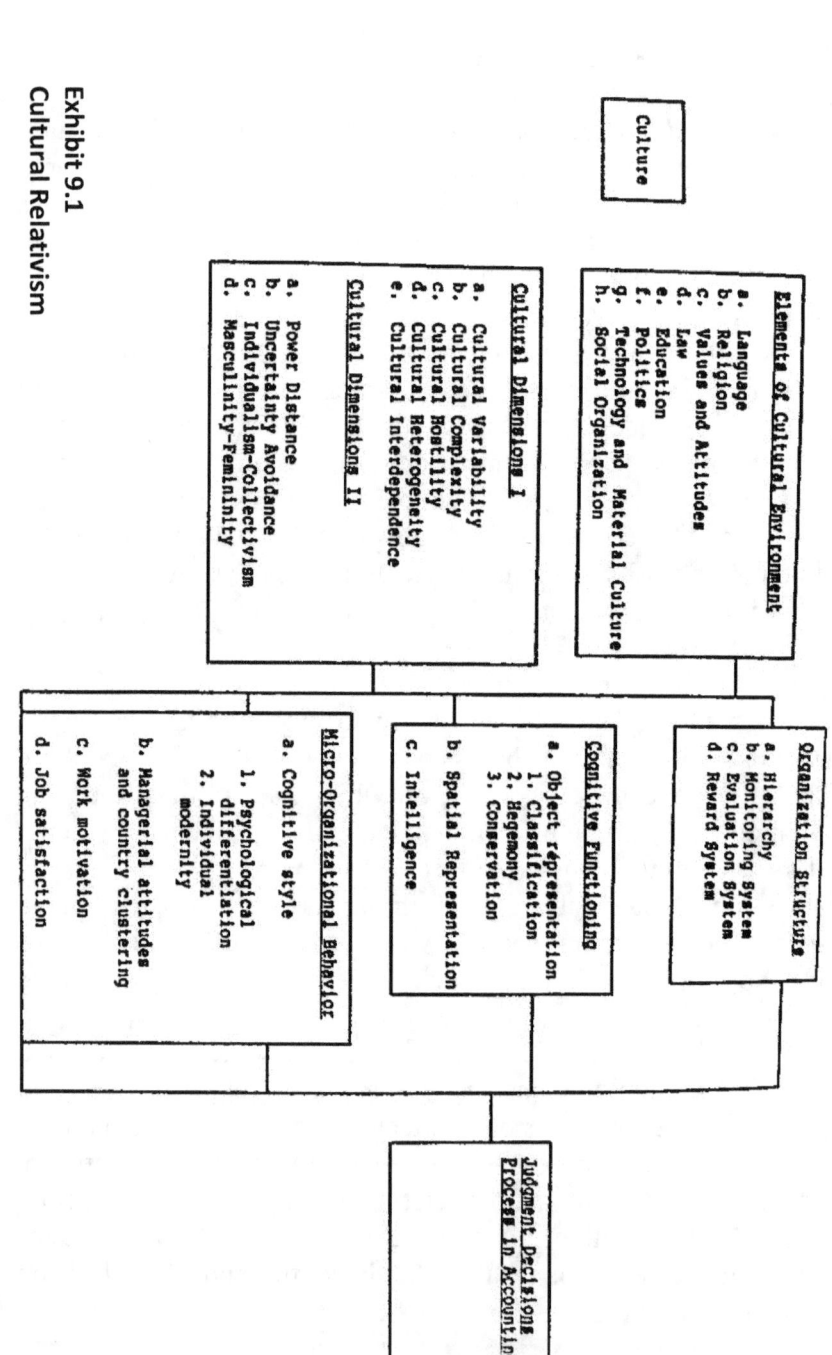

Exhibit 9.1
Cultural Relativism

Culture

Elements of Cultural Environment
a. Language
b. Religion
c. Values and Attitudes
d. Law
e. Education
f. Politics
g. Technology and Material Culture
h. Social Organization

Cultural Dimensions I
a. Cultural Variability
b. Cultural Complexity
c. Cultural Hostility
d. Cultural Heterogeneity
e. Cultural Interdependence

Cultural Dimensions II
a. Power Distance
b. Uncertainty Avoidance
c. Individualism-Collectivism
d. Masculinity-Femininity

Organization Structure
a. Hierarchy
b. Monitoring System
c. Evaluation System
d. Reward System

Cognitive Functioning
a. Object representation
1. Classification
2. Hegemony
3. Conservation
b. Spatial Representation
c. Intelligence

Micro-Organizational Behavior
a. Cognitive style
1. Psychological differentiation
2. Individual modernity
b. Managerial attitudes and country clustering
c. Work motivation
d. Job satisfaction

Judgment, Decisions Process in Accounting

Cultures vary along five dimensions: cultural variability, cultural complexity, cultural hostility, cultural heterogeneity, and cultural interdependence.[84] The first three dimensions refer to conditions within cultures while the latter two refer to conditions among cultures. These dimensions may be seen as potential sources of problems for the multinational corporation:

(1)*Cultural variability* generates uncertainty, which calls for organizational flexibility and adaptability; (2) *Cultural complexity* raises the difficulty of understanding, which necessitates organizational and individual contexting and preparation; (3) *Cultural hostility* threatens goal attainment and survival which demands the maintenance of social acceptability; (4) *Cultural heterogeneity* hinders centralized decision making with information overload, which calls for decentralization; and (5) *Cultural independence* increases the vulnerability of an organization to intergroup conflict, which necessitates less autonomy for individual subsidiaries and more system-wide coordination.[85]

This cultural relativism model assumes that differences in these five dimensions generate different cultural environments that have the potential of dictating the organizational structures adopted, the cognitive functioning of individuals, and the micro-organizational behavior, that may shape the judgment/decision process in accounting.

Cultures also vary along four dimensions that reflect the cultural orientations of a country and explain 50 percent of the differences in value systems among countries:[86] (1) individualism versus collectivism, (2) large versus small power distance, (3) strong versus weak uncertainty avoidance, and (4) masculinity versus femininity.

Individualism versus collectivism is a dimension that represents the degree of integration a society maintains among its members or the relationship between an individual and his/her fellow individuals. While individualists are expected to take care of themselves and their immediate families only, collectivists are expected to remain emotionally integrated into in-groups which protect them in exchange for unquestioning loyalty.

Large versus small power distance represents the extent to which members of a society accept the unequal distribution of power in institutions and organizations. In large power distance societies, there is a tendency for people to accept a hierarchical order in which everybody has a place which needs no justification, whereas in small power distance societies, people tend to live for equality and demand justification for any existing power inequalities.

Strong versus weak uncertainty avoidance is a dimension that represents the degree to which the members of a society feel uncomfortable with uncertainty and ambiguity. In strong uncertainty avoidance societies, people are intolerant of ambiguity and try to control it at all costs, whereas in weak uncertainty avoidance societies, people are more tolerant of ambiguity and tend to live with it.

Masculinity versus femininity is a dimension that represents the nature of the social divisions of sex roles. Masculine roles imply a preference for achievement, assertiveness, making money, sympathy for the strong, and the like. Feminine roles imply a preference for warm relationships, modesty, care for the weak, preservation of the environment, concern for the quality of life, and so on.

This cultural relativism model assumes that differences among these four dimensions create different cultural arenas that have the potential of dictating the organizational structures adopted, the type of cognitive functioning, and the micro-organizational behavior that may shape the judgment/decision process in accounting.

Culture and Organizational Structure

The cultural relativism model assumes that culture, through its elements and dimensions, dictates the type of organizational structure. The idea was first advanced by J. Child who stated that culture affects the design of organizational structure,[87] strongly refuting the "culture free" contingency theory of organizational structure proposed by D. J. Hickson and colleagues.[88-90] In fact, A. Sorge argued that all facts that bear upon organizational practices do so in the form of cultural constructs, and that organizations develop through a "nonrational" process of experimentation what is wholly cultured.[91]

There is no culture-free context of organization, because even if organizational solutions or contexts are similar, they are always culturally constructed and very imperfectly interpreted as the reaction to a given constraint. Culture enters organization through artful, unselfconscious, piecemeal experimentations with alternatives in business policy, finance, work/organization, industrial relations, education and training, and many other factors.[92]

Uman Sekaran and Carol R. Snodgrass carry the argument one step further by offering ideas on how specific cultural dimensions affect particular structural elements.[93] More specifically, they attempt to match the four structural aspects of the organization- hierarchy, monitoring system, evaluation system, and reward system- with the four cultural dimensions identified by Hofstede to synchronize with the preferred modes of behavior of organizational members.

Hierarchies refer to how organizations distribute power among their members while power distance refers to how a society accepts the fact that power in institutions and organizations is unequally distributed. It follows that the situation for large power distance culture groups calls for centralized and rigid hierarchies followed by emergent behavior of dependence and counterdependence while the situation for low power distance cultural groups calls for decentralized and fluid hierarchies followed by a behavior of independence.

The monitoring system refers to the process of collection and dissemination of information on performance, while uncertainty avoidance refers to the certainty of an unknown future and the difference in the way people react to it by experiencing different levels of anxiety. It follows that the situation for weak uncertainty avoidance calls for a simplistic monitoring system, while the situation for high uncertainty avoidance calls for a complete and comprehensive monitoring system followed by low levels of anxiety.

The evaluation system refers to the process of appraising the effectiveness and efficiency of organizational individual performance. Individual-collectivism refers to the type of relationship between a group and one of its members. It follows that a situation for individualistic cultural groups calls for an evaluation system based on individual achievement followed by a calculative behavior while a situation for collectivistic cultural groups calls for an evaluation system based on organizational performance followed by a moralistic behavior.

The reward system refers to the process of bestowing rewards for organizational or individual performance while masculinity-femininity refers to the nature of the social division of sex roles. It follows that a situation for "masculine" cultural groups calls for a reward system based on money, power, individual recognition and promotion, challenging assignments, status symbols, and the like, the catering to their machismo ideals, while a situation for "feminine" cultural groups calls for a reward system based on good quality of work life, security, a sense of belonging, a cooperative work system, and catering to their androgynous ideals.

Micro-Organizational Behavior and Culture

Cross-cultural research on micro-organizational behavior has examined various issues including cognitive style, work motivation, job satisfaction, and other important managerial attitudes and behaviors, and has highlighted the difference across various cultures.[94]

Research on cognitive style focuses on cultural differences in the structural aspects of an individual's cognitive system. It relied on the concept of psychological differentiation introduced by Witkin, Dyk, Faterson, Goodenough, and Karp,[95] and used by Witkin and Berry,[96] for an understanding of the effects of subjective culture on individual behavior. Known as the theory of psychological differentiation it relies on field dependence and field independence measures to categorize people along the dimension of field of articulation. Cultural differences were found in the level of field articulation among cultural groups in several countries.[97] Besides the concept of field dependence, the cognitive style approach known as individual modernity was used in cross-cultural research to explain how cultures change from traditional to modern.[98]

Research on attitudes and values focuses on cultural differences rather than similarities in personal, work-related, and ancestral values and attitudes. Various studies focus on a clustering of countries in terms of managerial and worker attitudes and values. Simcha Ronen and Oded Shenkar present a review of the published literature on country clustering and propose a map that integrates and synthesizes the available data.[99] The variables examined in these clustering studies include work goal importance, need deficiency, fulfillment and job satisfaction, managerial and organizational variables, and work role and interpersonal orientation. The resulting clusters discriminate on the basis of language, religion, and geography. Well-defined clusters are the Anglo, Germanic, Nordic, Latin-European, and Latin American ones. Ill-defined clusters are those describing the Far East and Arab countries as well as countries described as independent (e.g., Israel and Japan). Areas in Africa have not been studies at all while those in the Middle East and Far East have not been studied sufficiently. The review is, however, criticized by Peter Blunt[100] for alleged ethnocentrism and technocentrism defined as a lack of interdisciplinary approach in organizational studies.

Research on work motivation examines cross-cultural differences in motivation using one of the following theoretical bases: Atkinson's expectancy theory,[101] McClelland's achievement motivational theory,[102] vocation- and achievement-related motivation,[103] and Adam's equity theory.[104]

Research on job satisfaction focuses on cross-cultural differences in the relationships between satisfaction and other variables of interest, such as absenteeism or productivity. These studies rely on the following theoretical bases: Maslow's need theory,[105] the importance of various job dimension,[106] frame reference theory,[107] environmental theory,[108] Herzberg's two-factor theory,[109] and the alienation hypothesis.[110]

Cognitive Functioning

How people learn and think represents the study of human cognition. Cultural differences in cognitive functioning have also been subject to debate. Do people from different cultures perform differently on tasks that require certain cognitive skills? Two general hypotheses have been proposed. One maintains that cognitive processes are similar in individuals in different cultures, the other that cognitive processes are subject to cultural differences.[111,112] Evidence has been presented in support of both positions.[113,114] A third "situationist" hypothesis argues that cultural differences depend on the particular situation in the sense that "cultural differences in cognition reside more in the situations in which particular cognitive processes are applied than in the existence of a process in one cultural group and its absence in another."[115]

The debate needs to be continued to determine whether people from different cultures will perform differently on tasks that require certain cognitive skills. Certain conditions need to be met in order to be able to usefully interpret potential cultural differences in cognitive functioning in an accounting context.

When we consider intellectual growth or style in different cultures, we are confronted by three requirements. We need to obtain . . . some picture of skills, common to people from many backgrounds, as well as skills that differentiate among them. At the same time, we need to find the features of milieu that may account for the similarities and differences in skills. And finally, . . . we have to ask as we transpose a task from one culture to another, whether the same answer means the same thing in both worlds.[116]

To meet the requirements, two conditions need to be met. One is to assure the absence of ambiguous communication between the participants of the experiment and the preparers of the tasks, as differences in the way people perform may reflect different understandings of the requirements rather than differences in cognitive functioning. The second is to insure that the participants are truly representative of their respective cultures.

Are there any differences in the cognitive strategies used by people from different cultures when they represent information about objects? To answer this question, various studies have examined potential differences in classification, memory, and conservation.

There may be cultural differences in the way people classify objects, through the use of different attributes. Cultural differences in classification tasks have been observed although the variation may be attributable in some cases to differences in education and differences in familiarity with the items to be classified.[117] Similarly cultural differences in ability to abstract or to think in generalities have been observed in sorting tasks. However, in constrained classification tasks where the subjects learn to identify objects consistently on the basis of some feature, the skill in performing the task increases with age[118] and with education level.[119]

The recall of information from memory and its relation to culture is another research question of interest to object representation. In most experiments assessing the potential for cultural differences in the recall of information, age and education level were better related to the ways people from different cultures assess their memories.[120-122]

The concept of conservation, as introduced in Piaget's theory, refers to the ability of people to recognize the identity of objects or substances in spite of changes in their appearance. Cultural differences in the performance of conservation tasks are another research questions of interest to object representation. While there are some obvious common problems due to differences in testing and scoring methods, age range of subjects, amount and kind of verbalization elicited from subjects, and language of testing, the results of experiments confirm the existence of a similar sequence of conservation across cultures and the existence of a "lag" in development of conservation among some cultures.[123-125] Education, although not necessarily formal, as well as familiarity with the tasks are also associated with differences in conservation performance.

Are there any differences in the cognitive strategies used by people from different cultures when they organize and use spatial information? Various studies have examined the potential for cultural difference in spatial reference systems. Different spatial reference systems were found to be used by Puluwat sailors navigating among the islands in the Western Pacific,[126] and the Temme in West Africa.[127] Other studies determined that cultural differences in the degree of field dependence are a result of differences in child rearing and other socialization practices.[128] The evidence tends toward the existence of cultural differences in the organization and use of spatial information. More evidence is needed, however, to insure that the participants are more representative of their culture and are more familiar with tasks they can relate to.

There are also potential cultural differences in competence in cognitive behavior, which is equivalent to the Western notion of intelligence. A good definition follows:

Intelligence, a concept within the area of individual differences, reduces itself to two essentials, the power of the mind, and the skills through which this power expresses itself. The former aspect comes nearest to what the man in the street means by intelligence. It can be defined as "the ability to learn," "the capacity for understanding," "the ability to perceive essential relations between things," "insight into the nature of things." The "machines" through which this power expresses itself provide the foundation of abilities- from the highest abilities such as the solving of mathematical equations, right down to the simplest such as tying one's bootlaces.[128]

Attempts to provide possible cultural bases for differences in general intelligence have been criticized for a number of reasons: (1) most tests of intelligence are culture-specific; (2) conceptual abilities are used as the skills to be assessed as intelligence while members of non-European cultures are known to think concretely;[129] (3) the environmental conditions between different cultural groups are not necessarily identical;[130] (4) contact with Western culture, familiarity with test materials, and conditions of testing affect the results;[131-133] (5) rural versus urban environment, education level, and early nutrition can also affect general intellectual development, a phenomenon known as the deficit hypothesis.[134] Berry, however, emphasizes that one must accept that it is clever to do different things in different cultural systems, and if inferences about intelligence are made, the original observations must be based upon an adequate sample of what people are able to do in their own cultural system.[135] A similar point is made by Vernon:

We must try to discard the idea that intelligence (i.e., intelligence b) is a kind of universal faculty, a trait which is the same (apart from variations in amount) in all cultural groups. Clearly, it develops differently in different physical and cultural environments. It should be regarded as a name for all the various cognitive skills which are developed in, and valued by, the group. In Western civilization it refers mainly to grasping relations and symbolic thinking, and this permeates to some extent all the abilities we show at school, at work, or in daily life. We naturally tend to evaluate the intelligence of other ethnic groups on the same criteria, though it would surely be more psychologically sound to recognize that such groups require, and stimulate, the growth of different mental as well as physical skills for coping with their particular environments, i.e., that they possess different intelligences.[136]

CONCLUSION

The essence of cultural relativism in is the presence of a cultural process that is assumed to guide the judgment/decision process in accounting. The model in this chapter postulates that culture, through its components, elements, and dimensions, dictates the organizational structures adopted, micro-organizational behavior, and the cognitive functioning of individuals faced with a phenomenon.

NOTES

1. Adam Smith, *A Inquiry into the Nature and Causes of the Wealth of Nations* (London: J. Maynard, 1811).

2. Adam Ferguson, *An Eye on the History of Civil Society* (New York: Garland, 1971).

3. Anne Robert Jacques Turgot, *Reflections on the Formation and Distribution of Rides* (New York: A. M. Welly, 1963).

4. Denis Diderot, *Pensees Flu Consophiques* (Geneve: E. Droz, 1950).

5. Auguste Comte, *A General View of Positivism* (London: Rutledge, 1907).

6. Georg Wilhelm Friedrich Hegel, *Lectures on the Philosophy of World History: Introduction* (New York: Cambridge University Press, 1975).

7. Lewis Henry Morgan, *Ancient Society* (New York: Holt, Rinehart and Winston, 1877).

8. Ibid.

9. Comte, *General View of Positivism.*

10. Thomas R. Nalthus, *An Essay on the Principle of Population* (London: T. Bensley, 1803).

11. Herbert Spencer, *Education: Intellectual, Moral and Physical* (New York: D. Appleton, 1961).

12. Charles Darwin, *The Descent of Man* (New York: H. M. Caldwell, 1874).

13. Karl Marx, *Capital* (Chicago: Encyclopedia Britannica, 1955).

14. Frederich Engels, *The Origin of the Family, Private Property and the State* (New York: International, 1979).

15. Franz Boas, *Anthropology and Modern Life* (New York: W. W. Norton, 1928).

16. R. J. Harner, "Population Pressure and Ten Social Evolutions of Agriculturalists," *South Western Journal of Anthropology* 26 (1970): 67-86.

17. Bronislaw Malinowski, *Argonauts of the Western Pacific* (New York: Dutton, 1950).

18. A. R. Radcliffe-Brown, *Structure and Function in Primitive Society* (London: Cohen and West, 1961).

19. Ruth Benedict, *Patterns of Culture* (New York: Houghton Mifflin, 1934).

20. Margaret Mead, *Coming of Age in Samoa: A Psychological Study of Primitive Youth for Western Civilization* (New York: Morrow, 1961).

21. Leslie White, *The Science of Culture* (New York: Grove Press, 1949).

22. Ibid., 368-69.

23. In the words of Karl Marx: "The mode of production in material life determines the general character of the social, political

and spiritual processes of life. It is not the consciousness of men that determines their existence, but on the contrary, their social existence determines their consciousness" (*A Contribution to the Critique of Political Economy* [New York: International, 1970], 21).

24. Claude Levi-Strauss, *Le Cru and Le Cuit* (Paris: Pbon, 1964).

25. White, *Science of Culture*.

26. Simcha Ronen, *Comparative and Multinational Management* (New York: Wiley, 1986), 20-27.

27. G. P. Murdock, "Common Denominator of Cultures," in R. Linten, ed., *The Science of Man in the World Crises* (New York: Columbia University Press, 1945), 12-42.

28. G. W. Allport, P. E. Vernon, and Q. Lindzey, *A Study of Values* (Boston: Houghton Mifflin, 1960).

29. C. Morris, *Varieties of Human Value* (Chicago: University of Chicago Press, 1956).

30. F. R. Kluckhohn and F. Strodtbeck, *Variations in Value Orientations* (Westport, Conn.: Greenwood Press, 1961).

31. I. Sarnoff, *Society with Tears* (Secaucus, N.J.: Citadel Press, 1966).

32. J. Rokeach, *The Nature of Human Values* (New York: Free Press, 1966).

33. P. R. Harris and R. T. Moran, *Managing Cultural Differences* (Houston: Cruff, 1979).

34. Paul Bohannan, "Rethinking Culture: A Project for Current Anthropologists," *Current Anthropology* 14/4 (Oct. 1973): 357-65.

35. Harris and Moran, *Managing Cultural Differences*, 8.

36. Marvin Harris, *Culture, Man and Nature* (New York: Thomas Y. Crowell, 1971), 141.

37. Carol R. Ember, and Melvin Ember, *Cultural Anthropology*, 3d ed. (Englewood Cliffs, N.J.: Prentice-Hall, 1981), 32.

38. Marvin Harris, *Cows, Rigs, Wars and Witches: The Riddles of Culture* (New York: Vintage Books, 1974).

39. Linda Smircich, "Concepts of Culture and Organizational Analysis," *Administrative Science Quarterly* 28 (1983): 339-58.

40. B. Malinowski, *A Scientific Theory of Culture* (Chapel Hill: University of North Carolina Press, 1944).

41. A. R. Radcliffe-Brown, *Structure and Function in Primitive Society* (New York: Free Press, 1968).

42. Ward H. Goodenough, *Culture, Language and Society* (Reading, Mass.: Addison-Wesley, 1971).

43. Clifford Geertz, *The Interpretation of Cultures* (New York: Basic Books, 1973).

44. Claude Levi-Strauss, *Structural Anthropology* (Chicago: University of Chicago Press, 1983).

45. Nancy Adler, "A Typology of Management Studies Involving Culture," *Journal of International Business Studies* (Fall 1983): 24-47.

46. Walter J. Lonner, "The Search for Psychological Universals," in H. C. Triandis and W. W. Lambert, eds., *Handbook of Cross-Cultural Psychology* (Boston: Allyn and Bacon, 1980), 46.

47. Ibid., 147-48.

48. Fons J. R. Van de Vijver and Ype H. Poortinga, "Cross-Cultural Generalization and Universality," *Journal of Cross-Cultural Psychology* (Dec. 1982): 387-408.

49. Ibid., 351.

50. C. Geertz, "The Impact of the Concept of Culture on the Concept of Man," in J. R. Platt, ed., *New Views on the Nature of Man* (Chicago: University of Chicago Press, 1965), 103.

51. R. L. Monroe and R. H. Monroe, "Perspectives Suggested by Anthropological Data," in H. C. Triandis and W. W. Lambert, eds., *Handbook of Cross-Cultural Psychology* (Boston: Allyn and Bacon, 1980), 254.

52. R. A. Lennie, *Culture, Behavior and Personality* (Chicago: Aldrine, 1973), 217.

53. John W. Berry, "On Cross-Cultural Comparability," *International Journal of Psychology* 4/2 (1969): 125.

54. K. L. Pike, *Language in Relation to a Unified Theory of the Structure of Human Behavior*, ed ed. (The Hague: Mouton, 1967).

55. Berry, "On Cross-Cultural Comparability," 119-28.

56. J. W. Berry, "Introduction to Methodology," in H. C. Triandis and J. W. Berry, eds., *Handbook of Cross-Cultural Psychology*, vol. 2 (Boston: Allyn and Bacon, 1980).

57. Marvin Harris, *Cultural Materialism: The Struggle for a Science of Culture* (New York: Random House, 1979), 32.

58. Ibid.

59. Berry, "Our Cross-Cultural Comparability," 119-28.

60. Harry C. Triandis and Marvin Gerardo, "Etic Plus Emic versus Pseudoetic: A Test of a Basic Assumption of Contemporary Cross-Cultural Psychology," *Journal of Cross-Cultural Psychology* 14/4 (1979): 490.

61. S. H. Irvine and W. K. Carroll, "Testing and Assessments Across Cultures: Issues in Methodology and Theory," in H. C. Traindis and J. W. Berry, eds., *Handbook of Cross-Cultural Psychology*, vol. 2 (Boston: Allyn and Bacon, 1980).

62. C. O. Frake, "Cultural Ecology and Ethnography," in S. A. Dil, ed., *Language and Cultural Description: Essays by Charles O. Frake* (Stanford, Calif.: Stanford University Press, 1980), 18-25.

63. W. C. Sturevant, "Studies in Ethnoscience," In A. K. Romney and R. G. D'Andrade, eds., *Transcultural Studies in Cognition* (American Anthropologist Special Publication, 1964), 99-131.

64. H. C. Triandis and L. M. Triandis, "A Cross-Cultural Study of Social Distance," *Psychological Monographs* 76/21 (1962).

65. H. C. Triandis, E. E. Davis, and S. I. Takezawa, "Some Determinants of Social Distance among American, German and Japanese Students," *Journal of Personality and Social Psychology* 2 (1965): 540-41.

66. Nancy C. Morey and Fred Luthans, "An Emic Perspective and Ethnoscience Methods for Organizational Research," *Academy of Management Review* 9/1 (1984): 27-36.

67. J. P. Spradley, *The Ethnographic Interview* (New York: Holt, Rinehart and Winston, 1979).

68. J. P. Spradley, *Participant Observation* (New York: Holt, Rinehart and Winston, 1980).

69. J. P. Spradley, and D. W. McCurdy, *The Cultural Experience: Ethnography in Complex Society* (Chicago: Science Research Associates, 1978).

70. P. J. Pelto, *Anthropological Research: The Structures of Inquiring* (New York: Harper and Row, 1970).

71. Morey and Luthans, "An Emic Perspective and Ethnoscience Methods of Organizational Research," 30.

72. H. C. Triandis, *The Analysis of Subjective Culture* (New York: Wiley, 1972).

73. Van De Vijver and Poortinga, "Cross-Cultural Generalizations and Universality," 405.

74. T. A. Cleary and T. L. Hilton, "An Investigation of Item Bias," *Educational and Psychological Measurement* 28 (1968): 61-75.

75. L. J. Cronbach et al., *The Dependability of Behavioral Measurements* (New York: Wiley, 1972).

76. L. J. Cronbach and P. E. Meehl, "Contrast Validity in Psychological Tests," *Psychological Bulletin* 52 (1955): 281-302.

77. Van de Vijver and Poortinga, "Cross-Cultural Generalization and Universality."

78. Ibid.

79. Ibid., 405.

80. E. T. Hall, *Beyond Culture* (Garden City: Anchor Books, 1977), 16-17.

81. J. Child, "Culture, Contingency and Capitalism in the Cross-National Study of Organizations," in L. L. Cummings and C. M. Staw, eds., *Research in Organizational Behavior* (Greenwich, Conn.: JAI Press, 1981), 3:303-56.

82. G. Hofstede, *Culture's Consequences: International Differences in Work-Related Values* (Beverly Hills, Calif.: Sage, 1980).

83. Uma Sekaran and Carol R. Snodgrass, "A Model for Examining Organizational Effectiveness Cross-Culturally," *Advances in International Comparative Management* (Greenwich, Conn.: JAI Press, 1986), 2:213.

84. Ven Terpstra, *The Cultural Environment of International Business* (Cincinnati: South Wester, 1978), xvii.

85. Ibid., xxii.

86. G. Hofstede, "Dimensions of National Cultures in Fifty Countries and Three Regions," in J. B. Deregowski, S. Dziuarawiec, and R. S. Annis, eds., *Explications in Cross-Cultural Psychology* (Lisse, The Netherlands: Soviets and Zeilinger, 1983), 335-55.

87. Child, "Culture, Contingency and Capitalism in the Cross-National Study of Organizations," 313.

88. The argument that context-structure relations will be stable across societies is stated as follows:

This hypothesis implicitly rests on the theory that there are imperative, or causal relationships, from the resources of customers, of employees, of materials and finance, etc., and of operating technology of an organization, to its structure, which take effect whatever the surrounding societal differences. (pp. 63-64)

In D. J. Hickson, et al., "The Culture-Free Context of Organizational Structure: A Tri-National Comparison," *Sociology* 8 (1974).

89. D. J. Hickson, et al., "Grounds for Comparative Organizational Theory: Quicksands or Hard Core?" in C. J. Lammers and D. J. Hickson, eds., *Organizations Alike and Unlike* (London: Rutledge and Kegan Paul, 1979), chap. 2.

90. J. H. K. Inkson, D. J. Hickson, and D. S. Pugh, "Administrative Reduction of Variance in Organization and Behavior: A Comparative Study," in D. S. Pugh and R. L. Payne, eds., *Organizational Behavior in Its Context: The Aston Programme III* (Farnborough, Hants: Sasoon House, 1977), chap. 2.

91. A Sorge, "Cultured Organization" (discussion paper 80-56, Berlin: International Institute of Management, 1980).

92. Ibid.

93. Sekaran and Snodgrass, "Model for Examining Organizational Effectiveness Cross-Culturally," 216-20.

94. Rabi S. Bhagat and Sara J. McQuaid, "Role of Subjective Culture in Organizations: A Review and Directions for Future Research," *Journal of Applied Psychology Monograph* (Oct. 1982): 653-85.

95. H. A. Witkin, et al., *Psychological Differentiation* (Potomac, Md.: Erlbaum, 1974).

96. H. A. Witkin and J. W. Berry, "Psychological Differentiation in a Cross-Cultural Perspective," *Journal of Cross-Cultural Psychology* 6 (1975): 4-87.

97. L. W. Gruenfeld, "Field Dependence and Field Independence as a Framework for the Study of Task and Social Orientations in Organizational Leadership," in D. Graves, ed., *Management Research: A Cross-Cultural Perspective* (Amsterdam, The Netherlands: Eisener North Holand Biomedical Press, 1973).

98. A. Inkeles and D. H. Smith, *Becoming Modern: Individual Change in Six Developing Countries* (Boston: Harvard University Press, 1974).

99. Simcha Ronen and Oded Shenkar, "Clustering Countries on Attitudinal Dimensions: A Review and Synthesis," *Academy of Management Review* 10/3 (1985): 435-54.

100. Peter Blunt, "Techno and Ethnocentrism in Organization Studies: Comment and Speculation Prompted by Ronen and Shenkar," *Academy of Management Review* 11/4 (1986): 857-59.

101. J. W. Atkinson, "Motivational Determinants of Risk Taking Behavior," *Psychological Review* 64 (1957): 359-72.

102. D. C. McClelland, *The Achieving Society* (Princeton, N.J.: Van Nostrand, 1961).

103. P. C. Smith, L. M. Kendal, and C. L. Hulin, *The Measurement of Satisfaction in Work and Retirement: A Strategy for the Study of Attitudes* (Chicago: Rand McNally, 1965).

104. J. C. Adam, "Toward an Understanding of Inequity," *Journal of Abnormal and Social Psychology* 67 (1963): 422-36.

105. A. Maslow, *Motivation and Personality* (New York: Harper and Row, 1954).

106. F. Sahili, "Determinants of Achievement Motivation for Women in Developing Countries," *Journal of Vocational Behavior* 14 (1974): 297-305.

107. H. Soliman, "Motivation-Hygiene Theory of Job Satisfaction: An Empirical Investigation and an Attempt to

Reconcile Both the One-and-Two Factor Theories of Job Attitudes," *Journal of Applied Psychology* 54 (1970): 452-61.

108. Ibid.

109. F. Herzberg, B. Mausner, and B. Snyderman, *The Motivation to Work* (New York: Wiley, 1959).

110. C. L. Hulin and M. R. Blood, "Job Enlargement, Individual Differences and Worker Responses," *Psychological Bulleting* 69 (1968): 41-55.

111. M. Cole, et al., *The Cultural Context of Learning and Thinking* (New York: Banc Books, 1971).

112. B. B. Lloyd, *Perception and Cognition: A Cross-Cultural Perspective* (Middlesex, England: Penguin, 1972).

113. H. C. Triandis, R. S. Malpass, and A. R. Davidson, "Psychology and Culture," *Annual Review of Psychology* 24 (1973): 356.

114. J. Kagan, M. M. Haith, and F. J. Morrison, "Memory and Meaning in Two Cultures," *Child Development* 44 (1973): 356.

115. M. Cole, J. Gray, J. Glick, and D. Sharp, *The Cultural Context of Learning and Thinking* (New York: Banc Books, 1971).

116. J. Goodnow, "Problems in Research on Culture and Thought," in D. Ekland and J. Flavell, eds., *Studies in Cognitive Developments* (New York: Oxford University Press, 1969).

117. P. M. Greenfield, "Comparing Dimensional Categorization in Natural and Artificial Contents: A Developmental Study among the Zimacantecos of Mexico," *Journal of Social Psychology* 93 (1974): 157-71.

118. A. C. Mundy-Castle, "An Experimental Study of Prediction among Ghancian Children," *Journal of Social Psychology* 73 (1967): 161-68.

119. M. Cole, J. Gray, and J. Glick, "Some Experimental Studies of Kjello Quantitative Behavior," *Psychonomic Monographs Supplements* 2 (1968): 173-90.

120. D. A. Wagner, "The Development of Short-Term and Incidental Memory: A Cross-Cultural Study," *Child Development* 45 (1974): 389-96.

121. S. Scribner, "Development Aspects of Categorized Recall in a West African Society," *Cognitive Psychology* 6 (1974): 475-94.

122. J. A. Meacham, "Patterns of Memory Abilities in Two Cultures," *Developmental Psychology* 11/1 (1975): 50-53.

123. P. R. Dasen, "Cross-Cultural Piagetian Research: A Summary," *Journal of Cross-Cultural Psychology* 3 (1972): 23-39.

124. P. R. Dasen, "The Influence of Ecology, Culture and European Contacting Cognitive Development in Australian Aborigines," in J. Berry, and P. Dasen, eds., *Culture and Cognition: Reading in Cross-Cultural Psychology* (London: Methuen, 1974).

125. P. R. Dasen, "Concrete Operational Development in Three Cultures," *Journal of Cross-Cultural Psychology* 6/2 (1975): 156-72.

126. T. Gladwin, *East Is a Big Bird* (Cambridge, Mass.: Harvard University Press, 1970).

127. J. Littlejohn, "Cultural Relationism," *Anthropological Quarterly* 36, (1963): 1-17.

128. H. A. Witkin, et al., *Psychological Differentiation* (New York: Wiley, 1962).

129. S. Biesheuvel, "The Nature of Intelligence: Some Practical Implications of Its Measurement," in J. B. Jeffrey, ed., *Culture and Cognition: Readings in Cross-Cultural Psychology* (London: Methuen, 1974), 221.

130. A. G. J. Cryrs, "African Intelligence: A Critical Survey of Cross-Cultural Intelligence Research in Africa South of the Sahara," *Journal of Social Psychology* 57 (1962): 283-301.

131. S. Biesheuvel, "Psychological Tests and Their Applications to Non-European People," in J. B. Jeffrey, ed., *The Yearbook of Education* (London: Evans, 1949).

132. E. T. Abiola, "The Nature of Intelligence in Nigerian Children," *Teacher Education* 6 (1965): 37-58.

133. J. M. Faverge and J. C. Falmagne, "On the Interpretation in Intercultural Psychology: A Page Written in Recognition of the Work Done in This Field by Dr. S. Biesheuval," *Psychologia Africana* 9 (1962): 22-36.

134. P. E. Vernon, "Administration of Group Intelligence Tests to East African Pupils," *British Journal of Educational Psychology* 37 (1967): pt. 3, pp. 251-82.

135. M. Cole and J. Bruna, "Cultural Differences and Influences about Psychological Processes," *American Psychologist* 26 (1971): 867-76.

136. J. W. Berry, "Radical Cultural Relativism and the Concept of Intelligence," in J. Berry and P. Dasen, eds., *Culture and Cognition: Readings in Cross-Cultural Psychology* (London: Methuen, 1974).

137. P. E. Vernon, *Intelligence and Cultural Environment* (London: Methuen, 1969), 10.

CHAPTER 10
LINGUISTIC RELATIVISM

INTRODUCTION

Speakers of different languages react differently to a phenomena, resulting in difficulties in interlinguistic communication internationally. Basically, the model in this chapter postulates that as a result of three theses: the linguistic relativity thesis, the sociolinguistic thesis, and the bilingual thesis, the linguistic characteristics dictate the judgment/decision process.

LINGUISTIC RELATIVITY IN ACCOUNTING
The Sapir-Whorf Hypothesis of Linguistic Relativity

Anthropologists have always emphasized the study of language in their studies of culture. E. Sapir referred to the linguistic symbolism of a given culture. He perceived language as an instrument of thought and communication of thought. In other words, a given language predisposes its users to a distinct belief. All these premises led to the formulation of the principle of linguistic relativity: language is an active determinant of thought. Similarly, B. L. Whorf maintained that the ways of speaking are indicative of the metaphysics of a culture. Such a metaphysics consists of unstated premises which shape the perception and thought of those who participate in that culture and predisposes them to a given method of perception.[1]

Formulation of ideas is not an independent process, strictly rational in the old sense, but is part of a particular grammar, and differs, from slightly to greatly, between different grammars. . . . We are thus introduced to a new principle of relativity, which holds that all observers are not led by the same physical evidence to the same picture of the universe, unless their linguistic backgrounds are similar, or in some way may be calibrated.[2]

The linguistic relativity hypothesis is in fact preceded by linguistic determinism hypothesis. Linguistic determinism implies that the structure of language determines the structure of thought.

The deterministic aspect of such a position is well expressed by Whorf:

It was found that the background linguistic system (in other words, the grammar) of each language is not merely a reproducing instrument for voicing ideas but rather is itself the shaper of ideas, the program and guide for the individual's mental activity, for his analysis of impressions, for his synthesis of his mental stock and trade.

Formulation of ideas is not an independent process, strictly rational in the old sense, but is part of a particular grammar, and differs, from slightly to greatly, between different grammars. We dissect nature along lines laid down by our native languages. The categories and types that we isolate in the world of phenomena we do not find these because they stare every observer in the face; on the contrary, the world is presented in a kaleidoscopic flux by our minds- and this means largely by the linguistic system in our minds.[3]

These arguments were used to demonstrate the relativity of language. Whorf went even further by showing that in certain domains American Indian languages are superior to European languages:

It takes but little real scientific study of preliterate languages, especially those of America, to show how much more precise and finely elaborated is the system of relationship in many such tongues than ours. By comparison with many American languages, the formal systematic organization of ideas in English, German, French, or Italian is poor and jejeune. Why for instance, do we not like the Hopi, use a different way of expressing the relation of channel of sensation (seeing) to result in consciousness, as between "I see that it is red" and "I see that it is new"? We fuse the two different types of relationship into a vague sort of connection expressed by "that" whereas the Hopi indicates that in the first case seeing presents unspecified evidence from which is drawn the inference of newness. . . . Does the Hopi language show here a higher plan of thinking, a more rational analysis of situations, than our English? Of course, it does. In this field and in others, English compared to Hopi is like a bludgeon compared to a rapier.[4]

The basic view in the Sapir-Whorf hypothesis is that the characteristics of language have determining influences on cognitive processes. Basically monolingual individuals speaking completely different languages in terms structural, grammatical, and other characteristics, should adopt different mediated behaviors.

The (real world) is to a large extent unconsciously built up on the language habits of the group. The worlds in which different societies live are *distinct* worlds, merely the same world with different labels attached. We [as individuals] see and hear and otherwise experience very largely as we do because the language habits of our community predispose certain choices of interpretation.[5]

Thus, language is more than a communication vehicle about the objective reality existing independently of language but instead represents an objective reality that man uses to organize the realities around him. The scheme used by speakers of different languages when speaking about the nonlinguistic world will differ drastically. As stated by Sapir, "language does not as a matter of actual behavior stand apart from or run parallel to direct experience- but completely penetrates with it."[6] Or as stated by Whorf, "observers are not led by the same picture of the universe, unless their linguistic backgrounds are similar or can in some way be calibrated."[7]

That the real world is to a large extent unconsciously built on the language of a given group and that the intellectual system embodied in each language shapes the thought of its speakers in a quite general way is the essence of the linguistic relativity hypothesis.

The categories and types we isolate from the world of phenomena we do not find these because they stare every observer in the face. On the contrary the world is presented in a kaleidoscopic flux of impressions which have to be organized in our minds. This means largely, by the linguistic system in our minds.[8]

In its extreme position, the linguistic relativity hypothesis claims that cognitive organization is directly constrained by linguistic structure. J. A. Fishman explains this claim as follows:

Some languages recognize far more tenses than do others. Some languages recognize a gender of norms (and, therefore, also require markers of gender in the verb and adjective systems), whereas others do not. Some languages build into the verb system recognition of certainty or uncertainty of past, present, or future action. Other languages build into the verb system a recognition of the size, shape and color of norms referred to.[9]

In a summary of the linguistic relativity hypothesis, Roger Brown distinguishes two main hypotheses:[10]

I.   Structural difference between language systems will, in general, be paralleled by nonlinguistic cognitive differences, of an unspecified sort, in the native speakers of two languages.

II. The structure of anyone's native language strongly influences or fully determines the world-view he will acquire as he learns the language.[11]

Paul Kay and Willett Kempton add a third hypothesis:

III. The semantic systems of different languages vary without constraint.[12]

The evidence on the three hypotheses is, however, mixed.

That the linguistic relativity hypothesis indicates that the characteristics of language have determining influences on cognitive processes generates both delight and horror. The delight resides in the knowledge that the mastery of the language is followed by the influence on our cognitive abilities. Fishman, however, mentions the horror:

The first is the *horror of helplessness*, since all of us in most walks of life and most of us in all walks of life are helplessly trapped by the language we speak. We cannot escape from it- and, even if we could flee, where would we turn but to some other language with its own blinders and its own vicelike embrace on what we think, what we perceive, and what we say. The second horror is the *horror of hopelessness*- for what hope can there be for mankind? What hope that our group will ever understand the other? What hope that one nation will ever communicate with the other?[12]

While these two horrors are exaggerated, the challenge remains to understand the full consequences of the linguistic relativity thesis in the social sciences in general and in accounting in particular.

Systematization of the Sapir-Whorf Hypothesis

Using a double dichotomy, Fishman systematized the Sapir-Whorf hypothesis as shown in Exhibit 10.1.[13] Fishman's model views the characteristics of language as either lexical or grammatical, and the behavior of the speaker as either verbal behavior per se (generally interpreted in terms of cultural themes or *Weltanschauung*) and individual behavior data which is nonverbal in nature. Four cells correspond to four levels of the Sapir-Whorf hypothesis of linguistic relativity.

Cell 1 corresponds to linguistic codifiability and cultural reflections. It implies a relationship between the lexical properties of a language and the speaker's linguistic behavior.

Exhibit 10.1

Fishman's Systematic Version of the Sapir-Whorf Hypothesis

Data about language Characteristics	Data of Speaker's Behavior	
	Linguistic Data	Nonlinguistic Data
Lexical Characteristic	1	2
Grammatical Characteristics	3	4

Phenomena are codified differently in each language, which structures their verbal behavior. The absence of an English equivalent for German *Gemutlichkeit* makes it easier for Germans to be aware of and to express the phenomena. The French use of one word for both "conscience" and "consciousness" is shown by R. Linderman to have led to a greater conceptual fusion between these two usages on the part of French philosophers than for English or German thinkers.[14] Because of the different codifications the linguistic behavior and communication will differ. For example, the fact that Arabs have different terms for horses and the Eskimos have different terms for snow, makes it easier for Arabs to communicate about horses and Eskimos about snow. This analysis is applicable to R. D. Gastil's concept of polysemy that may be more easily expressible in one language than another.[15]

Languages differ as to the presence or absence of the field distinctions which they make. A language may be seen as a limited group of words and forms available for the use of a man thinking or expressing himself in the medium of that language. If he does not have the means to do a certain job of thinking or expressing, that job will not be accomplished as well as if he had such means.[16]

Cell 2 corresponds to linguistic codifiability and behavioral concomitants. It implies a relationship between lexical properties of a language and then on linguistic behavior of the users of a language. This level is more crucial than level 1 for the testing of the linguistic relativity hypothesis.

In order to find evidence to support the linguistic relativity hypothesis it is no sufficient merely to point to differences between languages and to assume that users of these languages have correspondingly different mental experiences. If we are not to be guilty of circular inference, it is necessary to show some correspondence between the presence of absence of a certain linguistic phenomenon and the presence or absence of a certain kind of non-linguistic response.[17]

The second level implies that speakers of a language that make certain lexical distinctions will be able to perform certain nonlinguistic tasks better and more rapidly than the speakers of languages that do make these lexical distinctions. R. W. Brown and E. H. Lenneberg,[18] Lenneber,[19,20] and De Lee Lantz and Volney

Steffbre[21] showed a shorter response latency in naming culturally encoded colors (i.e., colors that can be named with a single word) than colors which are not culturally encoded.

Cell 3 corresponds to linguistic structure and its cultural concomitants. It implies a relationship between grammatical characteristics and linguistic behavior. In essence, the concern is with the relation between language and worldview. It is best illustrated by Whorf's statement:

The background linguistic system (in other words, that grammar) of each language is not merely a reproducing instrument for voicing ideas, but rather is itself the shaper of ideas, the program and guide for the individual's mental activity, for his analysis of impressions, for his synthesis of is mental stock in trade. Formulation of ideas is not an independent process, strictly rational in the old sense, but is part of a particular grammar and differs, from slightly to greatly, between grammars.[22]

The thesis is best echoed by G. L. Trager:

Language as a whole has structure and all its parts and subdivisions also have structure. . . . [If] the rest of cultural behavior has been conditioned by language, then there must be a relationship between *the structure* of language and the *structure* of behavior.[23]

Basically the level of the hypothesis in cell 3 assumes that speakers of one language who use specific grammatical rules are predisposed to a given worldview different from the speakers of other languages. Whorf bases hi conclusions on an analysis of Hopi and compares it with standard average European languages (SAE) (including English).[24] He highlights specific grammatical structures (absence of tenses, the classification of events by duration categories, the use of grammatical forms to indicate the type of validity intended by the speaker, etc.). H. Hoijer argued the same position by analyzing Navaho.[25] The work of Susan Ervin-Tripp on bilingualism may also be used to support this level of the linguistic relativity hypothesis.[26] Bilingual Japanese women married to U.S. servicemen were asked to converse in Japanese with the result that the context of their conversation was more typical of women in Japan. When asked to converse in English, the context was more typical of women in the United States.

Cell 4 corresponds to the linguistic structure and its behavioral concomitants. It implies a relationship between grammatical characteristics and nonlinguistic behavior. J. B. Carroll and T. S. Casagrande provide support for this level of the hypothesis.[27] They examined whether the speakers of language that codes verbally for color, shape, and size, as the Navaho language, will classify objects differently from the speakers of a language that codes verbally for tense, person, and number, as in English.

(a). . . This feature of the Navaho language would affect the relative potency or order of emergency of such concepts as color, size, shape or form, and number in the Navaho-speaking child (specifically that shape or form would develop earlier and increase more regularly with age, since this is the aspect provided for in the verb forms themselves), and (b) that he (i.e. the Navaho child) would be more inclined to perceive formal similarities(i.e. shape or form similarities) between objects than would English-speaking Navaho children of the same age.[28]

The results showed that Navaho-dominant Navahos made object choice as predicted by the grammatical verb more often than did the English-dominant Navahos.

THE SOCIOLINGUISTIC THESIS

Speech systems are generated, or controlled, by social relations. This role of language in defining communities and social relationships is the realm of sociolinguistics. It argues that the roots of social class are carried through a communication code that social class itself promotes.

If a social group, by virtue of its class relation, i.e., as a result of its common occupational function and social status, has developed strong communal bonds; if the work relations of this group offer little variety; little exercise in decision making; if asserting, if it is to be successful must be a collective rather than an individual act; if the work task requires physical manipulation and control rather than symbolic organization and control; if the diminished authority of the man at work is transformed into an authority of power at home; if the home is over crowded and limits the variety of situations it can offer; if the children socialize each other in an environment offering little intellectual stimuli; if all these attributes are found in one setting, then it is plausible to assume that such a social setting will generate a particular form of communication which will shape the intellectual, social and affective orientation of the children.[29]

The linguistic thesis implies that different forms of social relations generate very different speech systems, linguistic repertoires, or communications codes.[30-33] In other words, people learn their social roles through the process of communication. Social role is best defined as follows: "A social role can then be considered as a complex coding activity controlling both the creation and organization of specific meanings and the conditions for their transmission and reception.[34]

Communication codes can be either elaborated or restricted, depending whether it is difficult or easy to predict their linguistic alternatives. Similarly role systems are either open or closed, according to whether they permit or reduce the range of alternatives for realization of verbal meanings. Basil Bernstein used this simple dichotomy to identify the contextual nature of the use of repertoires and to show a causal connection between role systems, communication codes, and the realization of different orders of meaning and relevance. As shown in Exhibit 10.2, in distinguishing between object and person orders of meaning, an individual will use an elaborated or restricted code depending on whether the role system is closed and the verbal meanings are likely to be assigned or the role system is open and the verbal meanings are likely to be novel. As stated by Bernstein:

We can begin to see that in the area where the role system is open, there is an induced motivation to explore and actively seek out and extend meanings; where the role is closed, there is little induced motivation to explore and create novel meanings. . . .

Where the role system is open, the individual child learns to cope with ambiguity and isolation in the creation of verbal meanings; where the role system is closed, the individual or child forges such learning. On the contrary, he learns to create verbal meanings in social contexts which are unambiguous and communalized.[35]

Thus the social role determines the communication code or linguistic repertoires used.

Exhibit 10.2
Role Systems

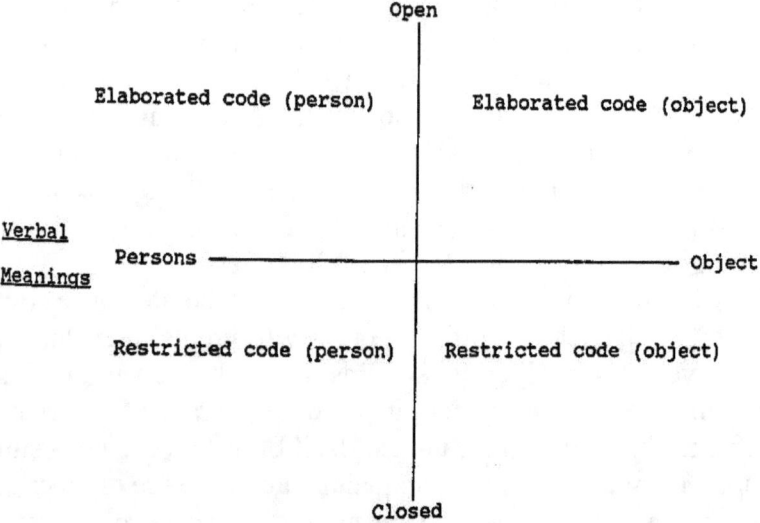

Bernstein's Causal Connection Between Role Systems, Communication Codes, and the Realization of Different Orders of Meaning and Relevance

Accounting situations also involve different role relationships that result from a number of factors, including membership in different professional associations, difference in education levels and fluency in accounting, and difference in economic and social positions. These role relationships in turn determine either an elaborated accounting communication code if the role system is open or a restricted accounting communication code if the system is closed. In essence the sociolinguistic thesis implies the existence of different linguistic repertoires as a result of the different social role relationships. For example, various professional affiliations in accounting create different linguistic repertoires or codes for intragroup communications and/or intergroup communications which lead to a differential understanding of accounting and social relationships.[36] Specifically, a select set of accounting concepts was subjected to analysis using multidimensional scaling techniques to evaluate the intergroup perceptual differences between three groups of users. A sociolinguistic construct was used to justify the possible lack of consensus on the meaning of accounting concepts. The dimensions of the common perceptual space were identified and labeled as conjunctive, relational, and disjunctive by analogy to the process of concept formation. The sociolinguistic thesis was verified for both the conjunctive and the disjunctive concepts.

THE BILINGUAL THESIS

The best tests of the Sapir-Whorf hypothesis can be provided by bilinguals as they are the only ones who can personally testify to the different *Weltanschauungs* created by different languages. There are various expressions of the differential effect of the worldview imposed by different languages. Consider the following statement: "Language is so intimately interwoven with the whole of social behavior that a bilingual, for better or worse, is bound to differ from the monoglot.[37]

But bilingualism is not the only situation that may result in different worldviews created by different languages. Diglossia is another case. Diglossia occurs when a society uses two or more languages for intrasociety communication. It is basically manifested by the existence of stable and separable communication codes that depend on each other but serve different social functions. Basically some societies rely no separate dialects or functionally differentiated language varieties.[38] Fishman, in fact, makes the separation between high (H) language, used in conjunction with religion, education, and other aspects of high culture, and low (L) language used in conjunction with everyday aspects of society.[49] Charles A. Ferguson, who introduced the concept of diglossia, perceived H and L as superposed language.[40] Fishman distinguishes several different kinds of linguistic relationships between H and L language as follows:

1. H is classical and L is vernacular, the two being genetically related, as in classical and vernacular Arabis, classical or classicized Greek (Katarevusa) and Demotiki, to name only a few.
2. H is classical and L is vernacular, the two not being genetically unrelated, as in Loshn Koydesh (textual Hebrew/Aramaic) and Yiddish.
3. H is written/formal spoken and L is vernacular, the two being genetically related to each other, as in Spanish and Guarani in Paraguay.
4. H is written/formal and L is vernacular, the two being genetically related to each other, as in High German and Swiss German.[41]

The important fact is that different social roles and relationships dictate the use of different languages or dialects resulting in different worldviews and attitudes:

Where one set of behaviors, attitudes and values supported, and was expressed in, one language, another set of behaviors, attitudes and values supported and was expressed in the other. Both sets of behaviors, attitudes and values were fully accepted as culturally legitimate and complementary (i.e. nonfictual) and indeed, little if any conflict between them was possible in view of the functional separation between them.[42]

Both bilingualism and diglossia have an impact on the use of accounting language. Speakers of multiple languages or different dialects will experience different worldviews in their use of accounting languages from unilinguals. Different languages or dialect systems may provide cognitive enrichment or linguistic and perceptual confusion. Switching from one language or dialect to another may lead to better perception. In effect, language switching has been found to be related to higher levels of creativity and cognitive feasibility,[43] concept formation,[44] verbal intelligence,[45] and psycholinguistic abilities.[46] The three problems identified can affect the perception of accounting concepts by bilingual and unilingual speakers of languages or dialects. Janice Monti-Belkaoui and Ahmed Belkaoui conducted an experiment to evaluate the extent of these problems in accounting.[47] The findings supported the contention that unilingual speakers of separate languages differ from each other and from bilingual speakers in their perception of concepts. Some of these findings also provided support for the contention that language switching may enhance understanding. The evidence suggests that fluency in more than one language aids in the uniform acquisition and comprehension of concepts.

LINGUISTIC RELATIVISM: A MODEL

A phenomenon may be represented as language-based given the existence of the two components of symbolic representations and grammatical characteristics. The judgment/decision process is determined by the impact of language on behavior and attitudes as hypothesized by the linguistic relativity hypothesis, the sociolinguistic hypothesis, and the bilingual thesis. Basically the linguistic codifiability or structure of language affects the linguistic and nonlinguistic behavior of users. The social roles created by different professional memberships, social classes, and education lead to different communication codes, either elaborate or restricted, that affects concept formation, understanding, and decision making. Finally, the use of different languages or dialects, as in bilingualism or diglossia, provides speakers with a different understanding of a phenomena as well as different cognitive abilities. The three results contribute to a linguistic relativism model, as portrayed in Exhibit 3.3, which is assumed to determine the judgment/decision process.

CONCLUSION

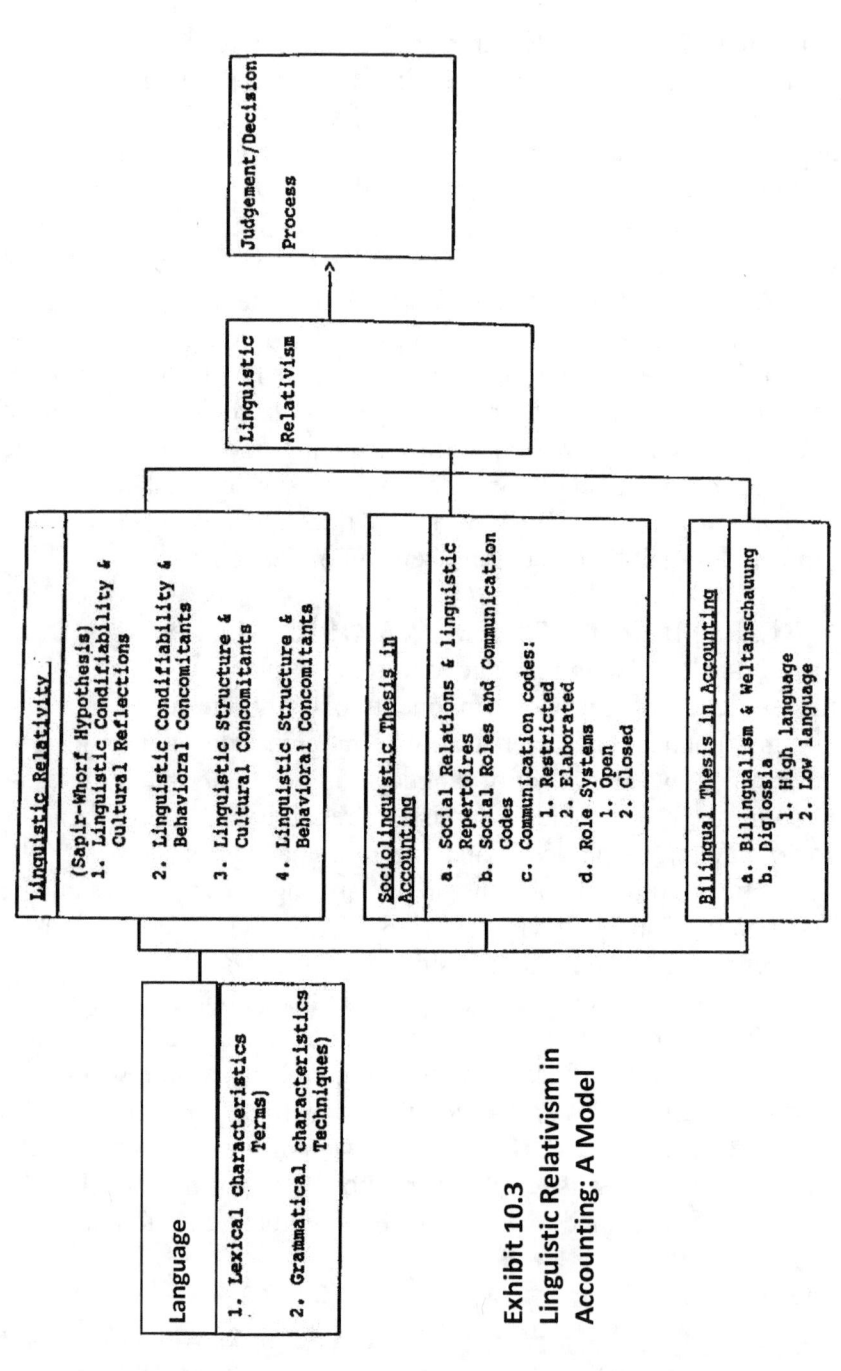

Exhibit 10.3
Linguistic Relativism in
Accounting: A Model

The essence of bilinguistic relativism is the presence of a linguistic process that is assumed to guide the judgment/decision process. The model in this chapter postulates that phenomenon as a language based affects the judgment/decision process as result of the theory and findings underlying the Sapir-Whorf hypothesis of linguistic relativity, the sociolinguistic thesis, and the bilingualism or diglossia thesis.

NOTES

1. E. Sapir, in D. G. Mandelbaum, ed., *Culture, Language and Personality: Selected Essays*, (Cambridge, Mass.: MIT Press, 1956).

2. B. L. Whorf, *Language, Thought and Reality* (Boston: MIT Press, 1951).

3. Ibid., 214.

4. Ibid., 212.

5. Ibid., 84-85.

6. E. Sapir, "The Status of Linguistics as a Science," *Language* 5 (1929): 207-14.

7. B. L. Whorf, "Science and Linguistics," *Technological Review* 44 (1940): 229-31, 247, 248.

8. Ibid., 212.

9. J. A. Fishman, *The Sociology of Language* (New York: Newbury House, 1972), 156.

10. Roger Brown, "Reference: In Memorial Tribute to Eric Lenneberg," *Cognition* 4 (1976): 125-53.

11. Ibid., 128.

12. Paul Kay and Willett Kempton, "What Is the Sapir-Whorf Hypothesis?" *American Anthropologist* 86 (1984): 66.

13. J. A. Fishman, "A Systematization of the Whorfian Hypothesis," *Behavioral Science* 5/4 (1960): 332.

14. Ibid.

15. R. Linderman, *Der Begriff Der Conscience in Franzosichen Den ken* (Leipzig: Jena, 1938).

16. R. D. Gastil, "Relative Linguistic Determinism," *Anthropological Linguistics* 1/9 (1959): 24-38.

17. Ibid., 37.

18. J. B. Carroll and T. S. Casagrande, "The Function of Language Classification in Behavior," in E. E. Maccoby, T. M. Newcomb, and E. L. Hartley, eds., *Readings in Social Psychology* (New York: Holt, Rinehart and Winston, 1958), 13.

19. R. W. Brown and E. H. Lenneberg, "A Study in Language and Cognition," *Journal of Abnormal and Social Psychology* 49 (1954): 454-62.

20. E. H. Lenneberg, "Cognition in Ethnolinguistics," *Language* 29 (1953): 463-71.

21. E. H. Lenneberg, "A Probabilistic Approach to Language Learning," *Behavioral Science* 2 (1957): 1-12.

22. De Lee Lantz and Volney Steffbre, "Language and Cognition Revisited," *Journal of Abnormal and Social Psychology* 2 (1953): 454-62.

23. Whorf, "Science and Linguistics," 247.

24. G. L. Trager, "The Systematization of the Whorf Hypothesis," *Anthropological Linguistics* 1 (1959): 31-35.

25. Whorf, "Science and Linguistics."

26. H. Hoijer, "Cultural Implications of the Navaho Linguistic Categories," *Language* 27 (1951): 111-20.

27. Susan Erwin-Tripp, "Sociolinguistics," in L. Berkowitz, ed., *Advances in Experimental Social Psychology* (New York: Academic Press, 1969), 91-163.

28. J. B. Carroll and T. S. Casagrande, "Function of Language Classification in Behavior."

29. Ibid.

30. Basil Bernstein, "A Sociolinguistic Approach to Socialization, with Some Reference to Educability," in John J. Gumperz and Dell Hymes, eds., *Direction in Sociolinguistics: The Ethnography of Communication* (New York: Holt, Rinehart and Winston, 1972), 472.

31. Susan M. Erwin-Tripp, "An Analysis of the Interaction of Language, Topic and Listener," *American Anthropologist* 66/6 (1964): 86-102.

32. Erwin-Tripp, "Sociolinguistics," 91-165.

33. John J. Grumperz, "Linguistic and Social Interaction in Two Communities," *American Anthropologist* 66/6 (1964): 137-54.

34. Dell Hynes, "Modes of the Interaction of Language and Social Setting," *Journal of Social Issues* 23/2 (1967): 8-28.

35. Bernstein, "Sociolinguistic Approach to Socialization with Some Reference to Educability," 474.

36. Ibid., 478-79.

37. Ahmed Belkaoui, "The Interprofessional Linguistic Communication of Accounting Concepts: An Experiment in Sociolinguistics," *Journal of Accounting Research* (Fall 1980): 362-74.

38. Robert H. Lowie, "A Case of Bilinguialism." *World* 1 (1945): 249-59.

39. J. A. Fishman, "Bilingualism with and without Diglossia; Diglossia with or without Bilingualism," *Journal of Social Issues* 2 (1967): 29-39.

40. Ibid., p. 30.

41. Charles A. Ferguson, "Diglossia," *World* 15 (1959): 325-40.

42. J. A. Fishman, "Bilingualism and Biculturalism, as Individual and Social Phenomena," *Journal of Multilingual and Multicultural Development* 1 (1980): 3-15.

43. Fishman, "Bilingualism with or without Diglossa; Diglossia with or without Bilingualism," 29-30.

44. E. Peal and W. E. Lambert, "The Relationship of Bilingualism to Intelligence," *Psychological Monographs* 1 (1962): 76-84.

45. W. W. Liedke and L. D. Nelson, "Concept Formation and Bilingualism," *Alberta Journal of Educational Research* 2 (1968): 4-20.

46. W. E. Lambert, and G. R. Tucker, "The Benefits of Bilingualism," *Alberta Journal of Educational Research* (Sept. 1973): 115-22.

47. M. C. Casserby and A. P. Edwards, *Detrimental Effects of Grade One Bilingualism Programs: An Exploratory Study*, paper

presented at the annual conference of the Canadian Psychological Association (Toronto 1979).

48. Janice Monti-Belkaoui and Ahmed Belkaoui, "Bilingualism and the Perception of Professional Concepts," *Journal of Psycholinguistic Research* 12/2 (1983): 111-27.

CHAPTER 11
ORGANIZATIONAL CULTURE
RELATIVISM

INTRODUCTION

The reaction of individuals working in different firms to a given phenomenon differs. The reason for this difference is the organizational culture unique to each firm. The organizational culture relativism model in this chapter postulates that various organizational phenomena and characteristics create a distinct corporate culture in each firm that influences and/or dictates the judgment/decision process.

ORGANIZATIONAL CULTURE RELATIVISM: A MODEL

The efficiency of a corporate culture requires the development of a general paradigm that helps members determine what is in the best interests of the corporation.

The paradigm provides members with a sort of master routine that enables them to solve two related problems stemming from the boundedness of their rationality. The first problem is they, as individuals, are limited in their ability to comprehend and process information. The paradigm may give them categories, processing routines, and examples of good and bad solutions, that will greatly increase their ability to determine how to operate in the class. . . .

[The paradigm] may provide shared frameworks, language, and referents that can help members start from similar assumptions in deriving solutions to previously unfamiliar problems.[1]

The corporate culture paradigm gives the individual faced with an accounting phenomenon categories, processing routines, and schemes that helps solve problems in the best interest of the culture. This is in essence an organizational culture relativism thesis that states that organizational culture through shared frameworks, languages, and reflections determines the judgment/decision process in accounting. The model, as illustrated in Exhibit 11.1, postulates that various organizational factors, including metaphors, symbolisms, internalization, modes of governing transactions, and type of executive personality affect both the processes of organizational commitment and organizational socialization in such a way as to create a specific corporate culture, which in turn determines the judgment/decision process of individuals faced with a phenomenon.

1. **Metaphors**
   a. Organism
   b. Machine
   c. Theater
   d. Political Arena
2. **Symbolism**
   a. Myth
   b. Rituals
   c. Legends
   d. Specialized knowledge
   e. Ideology
3. **Internalization**
   a. Process of character formation
   b. Creation of organization sagas

Modes for Governing Transaction
1. Markets and Bureaucracies
2. Clans

Executive Personality
1. Suspicious
2. Depressive
3. Dramatic
4. Compulsive
5. Detached

Organizational Commitment
1. **Aspects**
   a. Retention of Numbers
   b. Group Cohesiveness
   c. Social Control
2. **Types**
   a. Instrumental Commitment
   b. Commitment
   c. Affective Commitment
   c. Moral Commitment

Organizational Socialization
1. **Sequents and Boundaries**
   a. Functional
   b. Hierarchical
   c. Inclusionary
2. **Organizationally Defined Roles**
   a. Knowledge
   b. Strategy
   c. Mission
3. **Tactical Dimensions of Socialization**
   a. Collective vs. Individual
   b. Formal vs. informal
   c. Sequential vs. Variable
   d. Fixed vs. variable
   e. Serial vs. disjunctive
   f. Investiture vs. divestiture

Organizational Culture
a. Strong vs. Weak Cultures
b. Culture in Research Paradigms
   b1. Functionalist
   b2. Interpretive
   b3. Structurationist
c. Accounting Oriented Organizational Culture (AOAC)
d. Executive Personality Created Culture
   d1. Paranoid Culture
   d2. Avoidant Culture
   d3. Characteristic Culture
   d4. Bureaucratic Culture
   d5. Politicized Culture

Judgment/Decision Process in Accounting

Exhibit 11.1
Organizational Cultural Relativism

UNDERLYING ASSUMPTIONS AND METAPHORS OF ORGANIZATION

Various metaphors or images have been used to illustrate the type of experience generally referred to as an "organization." This is a result of the tendency of scientists to create knowledge about the world by examining the effects of different metaphoric categorization of their subjects.[2] Organizations, for example, have been viewed, using metaphors from the physical world, as organism and machine.[3] Other metaphors include "theaters" for performance of roles, dramas, and scripts,[4,5] and "political arenas," aimed at the pursuit and display of power.[6,7]

Underlying these metaphors is the presence of a culture that expresses the values or social ideas and the beliefs that organizational members come to share. The manifestation of these values or patterns of belief is in the form of symbolic devices such as myths,[8] rituals,[9] legends,[10,11] and specialized language.[12] These symbolisms constitute aspects of the more cultural and expressive components of organizational life.[13] They are internalized either through a process of character formation (an embodiment of values in an organizational structure through statements of mission, program of activity, selective recruitment, and specialization)[14] or the creation of organizational sagas (a system of collective understanding of unique accomplishment in a formally established group).[15]

In the context of our model, the metaphors, the values held by the members of the organization, the symbolisms adopted, the process of character formation, and the creation of organizational sagas affect and determine the type of organizational socialization and commitment processes adopted.

MODELS FOR GOVERNING TRANSACTIONS

W. G. Ouchi proposed three alternative modes for governing exchanges or transactions: markets, bureaucracies, and clans.[16] They are explicated as follows.

A market form of governance uses the price mechanism in competitive situations as a mode of governing exchanges and as an efficient mechanism of control. Contracts between parties are made at a "fair price," insuring a perception of equity among self-interested parties bounded by a given rationale. Those conditions are not, however, always prevalent.

Under conditions of increased ambiguity (a unique product of rapidly changing environmental conditions), however, the bounded rationality of parties makes transactions more costly because the parties have difficulty writing a sufficiently detailed and prescient contract to insure the equitable assessment of value and prohibit self-interested individuals from taking unfair advantage of the ambiguity. Under such conditions, markets may fail.[17]

Bureaucracies as a form of governance under conditions of ambiguity rely upon a mixture of close evaluation with a socialized acceptance of common objectives and the creation of incomplete contracts in the form of employment contracts. While markets rely on prices, bureaucracies rely on rules. This creates important differences.

In any case, rules differ from prices in the important sense that they are partial rather than complete handles of information. A price implies that a comparison has taken place, a comparison between alternative buyers or sellers of the value of the object in question. A rule, however, is essentially an arbitrary standard against which a comparison is yet to be made. In order to use a rule (e.g., a budget, or cost standard) a manager must observe some actual performance, assign some value to it, and then compare that assigned value to the rule in order to determine whether the actual performance was satisfactory or not. All this consumes a great deal of administrative overhead. If the rule is expressed qualitatively rather than quantitatively, the cost of administration can be expected to be higher.[18]

As the third mode of governing transactions, clans socialize the parties to the exchange in such a way that though self-interested, they see a common benefit in the exchange and congruence with their objectives. Clans basically rely upon a relatively complete socialization process that effectively eliminates goals in congruence between individuals.

The clan as a governing mechanism is tantamount to the creation of a specific organizational culture. In fact, "the clan requires such a relatively greater degree of social understanding, specific to the organization, about the general objectives, methods, and values of the collective that it clearly may be thought of as control or governance by means of a local culture that is analogous to the paradigmatic anthropological culture."[19]

Conditions conducive to the development of clans include: (1) a long history and a stable membership, allowing one generation of members to pass on knowledge to successive generations, in the process contributing to the institutionalization of social knowledge;[20] (2) the absence of institutional alternatives, given that contradiction may lead to a loss of the sense of taken-for-granted reality;[21] and (3) interactions among members, as a way of encouraging the continued reinforcement and development of shared knowledge about the social world.[22]

In addition to the market, bureaucracy, and clan categories, Max Boisot and John Child introduce the category of fief to take into account other transaction-governance possibilities that may be more consistent with the social preferences emanating from traditional culture.[23] By focusing on the informational aspect of economic transaction and by differentiating between levels of information codification and diffusion, they propose a taxonomy of four transaction-governance structure (see Exhibit 11.2).[24] This transaction-governance structure employs both uncodified and undiffused information.

One is characterized by transacting with relatively noncodified information that is asymmetrical distributed within the relevant population (i.e., has low diffusion). Historically this mode is exemplified by the fief as a social organization, i.e., small numbers, hierarchically structured through face-to-face and personalized power relationships that often have to be charismatically legitimated- by such means as the laying-on of hands, initiation of rites, commendation ceremonies, and the like.[25]

In the context of the model shown in Exhibit 11.1, the modes for governing transactions in general and clans and fiefs in particular contribute to the process of organizational commitment and organizational socialization that result ultimately in a distinct organizational culture.

Exhibit 11.2
Typology of Transaction-Governance Structures

Codified Information	**2. Bureaucracies** – Information diffusion limited and under central control – Relationships impersonal and hierarchical – Submission to superordinate goals – Hierarchical coordination – No necessity to share values and beliefs	**3. Markets** – Information widely diffused, no control – Relationships impersonal and competitive – No superordinate goals—each one for himself – Horizontal coordination through self-regulation – No necessity to share values and beliefs
Uncodified Information	**1. Fiefs** – Information diffusion limited by lack of codification to face-to-face relationships – Relationships personal and hierarchical (feudal/charismatic) – Submission to superordinate goals – Hierarchical coordination – Necessity to share values and beliefs	**4. Clans** – Information is diffused, but still limited by lack of codification to face-to-face relationships – Relationships personal but nonhierarchical – Goals are shared through a process of negotiation – Horizontal coordination through negotiation – Necessity to share values and beliefs

Source: Reprinted from "The Iron Law of Fiefs: Bureaucratic Failure and the Problem of Governance in the Chinese Economic Reforms" by Max Boisot and John Child published in *Administrative Science Quarterly* (vol. 33, no. 4) by permission of *Administrative Science Quarterly* © 1988 by Cornell University, 0001-8392/88/3304-0507/$1.

THE EXECUTIVE PERSONALITY

Where power is consolidated in the hands of a top executive or a small, homogeneous dominant coalition, there is a potential link between the executive personality and the organizational culture. Where the problem of culture becomes a concern is in firms with relatively dysfunctional, neurotic executives. For example, Kets de Vries, F. R. Manfred, and D. Miller identify five potential neurotic styles, their fantasies, and their impact on organizational culture and the organization.[26]

1. The suspicious style is associated with a fantasy of persecution that leads to a paranoid culture and a paranoid organization. Hypotheses for the paranoid constellation are shown in Exhibit 11.3.
2. The depressive style is associated with a fantasy of helplessness that leads to an avoidant culture and a depressive organization. Hypotheses for the depressive constellation are shown in Exhibit 11.4.
3. The dramatic style is associated with a fantasy of grandiosity that leads to a charismatic culture and a dramatic organization. Hypotheses for the dramatic style are shown in Exhibit 11.5.
4. The compulsive style is associated with a fantasy of control that leads to a bureaucratic culture and a compulsive organization. Hypotheses for the compulsive style are shown in Exhibit 11.6.
5. The detached style is associated with a fantasy of detachment that leads to a politicized culture and a schizoid organization. Hypotheses for the detached style are shown in Exhibit 11.7.

Where firms are healthy because of a mixture of personality styles, the impact on culture and the organization will be more salutary. In the context of the model shown in Exhibit 11.1, the type of executive personality affects the processes of organizational commitment and socialization to produce a specific corporate culture.

ORGANIZATIONAL COMMITMENT

Commitment to a utilitarian organization, in which the sources of control and motivation are material rather than psychological or symbolic, is difficult given that such an organization generally lacks a compelling ideology and is impersonal and rational, involving only segmental portions of the self.

Exhibit 11.3
Hypotheses for the Paranoid Constellation

1. The persecutory fantasy and the suspicious style will go together.
2. The more pronounced these personality and cultural factors are in the CEO and his/her top managers, the more the organizational culture will be plagued by; suspiciousness and mistrust; the search for and identification of enemies in the environment; poor morale; fight/flight attitudes; uniform but distorted perceptions; and the use of information as a power resource.
3. The more pronounced these personality and cultural factors, the more the structure of the organization will use: sophisticated control and information systems; centralized power for decision making; and a sophisticated scanning apparatus to study the environment.
4. The more pronounced these personality and cultural factors, the more wariness enters into decision making; the more reactive and fragmented the strategy; and the greater the proclivity to diversify.

Source: Manfred F. R. Kets de Vries and Danny Miller, "Personality, Culture, and Organization," *Academy of Management Review* (Apr. 1986): 271. Reprinted with permission.

Exhibit 11.4

Hypotheses for the Depressive Constellation

1. The fantasy of helplessness and the depressive (avoidant/dependent) style will be found in the same CEO's.

2. The more pronounced these personality and cultural factors are in the CEO and his/her managers, the more the organizational culture will be characterized by: a lack of initiative; unmotivated absentee executives; buck-passing; delays; "decidophobia"; passivity; and a sense of futility.

3. The more prominent these personality and cultural factors, the more the structure of the firm will be: bureaucratic; rigid; impersonal; and based on formal position (mechanistic). There will be very little scanning of the environment or communication among managers.

4. The more prominent these factors, the more moribund the strategy-which will be less likely to have changed materially in a long time, and which will be anachronistic, even in the mature industries in which these firms are usually found. Extreme conservatism, a very vague set of goals and strategies, and an absence of plans will also be more common.

Source: Manfred F. R. Kets de Vries and Danny Miller, "Personality, Culture and Organization," *Academy of Management Review* (Apr. 1986): 272. Reprinted with permission.

Exhibit 11.5
Hypotheses for the Dramatic Constellation
1. The fantasy of grandiosity and the dramatic (histrionic/narcissistic) style will be found in the same personality.
2. The more pronounced these personality and cultural factors are in the CEO and his/her managers, the more the organizational culture will be characterized by dependent subordinates who: idealize the leader; home him/her infallible; and never question him/her. There will be an enthusiastic adherence to the beliefs and goals of the CEO, and a paucity of independent-minded executives. A charismatic culture will prevail.
3. The more prominent these personality and cultural factors, the more the structure of the organization will be: extremely centralized; too informal for its administrative task; too primitive in its scanning and information processing apparatus; and too constrained in its bottom-up communications.
4. The more prominent these factors, the more intuitive, impulsive, and risky the decision making, and the more proactive, expansionalistic, and acquisitions-oriented the strategy.

Source: Manfred F. R. Kets de Vries and Danny Miller, "Personality, Culture and Organization," *Academy of Management Review* (Apr. 1986): 242. Reprinted with permission.

Exhibit 11.6

Hypotheses for the Compulsive Constellation

1. The fantasy of control will conjoin with the compulsive style.
2. The more pronounced these personality and cultural factors are in the CEO and his/her managers, the more the culture of the organization will center around issues of control. Efficiency or the slavish adherence to an archaic set of standards and the prevalence of risk averse, bureaucracy-loving managers will prevail. Ritual will rule.
3. The more prominent these personality and cultural factors, the more the structure of the organization will be: bureaucratic; hierarchical; rigid; rule-oriented; inwardly focused; formalized; and centralized. Programmed, routinized, and standardized practices will dominate. Cost controls will monitor efficiency but there will be very little analysis of the environment.
4. The more prominent these factors, the more decision making will focus on details and established procedures. A fixed strategy will prevail; this is never questioned but merely "implemented," through action plans, capital budget, etc.

Source: Manfred F. R. Kets de Vries and Danny Miller, "Personality, Culture and Organization," *Academy of Management Review* (Apr. 1986): 276. Reprinted with permission.

Exhibit 11.7
Hypotheses for the Schizoid Constellation

1. The fantasy of detachment will coincide with the detached (schizoid/avoidant) style.
2. The more pronounced these personality and cultural factors are in the CEO, the more the culture of the organization will be characterized by a leadership vacuum, and dominated by a second tier of politicized "gamesmen" who jocky for power and position. Coordination and cooperation will be neglected.
3. The more prominent these personality and culture factors, the more the structure the organization will be fragmented into uncooperative "fiefdoms." Political battles will use information systems as power resources and effective communication and collaboration will be thwarted. Power will be distributed among an altering coalition of second tier managers.
4. The more prominent these factors, the more fragmented, vacillating, and inconsistent the strategies. The absence of consensus will make concerted and adaptive change less possible. Politics will be a far more important influence on decisions than rationality; a muddling-through orientation will be common.

Source: Manfred F. R. Kets de Vries and Danny Miller, "Personality, Culture and Organization," *Academy of Management Review* (Apr. 1986): 277. Reprinted with permission.

In addition, involvement in such an organization tends to be largely calculative. What, then, leads to commitments in these organizations? Before examining this question, the concept of commitment must be explicated.

Commitment was first viewed as a form of institutionalization, "the integration of the expectations of actors in a relevant interactive system of roles with a shared normative pattern of values."[27] An elaboration of the concept of commitment from norms to other aspects of a social system was provided by R. M. Kantor as follows: "Commitment may be defined as the process through which individual interests become attached to the carrying out of socially organized patterns of behavior which are seen as fulfilling those interests, as expressing the nature and needs of the person."[28] Three major aspects of a social system affect commitment, namely, retention of members, group cohesiveness, and social control.[29]

Retention refers to people's willingness to stay in the system, to continue to staff it and carry out their roles. Group cohesiveness denotes the ability of people to "stick together," to develop the mutual attraction and collective strength to withstand threats to the group's existence. And social control involves the readiness of people to obey the demands of the system, to conform to its values and beliefs and take seriously its dictates.[30]

Commitment involves, then, the desire to stay in the group, to stick with the other members, and to abide by the rules, a three-level process involving *instrumental* commitment (commitment to a social role) *affective* commitment (commitment to relationships), and *moral* commitment (commitment to norms and values). In the context of social action theory, the person cognizes, and evaluates.[31] "That is, he orients himself with respect to the rewards and costs that are involved in participating in the system, with respect to his emotional attachment to the people in the system, and with respect to the moral compellingness of the norms and beliefs of the system."[32]

Bruce Buchanan distinguishes between three components of commitment: "(a) identification- adoption as one's own the goals and values of the organization, (b) involvement-psychological immersion or absorption in the activities of one's work role, and (c) loyalty- a feeling of affection for and attachment to the organization."[33]

Various empirical studies have sought to identify the correlates of commitment. First, social involvement with colleagues and personal investments such as length of organizational service, age, and hierarchical position were found to be related to commitment.[34] Second, organization identification was found to be determined by a sense of work accomplishment, relations with supervisors, and length of organizational service.[35] Third, identification was found to be related to opportunities for personal achievement provided by the organization, access to power within the organization, and absence of competing objects of identification.[36] Finally, role tension, years of organizational service, and dissatisfaction with the bases of organizational advancement were also found to be good predictors of commitment.

In the context of the model shown in Exhibit 11.1, the underlying assumptions and metaphors, the modes for governing transactions, and the type of executive personality affect the process of organizational commitment so as to produce a specific corporate culture.

ORGANIZATIONAL SOCIALIZATION

The organizational socialization process is an attempt by the experienced members of an organization to teach new members their view of the organizational world and its traditions. As defined by John Van Maanen and Edgar H. Scheim, it is the process by which these new individuals learn the social knowledge and skills demanded by their new organizational role, that is, the cultural perspective of the role[37] required for all the moves made in the organization, whether upward, downward, or lateral.

A descriptive conceptual scheme of organizational socialization, proposed by Van Maanen and Scheim, is adopted here. Six assumptions are made: (1) the individual undergoing the organizational transition is in an anxiety-producing situation; (2) the socialization process does not take place in a vacuum; (3) the socialization process is vital to the stability and productivity of the organization; (4) there is great variation in the way people adjust to novel circumstances; (5) individuals, not organizations, create and sustain beliefs; and (6) the descriptive scheme proposed transcends the particular and peculiar and aims for the general and typical.[38]

Organizationally defined roles are assumed to exist, guarded by segments and boundaries. The organizationally defined roles are assumed to assess a content or knowledge base, a strategic base suggesting the ground rules for the choosing of particular solutions, and an explicit/implicit mission, purpose, and mandate. These segments and boundaries are derived from the three dimensions of an organizationally defined role: functional, hierarchical, and inclusionary.[39] The functional dimension or boundary refers to the various tasks performed by members of an organization, including marketing, finance, production, administrative staff, personnel, research, and development. The hierarchical dimension or boundary refers to the distribution of rank within an organization and the definition of responsibilities. The inclusionary dimension or boundary refers to the individual's inclusion within the organization. For the newcomer each of these dimensions represents boundaries to be eventually crossed by submitting to the appropriate organizational socialization process and ultimately becoming an insider. The filtering process differs depending on the type of boundary.

Hierarchical boundaries crossed by persons moving upward are associated usually with filtering processes carrying notions of merit, potential, and judged past performance, although age and length of service are often utilized as surrogate measures of "readiness" to move upward in an organization. Functional boundaries usually filter people on the basis of their demonstrated skill or assumed aptitude to handle a particular task. However, when functional boundaries are relatively permeable, as they often are, the filtering process may operate on the premise that there are people in the organization who "need" or "wish" to broaden their work experiences. Finally, inclusionary filters, in the main, represent evaluations made by others on the scene as to another's "fitness" for membership.[40]

Once barriers are crossed, the newcomer reacts to the role either as a caretaker[41] or as an innovator. What leads to the change is the use of a tactic of organizational socialization, which refers to the ways in which the experiences of persons from one role to another are structured for them by others in the organization.[42] Six major tactical dimensions that characterize the structural side of organizational socialization are proposed.[43] They include: (1) *collective* versus *individual socialization processes*; (2) *formal* versus *informal socialization processes*; (3) *sequential* versus *variable socialization processes*; (4) *fixed* versus *variable socialization processes*; (5) *serial* versus *disjunctive socialization processes*; and (6) *investiture* versus *divestiture socialization processes*.

While collective socialization involves the socialization of a group of new members together through a common set of experiences, individual socialization involves the processing of an individual through individual experiences. Formal socialization involves putting the newcomer through a set of experiences specifically tailored for him/her while informal socialization does not differentiate the newcomer from the other organizational members through the use of the informal tactics. Sequential socialization involves the use of a given sequence of discrete and identifiable steps leading to a target role while random specialization involves changing the sequence of steps. In fixed socialization, the newcomer is aware of the time required to complete a given passage while in variable socialization, he/she is not provided any clues about when to expect a given boundary passage. In the serial socialization process, the newcomer follows the footsteps of predecessors who serve as role models while in the disjunctive process the newcomer is left on one's own, to perform the "heroic myth,"[44] prevalent in Western fairy tales.[45] In the investiture socialization process, the individual is praised for one's personal characteristics while in the divestiture socialization process, the person is denied and stripped of the same personal characteristics, a process similar to Goffman's "total institutions,"[46] with the deliberate "mortifications to self" which entry into them entails.

In the context of our model, the various identified organizational characteristics affect the process of organizational socialization so as to create a specific corporate culture that will shape the judgment/decision process.

ORGANIZATIONAL CULTURE

The concept of organizational culture or corporate culture has been given various definitions. It was assumed to be embodied and transmitted by "stories," "myths," and symbols." It was referred to as a set of shared understanding, interpretations, or perspectives that allow members to articulate contextually appropriate accounts. Stephen R. Barley provided a definition that integrates all these terms:

From the observation that this family of terms is repeatedly associated with the notion of culture, one may infer that in organization studies "culture" is somehow implicitly tied to notions of social cognition and contextual sense making. Whatever else it may be said to be, culture appears to have something to do with the way members of a collective organize their experience.[47]

Basically members of a group develop a system of publicly and collectively accepted meanings, such as terms, forms, categories, and images, that allows them to explain their own situation to themselves,[48] and symbolically create an ordered world.

Various characterizations of organizational culture are of importance to the model illustrated in Exhibit 11.1.

Attempts have been made to contrast "strong" homogeneous cultures with "weak" heterogeneous cultures that deviate from management philosophy and are assumed to lack integration.[49,50] Katheleen L. Gregory criticized this type of dichotomization, arguing that it would be more accurate to separate cultural integration from organizational integration and to describe organizations rather than cultures as either strong or weak in terms of integration:

Organizations that lack integration may be comprised of members acting from numerous internally consistent but externally conflicting cultures. Ethnocentrism exacerbates the intensity of conflicts, since each coalition takes its position for granted or may even assume meanings and priorities are shared. The cultures may conflict only in a few situations, or in many.[51]

Organizational cultures may be viewed from at least three perspectives.[52,53] The functionalist research paradigm views culture as an organizational variable. The interpretive research paradigm views it as a pattern of symbolic discourse, something the organization is. The structuralist research paradigm views it as a system of integrated subcultures, not as a unified set of values to which all organizational members subscribe.

Organizational cultures may also be accounting-oriented. More specifically, Andrew P. Thomas argued that enterprises can be conceptualized in terms of the extent to which they have an accounting-oriented organizational culture.[54] It is assumed to take the form of a continuum representing the extent to which accounting is used as a symbol,[55,56] a language,[57,58] ideology,[59,60] rituals,[61] myths,[62] and witchcraft, magic, and ceremony.[63]

The analogy follows from Andrew Pettigrew's suggestion that culture has five elements: symbols, language ideology, rituals, and myths.[64] The accounting-oriented organizational culture is shown by Andrew P. Thomas to have an impact on choices of corporate reporting practices.[65] In the context of our model, the concept of accounting-oriented organizational culture is assumed to depend on the organizational socialization process and to affect the judgment/decision process.

The neurotic styles of the executive can create a distinct neurotic culture.[66,67] More specifically, the following associations are hypothesized: (1) suspicious style creates a paranoid culture; (2) depressive style creates an avoidant culture; (3) compulsive style creates a bureaucratic culture; (4) dramatic style creates a charismatic culture, and (5) detached style creates a politicized culture.[68]

CONCLUSION

An efficient organizational culture requires the sharing of frameworks, referents, and language that shape the schemes individuals use when faced with accounting phenomena. The model in this chapter argues in favor of such relativism whereby the organizational culture ultimately determines the judgment/decision process.

NOTES

1. Alan Wilkins and William, G. Ouchi, "Efficient Cultures: Exploring the Relationship Between Culture and Organizational Performance," *Administrative Science Quarterly* 28 (1983): 475.

2. R. H. Brown, *A Poetic for Sociology* (Cambridge: Cambridge University Press, 1977).

3. Gareth Morgan, "Paradigms, Metaphors and Puzzle Solving in Organization Theory," *Administrative Science Quarterly* 25 (1980): 605-22.

4. Erving Goffman, *The Presentation of Self in Everyday Life* (New York: Double Day, 1959).

5. I. L. Mangham and M. A. Overington, "Dramatism and the Theatrical Metaphor," in M. Gareth, ed., *Beyond Method: Social Research Strategies* (Beverly Hills, Calif.: Sage, 1983), 219-33.

6. Michel Cozier, *The Bureaucratic Phenomenon* (Chicago: University of Chicago Press, 1964).

7. Jeffrey Pfeffer, "Management as Symbolic Action: The Creation and Maintenance of Organizational Paradigms," in Larry L. Cummings and Barry M. Staw, eds., *Research in Organizational Behavior* (Greenwich, Conn.: JAI Press, 1981), 1-52.

8. D. M. Boje, D. B. Fedor, and K. M. Rowland, "Myth Making: A Qualitative Step in OD Interventions," *Journal of Applied Behavioral Science* 18 (1982): 17-28.

9. Terrence E. Deal and Allan A. Kennedy, *Corporate Cultures* (Reading, Mass.: Addison-Wesley, 1982).

10. I. I. Mitroff and R. H. Kilmann, "On Organization Stories: An Approach to the Design and Analysis of Organizations Through Myths and Stories," in R. H. Kilmann, L. R. Pondy, and D. P. Slevin, eds., *The Management of Organizational Design* (New York: Elsevier, 1976), 183-207.

11. Alan Wilkins and Joanne Martin, "Organizational Legends" (working paper, Graduate School of Business, Stanford University, 1980).

12. John A. Y. Andrews and P. M. Hirsch, "Ambushes, Shootouts, and Knights of the Roundtable: The Language of Corporate Takeovers," in Louis R. Pondy, et al., eds., *Organizational Symbolism* (Greenwich, Conn.: JAI Press, 1982).

13. Andrew M. Pettigrew, "On Studying Organizational Cultures," *Administrative Science Quarterly* (Dec. 1974): 520-81.

14. P. Selznick, *Leadership in Administration* (Evanston, Ill.: Row, Peterson, 1957).

15. Burton R. Clark, "The Organizational Saga in Higher Education," *Administrative Science Quarterly* 17 (1979): 174-84.

16. W. G. Ouchi, "A Conceptual Framework for the Design of Control Mechanisms," *Management Science* (Sept. 1975): 831-47.

17. Alan L. Wilkins and William G. Ouchi, "Efficient Cultures: Exploring the Relationship Between Culture and Organizational Performance," *Administrative Science Quarterly* 28 (1983): 470.

18. Ouchi, "A Conceptual Framework for the Design of Control Mechanisms," 831.

19. Wilkins and Ouchi, "Efficient Cultures," 472.

20. P. L. Berger and T. Luckmann, *The Social Construction of Reality* (Garden City: Anchor Books, 1967).

21. Ibid.

22. Wilkins and Ouchi, "Efficient Cultures," 472-74.

23. Max Boisot and John Child, "The Iron Law of Fiefs: Bureaucratic Failure and the Problem of Governance in the Chinese System Reforms," *Administrative Science Quarterly* 33 (Dec. 1988): 507-27.

24. Ibid., 509.

25. Ibid., 508.

26. Manfred F. R. Kets de Vries and D. Miller, "Personality, Culture, and Organization," *Academy of Management Review* 11 (1986): 266-79.

27. T. Parsons and E. A Shils, *Toward a General Theory of Action* (New York: Harper and Row, 1962), 20.

28. R. M. Kantor, "Commitment and Social Organization: A Study of Commitment Mechanisms in Utopian Societies," *American Sociological Review* (Aug. 1968): 500.

29. R. M. Kantor, *Commitment and Community* (Cambridge, Mass.: Harvard University Press, 1972), 67.

30. Ibid., 65.

31. Ibid., 68.

32. M. E. Sheldon, "Investments and Involvements as Mechanisms Producing Commitment to the Organization," *Administrative Science Quarterly* 16 (1971): 143-50.

33. Bruce Buchanan, "Building Organizational Commitment: The Socialization of Managers in Work Organizations," *Administrative Science Quarterly* 18 (1974): 533.

34. Sang M. Lee, "An Empirical Analysis of Organizational Identification," *Academy of Management Journal* 14 (1971): 213-26.

35. M. E. Brown, "Identification and Some Conditions of Organizational Involvement," *Administrative Science Quarterly* 14 (1969): 346-55.

36. L. c. Hrebiniak and J. A. Alutto, "Personal and Role-Related Factors in the Development of Organizational Commitment," *Administrative Science Quarterly* 18 (1973): 555-72.

37. John Van Maanen and Edgar H. Schein, "Toward a Theory of Organizational Socialization," in Barry M. Staw, ed., *Research in Organizational Behavior* (Greenwich, Conn.: JAI Press, 1979), 211.

38. Ibid., 215-16.

39. E. H. Schein, "The Individual, the Organization and the Career: A Conceptual Scheme," *Journal of Applied Behavioral Science* 7 (1971): 410-26.

40. Van Maanen and Schein, "Towards a Theory of Organizational Socialization," 224.

41. E. H. Schein, "Occupational Socialization in the Professions: The Case of the Role Innovator," *Journal of Psychiatric Research* (1971): 521-30.

42. John Van Maanen, "People Processing: Major Strategies of Organizational Socialization and Their Consequences," in J. Paap,

ed., *New Directions in Human Resource Management* (Englewood Cliffs, N.J.: Prentice-Hall, 1978).

43. Ibid.

44. T. Campbell, *The Hero with a Thousand Faces* (New York: Anchor Books, 1956).

45. B. Bettelheim, *The Uses of Enchantment: The Meaning of Importance of Fairy Tales* (New York: Alfred A. Knopf, 1976).

46. E. Goffman, *Asylums* (New York: Random House, 1961).

47. Stephen R. Barley, "Semiotics and the Study of Occupational and Organizational Cultures," *Administrative Science Quarterly* 28 (1983): 393.

48. Andrew M. Pettigrew, "On Studying Organizational Cultures," *Administrative Science Quarterly* (Dec. 1979): 574.

49. Terrence E. Deal and Allan A. Kennedy, *Corporate Cultures: The Rites and Rituals of Corporate Life* (Reading, Mass.: Addison-Wesley, 1982).

50. Thomas T. Peters and Robert H. Waterman, Jr., *In Search of Excellence* (New York: Harper and Row, 1982).

51. Katheleen L. Gregory, "Native-View Paradigms: Multiple Cultures and Culture Conflicts in Organizations," *Administrative Science Quarterly* 28 (1983): 365.

52. Linda Smircich, "Concepts of Culture and Organizational Analysis," *Administrative Science Quarterly* 28 (1983): 339-58.

53. Patricia Riley, "A Structuralionist Account of Political Culture," *Administrative Science Quarterly* 28 (1983): 414-37.

54. Andrew P. Thomas, "The Effects of Organizational Culture on Choices of Accounting Methods" (paper presented at the American Accounting Association annual meeting, Orlando, Fla., 1988).

55. S. Burchell, et al., "The Roles of Accounting in Organization and Society," *Accounting, Organizations and Society* (1980); 5-27.

56. R. J. Boland and L. R. Pondy, "Accounting in Organizations: A Union of Natural and Rational Perspectives," *Accounting, Organizations, and Society* 3 (1980): 5-27.

57. D. Cooper, "A Social and Organizational View of Management Accounting," in M. Brownwich and A. G. Hopwood,

eds., *Essays in British Accounting Research* (London: Pitman, 1981), 178-205.

58. Ahmed Belkaoui, "Linguistic Relativity in Accounting," *Accounting, Organizations and Society* (Oct. 1978): 97-104.

59. D. Cooper, "Discussion Towards a Political Economy of Accounting," *Accounting, Organizations and Society* 3 (1980): 161-66.

60. D. Cooper and M. J. Sherer, "The Value of Corporate Accounting Reports: Arguments for a Political Economy of Accounting," *Accounting, Organizations and Society* 3 (1984): 207-32.

61. A. Wildavsky, "Economy and Environment/Rationality and Ritual: A Review Essay, *Accounting, Organizations and Society* (1976): 117-29.

62. R. J. Boland, "Myth and Technology in the American Accounting Profession," *Journal of Management Studies* 19/1 (1982): 109-27.

63. T. E. Gambling, "Magic, Accounting and Morale," *Accounting, Organizations and Society* (1977): 141-51.

64. Pettigrew, "On Studying Organizational Cultures."

65. Thomas, "Effects of Organizational Culture on Choices of Accounting Methods."

66. D. Miller and P. H. Friesen, "Archetypes of Strategy Formulation," *Management V Science* 24 (1978): 921-33.

67. D. Miller and P. H. Friesen, *Organizations: A Quantum View* (Englewood Cliffs, N.J.: Prentice-Hall, 1984).

68. de Vries and Miller, "Personality, Culture, and Organization," 266-79.

CHAPTER 12
CONTRACTUAL RELATIVISM

INTRODUCTION

People in organizations are bound by the covenants and limitations of their employment contracts. Similarly, various financing contracts limit and define the type of financial transactions permissible for a given firm. What these contracts imply in the organization is an effort to monitor the behavior and actions of individuals toward an efficient realization of organizational goals. Therefore, the model in this chapter postulates that the judgment/decision process may be shaped by the permissible behavior and actions defined in the contracts entered by the organization with individuals seeking employment or provision of services.

THE AGENCY THEORY: CONTRACTUAL VIEWS OF THE FIRM

The agency theory was developed in response to the concern about risk sharing, a problem that arises when cooperating parties have different attitudes toward risk.[1,2] Cooperating parties, however, may have different goals and division of labor.[3,4] Organizations are in fact "legal frictions which serve as a nexus for a set of contracting relationships among individuals."[5] Basically contractors or providers of capital (principals) supply the factors of production. The principal delegates to manager, or agent, the coordination of the contracts and the implementation of the work. Therefore, the agency relationship is secured by a contract under which the principal engages the agent to perform some services on his or her behalf. The agency problem arises because the goals of the principal and agent differ and the monitoring of the agent's effort and action is difficult or expensive. The agent, therefore, will not always act in the best interests of the principal. As a result agency costs are incurred. They are equal to the sum of: (1) the monitoring expenditure by the principal, designed to limit the aberrant activities of the agent; (2) the bonding expenditures by the agent to guarantee that he/she will not take certain actions that may be harmful to the principal and to ensure that the principal will be compensated for any losses; (3) the residual loss due to the divergence between the agent's decisions and those decisions which would maximize the welfare of the principal.[6] The focus of agency then becomes the design of an optimal contract between a principal and an agent that are engaged in cooperative behavior, have different goals and attitudes toward risk, and are assumed to be motivated solely by self-interest.

THE STEWARDSHIP/ACCOUNTABILITY MODEL

Generally, accounting has been viewed as a means of providing the history of an organization and its transactions with its environment. For either the owner or the shareholders of a firm, accounting records provide a history of the manager's stewardship of the owner's resources. The stewardship concept is basically a feature of the principal-agent relationship whereby the agent is assumed to safeguard the resources of the principal and to provide information to the principal on the uses of the resources. The accountability model can be defined as follows:

The primary role of the accountant is to assist the account or in accounting for his activities and their consequences and, at the same time, provide information to the accountee. . . . [T]he accountability approach . . . includes not only the traditional stewardship issues centered on the compliance with established rules but also the modern performance issues oriented toward the efficiency and effectiveness notions.[7]

Measurement of the stewardship concept has evolved over time. J. G. Birnberg distinguished four periods: (1) the pure custodial period, (2) the traditional custodial period, (3) the asset-utilization period, and (4) the open-ended period.[8]

The first two periods refer to the need for the agent to return the resources intact to the principal by performing minimal tasks to fulfill the custodial function. In these two periods, the disclosure of the balance sheet data is considered adequate. The third period refers to the need for the agent to provide initiative and insight in using the assets in conformity with agreed-upon plans.

In addition to using the balance sheet, this period requires the acquisition of performance-evaluation data on the effectiveness of the use of the assets. Finally, the open-ended period differs from the asset-utilization period by providing more flexibility in the use of assets and enabling the agent to chart the course of asset utilization. J. C. Birnberg elaborates on this last concept:

This involves not only the initial direction, but also ascertaining the critical point in time when such directions must be changed. Like strategic control, the stewardship function requires that a significant degree of responsibility be assumed by the servant. The task force is probably characterized by a lack of structure and a significant amount of uncertainty. This suggests that we may find our reporting system to the master caught between the rock and hard space of communication- the need for the detail on one hand and the risk of overload and excessive complexity on the other.[9]

The stewardship model, in the open-ended period, views the accounting reporting system as a way of mitigating the loss of efficiency produced by the fact that the steward knows more about his actions and the state of the world than the owner, and the conflict of interest caused by the fact that each individual acts in his/her own best interest. The role of the accounting system in mitigating the loss of efficiency is made possible by the strong assumption that the accountant is selfless, honest, and independent.[10]

THE TRANSACTION-COST ECONOMICS MODEL

The transaction-cost economics model attempts to develop a systematic answer to why firms exist, and to explain the circumstances under which hierarchically directed transactions within firms replace market-mediated transactions.

The general approach to economic organization employed here can be summarized compactly as follows: (1) Markets and firms are alternative instruments for completing a related set of transactions; (2) whether a set of transactions ought to be executed across markets or within a firm depends on the relative efficiency of each mode; (3) the coast of writing and executing complex contracts across a market *varies with the characteristics of the human decision makers who are involved with the transactions on the one hand, and the objective properties of the market on the other*; and (4) although the human and environmental factors that impede exchanges between firms (across a market) manifest themselves somewhat differently within the firm, the same set of factors applies to both.[11]

Two human characteristics are assumed to affect this governance choice, namely, bounded rationality and opportunism.

Opportunistic behavior is any action used by one party, enjoying an informational (or other) advantage to exploit that advantage to the economic detriment of others. In its crassest form, Williamson uses it to refer to "lying, stealing, and cheating" or other "self-disbelieved statements."[12]

Bounded rationality is the limited computation ability of individuals and their limited ability to acquire and process information. Given the existence of a small number of parties to an exchange, which increases the likelihood of opportunistic behavior, and given the existence of uncertainty/complexity that also increases the likelihood of opportunism, the costs of the transaction are prohibitive and hierarchy rather than the market would be the best way of carrying forward the transaction. The transaction costs of negotiating, monitoring, harmonizing, and enforcing contrasts between parties are incurred by each. These contracts are, however, assumed to be incomplete as one cannot- given the bounded rationality assumption- incorporate all contingencies, and courts are to be imperfect enforcers of contracts. Lessening the impact of the incompleteness of contrast is an issue, as parties may take advantage of the rise of an unforeseen contingency. The latter behavior is labeled as a hold-up behavior. This situation, characterized by the incompleteness of contracts and self-interested behavior, prevents a cooperative solution from being achieved. How the parties can resolve these problems between themselves (referred to as private ordering) rather than using the courts (referred to as legal ordering) is the question of essence in transaction-cost economics. Governance procedures are devised to achieve the objective of meeting transaction costs arising from the opportunistic behavior caused by the rise of the unforeseen contingencies. One of the opportunistic behaviors most in need of control is the distortion of ex-ante investments in relation-specific assets. More precisely, assets are characterized by a high asset specificity when their use inside the relationship is higher than their use outside the relationship. An opportunistic behavior arises when the same asset is subject to an ex-post hold up behavior.

THE PRINCIPAL-AGENT MODEL

The concern in this model is a general theory of the principal-agent relationship and the derivation of the optimal employment contract within a well-specified model of the agency relationship. Various assumptions are made in the principal-agent model: (1) there is goal conflict between the principal and the agent; (2) the agent is more risk averse than the principal; (3) both agent and principal are rational and have unlimited computational ability; (4) contracts are complete in the sense that first, all contingencies which are verifiable can be used as arguments in the contracts and second, the contracts are accurately enforced by the courts.

Given that the principal cannot determine that the agent has acted well and given their different goals, two agency problems arise generally denoted as moral hazard or hidden action and adverse selection or hidden information.

The moral hazard or hidden action problem refers to the lack of effort exercised by the agent given that effort is a disutility to the agency. The term *moral hazard* originated from the fact that fire insurance dulls incentives for caution and even creates incentives for arson.

The adverse selection or hidden information problem involves a misrepresentation of skill or validity by the agent. It is a case where the agent uses information in making decisions that the principal does not have.

Given the presence of the unobservable behavior due to moral hazard and adverse selection, the principal has two options: either to design an information system that reveals the agent's behavior to the principal or to design employment contracts that mitigate the divergence between the cooperative behavior that will maximize the welfare of the individuals and the self-interested behavior that is achievable.

The solution to the basic agency problem consists of:
i) the employment contract, which incorporates:
    1. the payment schedule for the agent;
    2. the information system choices . . . ;
    3. specification of how the agent *promises* to act;

ii) the agent's actual action[13]

The optimal choices of these variables and their welfare effects (i.e., risk sharing and production) are the main concern of principal-agent research.

THE POSITIVIST AGENCY THEORY

The positivist agency theory explains why certain contractual relationships arise. It describes specifically the governance mechanisms that limit the agent's self-serving behavior in those cases where the principal and the agent are likely to have conflicting goals. For example, M. Jensen and W. H. Meckling showed how increased ownership equity by managers aligns managers' interests with those of the owners.[14] The capital and labor markets are assumed to be efficient and to act as information mechanisms to control the opportunism of top executives.[15]

Similarly, the board of directors is assigned the same information and control roles.[16] In addition, there is evidence in support of agency problems between shareholders and executives across situations in which their interests diverge- such as in takeover attempts,[17] debt versus equity financing,[18] and acquisitions and divestitures.[19] The mitigation of agency problems is shown to be possible through outcome-based contracts such as golden parachutes[20,21] and executive stock holdings,[22] and through information systems such as boards,[23] and efficient markets.[24]

Unlike the principal-agent theory, the positivist agency theory assumes that the observed employment and financial contracts are optimal given transaction costs. However, the same transaction costs make the contract incomplete and coupled with the opportunistic behavior of agents make the genesis of cooperation very difficult.

As a result of the above situation, the focus of the positivist agency theory becomes to explain the use of those observed contracts through an examination of the effect that changes in employment and financing contracts have on the behavior of management (i.e., their financing and investment) decisions and on the stock price of the firm.[25]

Design and changes in these contracts may be made through the choice of accounting policies. Positive accounting theory (the Rochester School of Accounting) aims at investigating the economic consequences of voluntary and mandatory choices of accounting techniques and standards.

In general, the prediction of economic consequences theories is driven by contracting and monitoring costs associated with management compensation contracts, bond covenants, regulation, and/or political visibility.[26] These theories assume that changes in the accounting rules used to calculate accounting numbers have economic consequences because they change the distribution of expected cash flows or the claims of various parties to those cash flows. Accordingly, R. L. Watts and J. L. Zimmerman offer the following hypotheses:

Bonus plan hypothesis. Managers of firms with bonus plans are more likely to choose accounting procedures that shift reported earnings from future periods to the current periods.[27]

Debt/equity hypothesis. The larger a firm's debt/equity ratio, the more likely the firm's manager is to select accounting procedures that shift reported earnings from future periods to the current period.[28]

Size hypothesis. The larger the firm, the more likely the manager is to choose accounting procedures that defer reported earnings from current to future periods.[29]

Compensation contracts may also be designed to overcome agency problems. This is evidenced by the association between compensation and firm performance,[30-32] positive stock-price reactions to the adoption of golden parachutes,[33] short-term performance plans,[34] and long-term performance plans.[35]

CONTRACTUAL RELATIVISM

A firm is assumed to be a nexus of contracts, whereby contractors or shareholders are suppliers of production factors. The agents coordinates these contracts, initiating and implementing exchanges between shareholders, creditors, employees, customers, and suppliers.

The behavior and action of each of these individuals is assumed to be determined by the specifications of the contract that defines what is permissible and acceptable to the firm. Each of the components of agency theory- the stewardship/accountability model, the transaction-cost economics model, the principal-agent model, and the positivist agency model- adheres to the notion of the contract that is the guide to permissible behavior and actions in the firm. The situation is also applicable to the individual in the firm faced with the task of providing a solution to a phenomenon. The covenants of the contract defining the relationship between this individual and the firm may provide the necessary guidelines for this individual in dealing with phenomena. This is the essence of the contractual relativism model, portrayed in Exhibit 12.1. As a result of the assumptions and implications of the four models of agency theory, contracts through their definition of permissible behavior and actions determine the judgment/decision process.

CONCLUSION

The essence of the model portrayed in this chapter is that contracts define permissible behavior and actions that determine the judgment/decision process. The importance of these contracts results from the assumptions and implications inherent in the four models of agency theory, namely, the stewardship/accountability model, the transaction-cost economics model, the principal-agent model, and the positivist agency model.

NOTES

1. K. Arrow, *Essays in the Theory of Risk Bearing* (Chicago: Markham, 1971).

2. R. Wilson, "On the Theory of Syndicates," *Econometrica* 16 (1968): 119-32.

3. M. Jensen and W. Meckling, "Theory of the Firm: Managerial Behavior, Agency Costs and Ownership Structure," *Journal of Financial Economics* (Oct. 1976): 305-60.

4. S. Ross, "The Economic Theory of Agency: The Principal's Problem," *American Economic Review* 63 (1973): 134-35.

5. Jensen and Meckling, "Theory of the Firm."

6. Ibid., 308.

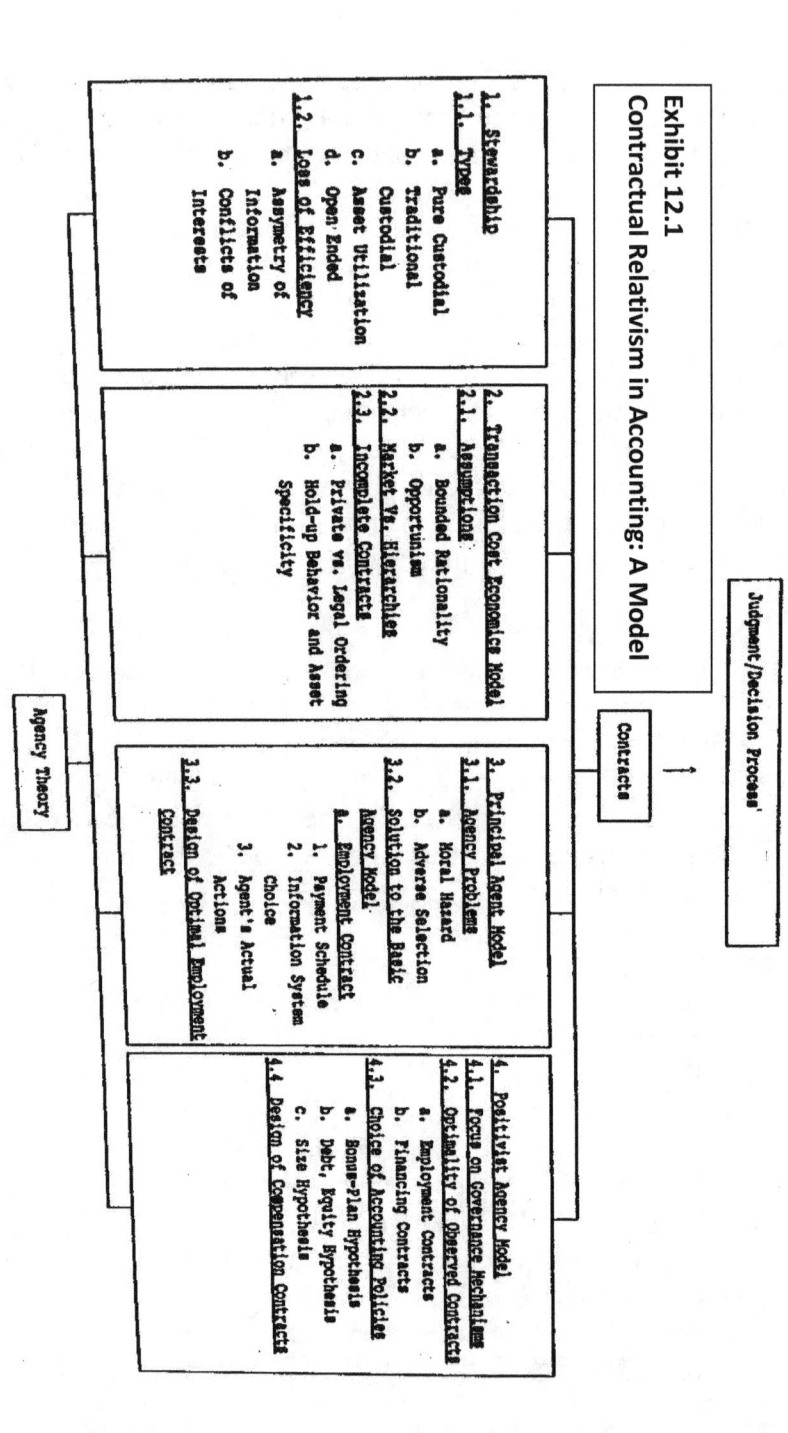

Exhibit 12.1
Contractual Relativism in Accounting: A Model

Judgment/Decision Process

Contracts →

Agency Theory

1. Stewardship
1.1. Types
  a. Pure Custodial
  b. Traditional Custodial
  c. Asset Utilization
  d. Open Ended
1.2. Loss of Efficiency
  a. Asymmetry of Information
  b. Conflicts of Interests

2. Transaction Cost Economics Model
2.1. Assumptions
  a. Bounded Rationality
  b. Opportunism
2.2. Market Vs. Hierarchies
2.3. Incomplete Contracts
  a. Private vs. Legal Ordering
  b. Hold-up Behavior and Asset Specificity

3. Principal Agent Model
3.1. Agency Problems
  a. Moral Hazard
  b. Adverse Selection
3.2. Solution to the Basic Agency Model
  a. Employment Contract
    1. Payment Schedule
    2. Information System
    3. Agent's Actual Actions
3.3. Design of Optimal Employment Contract

4. Positivist Agency Model
4.1. Focus on Governance Mechanisms
4.2. Optimality of Observed Contracts
  a. Employment Contracts
  b. Financing Contracts
4.3. Choice of Accounting Policies
  a. Bonus-Plan Hypothesis
  b. Debt/Equity Hypothesis
  c. Size Hypothesis
4.4 Design of Compensation Contracts

7. Y. Ijiri, *The Theory of Accounting Measurement*, Studies in Accounting Research No. 10 (Sarasota, Fla.: American Accounting Association, 1975), ix-x.

8. J. C. Birnberg, "The Role of Accounting in Financial Disclosure," *Accounting, Organizations and Society* (June 1980): 73.

9. Ibid., 74.

10. Gjesdeal has analyzed the stewardship problem using a principal-agent model. See F. Gjesdal, "Accounting for Stewardship," *Journal of Accounting Research* (Spring 1981): 208-31.

11. O. E. Williamson, *Markets and Hierarchies: Analysis and Antitrust Implications* (New York: Free Press, 1975), 8.

12. Ibid.

13. Stanley Baiman, "Agency Research in Managerial Accounting: A Survey," *Journal of Accounting Literature* (Spring 1982): 154-213.

14. Jensen and Meckling, "Theory of the Firm," 305-60.

15. E. Fama, "Agency Problems and the Theory of the Firm," *Journal of Political Economy* 88 (1980): 288-307.

16. E. Fama and M. Jensen, "Separation of Ownership and Control," *Journal of Law and Economics* 26 (1983): 301-25.

17. R. Walking and M. Long, "Agency Theory, Managerial Welfare and Takeover Bid Resistance," *Rand Journal of Economics* 15 (1984): 54-68.

18. A. Argawal and G. Mandelker, "Managerial Incentives and Corporate Investment and Financing Decision," *Journal of Finance* 42 (1987): 823-37.

19. Y. Amihud and B. Lev, "Risk Reduction as a Managerial Motive for Conglomerate Mergers," *Bell Journal of Economics* 12 (1981): 823-37.

20. H.Singh and F. Hariomto, "Management Brand Relationships, Takeover Risk and the Adoption of Golden Parachutes: An Empirical Investigation," *Academy of Management Journal* (forthcoming).

21. M. Jensen and R. Roeback, "The Market for Corporate Control: Empirical Evidence," *Journal of Financial Economics* 3 (1976): 305-60.

22. Argawal and Mandelker, "Managerial Incentives and Corporate Investment and Financing Decision."

23. R. Kosnik, "Greenmail: A Study in Board Performance in Corporate Governance," *Administrative Science Quarterly* 32 (1987): 163-85.

24. M. Wolfson, "Empirical Evidence of Incentive Problems and Their Mitigation in Ore and Gas Shelter Programs," in J. Pratt and R. Zechhauser, eds, *Principals and Agents: The Structure of Business* (Boston: Harvard Business School Press, 1982), 101-26.

25. Stanley Baiman, "Agency Research in Managerial Accounting: A Second Look" (paper presented at the Inaugural Management Accounting Research conference, School of Accounting, University of New South Wales, Sept. 9-10, 1988, 12).

26. R. W. Holthausen and R. W. Leftuwich, "The Economic Consequences of Accounting Choice: Implications of Costly Contracting and Monitoring," *Journal of Accounting and Economics* (Aug. 1983): 77-118.

27. R. L. Watts and J. L. Zimmerman, *Positive Accounting Theory* (Englewood Cliffs, N.J.: Prentice-Hall, 1986), 208.

28. Ibid., 216.

29. Ibid., 235.

30. Ahmed Belkaoui, "Executive Compensation, Economic Performance, Organizational Effectiveness and Social Performance," *Research in Corporate Social Performance and Policy* (forthcoming).

31. K. Murphy, "Incentives, Learning and Compensation: A Theoretical and Empirical Investigation of Managerial Labor Contracts," *Rand Journal of Economics* (Spring 1986): 59-76.

32. A. Coughlin and R. Schmidt, "Executive Compensation, Management Turnover, and Firm Performance: An Empirical Investigation," *Journal of Accounting and Economics* (Apr. 1985): 43-66.

33. R. Lambert and D. Larcher, "Golden Parachutes, Executive Decision-Making and Shareholder Wealth," *Journal of Accounting and Economics* (Apr. 1985), 179-204.

34. H. Tehranian and J. Waegelein, "Market Reaction to Short-Term Executive Compensation Plan Adoption," *Journal of Accounting and Economics* (Apr. 1985): 131-45.

35. J. Brickley, S. Bhagat, and R. Lease, "The Impact of Long-Range Management Compensation Plans on Shareholders Wealth," *Journal of Accounting and Economics* (Apr. 1985): 115-30.

www.ingramcontent.com/pod-product-compliance
Lightning Source LLC
Chambersburg PA
CBHW071325280526
45787CB00001B/1